TH

GREAT RED

DRAGON;

OR THE

MASTER-KEY TO POPERY.

BY

ANTHONY GAVIN,

**FORMERLY ONE OF THE ROMAN CATHOLIC PRIESTS
OF SARAGOSSA, SPAIN.**

"And behold a GREAT RED DRAGON, having seven heads and
ten horns," etc.—REV xii. 3.

FORTY-FIFTH THOUSAND.

BOSTON:
PUBLISHED BY SAMUEL JONES,
86 WASHINGTON STREET.
1854.

MYSTERY; BABYLON THE GREAT, THE MOTHER OF HARLOTS, AND ABOMINATIONS OF THE EARTH.—REV. 17, 5.

F. HEDGE. SC.

Allegorical view of Popery, as described in the Book of Revelations.

CONTENTS.

3

PREFACE.

WHEN I first designed to publish the following sheets, it was a matter of some doubt with me, whether or no I should put my name to them; for if I did, I considered that I exposed myself to the malice of a great body of men, whc would endeavor on all occasions to injure me in my reputation and fortune, if not in my life; which last (to say no more) was no unnatural suspicion of a Spaniard, and one in my case, to entertain of some fiery zealots of the Church of Rome.

But on the other hand, I foresaw, that if I concealed my name, a great part of the benefit intended to the public by this work, might be lost. For I have often observed, as to books of this kind, where facts only are related, (the truth of which in the greatest measure must depend on the credit of the relater,) that wherever the authors, out of caution or fear, have concealed themselves, the event commonly has been, that even the friends to the cause, which the facts support, give but a cold assent to them, and the enemies reject them entirely as calumnies and forgeries, without ever giving themselves the trouble of examining into the truth of that which the relater dares not openly avow. On this account, whatever the consequences may be, I resolved to put my name to this; and accordingly did so to the first proposals which were made for printing it.

But, by this means, I am at the same time obliged to say something in vindication of myself from several aspersions which I lie under, and which indeed I have already in a great degree been a sufferer by, in the opinion of many worthy gentlemen. The first is, that I never was a priest, because I have not my letters of orders to produce. This, it must be confessed, is a testimonial, without which no one has a right, or can expect to be regarded as a person of that character; unless he has very convincing arguments to offer the world, that, in his circumstances, no such thing could reasonably be expected from him; and whether or no mine are such, I leave the world to judge. My case was this:

As soon as it had pleased God by his grace to overcome in me the prejudices of my education in favor of that corrupt church, in which I had been raised, and to inspire me with a resolution to embrace the protestant religion, I saw, that in order to preserve my life, I must immediately quit Spain, where all persons, who do not publicly profess the Romish religion, are condemned death. Upon this I resolved to lose no time in making my escape, but how to make it was a matter of the greatest difficulty and danger. However, I determined rather to hazard all events, than either to continue in that church, or expose myself to certain death; and accordingly made choice of disguises as the most probable method of favoring my escape. The first I made use of, was the habit of an officer in the army: and as I was sure there would be strict inquiry and search made after me, I durst not bring along with me my letters of orders, which, upon my being suspected in any place, for the person searched after, or any other unhappy accident, would have been an undeniable evidence against me, and consequently would have condemned me to the inquisition. By this means I got safely to London, where I was most civilly received by the late Earl Stanhope, to whom I had the honor to be known when he was in Saragossa. He told me that there were some other new converts of my nation in town, and that he hoped I would follow the command of Jesus to Peter, viz. When thou art converted strengthen thy brethren.

Upon this I went to the late Lord Bishop of London, and by his lordship's order, his domestic chaplain examined me three days together; and as I could not produce the *letters of orders*, he advised me to get a certificate from my Lord Stanhope, that he knew me, and that I was a priest, which I obtained the very same day; and upon this certificate, his lordship received my recantation, after morning prayers in his chapel of Somerset-house, and licensed me to preach and officiate in a Spanish congregation composed of my Lord Stanhope, several English officers, and a few Spanish officers, new converts. By virtue of this license, I preached two years and eight months, first in the chapel of Queen's Square, Westminster, and afterwards in Oxenden's chapel, near the hay-market. But my benefactor, desirous to settle me in the English church, advised me to go chaplain to the Preston man of war, where I might have a great deal of leisure to learn the language; and being presented and approved by the Bishop of London, the Lords of the Admiralty granted me the warrant or commission of chaplain. Then his lordship, though he had given his consent in writing, to preach in Spanish, enlarged it in the warrant of the Admiralty, which license I shall take leave to insert here at large.

Whereas the Reverend Mr. Anthony Gavin was recommended to me by the right honorable Lord Stanhope, and by the same and other English gentlemen, I was certified that the said Reverend Mr. Gavin was a secular priest, and master of arts in the university of the city of Saragossa, in the kingdom of Arragon, in Spain, and that they knew him in the said city, and conversed with him several times: This is to certify that the said Reverend Mr. Gavin, after having publicly and solemnly abjured the errors of the Romish religion, and being thereupon by me reconciled to the church of England, on the 3d day of January, 1715-16, he then had my leave to officiate, in the Spanish language, 'n the chapel of Queen's Square, Westminster; and now being appointed chaplain of his Majesty's ship, the Preston, has my license to preach in English, and to administer the sacraments, at home and abroad, in all the churches and chapels of my diocess. •

Given under my hand, in London, the 13th of July, 1720.

Signed,   JOHN LONDON.

The certificate, license, and warrant, may be seen at any time, for I have them by me.

After that, the ship being put out of commission, and my Lord Stanhope being in Hanover with the king, I came over to Ireland on the importunity of a friend, with a desire to stay here until my lord's return into England : But when I was thinking of going over again, I heard of my lord's death, and having in him lost my best patron, I resolved to try in this kingdom, whether I could find any settlement; and in a few days after, by the favor of his grace my Lord Archbishop of Cashel, and the Reverend Dean Percival, I got the curacy of Gowran, which I served almost eleven months, by the license of my Lord Bishop of Ossory, who afterwards, upon my going to Cork, gave me his letters dismissory.

I was in Cork very near a year, serving the cure of a parish near it, and the Rev. Dean Maule being at that time in London, and I being recommended to him to preach in his parish church of Shandon, he went to inquire about me to the Bishop of London, who, and several other persons of distinction, were pleased to give me a good character, as the Dean on my leaving him did me the favor to certify under his hand, together with my good behaviour during my stay in Cork.

Now my case being such as I have represented it, I freely submit it to the judgment of every gentleman of ingenuity and candor to determine, whether it could be expected from me, that I should have my *letters of orders* to show : and yet whether there can be any tolerable reason to suspect my not having been a priest. I think it might be enough to silence all suspicions on this account, that I was received as a priest into the church of England, and licensed as such to preach and administer the sacraments both in that kingdom and this; and I hope no one can imagine, that any of the bishops of the best constituted and governed churches upon earth, would admit any person to so sacred a trust, without their being fully satisfied that he was in orders.

I shall, on this occasion, beg leave to mention what the Bishop of London said to me, when I told him I had not my letters of orders, but that my Lord Stanhope, and other gentlemen of honor and credit, who knew me in my native city of Saragossa, would certify, that I there was esteemed, and officiated as a priest. Bring such a certificate, said he, and I will receive and license you; for I would rather depend upon it, than any *letters of orders* you could produce, which, for ought I could tell you might have forged.

I hope what I ha e here said may convince even my enemies, of my beirg a clergyman: And how I have behaved myself as such, since I came into this kingdom, I appeal to those gentlemen I conversed with in Gowran, Gortroe and Cork, and for this last year and a half, to the officers of Col. Barrel, Brigadier Napper, Col. Hawley, Col. Newton, and Col. Lanoe's regiments, who : am sure will do me justice, and I desire no more of them; and upon an inquiry into my behaviour, I flatter myself that the public will not lightly give credit to the ill reports spread abroad by my enemies.

Another objection raised against me is, that I have perjured myself in discovering the private confessions which were made to me. In one point indeed they may call me perjured, and it is my comfort and glory that I am so in it, viz: That I have broke the oath I took, when I was ordained priest, which was, to live and die in the Roman Catholic faith. But as to the other perjury charged upon me, they lie under a mistake; for there is no oath of secrecy at all administered to confessors, as most protestants imagine. Secrecy indeed is recommended to all confessors by the casuists, and enjoined by the councils and popes so strictly, that if a confessor reveals (except in some particular cases) what is confessed to him, so as the penitent is discovered, he is to be punished for it in the inquisition; which, it must be owned, is a more effectual way of enjoining secrecy than oaths themselves.

However, I am far from imagining, that because in this case I have broken no oath, I should therefore be guilty of no crime, though I revealed every thing which was committed to my trust as a confessor, of whatever ill consequence it might be to the penitent; no, such a practice I take to be exceedingly criminal, and I do, from my soul, abhor it.

But nevertheless there are cases where, by the constitution of the church of Rome itself, the most dangerous secrets may and ought to be revealed: Such as those which are called " reserved cases," of which there are many; some reserved to the pope himself, as heresy; some to his apostolic commissary or deputy, as incest in the first degree; some to the bishop of the diocess, as the setting a neighbor's house on fire. Now in such cases the confessor cannot absolve the penitent, and therefore he is obliged to reveal the confession to the person to whom the absolution of that sin is reserved; though indeed he never mentions the penitent's name, or any circumstance by which he may be discovered.

Again, there are other cases (such as a conspiracy against the life of the Prince, or a traitorous design to overturn the government) which the confessor is obliged in conscience, and for the safety of the public, to reveal.

But besides all these, whenever the penitent's case happens to have any thing of an uncommon difficulty in it, common prudence, and a due regard to the faithful discharge of his office, will oblige a confessor to discover it to men of experience and judgment in casuistry, that he may have their advice now to proceed in it: And that is what confessors in Spain not only may do, but are bound by the word of a priest to do wherever they have an opportunity of consulting a college of confessors, or, as it is commonly called, a *moral academy.*

I believe it may be of some service on the present occasion, to inform my readers what those *moral academies* are, which are to be met with through Spain, in every city and town where there is a number of secular and regular priests: But I shall speak only of those in the city of Saragossa, as being the most perfectly acquainted with them.

A moral academy is a college or assembly consisting of several Father Confessors, in which each of them proposes some moral case which has happened to him in confession, with an exact and particular account of the confession, without mentioning the penitent's name: And the proponent having done this, every member is to deliver his opinion upon it. This is constantly practised every Friday, from two of the clock in the afternoon, till six, and sometimes till eight, as the cases proposed happen to be more or less difficult. But when there is an extraordinary intricate case to be resolved, and the members cannot agree in the resolution of it, they send one of their assembly to the *great academy*, which is a college composed of sixteen casuistical doctors, and four professors of divinity, the most learned and experienced in moral cases that may be had: and by them the case in debate is resolved, and the resolution of it entered in the books of the academy by the consent of the president and members.

The academy of the holy trinity, founded and very nobly endowed by Archbishop Gamboa, is one of the most famous in the city of Saragossa; and of it I was member for three years. I was very young and inexpert in cases of conscience, when I was first licensed to be a confessor; for the pope having dispensed with thirteen months of the time required by the canons for the age of a priest (for which I paid sixty pistoles) I was ordained before I was twenty three years old, by Don Antonio Ibannez de la Rivia de Herrera, Archbishop of Saragossa, and Viceroy of Arragon, and at the same time licensed by him to hear confessions of both sexes. In order then the better and more speedily to qualify myself for the office, I thought it my most prudent way to apply as soon as possible, to be admitted into this learned society, and as it happened, I had interest enough to succeed.

Now among many statutes left by the founder to this academy, one is this, viz: That every person who is chosen a member of it, is, on his admission, to promise upon the word of a priest, to give the whole assembly a faithful account of all the private confessions he has heard the week before, which have any thing in them difficult to be resolved: yet so as not to mention any circumstance by which the penitents may be known.

And for this end there is a book, where the secretary enters all the case proposed and resolved every Friday; and every third year there is, by the consent of the president and members of the academy, and by the approbation of the *great one*, a book printed containing all the cases resolved for three years before, and which is entitled, " compendium casuum moralium academiæ S. S. trinitatis." The academy of the holy trinity is always composed of twenty members, so that every one may easily perceive, that each of the members may be acquainted in a year or two, with many hundreds of private confessions of all ranks and conditions of people; besides those which were made to themselves: Which remark I only make, by the by, to satisfy some men, who, I am told, find fault with me for pretending to impose on the public for genuine, several confessions which were not made to myself, and consequently for the reality of which, I can have no sufficient authority.

Now after all that has been said on this head, I believe I need not be at much trouble to vindicate myself from the imputation of any criminal breach of secrecy; for if the reader observe, that on the foregoing grounds, there is no confession whatever which may not lawfully be revealed, (provided the confessor do not discover the penitent,) he cannot in justice condemn me for publishing a few, by which it is morally impossible, in the present circumstances, that the penitents should be known. Had I been much more particular than I am in my relations, and mentioned even the names and every thing else I knew of the persons, there would scarce be a possibility (considering the distance and little intercourse there is between this place and Saragossa) of their suffering in any degree by it: And I need not observe that the chief, and indeed only reason of enjoining and keeping secrecy, is the hazards the penitent may run by discovery, but I do assure the reader, that in every confession I have related, I have made use of feigned names, and avoided every circumstance by which I had the least cause to suspect the parties might be found out. And I assure him further, that most of the cases here published by me, are, in their most material points, already printed in the *compendiums* of that *moral academy* of which I was a member.

As for the reasons which moved me to publish this book, I shall only say, that as the corrupt practices, which are the subject of it, first set me upon examining into the principles of the church of Rome, and by that means of renouncing them; so I thought that the making of them public might happily produce the same effect in some others.

I did design on this occasion to give a particular account of the motives of my conversion, and leaving Spain; but being confined to three hundred pages, I must leave that and some other things relating to the sacraments of the church of Rome, to the second part, which I intend to print if the public think fit to encourage me.

I must beg the reader's pardon for my presumption in writing to him in his own language, on so short an acquaintance as I have with it. I hope he will excuse the many mistakes I have committed in the book: I shall be very well pleased to be told of, and I shall take the greater care to avoid them in the second part.

PREFACE TO THIS EDITION.

The preceding preface, which was written by the original author of this valuable work, is published in his own words, in order that the reader may understand his motives and views in disclosing the important facts which had come to his knowledge in relation to Popery. Having abjured the errors of the Romish religion, he felt constrained to warn others of the insidious arts to which he had been himself the victim, and to point out the absurd contrivances by which the priesthood of that denomination impose upon the credulity of the ignorant and unsuspecting. In doing this he has given to the world a mass of facts which cannot be disbelieved, nor controverted, and which must satisfy every intelligent mind of the gross fallacy of the doctrines of that ancient church, and the dreadful corruptions practised by those who administer its concerns.

As a christian people, it becomes us to examine carefully the grounds of our belief, and to decide with due caution for ourselves, whether the doctrines and standards of faith proposed for our acceptance by any set of men, conform with those handed down to us by the fathers. By placing this book in the hands of the American reader, he will be enabled to compare it with the only safe rule of faith and practice, the blessed Gospel of Christ, which is all truth, purity, and wisdom, and cannot mislead.

The American reader will also decide, whether the forms of the Roman catholic religion are suited to the circumstances of a republican people. If even the doctrines of that faith, were safe and pure, we cannot believe that the complicated machinery, the expensive and unmeaning parade, and the despotic principles of its church government, could ever be received into practice by the good sense of intelligent and free people.

To make this compilation more complete, we have added to the original work of Mr. Gavin, an account of " The Inquisition of Goa," by the celebrated Dr. Buchanan, who travelled and resided in Asia; an account of " The Inquisition at Macerata in Italy," by Mr. Bower; and a Summary of the Roman catholic faith, carefully prepared from their own works, and which will place the whole subject clearly within the comprehension of the plainest understanding.

Flagellation of a Prince by the Roman Clergy in the 18th century.

THE GREAT RED DRAGON.

PART I.

AURICULAR confession being one of the five commandments
of the Roman-Catholic Church, and a condition necessarily
required in one of their sacraments; and being too an article
that will contribute very much to the discovery of many other
errors of that communion, it may be proper to make use of
the Master-Key, and begin with it: And first of all, with the
Father confessors, who are the only key-keepers of it.

Though a priest cannot be licensed, by the canons of their
church, to hear men's confessions, till he is thirty years, nor
to confess women till forty years of age, yet ordinarily he
gets a dispensation from the bishop, to whom his probity, secrecy, and sober conversation are represented by one of the
diocesan *examinators, his friend, or by some person of interest with his lordship; and by that means he gets a confessor's
license, most commonly, the day he gets his letters of orders,
viz.: Some at three-and-twenty, and some at four-and-twenty
years of age, not only for men, but for women's confessions
also. I say, some at three-and-twenty; for the Pope dispenses
with thirteen months, to those that pay a sum of money; of
which I shall speak in another place.

To priests thus licensed, to be judges of the tribunal of conscience, men and women discover their sins, their actions, their
thoughts, nay, their very dreams, if they happen to be impure.
I say, judges of the tribunal of conscience; for when they are

---

* Those that are appointed by the bishop, to examine those that are to be
ordained or licensed to preach and hear confessions.

licensed, they ought to resolve any case (let it be ever so hard) proposed by the penitent: And by this means it must often happen, that a young man who, perhaps, does not know more than a few definitions (which he has learned in a little manual of some casuistical authors) of what is sin, shall sit in such a tribunal, to judge, in the most intricate cases, the consciences of men, and men too that may be his masters.

I saw a reverend father* who had been eight-and twenty years professor of divinity in one of the most considerable† universities of Spain, and one of the most famous men for his learning, in that religion, kneel down before a young‡ priest of twenty-four years of age, and confess his sins to him. Who would not be surprised at them both? A man fit to be the judge, to act the part of a criminal before an ignorant judge, who, I am sure, could scarcely then tell the titles of the Summæ Morales.

Nay, the Pope, notwithstanding all his infallibility, doth kneel down before his confessor, tell him his sins, heareth his correction, and receives and performs whatever penance he imposeth upon him. This is the only difference between the Pope's confessor, and the confessor of Kings and other persons, that all confessors sit down to hear Kings and other persons, but the Pope's confessor kneels down himself to hear the Holy Father. What, the holy one upon earth humble himself as a sinner? Holiness and sin in one and the same subject, is a plain contradiction in terms.

If we ask the Roman-Catholics, Why so learned men, and the Pope, do so? They will answer, that they do it out of reverence to such a sacrament, out of humility, and to give a token and testimony of their hearty sorrow for their sins. And as for the Pope, they say he does it to show an example of humility, as Jesus Christ did, when he washed the Apostles' feet.

This answer is true, but they do not say the whole truth in it; for, besides the aforesaid reasons, they have another, as Molina tells them, viz: That the penitent ought to submit entirely to his confessor's correction, advice, and penance; and he excepts no body from the necessary requisite of a true penitent. Who would not be surprised (I say again) that a man of noted learning would submit himself to a young, unexpe-

* Fr. James Garcia.
† The university of Saragossa, in the kingdom of Arragon, in Spain, which, according to their historians, was built by Sertorious.
‡ The thing happened to me when I was 24 years of age.
§ In this Moral Summ. Chap. xviii. of the requisites of a true penitent.

rienced priest, as to a judge of his conscience, take his advice, and receive his correction and penance?

What would a Roman-Catholic say, if he should see one of our learned bishops go to the college to consult a young collegian in a nice point of divinity; nay, to take his advice, and submit to his opinion? Really, the Roman would heartily laugh at him, and with a great deal of reason; nay, he could say, that his lordship was not right in his senses. What then can a protestant say of those infatuated, learned men of the church of Rome, when they do more than what is here supposed?

As to the Pope (I say) it is a damnable opinion to compare him, in this case, to our Saviour Jesus; for Christ knew not sin, but gave us an example of humility and patience, obedience and poverty. He washed the apostles' feet; and though we cannot know by the Scripture whether he did kneel down or not to wash them: Suppose that he did, he did it only out of a true humility, and not to confess his sins. But the Pope doth kneel down, not to give an example of humility and patience, but really to confess his sins: Not to give an example of obedience; for, being *supreme pontifex*, he obeys nobody, and assumes a command over the whole world: nor of poverty; for Pope and necessity dwell far from one another. And if some ignorant Roman-Catholic should say, that the Pope, as Pope, has no sin, we may prove the contrary with Cipriano de Valeria,* who gives an account of all the bastards of several Popes for many years past. The Pope's bastards, in *Latin*, are called *nepotes*. Now mind, O reader, this common saying in Latin, among the Roman-Catholics: *Solent clerici filios suos vocare sobrinos aut nepotes:* That is, The priests use to call their own sons *cousins* or *nephews*. And when we give these instances to some of their learned men, (as I did to one in London,) they say, *Angelorum est peccare, hominumque penitere:* i. e. It belongs to angels to sin, and to men to repent. By this they acknowledge that the Pope is a sinner, and nevertheless they call him His holiness, and the most Holy father.

Who then would not be surprised to see the most holy Jesus Christ's vicar on earth, and the infallible in whatever he says, and doth submit himself to confess his sins to a man, and a man too that has no other power to correct him, to advise and impose a penance upon the most holy one, than what his holiness has

---

* The lives of the Popes, and the sacrifice of Mass.

been pleased to grant him? Every body indeed that has a grain of sense of religion, and reflects seriously on it.

I come now to their *Auricular Confession,* and of the ways and methods they practise and observe in the confessing of their sins. There is among them two ranks of people, learned and unlearned. The learned confess by these three general heads, thought, word, and deed, reducing into them all sorts of sins. The unlearned confess the ten commandments, discovering by them all the mortal sins which they have committed since their last confession. I say mortal sins; for as to the venial sins or sins of a small matter, the opinion of their casuistical authors* is, they are washed away by the sign of the cross, or by sprinkling the face with the holy water. To the discovery of the mortal sins, the father confessor doth very much help the penitent; for he sometimes, out of pure zeal, but most commonly out of curiosity, asks them many questions to know whether they do remember all their sins or not? By these and the like questions, the confessors do more mischief than good, especially to the ignorant people and young women; for perhaps they do not know what simple fornication is? What voluntary or involuntary pollution? What impure desire? What simple motion of our hearts? What relapse, reincidence, or reiteration of sins? and the like; and then by the confessor's indiscreet questions, the penitents learn things of which they never had dreamed before; and when they come to that tribunal with a sincere, ignorant heart, to receive advice and instruction, they go home with light, knowledge, and an idea of sins unknown to them before.

I said, that the confessors do ask questions, most commonly out of curiosity, though they are warned by their casuistical authors to be prudent, discreet, and very cautious in the questions they ask, especially if the penitent be a young woman, or an ignorant; for as Pineda says,† It is better to let them go ignorant than instructed in new sins. But contrary to this good maxim, they are so indiscreet in this point, that I saw in the city of Lisbon, in Portugal, a girl of ten years of age, coming from church, ask her mother what deflouring was? For the father confessor had asked her whether she was defloured or

---

* *Parez, Irribarren, and Salazar,* in his compend. Moral. Sect. 12. *de vitiis et peccatis,* gives a catalogue of the venial sins, and says, among others, that to eat flesh on a day prohibited by the church, without minding it, was so. To kill a man, throwing a stone through the window, or being drunk, or in the first motion of his passion, are venial sins, &c.

† Tract, de Penit. Sect. 1. sect. vii.

not? And the mother, more discreet than the confessor, tola the girl, that the meaning was, whether she took delight in smelling flowers or not? And so she stopped her child's curiosity. But of this and many other indiscretions I shall speak more particularly by and by.

Now observe, that as a penitent cannot hide any thing from the spiritual judge, else he would make a sacrilegious confession; so I cannot hide any thing from the public, which is to be my hearer, and the temporal judge of my work, else I should betray my conscience: Therefore, (to the best of my memory, and as one that expects to be called before the dreadful tribunal of God, on account of what I now write and say, if I do not say and write the truth from the bottom of my heart,) I shall give a faithful, plain account of the Roman's auricular confession, and of the most usual questions and answers between the confessors and penitents; and this I shall do in so plain a style that every body may go along with me.

And first, it is very proper to give an account of what the penitents do, from the time they come into the church till they begin their confession. When the penitent comes into the church, he takes holy water and sprinkles his face, and, making the sign of the cross, says, *per signum crucis de inimicis nostris libera nos Deus noster: In nomine Patris et Filii, et Spiritus Sancti.* Amen. i. e. By the sign of the cross deliver us our God from our enemies, in the name of the Father, and of the Son, and of the Holy Ghost. *Amen.* Then the penitent goes on, and kneels down before the great altar, where the great host (of which I shall speak in another place) is kept in a neat and rich tabernacle, with a brass or silver lamp, hanging before it, and burning continually, night and day. There he makes a prayer, first to the holy sacrament of the altar, (as they call it) after to the Virgin Mary, and to the titular saints of the church. Then turns about upon his knees, and visits five altars, or if there is but one altar in the church, five times that altar, and says before each of them five times, *Pater noster,* &c. and five times *Ave Maria,* &c. with *Gloria Patria,* &c.

Then he rises, and goes to the confessionary: i. e. The confessing place, where the confessor sits in a chair like our hackney chairs, which is most commonly placed in some of the chapels, and in the darkest place of the church. The chairs, generally speaking, have an iron grate at each side, but none at all before: and some days of devotion, or on a great festival, there is such a crowd of people that you may see three penitents at once about the chair, one at each grate, and the other

at the door, though only one confesses at a time, whispering
in the confessor's ear, that the others should not hear what he
says; and when one has done, the other begins, and so on: But
most commonly they confess at the door of the chair, one after
another; for thus the confessor has an opportunity of knowing
the penitent: And though many gentlewomen, either out of
bashfulness, shame, or modesty, do endeavor to hide their faces with a fan, or veil, notwithstanding all this they are known
by the confessor, who, if curious, by crafty questions brings
them to tell him their names and houses, and this in the very
act of confession, or else he examines their faces when the
confession s over whilst the penitents are kissing his hand or
sleeve; and if he cannot know them this way, he goes himself
to give the sacrament, and then every one being obliged to
show her face, is known by the curious confessor, who doth
this not without a private view and design, as will appear at
the end of some private confessions.

The penitent then kneeling, bows herself to the ground before the confessor, and makes again the sign of the cross in
the aforesaid form; and having in her hand the beads, or rosary of the Virgin Mary, begins the general confession of sins,
which some say in Latin, and some in the vulgar tongue; therefore it seems proper to give a copy of it both in Latin and
English:—

Confiteor Deo Omnipotenti; beatae Mariae semper Virgini,
beato Michaeli Archangelo, beato Joanni Baptistae, sanctis
apostolis Petro et Paulo, omnibus sanctis, et tibi, Pater; quia
peccavi nimis cogitatione, verbo, et opere, mea culpa, mea
culpa, mea maxima culpa: Ideo precor beatam Mariam semper Virginem, beatum Michaelem Archangelum, beatum Joan-
nem Baptistam, sanctos apostolos Petrum et Paulum, omnes
sanctos, et te, Pater, orare pro me ad Dominum Deum nos-
trum. *Amen.*

I do confess to God Almighty, to the blessed Mary, always a
Virgin, to the blessed Archangel Michael, to the blessed John
Baptist, to the holy apostles Peter and Paul, to all the saints,
and to thee, O Father, that I have too much sinned by thought,
word, and deed, by my fault, by my fault, by my greatest fault.
Therefore I beseech the blessed Mary, always a Virgin, the
blessed Archangel Michael, the blessed John Baptist, the holy
apostles Peter and Paul, all the saints, and thee, O Father, to
pray to God our Lord for me. *Amen.*

This done, the penitent raises him from his prostration to his
knees, and touching with his lip either the ear or the cheek of

the Spiritual Father, begins to discover his sins by the ten commandments: And here it may be necessary to give a translation of their ten commandments, word for word.

The commandments of the law of God are ten: The three first do pertain to the honor of God; and the other seven to the benefit of our neighbor.

I. Thou shalt love God above all things.
II. Thou shalt not swear.
III. Thou shalt sanctify the holy days.
IV. Thou shalt honor thy father and mother.
V. Thou shalt not kill.
VI. Thou shalt not commit fornication.
VII. Thou shalt not steal.
VIII. Thou shalt not bear false witness, nor lie.
IX. Thou shalt not covet thy neighbor's wife.
X. Thou shalt not covet the things which are another's.

These ten commandments are comprised in two, viz: To serve and love God, and thy neighbor as thyself. *Amen.*

Now, not to forget any thing that may instruct the public, it is to the purpose to give an account of the little children's confessions; I mean of those that have not yet attained the seventh year of their age; for at seven they begin most commonly to receive the sacrament, and confess in private with all the formalities of their church.

There is in every city, in every parish, in every town and village, a Lent preacher; and there is but one difference among them, viz.: that some preachers preach every day in Lent; some three sermons a week; some two, viz.: on Wednesdays and Sundays, and some only on Sundays, and the holy days that happen to fall in Lent. The preacher of the parish pitches upon one day of the week, most commonly in the middle of Lent, to hear the children's confessions, and gives notice to the congregation the Sunday before, that every father of a family may send his children, both boys and girls, to church, on the day appointed, in the afternoon. The mothers dress their children the best they can that day, and give them the offering money for the expiation of their sins. That afternoon is a holy day in the parish, not by precept, but by custom, for no parishioner, either old or young, man or woman, misseth to go and hear the children's confessions. For it is reckoned, among them, a greater diversion than a comedy, as you may judge by the following account.

The day appointed, the children repair to church at three of the clock, where the preacher is waiting for them with a long reed in his hand, and when all are together, (sometimes 150 in number, and sometimes less,) the reverend Father placeth them in a circle round himself, and then kneeling down, (the children also doing the same,) makes the sign of the cross, and says a short prayer. This done, he exhorteth the children to hide no sin from him, but to tell him all they have committed. Then he strikes, with his reed, the child whom he designs to confess the first, and asks him the following questions:

Confessor. How long is it since you last confessed?

Boy. Father, a whole year, or the last Lent.

Conf. And how many sins have you committed from that time till now?

Boy. Two dozen.

Now the confessor asks round about.

Conf. And you?

Boy. A thousand and ten.

Another will say a bag full of small lies, and ten big sins; and so one after another answers, and tells many childish things.

Conf. But pray, you say that you have committed ten big sins, tell me how big?

Boy. As big as a tree.

Conf. But tell me the sins.

Boy. There is one sin I committed, which I dare not tell your reverence before all the people; for somebody here present will kill me, if he heareth it.

Conf. Well, come out of the circle, and tell it me.

They both go out, and with a loud voice, he tells him, tha such a day he stole a nest of sparrows from a tree of another boy's, and that if he knew it, he would kill him. Then both come again into the circle, and the father asks other boys and girls so many ridiculous questions, and the children answer him so many pleasant, innocent things, that the congregation laughs all the while. One will say, that his sins are red, another that one of his sins is white, one black, and one green, and in these trifling questions they spend two hours' time. When the congregation is weary of laughing, the Confessor gives the children a correction, and bids them not to sin any more, for a black boy takes along with him the wicked children Then he asks the offering, and after he has got all from them, gives them the penance for their sins. To one he says, I give you for penance, to eat a sweet cake; to another, not to go to school the day following; to another, to desire his mother to buy him a new hat and such things as these; and pronouncing

the words of absolution, he dismisseth the congregation with
Amen, so be it, every year.

These are the first foundations of the Romish religion for
youth. Now, O reader! You may make reflections upon it, and
the more you will reflect, so much more you will hate the corruptions of that communion, and it shall evidently appear to
you, that the serious, religious instruction of our church, as to
the youth, is reasonable, solid, and without reproach. O! that
all Protestants would remember the rules they learned from
their youth, and practise them while they live! Sure I am,
they should be like angels on earth, and blessed forever after
death, in heaven.

From seven till fifteen, there is no extraordinary thing to say
of young people, only that from seven years of age, they begin
to confess in private. The confessors have very little trouble
with such young people, and likewise little profit, except with
a Puella, who sometimes begins at twelve years the course of
a lewd life, and then the Confessor finds business and profit
enough, when she comes to confess. Now I come to give an
account of several private confessions of both sexes, beginning
from people of fifteen years of age. The confession is a dialogue between the Spiritual Father and the penitent; therefore I shall deliver the confessions in a way of dialogue. The
letter C. signifies Confessor, and several other letters the
names of the penitents.

The confession of a young woman in Saragossa, whom I shall call Mary.
And this I set down chiefly to show the common form of their confessing
penitents. The thing was not public; and therefore I give it under a supposed name.

Confessor. How long is it since you last confessed?

Mary. It is two years and two months.

Conf. Pray, do you know the commandments of our holy
mother, the church?

Mary. Yea, Father.

Conf. Rehearse them.

Mary. The commandments of our holy mother, the church,
are five. 1. To hear Mass on Sundays and Holy days. 2.
To confess, at least, once in a year, and oftener, if there be
danger of death. 3. To receive the eucharist. 4. To fast.
5. To pay tithes and Primitia.*

* Primitia is to pay, besides the tenth, one thirtieth part of the fruits of the
earth, towards the repair of the church vestments, &c.

Conf. Now rehearse the seven sacraments.

Mary. The sacraments of the holy mother, the church, are seven. 1. Baptism. 2. Confirmation. 3. Penance. 4. The Lord's supper. 5. Extreme unction. 6. Holy orders. 7. Matrimony.—*Amen.*

Conf. You see in the second commandment of the church, and in the third, among the sacraments, that you are obliged to confess every year. Why then have you neglected so much longer a time to fulfil the precept of our holy mother?

Mary. As I was young, and a great sinner, I was ashamed, reverend Father, to confess my sins to the priest of our parish, for fear he should know me by some passages of my life, which would be prejudicial to me, and to several other persons related to my family.

Conf. But you know that it is the indispensable duty of the minister of the parish, to expose in the church, after Easter, all those who have not confessed, nor received the sacrament before that time.

Mary. I do know it very well; but I went out of the city towards the middle of Lent, and I did not come back again till after Easter; and when I was asked in the country, whether I had confessed that Lent or not? I said, that I had done it in the city: and when the minister of the parish asked me the same question, I told him, I had done it in the country. So, with this lie, I freed myself from the public censure of the church.

Conf. And did you perform the last penance imposed upon you?

Mary. Yea, Father, but not with that exactness I was commanded.

Conf. What was the penance?

Mary. To fast three days upon bread and water, and to give ten reals of plate,* and to say five masses for the souls in purgatory. I did perform the first, but not the second, because I could not get money for it unknown to my parents at that time.

Conf. Do you promise me to perform it as soon as you can?

Mary. I have the money here, which I will leave with you, and you may say, or order another priest to say the Masses.

Conf. Very well: but tell me now, what reason have you to come and confess out of the time appointed by the church? Is it for devotion, to quiet your conscience, and merely to make your peace with God Almighty, or some worldly end?

Mary. Good Father, pity my condition, and pray put me in

* A real of plate is about seven pence of our money in Ireland.

the right way of salvation, for I am ready to despair of God's mercy, if you do not quiet and ease my troubled conscience. Now I will answer to your question: the reason is, because a gentleman who, under promise of marriage, has kept me these two last years, is dead two months ago; and I have resolved in my heart to retire myself into a monastery, and to end there my days, serving God and his holy mother, the Virgin Mary.

Conf. Do not take any resolution precipitately, for, may be if your passion grows cool, you will alter your mind; and I suspect, with a great deal of reason, that your repentance is not sincere, and that you come to confess out of sorrow for the gentleman's death, more than out of sorrow for your sins; and if it be so, I advise you to take more time to consider the state of your conscience, and to come to me a fortnight hence.

Mary. My Father, all the world shall not alter my mind, and the daily remorse of my conscience brings me to your feet, with a full resolution to confess all my sins, in order to obtain absolution, and to live a new life hereafter.

Conf. If it is so, let us, in the name of God, begin the confession, and I require of you not to forget any circumstance of sin, which may contribute to ease your conscience. Above all, I desire of you to lay aside shame, while you confess your sins; for, suppose that your sins exceed the number of stars, or the number of the sands of the sea, God's mercy is infinite, and accepts of the true, penitent heart; for he wills not the death of a sinner, but that he should repent and turn to him.

Mary. I do design to open freely my heart to you, and to follow your advice, as to the spiritual course of my life.

Conf. Begin then by the first commandment.

Mary. I do confess, in this commandment, that I have not loved God above all things; for all my care, these two years past, has been to please Don Francisco, in whatever thing he desired me, and, to the best of my memory, I did not think of God, nor of his mother, Mary, for many months together.

Conf. Have you constantly frequented the assemblies of the faithful, and heard Mass on Sundays, and holy days?

Mary. No, Father; sometimes I have been four months without going to church.

Conf. You have done a great injury to your soul, and you have given a great scandal to your neighbors.

Mary. As for the first, I own it, for every Sunday and holy day I went out in the morning, and in so populous a city, they could not know the church used to resort to.

Conf. Did it come into your mind all this while, that God would punish you for your sins?

Mary. Yea, Father: but the Virgin Mary is my advocate. I keep her image by my bedside, and used to address my prayer to her every night before I went to bed, and I always had a great hope in her.

Conf. If your devotion to the Virgin Mary is so fervent, you must believe that your heart is moved to repentance by her influence and mediation; and I charge you to continue the same devotion while you live, and fear nothing afterwards.

Mary. That is my design.

Conf. Go on.

Mary. The second commandment is, *Thou shalt not swear.* I never was guilty of swearing, but I have a custom of saying, *Such a thing is so, as sure as there is a God in heaven:* and this I repeat very often every day.

Conf. That is a sinful custom, for we cannot swear nor affirm any thing by heaven or earth, as the scripture tells us; and less by Him who has the throne of his habitation in heaven: so you must break off that custom, or else you commit a sin every time you make use of it. Go on.

Mary. The third is, *Thou shalt sanctify the holy days.* I have told you already, my spiritual Father, that I have neglected, sometimes, to go to Mass, four months together; and to the best of my memory, in these two years and two months, I have missed sixty Sundays and holy days going to Mass, and when I did go, my mind was so much taken up with other diversions, that I did not mind the requisite devotion, for which I am heartily sorry.

Conf. I hope you will not do so for the future; and so, go on.

Mary. The fourth is, *Thou shalt honor father and mother* I have father and mother; as to my father, I do love, honor and fear him; as to my mother, I do confess, that I have answered and acted contrary to the duty, respect, and reverence due to her, for her suspecting and watching my actions and falsesteps, and giving me a christian correction: I have abused her, nay, sometimes, I have lifted up my hand to threaten her; and these proceedings of mine towards my good mother, torture now my heart.

Conf. I am glad to observe your grief, and you may be sure, God will forgive you these and other sins upon your hearty repentance, if you persevere in it. Go on.

Mary. The fifth is, *Thou shalt not kill.* I have not trans-

gressed this commandment effectively and immediately, but I
have done it affectively and mediately, and at second hand;
for a gentlewoman, who was a great hindrance to my designs,
once provoked me to such a pitch, that I put in execution all
the means of revenge I could think of, and gave ten pistoles
to an assassin, to take away her life.

Conf. And did he kill her?

Mary. No, Father, for she kept her house for three months,
and in that time we were reconciled, and now we are very
good friends.

Conf. Have you asked her pardon, and told her your design?

Mary. I did not tell her in express terms, but I told her
that I had an ill will to her, and that at that time I could have
killed her, had I got an opportunity for it: for which I heartily begged her pardon: she did forgive me, and so we live
ever since like two sisters.

Conf. Go on.

Mary. The sixth, *Thou shalt not commit fornication.* In
the first place, I do confess that I have unlawfully conversed -
with the said Don Francisco, for two years, and this unlawful
commerce has made me fall into many other sins.

Conf. Did he promise solemnly to marry you.

Mary. He did, but could not perform it, while his father
was alive.

Conf. Tell me, from the beginning, to the day of his
death, and to the best of your memory, your sinful thoughts,
words, actions, nay, your very dreams, about this matter.

Mary. Father, the gentleman was our neighbor, of a good
family and fortune, and by means of the neighborly friendship
of our parents, we had the opportunity to talk with one another as much as we pleased. For two years together, we loved
one another in innocence, but at last he discovered to me one
day, when our parents were abroad, the great inclination he
had for me; and that having grown to a passion, and this to
an inexpressible love, he could no longer hide it from me:
that his design was to marry me as soon as his father should
die, and that he was willing to give me all the proofs of sincerity and unfeigned love I could desire from him. To this I
answered, that if it was so, I was ready to promise never to
marry another during his life: To this, he took a sign of the
crucifix in his hands, and bowing down before an image of the
Virgin Mary, called the four elements to be witnesses of the
sincerity of his vows, nay, all the saints of the heavenly court.

C

to appear against him in the day of judgment, if he was not true in heart and words; and said, that by the crucifix in his hands, and by the image of the Virgin Mary, there present, he, promised and swore never to marry another during my life.— I answered him in the same manner; and ever since, we have lived with the familiarities of husband and wife. The effect of this reciprocal promise was the ruin of my soul, and the beginning of my sinful life; for ever since, I minded nothing else, but to please him and myself, when I had an opportunity.

Conf. How often did he visit you?

Mary. The first year he came to my room every night, after both families were gone to bed; for in the vault of his house, which joins to ours, we dug one night through the earth, and made a passage wide enough for the purpose, which we covered on each side with a large earthen water-jar; and by that means he came to me every night. But my grief is double, when I consider, that, engaging my own maid into this intrigue, I have been the occasion of her ruin too; for by my ill example, she lived in the same way with the gentleman's servant, and I own that I have been the occasion of all her sins too.

Conf. And the second year did he visit you so often?

Mary. No, father; for the breach in the vault was discovered by his father, and was stopped immediately; but nobody suspected any thing of our intimacy, except my mother, who from something she had observed, began to question me, and afterwards became more suspicious and watchful.

Conf. Did any effect of these visits come to light?

Mary. It would, had I not been so barbarous and inhuman to prevent it, by a remedy I took, which answered my purpose.

Conf. And how could you get the remedy, there being a rigorous law against it?

Mary. The procuring it brought me into a yet wickeder life; for I was acquainted with a friar, a cousin of mine, who had always expressed a great esteem for me; but one day after dinner, being alone, he began to make love to me, and was going to take greater liberties than he had ever done before. I told him that if he could keep a secret, and do me a service, I would comply with his desire. He promised me to do it upon the word of a priest. Then I told him my business, and the day after he brought me the necessary medicine ; and ever since I was freed from that uneasiness. I have lived the same course of life with my cousin; nay, as I was under such an obligation to him, I have ever since been obliged to allow him many other liberties in my house.

Conf. Are those other liberties he took in your house sinful or not?

Mary. The liberties I mean are, that he desired me to gratify his companion too, several times, and to consent that my maid should satisfy his lusts; and not only this, but by desiring me to corrupt one of my friends, he has ruined her soul; for, being in the same condition I had been in before, I was obliged, out of fear, to furnish her with the same remedy, which produced the same effect. Besides these wicked actions, I have robbed my parents to supply him with whatever money he demanded.

Conf. But as to Don Francisco, pray tell me, how often did he visit you since?

Mary. The second year he could not see me in private but very seldom, and in a sacred place; for having no opportunity at home, nor abroad, I used to go to a little chapel out of the town; and having gained the hermit with money, we continued our commerce, that way, for six or eight times the second year.

Conf. Your sins are aggravated, both by the circumstance of the sacred place, and by your cousin's being a Priest, besides the two murders committed by you, one in yourself, and the other in your friend. Nay, go on, if you have any more to say upon this subject.

Mary. I have nothing else to say, as to the commandment, but that I am heartily sorry for all these my misdoings.

Conf. Go on.

Mary. The seventh, *Thou shalt not steal.* I have nothing to confess in this commandment but what I have told you already, i. e. that I have stolen many things from my father's house, to satisfy my cousin's thirst of money; and that I have advised my friend to do the same; though this was done by me, only for fear that he should expose us, if we had not given him what he desired.

Conf. And do you design to continue the same life with your cousin, for fear of being discovered?

Mary. No, Father; for he is sent to another convent, to be professor of divinity for three years; and if he comes back again, he shall find me in a monastery; and then I will be safe, and free from his wicked attempts.

Conf How long is it since he went away?

Mary. Three months, and his companion is dead; so, God

be thanked, I am without any apprehension or fear now, and I hope to see my good design accomplished.

Conf. Go on.

Mary. The eighth is, *Thou shalt not bear false witness nor lie.* The ninth, *Thou shalt not covet thy neighbor's wife.* The tenth, *Thou shalt not covet any things which are another's.* I know nothing in these three commandments, that trouble my conscience : Therefore, I conclude by confessing, in general and particular, all the sins of my whole life, committed by *thought, word* and *deed,* and I am heartily sorry for them all, and ask God's pardon, and your advice, penance and absolution.. *Amen.*

Conf. Have you trangressed the fourth commandment of the church?

M..ry. Yea, father; for I did not fast as it prescribes, for though I did abstain from flesh, yet I did not keep the form of fasting these two years past; but I have done it since the gentleman's death.

Conf. Have you this year taken the bull of indulgences?

Mary Yea, Father.

Conf. Have you visited five altars, the days appointed for his holiness to take a soul out of purgatory?

Mary. I did not for several days.

Conf. Do you promise me, as a minister of God, and as if you were now before the tribunal of the dreadful judge, to amend your life, and to avoid all the occasions of falling into the same or other sins, and to frequent for the future, this sacrament, and the others, and to obey the commandments of God, as things absolutely necessary to the salvation of your soul?

Mary. That is my design, with the help of God, and of the blessed Virgin Mary, in whom I put my whole trust and confidence.

Conf. Your contrition must be the foundation of your new life, for if you fall into other sins after this signal benefit you have received from God, and his blessed mother, of calling you to repentance, it will be a hard thing for you to obtain pardon and forgiveness. You see God has taken away all the obstacles of your true repentance; pray ask continually his grace, that you may make good use of these heavenly favors. But you ought to consider, that though you shall be freed by my absolution from the eternal pains your manifold sins deserve, you shall not be free from the sufferings of purgatory, where your soul must be purified by fire, if you in this present life do not take care to redeem your soul from that terrible flame, by ordering some masses for the relief of souls in purgatory.

Mary. I design to do it as far as it lies in my power.

Conf. Now, to show your obedience to God, and our mother, the church, you must perform the following penance: You must fast every second day, to mortify your lusts and passions, and this for the space of two months. You must visit five altars every second day, and one privileged altar, and say in each of them five times *Pater noster*, &c., and five times *Ave Mary*, &c. You must say too every day for two months' time, three-and-thirty times the *creed*, in honor and memory of the three-and-thirty years that our Saviour did live upon earth; and you must confess once a week; and by the continuance of these spiritual exercises, your soul may be preserved from several temptations, and may be happy forever.

Mary. I will do all that with the help of God.

Conf. Say the act of contrition by which I absolve you.

Mary. O God, my God, I have sinned against thee; I am heartily sorry, &c.

Conf. Our Lord Jesus Christ absolve thee; and by the authority given me, I absolve thee, &c.

A private confession of a woman to a Friar of the Dominican order, laid down in writing before the Moral Academy, 1710, and the opinions of the members about it. The person was not known, therefore I shall call her Leonore.

Leonore did confess to F. Joseph Riva the following misdo ings:

Leonore. My reverend Father, I come to this place to make a general confession of all the sins I have committed in the whole course of my life, or of all those I can remember.

Conf. How long have you been preparing yourself for this general confession?

Leon. Eight days.

Conf. Eight days are not enough to recollect yourself, and bring into your memory all the sins of your life.

Leon. Father, have patience till you hear me, and then you may judge whether my confession be perfect or imperfect.

Conf. And how long is it since you confessed the last time?

Leon. The last time I confessed was the Sunday before Easter, which is eleven months and twenty days.

Conf. Did you accomplish the penance then imposed upor you?

Leon. Yea, father.

Conf. Begin then your confession.

Leon. I have neglected my duty towards God, by whose holy name I have many times sworn. I have not sanctified his holy days as I was obliged by law, nor honored my parents and superiors. I have many and many times desired the death of my neighbors, when I was in a passion. I have been deeply engaged in amorous intrigues with many people of all ranks, but these two years past most constantly with Don Pedro Hasta, who is the only support of my life.

Conf. Now I find out the reason why you have so long neglected to come and confess; and I do expect, that you will tell me all the circumstances of your life, that I may judge the present state of your conscience.

Leon. Father, as for the sins of my youth, till I was sixteen years of age, they are of no great consequence, and I hope God will pardon me. Now my general confession begins from that time, when I fell into the first sin, which was in the following manner:

The confessor of our family was a Franciscan friar, who was absolute master in our house; for my father and mother were entirely governed by him. It was about that time of my life I lost my mother; and a month after her my father died, leaving all his substance to the father confessor, to dispose of at his own fancy, reserving only a certain part which I was to have, to settle me in the world, conditionally that I was obedient to him. A month after my father's death, on pretence of taking care of every thing that was in the house, he ordered a bed for himself in the chamber next to mine, where my maid also used to lie. After supper, the first night he came home, he addressed himself thus to me: My daughter, you may with reason call me your father, for you are the only child your father left under my care. Your patrimony is in my hands, and you ought to obey me blindly in every thing: So in the first place order your maid's bed to be removed out of your own chamber into another. Which being done accordingly, we parted, and went each one to our own room; but scarcely had an hour past away, when the father came into my chamber, and what by flattery and promises, and what by threatenings, he deprived me of my best patrimony, my innocence. We continued this course of life till, as I believe, he was tired of me: for two months after, he took every thing out of the house, and went to his convent, where he died in ten days time; and by his death I lost the patrimony left me by my father, and with it all my support; and as my parents had spared nothing in my education, and as I had always been kept in the greatest affluence, you may judge how I was affected by the miserable circumstances I was then left in, with servants to maintain, and nothing in the world to supply even the necessary expenses of my house. This made me the more ready to accept the first offer that should be made me, and my condition being known to an officer of the army, he came to offer me his humble services. I complied with his desire, and so for two years we lived together, till at last he was obliged to repair to his regiment at Catalonia; and though he left me appointments more than sufficient for my subsistence during his absence, yet all our correspondence was soon broken off by his death, which happened soon after. Then, resolving to alter my life and conversation, I went to confess, and after having given an account to my confessor of my life, he asked my name, did promise to come the next day to see me, and to put me into a comfortable and creditable way of living. I was very glad to get such a patron, and so the next day I waited at home for him.

The father came, and after various discourses, he took me by the hand into my chamber, and told me that if I was willing to put in his hands my jewels, and what other things of value I had got from the officer, he would engage to get a gentleman suitable to my condition to marry me. I did every thing as he desired me; and so taking along with him all I had in the world, he carried them to his cell.

The next day he came to see me, and made me another proposal, very different from what I expected; for he told me that I must comply with his desire, or else he would expose me, and inform against me before the holy tribunal of the inquisition: So, rather than incur that danger, I did for the space of six months, in which, having nothing to live upon, (for he kept my jewels,) I was obliged to abandon myself to many other gentlemen, by whom I was maintained.

At last, he left me, and I still continued my wicked life, unlawfully conversing with married and unmarried gentlemen a whole year, and not daring to confess, for fear of experiencing the same treatment from another confessor.

Conf. But how could you fulfil the precept of the church, and not be exposed in the church after Easter, all that while?

Leon. I went to an old easy father, and promised him a pis-

tole for a certificate of confession, which he gave me witr,
out further inquiring into the matter; and so I did satisfy the
curate of the parish with it. But last year I went to confess,
and the confessor was very strict, and would not give me absolution, because I was an habitual sinner; but I gave him five
pistoles for ten masses, and then he told me that a confessor's
duty was to take care of the souls in purgatory, and that upon
their account he could not refuse me absolution; so by that
way I escaped the censure of the church.

Conf. How long is it since you broke off your sinful life?

Leon. But six weeks.

Conf. I cannot absolve you now, but come again next
Thursday, and I will consult upon all the circumstances of
your life and then I will absolve you.

Leon. Father, I have more to say: For I stole from the
church a chalice, by the advice of the said confessor, and he
made use himself of the money I got for the silver, which I
cut in pieces; and I did converse unlawfully several times in
the church with him. To this I must add an infinite number
of sins by *thought, word* and *deed,* I have committed in this
time, especially with the last person of my acquaintance,
though at present I am free from him.

Conf. Pray give me leave to consult upon all these things,
and I will resolve them to you the next confession; now go
in peace.

The first point to be resolved was whether Leonore could
sue the Franciscan convent for the patrimony left by her father in the confessor's hands?

The president went through all the reasons, *pro* and *con,*
and after resolved, that although the said Leonore was never
disobedient to her confessor, she could not sue the community
without lessening her own reputation, and laying upon the order so black a crime as that of her confessor; and that it was
the common maxim of all casuists that, *In rebus dubiis, minimum est sequendum,* in things doubtful, that of the least evil
consequence is to be pursued; and seeing the losing of her
patrimony would be less damage than the exposing of the
whole Franciscan order, and her own reputation: It did seem
proper to leave the thing as it was.

The second point to be resolved was whether Leonore was
in *proxima occasione peccati,* in the next occasion of sin, with
such a confessor the two first months?

Six members of the academy did think that she was; for
immediate occasion of sin signifies, that the person may satisfy

his passions *toties quoties*, without any impediment which Leonore could do all that while. But the other members of the academy did object against it: That the nature of *occasio proxima*, besides the said ?eason, implies freedom and liberty, which Leonore did want at that time, being as she was, young, inexperienced, timorous, and under the confessor's care and power; so it was resolved, that she was not the first two months in *proxima occasione peccati*.

The third point: Whether she committed greater sin with the second confessor, who threatened her with the inquisition? And whether she was obliged to undergo all the hardships, nay, death itself, rather than comply with the confessor's desire?

It was resolved *nemine contradicente*, that she was obliged for self-preservation's sake, to comply with the friar's desire and therefore her sin was less than other sins. ·

The fourth: Whether she was obliged to make restitution of the chalice she stole out of the church by the advice of the confessor?

The members could not agree in the decision of this point, for some were of opinion that both she and the friar were obliged to make restitution grounded in the moral maxim: *Facientes, et consentientes eadem paena puniuntur*, those that act and those who consent are to be punished alike. Others said, that Leonore was only an instrument of theft, and that the friar did put her in the way of doing what she never had done, but for fear of him, and that she was forced to do it; therefore, that she had not committed sacrilege, nay, nor venial sin by it; and that the friar only was guilty of sacrilege and robbery, and obliged to make restitution. Upon this division, the Rev. Mr. Ant. Palomo, then professor of philosophy, was appointed to lay the case before the members of the great academy, with this limitation, that he should not mention any thing of the friar in it, except the members of the academy should ask him the aggravating circumstances in the case.

He did it accordingly, and being asked by the president about the circumstances, it was resolved that Leonore was free from restitution, taking a bull of pardons. And as for the friar, by his belonging to the community, and having noth-'ng of his own, and obliged to leave at his death, every thing to the convent, he must be excused from making such restitution, &c.

The fifth point: Whether the church was desecrated by their unlawful commerce? and whether the confesso? was obliged to reveal the nature of the thing to .he bishop ot not?

As to the first part, all did agree, that the church was pol luted. As to the second, four were of opinion, that the thing was to be revealed to the bishop in general terms; but sixteen did object against it, and said that the dominical, *asperges me Hysopo, et mundabor*, thou shalt sprinkle me with hysop, and I shall be clean, &c. When the priest with the holy water and hysop sprinkles the church, it was enough to restore and purify the church.

After which, the president moved another question, viz: Whether this private confession was to be entered in the academy's book; *ad perpetuam rei memoriam*, in perpetual memory of the thing. And it was agreed to enter the cases and resolutions, mentioning nothing concerning the confessors, nor their orders. *Item*, it was resolved that the proponent could safely in conscience absolve Leonore the next confession, if she had the bull of indulgences, and promised to be zealous in the correction and penance, which he was to give her &c. And accordingly he did, and Leonore was absolved.

The private confession proposed in the Academy, by father Gasca, Jesuit, and member of the Academy: of a woman of thirty-three years of age.

Most reverend and learned fathers, I have thought fit not to trouble you with the methodical way of private confession I heard last Sunday, but to give you only an account of the difficult case in it. The case is this: a woman of thirty-three years of age, came to confess, and told me, that from sixteen years of age, till twenty-four, she had committed all sorts of lewdness, only with ecclesiastical persons, having in every convent a friar, who, under the name of cousin, did use to visit her:—and notwithstanding the multiplicity of cousins, she lived so poorly, that she was forced to turn procuress at the same time, for new cousins, and that she had followed that wicked life till thirty-two years of age. The last year she dreamed that the devil was very free with her, and those dreams or visions continuing for a long while, she found herself with child; and she protests that she knew no man for fourteen months before.—She is delivered of a boy, and she says that he is the devil's son, and that her conscience is so troubled about it, that if I do not find some way to quiet her mind she will lay violent hands upon herself. I asked her leave to consult the case, with a promise to resolve it next Sunday. Now I ask your wise advice upon this case.

The president said, that the case was impossible, and that the woman was mad; that he was of the opinion to send the woman to the physicians to be cured of some bodily distemper sne was troubled with. The Jesuit proponent replied, that the woman was in her perfect senses, and that the case well required further consideration: upon which, F. Antonio Palomo, who was reputed the most learned of the academy, said, that saint Augustin treats *de Incubo et Sucubo*, and he would examine the case, and see whether he might not give some hght for the resolution of the case?

And another member said, that there was in the case something more than apparition and devilish liberty, and that he thought fit that the father Jesuit should inquire more carefully into the matter, and go himself to examine the house, and question the people of it; which being approved by the whole assembly, he did it the next morning, and in the afternoon, being an extraordinary meeting, he came and said,

Most reverend and learned fathers, the woman was so strongly possessed with such a vision, that she has made public the case among the neighbors, and it is spread abroad. Upon which the inquisitors did send for the woman and the maid, and this has discovered the whole story, viz: That father Conchillos, victorian friar, was in love with the woman, but she could not endure the sight of him. That he gained the maid, and by that means he got into the house every night, and the maid putting some opium into her mistress's supper, she fell fast asleep, and the said father did lie with her six nights together. So the child is not the son of the devil, but of father Conchillos. Afterwards it was resolved to enter the case for a *memorandum*, in the academy's book.

The friar was put into inquisition for having persuaded the maid to tell her mistress that it was the devil; for she had been under the same fear, and really she was in the same condition. What became of the friar I do not know, this I do aver for a truth, that I spoke with the woman myself, and with the maid; and that the children used to go to her door, and call for the son of the devil. And being so mocked, she left the city in a few days after, and we were told that she lived after a retired christian life in the country.

The private confession of a priest, being at the point of death, in 1710. I shall call him Don Paulo.

Don Paulo. Since God Almighty is pleased to visit me with his sickness, I ought to make good use of the time I have to live, and I desire of you to help me with your prayers, and to take the trouble to write some substantial points of my confession, that you may perform, after my death, whatever I think may enable me in some measure, to discharge my duty towards God and men. When I was ordained priest, I made a general confession of all my sins from my youth to that time; and I wish I could now be as true a penitent as I was at that time; but I hope, though I fear too late, that God will hear the prayer of my heart.

I have served my parish sixteen years, and all my care has been to discover the tempers and inclinations of my parishioners, and I have been as happy in this world as unhappy before my Saviour. I have in ready money fifteen thousand pistoles, and I have given away more than six thousand. I had no patrimony, and my living is worth but four hundred pistoles a year. By this you may easily know, that my money is unlawfully gotten, as I shall tell you, if God spare my life till I make an end of my confession. There are in my parish sixteen hundred families, and more or less, I have defrauded them all some way or other.

My thoughts have been impure ever since I began to hear confessions; my words grave and severe with them all, and all my parishioners have respected and feared me. I have had so great an empire over them, that some of them knowing of my misdoings, have taken my defence in public. They have had in me a solicitor, in all emergencies, and I have omitted nothing to please them in outward appearance; but my actions have been the most criminal of mankind; for as to my ecclesiastical duty, what I have done has been for custom's sake. The necessary intention of a priest, in the administration of baptism and consecration, without which the sacraments are of no effect, I confess I had it not several times, as you shall see, in the parish books; and observe there, that all these names marked with a star, the baptism was not valid, for I had no intention: And for this I can give no other reason than my malice and wickedness. Many of them are dead, for which I am heartily sorry. As for the times I have consecrated without intention, we must leave it to God Almighty's mercy, for the wrong done by it to the souls of my parishioners, and those in purgatory cannot be helped.

As to the confessions and wills I have received from my parishioners at the point of their death, I do confess, I have made myself master of as much as I could, and by that means I have gathered together all my riches. I have sent this morning for

fifty bulls, and I have given one hundred pistoles for the bene·
fit of the holy *crusade*, by which his holiness secures my soul
from eternal death.

As to my duty towards God, I am guilty to the highest degree, for I have not loved him; I have neglected to say the
private divine service at home every day; I have polluted his
holy days by my grievous sins; I have not minded my superiors in the respect due to them; and I have been the cause of
many innocent deaths. I have procured, by remedies, sixty
abortions, making the fathers of the children their murderers
besides many other intended, though not executed, by some
unexpected accident.

As to the sixth commandment, I cannot confess by particu·
lars, but by general heads, my sins. I confess, in the first
place, that I have frequented the parish club twelve years.—
We were only six parish priests in it; and there we did consult and contrive all the ways to satisfy our passions. Every body had a list of the handsomest women in the parish;
and when one had a fancy to see any woman, remarkable for
her beauty, in another's parish, the priest of her parish sent for
her to his own house; and having prepared the way for wickedness, the other had nothing to do but to meet her there, and
fulfil his desires; and so we have served one another these
twelve years past. Our method has been, to persuade the
husbands and fathers not to hinder them any spiritual comfort; and to the ladies to persuade them to be subject to our
advice and will; and that in so doing, they should have liberty
at any time to go out on pretence of communicating some
spiritual business to the priest. And if they refused to do it,
then we should speak to their husbands and fathers not to let
them go out at all; or, which would be worse for them, we
should inform against them to the holy tribunal of inquisition
And by these diabolical persuasions they were at our com
mand, without fear of revealing the secret.

I have spared no woman of my parish, whom I had a fancy
for, and many other of my brethren's parishes; but I cannot
tell the number. I have sixty *nepotes* alive, of several women:
But my principal care ought to be of those that I have by
the two young women I keep at home since their parents
died. Both are sisters, and I had by the eldest two boys, and
by the youngest, one; and one which I had by my own sister
is dead. Therefore I leave to my sister five thousand pistoles,
upon condition that she would enter nun in St Bernard's
monastery, and upon the same condition I leave two thousand

D

pistoles a-piece to the two young women; and the remainder
I leave to my three *nepotes* under the care of Mossen John
Peralta, and ordering that they should be heirs to one another
if any of them should die before they are settled in the world,
and if all should die, I leave the money to the treasury of the
church, for the benefit of the souls in purgatory. *Item:* I order that all the papers of such a little trunk be burnt after my
confession is over, (which was done accordingly,) and that the
holy bull of the dead be bought before I die, that I may have
the comfort of having at home the Pope's pass for the next
world. Now I ask your penance and absolution for all the
sins reserved in all the bulls, from the first Pope, for which
purpose I have taken the bull of privileges in such cases as
mine.

So I did absolve him, and assist him afterwards, and he died
the next day. What to do in such a case, was all my uneasiness after his death; for if I did propose the case before the
members of the academy, every body could easily know the
person, which was against one of the articles we did swear at
our admittance into it: And if I did not propose it, I should
act against another article. All my difficulty was about the
baptisms which he had administered without intention: For it
is the known opinion of their church, that the intention of a
priest is absolutely necessary to the validity of the sacrament,
and that without it there is no sacrament at all. I had exam
ined the books of the parish, and I found a hundred and fifty-
two names marked with a star, and examining the register of
the dead, I found eighty-six of them dead: According to the
principles of the church, all those that were alive were to be
baptized; which could not be done without great scandal, and
prejudice to the clergy. In this uneasiness of mind I continued, till I went to visit the reverend father John Garcia,
who had been my master in divinity, and I did consult him,
on the case, *sub secreto naturali.* He did advise me to propose the case to the assembly, upon supposition, that if such
a case should happen, what should be done in it; and he recommended to me to talk with a great deal of caution, and to insist that it ought to be communicated to the bishop; and if the
members did agree with me, then without further confession,
I was to go to the bishop, and tell his lordship the case, under
secrecy of confession: I did so, and the bishop said he would
send for the books, and take the list of all those names; and
as many of them as could be found he would send for, one by
one into his own chamber, and baptize them; commanding

them, under the pain of ecclesiastical censure, not to talk of it, neither in public or private. But as for the other sins, there was no necessity for revealing them, for by virtue of the bull of Crusade, (of which I shall speak in the second chapter,) we could absolve them all.

Hear, O heaven! Give ear, O earth! And be horribly astonished! To see the best religion in the world turned into superstition and folly; to see, too, that those who are to guide the people, and put their flock in the way of salvation, are wolves in sheep's clothing, that devour them, and put them into the way of damnation. O God, open the eyes of the ignorant people, that they may see the injuries done to their souls by their own guides!

I do not write this out of any private end, to blame all sorts of confessors; for there are some who, according to the principles of their religion, do discharge their duty with exactness and purity, and whose lives, in their own way, are unblamable, and without reproach among men. Such confessors as these I am speaking of, are sober in their actions: they mortify their bodies with fasting over and above the rules prescribed by the church, by discipline, by kneeling down in their closets six or eight hours every day, to meditate on the holy mysteries, the goodness of God, and to pray to him for all sorts of sinners, that they may be brought to repentance and salvation, &c. They sleep but few hours. They spend most of their spare time in reading the ancient fathers of the church, and other books of devotion.

They live poorly, because whatever they have, the poor are enjoyers of it. The time they give to the public is but very little, and not every day; and then whatever counsels they give are right, sincere, without flattery or interest. All pious, religious persons do solicit their acquaintance and conversation; but they avoid all pomp and vanity, and keep themselves, as much as they can, within the limits of solitude; and if they make some visits, it must be upon urgent necessity. Sometimes you may find them in the hospitals among the poor, sick, helping and exhorting them: but they go there most commonly in the night, for what they do, they do it not out of pride, but humility.

I knew some of these exemplary men, but a very few; and I heard some of them preach with a fervent zeal about the promoting of Christ's religion, and exhorting the people to put their lives voluntarily in the defence of the Roman-Catholic faith, and extirpate and destroy all the enemies of their

communion. I do not pretend to judge them, for judgmen.
belongeth to God: This I say with St. Paul, that if those religious men *have a zeal of God*, their *zeal is not according to
knowledge.*

The private confession of a Nun, in the convent of S. O.—Before I begin
 the confession, it will not be improper to give an account of the customs of the nuns, and places of their confessions.

By the constitutions of their order, so many days are ap
pointed, in which all the nuns are obliged to confess, from the
Mother Abbess to the very wheeler; i. e. the nun that turns
the wheel near the door, through which they give and receive
every thing they want. They have a father confessor and a
father companion, who live next to the convent, and have a
small grate in the wall of their chamber, which answers to
the upper cloister or gallery of the convent. The confessor
hath care of the souls of the convent, and he is obliged to say
mass every day, hear confessions, administer the sacraments,
and visit the sick nuns. There are several narrow closets in
the church, with a small iron grate: One side answers to the
cloister, and the other to the church. So the nun being on the
inside and the confessor on the outside, they hear one another. There is a large grate facing the great altar, and the
holes of it are a quarter of a yard square; but that grate is
double, that is, one within and another without, and the distance
between both is more than half a yard. And besides these,
there is another grate for relations, and benefactors of the
community, which grate is single, and consists of very thin
iron bars: the holes of such a grate are near a quarter and ι
half square. In all those grates the nuns confess their sins:
for, on a solemn day, they send for ten or twelve confessors;
otherwise they could not confess the fourth part of them, for
there are in some monasteries 110 nuns, in others 80, in others 40, but this last is a small number.

The nuns' father-confessor hath but little trouble with the
young nuns, for they generally send for a confessor who is a
stranger to them, so that his trouble is with the old ones, who
have no business at the grate. These trouble their confessor
almost every day with many ridiculous trifles, and will keep
the poor man two hours at the grate, telling him how many
times they have spit in the church, how many flies they have
killed, how many times they have flown into a passion with
their lap dogs, and other nonsensical, ridiculous things like
these; and the reason is because they have nothing to do, no-

body goes to visit them nor cares for them; so sometimes they
choose to be spies for the young nuns, when they are at the grate
with their gallants; and for fear of their Mother Abbess, they
place some of the old nuns before the door of the parlor, to watch
the Mother Abbess, and to give them timely notice of her coming;
and the poor old nuns perform this office with a great deal of
pleasure, faithfulness, and some profit too.   But I shall not say
any more of them, confining myself wholly to the way of
living among the young nuns.

Many gentlemen send their daughters to the nunnery when
they are some five, some six, some eight years old, under the
care of some nun of their relations, or else some old nun ot
their acquaintance; and there they get education till they
are fifteen years old.   The tutress takes a great deal of care
not to let them go to the grate, nor converse with men all the
while, to prevent in them the knowledge and love of the
world.   They are caressed by all the nuns, and thinking it
will be always so, they are very well pleased with their confinement.   They have only liberty to go to the grate to their
parents or relations, and always accompanied with the old
mother tutress.   And when they are fifteen years old, which
is the age fixed by the constitutions of all the orders, they receive the habit of a nun, and begin the year of noviciate,
which is the year of trial to see whether they can go through
all the hardships, fastings, disciplines, prayers, hours of divine
service, obedience, poverty, chastity, and penances practised
in the monastery: But the prioress or abbess, and the rest of
the professed nuns, do dispense with, and excuse the novices
from all the severities, for fear that the novices should be
dissatisfied with, and leave the convent: And in this they are
very much in the wrong; for, besides that they do not observe
the precepts of their monastical rule, they deceive the poor,
ignorant, inexperienced young novices, who, after their profession and vows of perpetuity, do heartily repent they had
been so much indulged.   Thus the novices, flattered in the
year of noviciate, and thinking they will be so all their life
time, when the year is expired, make profession, and swear to
observe *chastity, obedience* and *poverty*, during their lives, and
clausura, i. e. *confinement;* obliging themselves, by it, never
to go out of the monastery.

After the profession is made, they begin to feel the severity
and hardships of the monastical life; for one is made a door-
keeper; another turner of the wheel, to receive and deliver by
it all the nuns' messages; another bell nun, that is to call the

nuns, when any one comes to visit them; another baker; another book-keeper of all the rents and expenses, and the like; and n the performance of all these employments, they must expend a great deal of their own money. After this they have liberty to go to the grate, and talk with gentlemen, priests and friars, who only go there as a gallant goes to see his mistress. So when the young nuns begin to have a notion of the pleasures of the world, and how they have been deceived, they are heartily sorry, but too late, for there is no remedy. And minding nothing but to satisfy their passions as well as they can, they abandon themselves to all sorts of wickedness and amorous intrigues.

There is another sort of nuns, whom the people call *las forcadas*, the forced nuns; i. e. those who have made a false step in the world, and cannot find husbands, on account of their crimes being public. Those are despised and ill used by their parents and relations, till they choose to go to the nunnery: So by this it is easily known what sort of nuns they will make.

Now as to the spending of their time. They get up at six in the morning and go to prayers, and to hear mass till seven. From seven till ten, they work or go to breakfast, either in their chambers, or in the common hall. At ten they go to the great mass till eleven: After it, they go to dinner. After dinner, they may divert themselves till two. At two they go to prayers, for a quarter of an hour, or (if they sing vespers) for half an hour; and afterwards they are free till the next morning: So every one is waiting for her *devoto*, that is, a gallant, or spiritual husband, as they call him. When it is dark evening, they send away the devotos, and the doors are locked up; so they go to their own chamber to write a billet, or letter to the spiritual husband, which they send in the morning to them, and get an answer; and though they see one another almost every day, for all that, they must write to one another every morning: And these letters of love, they call the *recreation of the spirit* for the time the devotos are absent from them. Every day they must give one another an account of whatever thing they have done since the last visit; and indeed there are warmer expressions of love and jealousy between the nun and the devoto, than between real wife and husband.

Now I come to the private confession; and I wish I could have the style of an angel, to express myself with purity and modesty in this confession.

Nun. Reverend Father, as the number of my sins are so great, and so great the variety of circumstances attending them; mistrusting my memory, I have set down in writing this confession, that you may entirely be acquainted with every thing that troubles my conscience; and so I humbly beg of you to read it.

Conf. I did approve the method of writing, but you ought to read it yourself, or else it cannot be *oris confessio,* or confession by mouth.

Nun. If it is so, I begin. I thought fit to acquaint you with the circumstances of my past life, that you may form a right judgment of my monastical life and conversation, which in some measure, will excuse me before the world, though not before God, our righteous judge.

I am the only daughter of counsellor N. E. who brought me up in the fear of God, and gave me a writing master, which is a rare thing. I was not quite thirteen years of age, when a gentleman of quality, though not very rich, began his love to me by letters which he (gaining my writing master) sent to me by him. There was nothing in the world so obliging, civil, modest and endearing, as his expressions seemed to me, and at last having the opportunity of meeting him at the house of one of my aunts, his person and conversation did so charm my heart, that a few days after we gave one another reciprocal promises of an eternal union: But by a letter which was unfortunately miscarried, and fell into my father's hands, our honest designs were discovered; and without telling me any thing, he went to see the gentleman, and spoke to him in this manner: Sir, my daughter, in discharging of her duty to so good a father, has communicated to me your honorable designs, and I come to thank you for the honor you are pleased to do my family: But, being so young, we think proper to put off the performance of it, till she comes to be fifteen years of age Now she, and I also, as a father to you both, (for I look upon you as upon my own son) do desire of you the favor not to give any public occasion of censure to the watchful neighbors, and if you have any regard for her, I hope you will do this and more for her and for me: And to shew you my great affection, I offer you a captain's commission in the regiment that the city raiseth for the king, and advise you to serve two years, and afterwards, you may accomplish your desire. The gentleman accepted it, and the next day the commission was signed and delivered to him, with an order to go to Catalonia. At the same time the writing master was sent out of the town under pretence of receiving some money from my father; and I was kept close at home, so he could not get an opportunity of seeing or writing to me; for my father told him I was sick in bed. As soon as he left the town, my father told me that he was dead, and that I must retire myself into the nunnery, for that was his will: So immediately he brought me here, and gave severe directions to the mother abbess, not to let me see any body but himself. Indeed, he did spare nothing to please me, until I received the habit, and made the profession and vows of a monastical life: After which he told me the whole story himself; and the gentleman was killed in Catalonia the first campaign.

I do confess, that ever since, I did not care what should become of me, and I have abandoned myself to all the sins I have been capable to commit. It is but ten months since I made my profession, and bound myself to perpetuity; though as I did it without intention, I am not a nun before God, nor obliged to keep the vow of religion; and of this opinion are many other nuns, especially ten young nuns, my intimate friends, who, as well as I, do communicate to one another the most secret things of our hearts.

Each of this assembly has her devoto, and we are every day in the afternoon at the grate: We shew one another the letters we receive from them, and there is nothing that we do not invent for the accomplishment of our pleasures.

Conf. Pray, confess your own sins, and omit the sins of your friends.

Nun. I cannot, for my sins are so confounded with the sins of my friends, that I cannot mention the one without the other.

But coming now to my greatest sin, I must tell you, that a nun of our assembly has a friar her devoto, the most beautiful young man, and we contrived and agreed together to bring him into the convent, as we did, and have kept him two and twenty days in our chamber: During which time we went to the grate very seldom, on pretence of being not well. We have given no scandal, for nobody has suspected the least thing in the case. And this is the greatest sin I have committed with man.

Conf. Pray, tell me, how could you let him in without scandal?

Nun. One of the assembly contrived to mat all the floc. of her chamber, and sent for the mat-maker to take the measure of the length and breadth of the room, and to make it in one piece, and send it to the Sexton's chamber, who is a poor ignorant fellow. When the mat was there, and the man paid for it, one day in the evening we sent the sexton on several messages, and kept the key of his room. The friar had asked leave of his prior to go into the country for a month's time, and disguising himself in a layman's habit, feeing well two porters, came in the dusk of the evening, into the sexton's room, and rolling up himself in the mat, the porters brought the mat to the door, where we were waiting for it; and, taking it, we carried it up to one of our chambers. We were afraid that the porters would discover the thing, but by money we have secured ourselves from them; for we hired ruffians to make away with them. We put him out of the convent in a great chest which could be opened on the inside, and of which he had the key, and giving the chest to the sexton, he and the servant of the convent carried it into the sexton's room. We ordered him to leave the key at the door, for we expected some relations which were to take a collation there; and we sent him on some errand till the friar had got out of the chest and of danger.

A month after, three of our friends began to perceive the condition they were in, and left the convent in one night, by which they have given great scandal to the city, and we do not know what has become of them; as for me, I design to do the same, for I am under the same apprehensions and fear; for I consider that if I do continue in the convent, my unusual size will discover me, and though one life shall be saved, I shall lose mine by the rulers of our order in a miserable manner, and not only so, but a heavy reflection will fall upon the whole order, and the dishonor of my family shall be the more public: Whereas, if I quit the convent by night, I save two lives, and the world will reflect only upon me, and then I shall take care to go so far off that nobody shall hear of me; and as I am sure, in my conscience, that I am not a nun for want of intention, when I did promise to keep *obedience, chastity, poverty,* and *perpetuity,* I shall not incur the crime of apostacy in leaving the convent; and if I continue in it, I am fully resolved to prevent my ruin and death by a strong operating remedy

This is all I have to say, and I do expect from you not only
your advice, but your assistance too.

Conf. I do find the case so intricate, that I want experience and learning to resolve what to do in it; and I do think
it proper for you to send for another confessor of years and
learning, and then you shall have the satisfaction of being well
directed and advised.

Nun. Now, reverend father, I do tell you positively, that
I shall never open my heart to another confessor, while I live,
and if you do not advise me what to do, I shall call you before
God for it; and now I lay upon you whatever thing may hap
pen in my case.

Conf. Ignorance will excuse me from sin, and I tell you I
am ignorant how to resolve the case.

Nun. I am resolved for all events, and if you refuse me
this comfort, I shall cry out, and say, that you have been soliciting and corrupting me in the very act of confession, and you
shall suffer for it in the inquisition.

Conf. Well, have patience, means may be found out; and
if you give me leave to consult the case, I shall resolve you
about it in three days time.

Nun. How can you consult my case, without exposing the
order, and my reputation too, perhaps, by some circumstance?

Conf. Leave it to me, and be not uneasy about it, and I do
promise to come with the resolution on Sunday next.

Nun. Pray, Father, if it be possible, come next Monday
morning, and I shall be free from company.

Conf. It is very well: but in the mean time, have before
your eyes the wrath of God against those that abandon themselves and forget that he is a living God, to punish suddenly
great sinners; and with this, farewell.

My mind never before was so much troubled as it was after
this case. I was, more by the interests of others, than by my
learning, appointed penitentiary confessor in the cathedral
church of St. *Salvator;* and as the duty of such a confessor is
to be every day, in the morning, four hours in the confessiona
ry, from eight to twelve, except he be called abroad—every
body thinks that such a confessor must be able to resolve all
cases and difficulties: But it was not so with me; for I was
young and without experience. And as to this case, the next
academical day I proposed it in the following manner:

There is a person bound by word of mouth, but at the same
time without intention, nay, with a mind and heart averse to it.
bound, I say, to *obedience, chastity,* and *poverty*   If the person

leaves the convent, the crime of apostacy is not committed in *foro interno;* and if the person continues in the convent, the consequence is to be a great sin in *foro externo* and *interno.* The person expects the resolution, or else is fully resolved to expose the confessor to scandal and personal sufferings. This is the case which I humbly lay down before your learned reverences.

The president's opinion was, that in such a case, the confessor was obliged, in the first place, to reveal it in general terms to the holy inquisitors; for (said he) though this case is not mentioned in our authors, there are others very like this, which ought to be revealed, viz: all those that are against either the temporal or spiritual good of our neighbor, which cases are reserved to the bishop or to his deputy; and this case, by the last circumstance, being injurious to the holy tribunal, the confessor ought to prevent the scandal which might otherwise fall upon him, to reveal the last circumstance. As for the first circumstance of the case, in this and others, we must judge *secundum allegata and probata;* and we must suppose, that no penitent comes to confess with a lie in his mouth; therefore, if the person affirms that he was bound without intention, he is free before God: Besides, *in rebus dubiis minimum est sequendum;* so to prevent greater evil, I think the person may be advised to quit the convent; and this is agreeable to the Pope's dispensations to such persons, when they swear and produce witness, that (before they were bound to the vow) heard the person say they had no intention to it.

The reverend Mr. Palomo's opinion was, that the confessor was to take the safest part, which was to advise the penitent to send to Rome for a dispensation, which could be obtained by money, or to the Pope's *Nuncio,* who would give leave to quit the convent for six months, upon necessity of preserving or recovering bodily health; and in that time, may be the person would dissipate some fumes of grief or melancholy fancies, &c.

But I replied to this, that the person could not do the first, for want of witness, nor the second, for being in perfect health, the physician never would grant his certificate to be produced before the Pope's *Nuncio,* which is absolutely necessary in such cases; and as to revealing the case to the holy inquisitors, it is very dangerous, both to the person and the confessor, as we could prove by several instances.

To this, several members being of my opinion, it was resolved, that the confessor, first of all, was to absolve the penitent, having a bull of *cruzade* and *extra confessionem,* or out of confession give, as a private person, advice to the penitent to quit the convent and take a certificate: Wherein the penitent was to specify, that the confessor had given such advice *extra actum confessionis.* The case and resolution was entered in the academy's book. And accordingly Monday following, I went to the nun and performed what was resolved; and the very same week, we heard in the city, that such a nun had made her escape out of the convent.

Two years and a half after this, I saw this very nun one day at the court of Lisbon, but I did not speak with her, for as I was dressed like an officer of the army, I thought she would not know me; but I was mistaken, for she knew me in my disguise as well as I did her. The next day she came to my lodgings followed by a lacquey, who, by her orders, had dogged me the night before. I was so troubled for fear to be discovered, that I thought the best way I could take was to run away and secure myself in an English ship: But by her first words, I discovered that her fear was greater than mine: for after giving me an account of her escape out of the convent, and safe delivery, she told me that a Portuguese captain happening to quarter in the same town where she was, took her away one night, and carried her to Barcelona, but that she refusing to comply with his desires, on any but honorable terms, he had married her and brought her to Lisbon: That her husband knew nothing of her having been a nun; that she took another name, and that she was very happy with her husband, who was very rich, and a man of good sense. She begged me with tears in her eyes not to ruin her by discovering any thing of her life past. I assured her, that nothing should happen on my account, that should disoblige her; and afterwards she asked me why I was not dressed in a clerical habit? To which I desired her to take no notice of it, for I was there upon secret business and of great consequence, and that as there was nobody there who knew me in Saragossa, it was proper to be disguised. She desired my leave to introduce me to her husband, under the title of a country gentleman, who was come thither for Charles the 3d's sake. I thanked her, and she went home overjoyed with my promise, and I was no less with hers. The next day her husband came to visit me, and ever after, we visited almost every day one another, till I left that city. This I say, she was a better wife than she had been a nun, and lived more religiously in the world, than she had done in the cloister of the convent.

Now I must leave off the account of private cases and confessions, not to be tedious to the readers by insisting too long a time upon one subject. But, as I promised to the public to discover the most secret practices of the Romish priests, in this point of *auricular confession*, I cannot dismiss nor put an end to this first chapter, without performing my promise.

By the account I have already given of a few private confessions, every body may easily know the wickedness of the Romish priests, but more particularly their covetousness and thirst of money will be detected by my following observations.

First of all, if a poor countryman goes to confess, the father-confessor takes little pains with him, for, as he expects little or nothing from him, he heareth him, and with bitter words corrects the poor man, and, most commonly, without any correction, imposing upon him a hard penance, sends him away with the same ignorance he went to confess.

2. If a soldier happens to go to make his peace with God, (so they express themselves when they go to confess) then the confessor sheweth the power of a spiritual guide. He questions him about three sins only, viz. *thefts, drunkenness and uncleanness.* Perhaps the poor soldier is free from the two first, but if he is guilty of the last, the confessor draws the consequence that he is guilty of all the three, and terrifying him with hell, and all the devils, and the fire of it, he chargeth him with restitution, and that he is obliged to give so much money for the relief of the souls in purgatory, or else he cannot get absolution. So the poor man, out of better conscience than his confessor, offers a month's pay, which must be given upon the spot (for in the shop of confessors there is neither trust nor credit) to appease the rough, bitter confessor, and to get absolution ; and I believe this hard way of using the poor soldiers is the reason that they do not care at all for that act of devotion; and as they are so bad customers to the confessor's shop, the confessors use their endeavors, when they go to buy absolution, to sell it as dear as they can; so they pay at one time for two, three, or more years.

I heard a soldier, damning the confessors, say, " if I continue in the king's service 20 years, I will not go to confess, for it is easier and cheaper to lift up my finger* and be absolved

---

*The custom of the Spanish army in the field, and the day before the battle, or before the engagement, the chaplain goes through all the companies, to ask the officers whether they have a mind to confess, and if any one has any thing to say, he whispers in the chaplain's ear, and so through all the officers. As for the private men : Crying out, says, he that has a sin, let him lift up one finger, and gives a general absolution to all at once.

by our chaplain, than to go to a devilish friar, who doth noth- ing but rail and grumble at me, and yet I must give him money for masses, or else he will not absolve me: I will give him leave to bury me alive, if ever he gets me near him again."

If a collegian goes to confess, he finds a mild and sweet con- fessor, and without being questioned, and with a small penance, he generally gets absolution. The reason the confessors have to use the collegians with so great civility and mildness is, first, because if a collegian is ill-used by his confessor, he goes to a deaf friar, who absolves *ad dexteram and ad sinistram*, all sorts of penitents for a real of plate; and after, he inquireth and examineth into all the other confessor's actions, visits and intrigues; and when he has got matter enough, he will write a lampoon on him, which has happened very often in my time. So the confessor dares not meddle with the collegians, for fear that his tricks should be brought to light; and another reason is, because the collegians, for the generality are like the *filles de joye in Lent,* i. e. without money, and so the confessor can- not expect any profit by them.

I say, if absolution is denied to a collegian, he goes to a *deaf confessor;* for some confessors are called *deaf,* not be- cause they are really, but because they give small penance without correction; and never deny absolution, though the sins be reserved to the Pope. I knew two Dominican friars, who were known by the name of *deaf confessors,* because they never used to question the penitent.

Only one of such confessors has more business in Lent, than twenty of the others, for he (like our couple-beggars, who for six pence do marry the people) for the same sum gives abso- lution. And for this reason all the great and habitual sinners go to the *deaf confessor,* who gives, upon a bargain, a cer- tificate, in which he says that such a one has fulfilled the com- mandment of the church, for every body is obliged to pro- duce a certificate of confession to the minister of the parish before Easter, or else he must be exposed in the church: So as it is a hard thing for any old sinner to get absolution, and a certificate from other covetous confessors, without a great deal of money, they generally go to the *deaf confessors.* I had a friend in the same convent, who told me, that such confes- sors were obliged to give two-thirds of their profit to the community, and being only two *deaf confessors* in that con- vent, he assured me, that in one lent, they gave to the father prior 600 pistoles a piece. I found the thing incredible, thinking that only poor and debauched people used to go to them; but he satisfied me, saying, that rich and poor, men and women, priests and nuns, were customers to them, and that only the poor and loose people used to go to confess in the church; but as for the rich, priests and nuns, they were sent for by them, in the afternoon, and at night; and that the poor *Deafs* had scarcely time to get their rest; and that when they were sent for, the common price was a pistole, and sometimes ten pistoles, according to the quality and circumstances of the person. And thus much of *deaf confessors.*

4. If a friar or a priest comes to confess, every body ought to suppose, that the father-confessor has nothing to do, but to give the penance, and pronounce the words of absolution; for both penitent and confessor being of the same trade, and of the same corporation, or brotherhood; the fashion of this cloak of absolution is not paid among them, and they work one for another, without any interest, in expectation of the same return.

This must be understood between the friars only, not between a friar and a secular priest; for these do not like one another, and the reason is, because the friars, for the generality, are such officious and insinuating persons in families, that by their importunities and assiduity of visits, they become at last the masters of families, and goods; so the secular priest hath nothing to busy himself with; and observe, that there are twenty friars to one secular priest, so the small fish is eaten by the greater; therefore, if it happens sometimes upon necessity, that a priest goes to confess to a friar, or a friar to a priest, they make use of such an opportunity, to exact as much as they can from one another.

I know a good merry priest, who had been in company with a friar's *devota,* i. e. in proper terms, *mistress;* and jested a little with her: Afterwards, the poor priest having something to confess, and no other confessor in his way, but the *devoto* of that *devota,* he was forced to open his heart to him; but the confessor was so hard upon him, that he made him pay on the nail two pieces of eight, to get absolution. So he payed dear for jesting with the mistress of a friar; and *ie* protested to me, that if it ever happened, that that friar should come to confess to him, he should not go away at so cheap a rate.

This I can aver, that I went to a Franciscan convent the second day of August, to get the indulgences of the Jubilee of Porciunculæ, and my confessor was so hard, that he began to persuade me, he could not absolve me without a pistole in hand: I told him, that I had not confessed any reserved sin, and that he did not know I could ruin him: But the friar, knowing that it was a great scandal to get up from his feet without absolution, he insisted on it; and I was obliged to avoid scandal, to give him his demand. After the confession was over, as I had been in a great passion at the unreasonable usage of the friar; I thought it was not fit for me to celebrate the Mass without a new reconciliation (as we call the short confession,) so I went to the father-guardian or superior of the convent, and confessing that sin of passion, occasioned by the covetous usage of such a confessor, his correction to me was, to pay down another pistole for scandalizing both the friar and the Franciscan habit; I refused the correction, and went home without the second absolution. I had a mind to expose both of them; but upon second thoughts, I did nothing at all, for fear that the whole order should be against me.

5. If a modest, serious, religious lady comes to confess, he useth her in another way; for he knows that such ladies never come to confess, without giving a good charity for Masses; so all the confessor's care is, to get himself into the lady's favor, which he doth by hypocritical expressions of godliness and devotion, of humility and strictness of life. He speaks gravely and conscientiously, and if the lady has a family, he gives her excellent advices, as, to keep her children within the limits of sobriety and virtue, for the world is so deceitful, that we ought always to be upon our guard; and to watch continually over our souls, &c. And by that means and the like, (the good lady believing him a sincere and devout man,) he becomes the guide of her soul, of her house and family, and most commonly the ruin of her children, and sometimes her own ruin too. I will give the following instance to confirm this truth; and as the thing was public, I need not scruple to mention it with the real names. In the year 1706, F. Antonio Gallardo, Augustin friar, murdered Donna Isabella Mendez, and a child three weeks old sucking at her breast. The lady was but twenty-four years of age, and had been married eight years to Don Francisco Mendez. The friar had been her spiritual guide all that while, and all the family had so great a respect and esteem for him, that he was the absolute master of the house. The lady was brought to bed, and Don Francisco being obliged to go into the country for four days, desired the father to come and lie in his house, and take care of it in his absence. The father's room was always ready: so he went there the same day Don Francisco went into the country. At eight at night, both the father and the

:ady went to supper, and after he sent all the maids and servants into the hall to sup, the lady took the child to give him suck; and the friar told her, in plain and short reasons, his love, and that without any reply or delay, she must comply with his request. The lady said to him, Father, if you propose such a thing to t~y my faithfulness and virtue, you know my conscience these eight years past; and if you have any ill design, I will call my family to prevent your further assurance. The friar then in a fury taking a knife, killed the child, and wounded so deeply the mother, that she died two hours after. The friar made his escape, but whether he went to his convent or not, we did not hear. I myself saw the lady dead, and went to her burial in the church of the old St. John.

6. If a *Beata* goes to confess, which they do every day, or at least every other day, then the Confessor, with a great deal of patience, hears her (sure of his reward.) I cannot pass by without giving a plain description of the women called *Beatas*, i. e. *blessed women*. These are most commonly tradesmen's wives, [generally speaking, ugly] and of a middle age. But this rule has some exceptions, for there are some *Beatas* young and handsome. They are dressed with modesty, and walk, with a serious countenance. But since their designs in this outward modesty, were discovered, they are less in number and almost out of fashion, since king Philip came to the throne of Spain; for the French liberty and freedom being introduced amongst the ladies, they have no occasion of stratagems to go abroad when they please: So, as the design of a *Beata* was to have an excuse, on pretence of confession, to go out, *sublata causa tollitur effectus.*

The Confessor, I said, of a *Beata*, was sure of his reward; for she, watching the living and the dead, useth to gather money for masses, from several people, to satisfy her confessor for the trouble of hearing her impertinences every day. A *Beata* sometimes makes her confessor believe that many things were revealed to her by the Holy Spirit; sometimes she pretends to work miracles; and by such visions, fancies, or dreams, the confessors fall into horrible crimes before God and the world.

The following instance, which was published by .he inquisitors, wil t testimony of this truth. I give the real names of the persons in this accoun., because the thing was made public.

In the city of Saragossa, near the college of St. Thomas of Villaneuva, lived Mary Guerrero, married to a taylor; she was handsome, witty, and ambitious: but as the rank of a taylor's wife could not make her shine among the quality, she undertook the life of a *Beata*, to be known by it in the city. The first step she was to make was to choose a confessor of good parts, and of good reputation among the nobility; so she pitched upon the reverend Father Fr. Michael Navarro, a Dominican Friar, a man who was D. D. and a man universally well beloved for his doctrine and good behaviour. But, *quando Venus vigilat, Minerva dormit.* She began to confess to him, and in less than a year, by her feigned modesty, and hypocritical airs; and by confessing no sins, but the religious exercises of her life; the reverend father began to publish in the city her sanctity to the highest pitch. Many ladies and gentlemen of the first rank, desirous to see the new saint, sent for her, but she did not appear, but by her maid, gave a denial to all. This was a new addition to the fame of her sanctity, and a new incitement to the ladies to see her. So some, going to visit Father Navarro, desired the favor of him to go along with them, and introduce them to the blessed Guerrero: But the father, (either bewitched by her, or in expectation of a bishoprick, for the making of a saint, or the better to conceal his private designs,) answered, that he could not do such a thing; for, knowing her virtue, modesty, and aversion to any act of vanity, he should be very much in the wrong to give her opportunities of cooling her fervent zeal and purity.

By that means, rich and poor, old and young, men and women, began to resort to her neighbor's house, and the Dominican church, only to see the blessed Guerrero. She shewed a great displeasure at these popular demonstrations of respect, and resolved to keep close at home; and after a long consultation with the Father Navarro, they agreed that she should keep her room, and that he would go to confess her, and say mass in her room, (for the Dominicans, and the four Mendicant orders, have a privilege for their friars to say Mass, or, as they say, to set an altar every where.) To begin this new way of living, the father charged her husband to quit the house and never appear before his wife; for his sight would be a great hindrance to his wife's sanctity and purity; and the poor sot believing every thing, went away and took a lodging for himself and apprentice.

They continued this way of living, both she and the Father, a whole year; but the fatigue of going every day to say Mass and confess the *blessed*, being too great for the reverend, he asked leave from the reverend father Buenacasa, then prior of the convent, to go and live with her as a spiritual guide. The prior, foreseeing some great advantage, gave him leave, so he went for good and all to be her lodger and master of the house. When the father was in the house, he began by degrees to give permission to the people now and then to see the *blessed*, through the glass of a little window, desiring them not to make a noise, for fear of disturbing the *blessed* in her exercise of devotion: She was in her own room, always upon her knees, when some people were to see her through the glass, which was in the wall between her room and that of the reverend. In a few months after, the archbishop went to see her, and conversed with her and the father Navarro, who was in great friendship with, and much honored by his Grace. This example of the prelate put the nobility in mind to do the same. The viceroy not being permitted by his royal representation to go to her, sent his coach one night for her, and both the father and the *blessed* had the honor to sup in private with his Excellency. This being spread abroad, she was troubled with coaches and presents from all sorts and conditions of people. Many sick went there in hopes to be healed by her sight; and some that happened to go when nature itself was upon the crisis, or by the exercise of walking, or by some other natural operation, finding themselves better, used to cry out, a miracle, a miracle! She wanted nothing but to be carried on a pedestal upon the ignorant's shoulders: The fame of her sanctity was spread so far, that she was troubled every post day with letters from people of quality in other provinces, so the reverend was obliged to take a secretary under him, and a porter to keep the door; for they had removed to another house of better appearance and more conveniency. Thus they continued for the space of two years, and all this while the reverend was writing the life of the *blessed;* and many times he was pressed to print part of her life; but the time of the discovery of their wickedness being come, they were taken by an order from the holy inquisition.

The discovery happened thus: Ann Moron, a surgeon's wife, who lived next door to the *blessed*, had a child of ten months old; and, as a neighbor, she went to desire the reverend to beg of the *blessed* to take the child and kiss him, thinking, that by such an holy kiss, her child would be happy forever. But the reverend desiring her to go herself and make the request to the *blessed*, she did it accordingly. Mary Guerrero took the child, and bid the mother leave him with her for a quarter of an hour. Ann Moron then thought that her child was already in heaven; but when in a quarter of an hour after, she came again for the child, the *blessed* told her, that her child was to die the night following, for so God had revealed to her in a short prayer she made for the child. The child really died the night following, but the surgeon, as a tender father, seeing some spots and marks in his child's body, opened it, and found in it the cause of its unfortunate death, which was a dose of poison. Upon this suspicion of the child's being poisoned, and the foretelling of his death by the *blessed*, the father went to the inquisitors, and told the nature of the thing.

Don Pedro Guerrero, the first inquisitor, was then absent; so Don Francisco Torrejon, second inquisitor went himself to examine the thing, and seeing the child dead, and all the circumstances against the *blessed*, he then ordered that she and the reverend, and all their domestic servants, should be secured immediately, and sent to the holy inquisition. All things were done accordingly, and this sudden and unexpected accident made such a noise in town, that every body reasoned in his own way, but nobody dared to speak of the inquisitor. At the same time every thing in the house was seized upon, with the papers of the reverend, &c. Among the papers was found the life of the *blessed*, written by father Navarro's own hand. I said in the beginning that he was bewitched, and so many people believed; for it seemed incredible that so learned a man as he was in his own religion, should fall into so gross an ignorance as to write such a piece, in the method it was found composed; for the manuscript contained about six hundred sheets, which by an order of the inquisitors, were sent to the *qualificators of the holy office*, to be reviewed by them, and to have their opinions thereupon. I shall speak of these qualificators, when I come to treat of the inquisitors and their practices. Now it is sufficient to say, that all the qualificators, being examinators of the crimes committed against the holy catholic faith, examined the sheets, and their opinion was, that the book entitled *the life of the blessed Mary Guerrero*, composed by the reverend father Fr. Michael Navarro, was scandalous, false, and against revealed doctrines in the scripture, and good manners, and that it deserved to be burnt in the common yard of the holy office, by the mean officer of it.

After this examination was made, the inquisitors summoned two priests out of every parish church, and two friars out of every conven , to come such a day to the hall of the holy tribunal, to be present at the trial and examinations against Mary Guerrero, and Michael Navarro. It was my turn to go to that tria. for the cathedral church of St. Salvator. We went the day appointed, all the summoned priests and friars, to the number of one hundred and fifty, bes des the inquisitors, officers of the inquisition, and qualificatcrs; these had the cross of the holy office before their breasts, which is set upon their habits in a very nice manner. The number of qualificators I reckoned that day in the hall, were two hundred and twenty. When all the summoned were together, and the inquisitors under a canopy of black velvet, (which is placed at the right corner of the altar, upon which was an image of the crucifix, and six yellow wax candles, without any other light,) they made the signal to bring the prisoners to the bar, and immediately they came out of the prison, and kneeling down before the holy fathers, the secretary began to read the articles of the examination, and convictions of their crimes.

Indeed, both the father and the blessed appeared that day very much like saints, if we will believe the Roman's proverb, that paleness and thin visage is a sign of sanctity. The examination, and the lecture of their crimes was so long, that we were summoned three times more upon the same trial, in which to the best of my memory, I heard the following articles:

That by the blessed's confession to Michael Navarro, this in the beginning of her life says: 1st. That the blessed creature knew no sin since she was born into the world. 2d. She has been several times visited by the angels in her closet; and Jesus Christ himself has come down thrice to give her new heavenly instructions. 3d. She was advised by the divine spouse to live separately from her husband. 4th. She was once favored with a visit of the holy trinity, and then she saw Jesus at the left hand of the Father. 5th. The holy dove came afterwards and sat upon her head many times. 6th. This holy co nforter has foretold her, that her body after death shall be always incorruptible; and that a great king, with the news of her death, shall come to honor her sepulchre with this motto: " The soul of this warrior* is the glory of my kingdom." 7th. Jesus Christ, in a Dominican's habit, appeared to her at night, and in a celestial dream she was overshadowe: by the spirit. 8th. She had taken out of purgatory

---

* *Guerrero*, in Spanish, signifies varrior.

seven tir.es the soul of her companion's sister. (What folly!) 9th. The Pope and the whole church shall rejoice in her death; nay, his holiness shall canonize her, and put her in the litany before the apostles, &c.

After these things, her private miracles were read, &c., and so many passages of her life, that it would be too tedious to give an account of them. I only write these to show the stupidity of the reverend Navarro, who, if he had been in his perfect senses, could not have committed so gross an error.— (This was the pious people's opinion.)—The truth is, that the Blessed was not overshadowed by the spirit, but by her confessor; for she being at that time with child, and delivered in the inquisition, one article against the father was, that he had his bed near her bed, and that he was the father of the new child, or monster on earth.

Their sentences were not read in public, and what was their end we know not; only we heard that the husband of the blessed had notice given him by an officer of the holy office, that he was at liberty to marry any other he had a fancy for; and by this true account the public may easily know the extravagancies of the Romish-confessors, who, blinded either by their own passions, or by the subtleties of the wicked beatas; do commit so great and heinous crimes, &c.

There is another sort of beatas, whom we call endemonia das, i. e. demoniacs, and by these possessed the confessor gets a vast deal of masses. I will tell you, reader, the nature of the thing, and by it you will see the cheat of the confessor and the demoniac. I said before, that among the beatas there are two sorts, young, and of middle age, but all married; and that the young undertake the way of confessing every day, or three times a week, to get opportunity of going abroad, and be delivered a while from their husbands' jealousies: But many husbands being jealous of the flies that come near their wives, they scarcely give them leave to go to confess. Observe further, that those women make their husbands believe that out of spite, a witch has given them the evil spirit, and they make such unusual gestures, both with their faces and mouths, that it is enough to make the world laugh only at the sight of them. When they are in the fit of the evil spirit they talk blasphemously against God and his saints; they beat husbands and servants; they put themselves in such a sweat, that when the evil spirit leaves them for a while, (as they say,) they cannot stand upon their feet for excessive fatigue. The poor deceived husbands, troubled in mind and body, send for a physician;

but this says, he has no remedy for such a distemper, and that physic knows no manner of devil, and so, their dealing being not with the spirit, but with the body, he sends the husband to the spiritual physician; and by that means they are, out of a good design, procurers for their own wives; for really they go to the spiritual father, begging his favor and assistance to come to exorcise, i. e. to read the prayer of the church, and to turn out the evil spirit out of his wife's body. Then the father makes him understand, that the thing is very troublesome, and that if the devil is obstinate and positive, he cannot leave his wife in three or four nights, and may be, in a month or two; by which he must neglect other business of honor and profit. To this the deluded husband promises that his trouble shall be well recompensed, and puts a piece of gold in his hand, to make him easy; so he pays beforehand for his future dishonor. Then the father exorcist goes along with him, and as soon as the wife hears the voice of the exorcist, she flies into an unmeasurable fury, and cries out, do not let that man (meaning the exorcist) come to torment me (as if the devil did speak in her and for her.) But he takes the hysop with holy water and sprinkles the room. Here the demoniac throweth herself on the floor, teareth her clothes and hair, as if she was perfectly a mad woman. Then the priest tieth the blessed stole, i. e. a sort of scarf they make use of among other ornaments to say mass, upon her neck, and begins the prayers. Sometimes the devil is very timorous, and leaves the creature immediately easy; sometimes he is obstinate, and will resist a long while before he obeys the exorcisms of the church; but at last he retires himself into his own habitation, and frees the creature from his torments; for, they say, that the devil or evil spirit, sometimes has his place in the head, sometimes in the stomach, sometimes in the liver, &c. After the woman is easy for a while, they eat and drink the best that can be found in the town.

A while after, when the husband is to mind his own business, the wife, on pretence that the evil spirit begins again to trouble her, goes into her chamber and desireth the father to hear her confession. They lock the door after them, and what they do for an hour or two, God only knoweth. These private confessions and exercises of devotion continue for several months together, and the husband loth to go to bed with his wife, for fear of the evil spirit, goes to another chamber, and the father lieth in the same room with his wife on a field-bed, to be always ready, when the malignant spirit comes

to exorcise, and beat him with the holy *Stola*. So deeply
ignorant are the people in that part of the world, or so great
bigots, that on pretence of religious remedies to cure their
wives of the devilish distemper, they contract a worse distemper on their heads and honors, which no physician, either
spiritual or corporal, can ever cure.

When in a month or two, the father and the demoniac have
settled matters between themselves, for the time to come, he
tells the husband, that the devil is in a great measure tamed,
by the daily exorcisms of the holy mother, the church, and
that it is time for him to retire, and mind other business of his
convent; and that, it being impossible for him to continue longer in his house, all he can do, is to serve him and her in his
convent, if she goes there every day. The husband, with a
great deal of thanks, pays the father for his trouble, who, taking his leave, goes to his community, and gives to the father
prior two parts of the money (for the third part is allowed to
him for his own pains.) The day following, in the morning,
the demoniac is worse than she was before: Then the husband, out of faith, and the zeal of a good Christian, crieth out,
the father is gone, and the devil is loose: The exorcisms of
the church are not ready at hand, and the evil spirit thinks
himself at liberty, and begins to trouble the poor creature: Let
us send her to the convent, and the bold, malignant spirit shall
pay dear there for this new attempt. So the wife goes to the
father, and the father takes her into a little room, next to the
vestry, (a place to receive their acquaintance, only of the female sex,) and there, both in private, the father appeases the
devil, and the woman goes quiet and easy to her house, where
she continues in the same easiness till the next morning.
Then the devil begins to trouble her again; and the husband
says, O obstinate spirit! You make all this noise because the
hour of being beaten with the holy stola is near: I know that
your spite and malice against the exorcisms of the church is
great; but the power of them is greater than thine: Go, go to
the father, and go through all the lashes of the stola. So the
woman goes again to the father, and in this manner of life
they continue for a long while.

There is of these beatas, in every convent church, not a
few, for sometimes, one of these exorcists keeps six, and sometimes ten, by whom, and their husbands, he is very well paid
for the trouble of confessing them every day, and for taming
the devil. But the most pleasant thing among those demoniacs is, that they have different devils that trouble them; for,

by a strict commandment of the father, they are forced to tell
their names, so one is called Belzebub, another Lucifer, &c.:
And those devils are very jealous, one of another. I saw several times, in the body of the church, a battle among three of
those demoniacs, on pretence of being in the fit of the evil
spirit, threatening and beating one another, and calling one
another nicknames, till the father came with the hysop, holy
water and the stola, to appease them, and bid them to be silent, and not to make such a noise in the house of the Lord.
And the whole matter was, (as we knew afterwards,) that the
father exorcist was more careful of one than the others; and
jealousy (which is the worse devil) getting into their heads,
they give it to their respective devils, who, with an infernal
fury, fought one against another, out of pet and revenge for
the sake of their lodging-room.

In the city Huesca, where (as they believe) Pontius Pilate
was professor of law in the university, and his chair, or part
of it, is kept in the bishop's palace for a show, and a piece of
antiquity, (and which I saw myself,) I say, I saw, and conversed both with the father exorcist and the beata demoniac
about the following instance:

The thing not being publicly divulged, but among a few
persons, I will give an account of it under the names of father
John and Dorothea. This Dorothea, when 13 years old, was
married, against her inclinations, to a tradesman 50 years old.
The beauty of Dorothea, and the ugliness of her husband,
were very much, the one admired, and the other observed by
all the inhabitants of the city. The bishop's secretary made
the match, and read the ceremony of the church, for he was
the only executor of her father's will and testament. She
was known by the name of *Young dancing eyes.* Her husband was jealous of her, in the highest degree: She could not
go out without him; and so she suffered this torment for the
space of three years. She had an aversion, and a great an-
tipathy against him. Her confessor was a young, well-shaped
friar; and whether out of her own contrivance, or by the
friar's advice, one day, unexpected by her husband, the devil
was detected and manifested in her. What affliction this was
to the old, amorous, jealous husband, is inexpressible. The
poor man went himself to the jesuit's college, next to his
house, for an *exorcist,* but the jesuit could do nothing to appease that devil, to the great surprise of the poor husband, and
many others too, who believe, that a jesuit can command and
F

overcome the devil himself, and that the devils are more afraid of a jes.it, than of their sovereign prince in hell.

The poor husband sent for many others, but the effect did not answer the purpose; till at last her own confessor came to her, and after many exorcisms and private prayers, she was (or the devil in her) pacified for a while. This was a testimony of the father John's fervent zeal and virtue to the husband; so they settled how the case was to be managed for the future. Friar John was very well recompensed upon the bargain; and both the demoniac and friar John continued in daily battle with the evil spirit for two years together. The husband began to sleep quiet and easy, thinking that his wife, having the devil in her body, was not able to be unfaithful to him; for while the malignant torments the body, the woman begins to fast in public, and eat in private with the exorcist; and the exercises of such demoniacs are all of prayers and devotions; so the deceived husband believes it is better to have a demoniac wife, than one free from the evil spirit.

The exorcisms of friar John, (being to appease not a spiritual, but a material devil,) he and Dorothea were both discovered, and found in the fact, by a friar in the same convent, who, by many presents from friar John and Dorothea, did not reveal the thing to the prior, but he told it to some of his friends, which were enemies to friar John, from whom I heard the story. For my part, I did not believe it for a while, till at last, I knew, that the friar John was removed into another convent, and that Dorothea left her house and husband, and went after him; though the husband endeavored to spread abroad, that the devil had stolen his wife. These are the effects of the practices of the demoniacs and exorcists.

Now I come to the persons of public authority, either in ecclesiastical, civil, or military affairs, and to the ladies of the first quality or rank in the world. As to those, I must beg leave to tell the truth, as well as of the inferior people. But, because the confessors of such persons are most commonly all Jesuits, it seems very apropos to give a description of those Fathers, their practices and lives, and to write of them, what I know to be the matter of fact.

Almost in all the Roman-Catholic countries, the Jesuit fathers are the teachers of the Latin tongue, and to this purpose they have in every college, (so they call their convents) four large rooms, which are called the four classes for the grammar. There is one teacher in each of them. The city corporation, or political body, paying the rector of the Jesuits

so much a year and the young gentlemen are at no expense
at all for learning the Latin tongue. The scholars lodge in
town, and they go every day, from eight in the morning till
eleven, to the college; and when the clock strikes eleven,
they go along with the four teachers to hear mass: They go
at two in the afternoon, till half after four, and so they do all
the year long, except the holidays, and the vacations from
the fifteenth of August till the ninth of September. As the
four teachers receive nothing for their trouble, because the
payment of the city goes to the community, they have contrived how to be recompensed for their labor: There were
in the college of Saragossa, when I learned Latin, very near
six hundred scholars, noblemen, and tradesmen's sons; every
one was to pay every Saturday a real of plate for the rule (as
they call it.) There is a custom, to have a public literal act
once every day, to which are invited the young gentlemen's
parents, but none of the common people. The father rector
and all the community are present, and placed in their velvet
chairs. To the splendid performance of this act, the four
teachers chuse twelve gentlemen, and each of them is to make,
by heart, a Latin speech in the pulpit. They chuse besides
the twelve, one emperor, two kings, and two pretors, which
are always the most noble of the young gentlemen: They
wear crowns on their heads that day, which is the distinguishing character of their learning. The emperor sits under a
canopy, the pretors on each side, and the kings a step lower,
and the twelve senators in two lines next to the throne. This
act lasts three hours; and after all is over, the teachers and
the father rector invite the nobility and the emperor, with
the pretors, kings and senators, to go to the common hall of
the college, to take refreshment of the most nice sweetmeats
and best liquor. The fathers of the emperor, kings, pretors,
and senators, are to pay for all the charges and expenses,
which are fixed to be a hundred pistoles every month. And
every time there are new emperors or kings, &c. by moderate
computation, we were sure, that out of the remainder of the
hundred pistoles a month, and a real of plate every week from
each of the scholars, the four father teachers had clear, to
be divided among themselves every year, sixteen hundred
pistoles.

We must own that the jesuits are very fit, and the most proper
persons for the education of youth, and that all these exercises
and public acts (though for their interests) are great stimula-
tions and incitements to learning in young gentlemen; for one

of them will study night and day only to get the empty title o emperor, &c. once in a month; and their parents are very glad to expend eight pistoles a year to encourage their sons and besides that, they believe, that they are under a great obligation to the Jesuits' college, and the jesuits knowing their tempers, become, not only acquainted with them, but absolute masters of their houses: I must own, likewise, that I never heard of any jesuit father, any thing against good manners or Christian conversation; for really, they behave themselves, as to outward appearance, with so great civility, modesty, and policy, that nobody has any thing to say against their deportment in the world, except self-interest and ambition.

And really, the Jesuits' order is the richest of all the orders in Christendom; and because the reason of it is not well known, I will now tell the ways by which they gather together so great treasures every where. As they are universally teachers of the Latin tongue, and have this opportunity to know the youth, they pitch upon the most ingenious young men, and upon the richest of all, though they be not very witty; they spare neither time, nor persuasions, nor presents, to persuade them to be of the society of Jesus (so they name their order): the poor and ingenious are very glad of it, and the noble and rich too, thinking to be great men upon account of their quality: so their colleges are composed of witty and noble people. By the noble gentlemen they get riches; by the witty and ingenious they support their learning, and breed up teachers and great men to govern the consciences of princes, people of public authority, and ladies of the first rank.

They do not receive ladies in private in their colleges, but always in the middle of the church or chapel; they never sit down to hear them. They do not receive charity for masses, nor beatas, nor demoniacs in their church, (I never saw one there) their modesty and civil manners charm every one that speaks with them; though I believe, all that is to carry on their private end and interests. They are indefatigable in the procuring the good of souls, and sending missionaries to catechise the children in the country; and they have fit persons in every college for all sorts of exercises, either of devotion, of law, or policy, &c. They entertain nobody within the gate of the college, so nobody knows what they do among themselves. If it sometimes happens that one doth not answer their expectation, after he has taken the habit, they turn him out; for they have fourteen years trial but as soon as they turn him out, they underhand procure a handsome settlement for him so that he who is expelled dares not say any thing against them, for fear of losing his bread. And if, after he is out, he behaves himself well, and gets some riches, he is sure to die a jesuit.

I heard of Don Pedro Segovia, who had been a jesuit, but was turned out, but by the jesuits' influence, he got a prebendary in the cathedral church, and was an eminent preacher. He was afterwards constantly visited by them, and when he came to die, he asked again the habit, and being granted to him, he died a jesuit, and by his death the jesuits became heirs of twenty thousand pistoles in money and lands.

There are confessors of kings and princes, of ministers of state, and generals, and of all the people of distinction and estates. So it is no wonder if they are masters of the tenth part of the riches in every kingdom, and if God doth not put a stop to their covetousness, it is to be feared, that one way or other, they will become masters of all, for they do not seek dignities, being prohibited by the constitutions of their order, to be bishops and popes; it is only allowed to them to be cardinals, to govern the pope by that means, as well as to rule emperors, kings, and princes. At this present time all the sovereigns of Europe have jesuits for their confessors.

Now it is high time to come to say something as to their practices in confessions; and I will only speak of those I knew particularly well.

First, The reverend father Navasques, professor of divinity in their college, was chosen confessor of the countess of Fuentes, who was left a widow at twenty-four years of age. This lady, as well as other persons of quality, kept a coach and servant for the father confessor. He has always a father companion to say mass to the lady. She allows so much a year to the college, and so much to her confessor and his companion. All persons have an oratory or chapel in their houses, by dispensation from the pope, for which they pay a great deal of money. Their way of living is thus, in the morning they send the coach and servant to the college, most commonly at eleven of the clock: the father goes every day at that time, and the lords and ladies do not confess every day; they have mass said at home, and after mass, the reverend stays in the lady's company till dinner-time. then he goes to the college till six in the evening, and at six goes again to see the lady or lord, till eleven. What are their discourses I do not know. This I know, that nothing is done in the family without the reverend's advice and approbation. So it was

with the countess' family, and when she died, the college got
four thousand pistoles a year from her.

The reverend father Muniessa, confessor of the duchess of
Villahermosa, in the same manner got at her death thirty
thousand pistoles, and the reverend father Aranda, confessor
to the countess of Aranda, got two thousand pistoles yearly
rent from her, all for the college. Now what means they make
use of to bewitch the people and to suck their substance, every
body may think, but no body may guess at. An ingenious
politician was asked how the jesuits could be rightly described
and defined, and he gave this definition of them. *Amici
frigidi, and inimici calidi,* i. e. cold friends and warm enemies. And this is all I can write concerning their manners
and practices.

Before I dismiss this subject, I cannot pass by one instance
more, touching the practices of confessors in general, and that
is, that since I came to these northern countries, I have been
told by gentlemen of good sense, and serious in their conversation, that many priests and friars were procurers (when they
were in those parts of the world) and shewed them the way
of falling into the common sin. It is no doubt they know all
the lewd women by auricular confession, but I could not believe
they would be so villanous and base, as to make a show of
their wickedness before strangers. This I must say in vindication of a great many of them (for what I write is only of the
wicked ones,) that they are many times engaged in intrigues
unknown to themselves, and they are not to be blamed, but
only the persons that with false insinuations, make them believe a lie for a truth, and this under a pretence of devotion.
To clear this I will tell a story, which was told me by a colonel
in the English service, who lives at present in London.

He said to me that an officer, a friend of his, was a prisoner
in Spain: his lodgings were opposite to a counsellor's house.
The counsellor was old and jealous, the lady young, handsome,
and confined, and the officer well shaped and very fair. The
windows and balconies of the counsellor were covered with
narrow lattices, and the officer never saw any woman of that
house. But the lady, who had several times seen him at his
window, could not long conceal her love; so she sent for her
father confessor, and spoke with him in the following manner:
My reverend father, you are my spiritual guide, and you must
prevent the ruin of my soul, reputation, and quietness of my
life. Over the way, said she, lives an English officer, who is
constantly at the window, making signs and demonstrations of

love to me, and though I endeavor not to haunt my balcony, for fear of being found out by my spouse; my waiting maid tells me that he is always there. You know my spouse's temper and jealousy, and if he observes the least thing in the world, I am undone forever. So to put a timely stop to this, I wish you would be so kind as to go over and desire him to make no more signs; and that if he is a gentleman, as he seems to be, he will never do any thing to disquiet a gentlewoman. The credulous confessor, believing every syllable, went over to the English officer, and told him the message, asking his pardon for the liberty he took; but that he could not help it, being as he was the lady's confessor.

The officer, who was of a very fiery temper, answered him in a resolute manner. Hear, friar, said he to the confessor, go your way, and never come to me with such false stories, for I do not know what you say, nor I never saw any lady over the way. The poor father, full of shame and fear, took his leave, and went to deliver the answer to the lady. What, said she, doth he deny the truth? I hope God will prove my innocence before you, and that before two days. The father did comfort her, and went to his convent. The lady seeing her designs frustrated this way, did contrive another to let the officer know her inclination. So one of her servants wrote a letter to her in the officer's name, with many lovely expressions, and desiring her to be in her garden at eight in the dark evening, under a figtree next to the walls. And recommending to her servant the secret, sealed the letter directed to her. Two days after, she sent for her confessor again, and told him, Now my reverend father, God has put a letter, from the officer, into my hands to convince him and you of the truth. Pray take the letter and go to him, and if he denies, as he did before, show him his own letter, and I hope he will not be so bold as to trouble me any more. He did accordingly, and the English gentleman answered as the first time; and as he flew into a passion, the father told him, Sir, see this letter, and answer me: which the officer reading, soon understood the meaning, and said, Now, my good father, I must own my folly, for I cannot deny my handwriting, and to assure you, and the lady, that I shall be quite a different man for the future, pray tell her that I will obey her commands, and that I will never do any thing against her orders. The confessor, very glad of so unexpected good success, as he thought, gave the answer to the lady, adding to it, Now, madam, you may be quiet, and without any fear, for he will obey you. Did not I

tell you, said she, that he could not deny the fact of the letter
So the confessor went home, having a very good opinion of the
lady, and the English officer too, who did not fail to go to the
rendezvous, &c.

Every serious, religious man, will rather blame the wicked
lady, than the confessor: for the poor man, though he was a
procurer and instrument of bringing that intrigue to an effect,
really he was innocent all the while; and how could he suspect any thing of wantonness in a lady so devoutly affected,
and so watchful of the ruin of her soul, honor, and quietness
of her life? We must excuse them in such a case as this was,
and say, That many and many confessors, if they are procurers, they do it unknown to themselves, and out of pure zeal
for the good of the souls, or to prevent many disturbances in a
family: But as for those that, out of wickedness, busy themselves in so base and villanous exercises, I say, heaven and
earth ought to rise in judgment against them. They do deserve to be punished in this world, that, by their example, the
same exercise might be prevented in others.

I have given an account of some private confessions of
both sexes, and of the most secret practices of some of the
Roman-Catholic priests, according to what I promised the public in my printed proposals. And from all that is written and
said, I crave leave to draw some few inferences.

First, I say, that the pope and councils are the original
causes of the aforesaid misdoings and ill practices of the
Romish priests. Marriage being forbidden to a priest, not by
any commandment of God or divine scripture, but by a strict
ordinance from the pope, an indisputable canon of the council.
This was not practised by them for many centuries after the
death of our saviour; and the priests were then more religious and exemplary than they are now. I know the reasons
their church has for it, which I will not contradict, to avoid all
sort of controversy: But this I may say, that if the priests,
friars and nuns were at lawful liberty to marry, they would
be better Christians, the people richer in honor and estates,
the kingdom better peopled, the king stronger, and the Romish
religion more free from foreign attempts and calumnies.

They do make a vow of chastity, and they break it by
living loose, lewd, and irregular lives. They do vow poverty,
and their thirst for riches is unquenchable; and whatever they
get, is most commonly by unlawful means. They swear
obedience, and they only obey their lusts, passions and inclination. How many sins are occasioned by binding them

selves with these three vows in a monastical life, it is inexpressible: And all, or the greater number of sins committed
by them, would be hindered, if the pope and council were to
imitate the right foundations of the primitive church, and the
apostles of Jesus Christ our Saviour.

As to particular persons, among the priests and friars,
touching their corruptions and ill practices in auricular confession, I say, they do act against divine and human law in
such practice, and are guilty of several sins, especially sacrilege and robbery. It is true, the Moral Summs are defective in the instruction of confessors, as opinions, grounded in
the erroneous principles of their church: But as to the settled
rules for the guiding and advising the penitent, what he ought
to do, to walk uprightly, they are not defective; so the confessors cannot plead ignorance for so doing, and consequently
the means they make use of in the tribunal of conscience,
are all sinful, being only to deceive and cheat the poor, ignorant people.

Their practices then, are against divine and human law,
contrary to the holy scriptures, nay, to humanity itself: For,
*Thou that teachest another, thou shalt not kill, nor commit adul-
tery, nor steal, nor covet thy neighbor's goods, nor wife:* Dost
thou all those things? And to insist only on *sacrilege* and
robbery. What can it be but *robbery,* and *sacrilege,* to sell
absolution, or, which is the same thing, to refuse it to the penitent, if he does not give so much money for masses ?

This may be cleared by their own principles, and by the
opinions of their casuistical authors, who agree in this, viz. :
That there are three sorts of sacrilege, or a sacrilege which
may be committed three different ways. These are the expressions they make use of: *Sacrum in sacro: Sacrum ex
sacro: Sacrum pro sacro.* That is, to take a sacred thing for
a sacred thing, a sacred thing in a sacred place; and a sacred
thing out of a sacred place. All these are robbery and sacrilege together, according to their opinions; and I said that the
confessors in their practices are guilty of all three; for in their
opinion, the holy tribunal of conscience is a sacred thing;
the absolution and consecrated church are sacred likewise.
As for the money given for the relief of the souls in purgatory, Corella, in his Moral Sum, says, that that is a sacred
thing too. Now it is certain among them, that no priest can
receive money for absolution, directly nor indirectly. Those
then that take it, rob that money which is unlawfully taken
from the penitent; and it is a sacrilege too, because they take

a sacred thing for a sacred thing, viz.: the sacred money for masses taken for absolution. They take that sacred thing in a sacred place, viz.: in the sacred tribunal of conscience: and they take a sacred thing out of a sacred place, viz.: the church.

Again: Though most commonly, *Quodcumque ligaveris super terram; erit ligatum et in cælis,* is understood by them litera'ly, and the pope usurps the power of absolving men without contrition, provided they have attrition, or only confession by mouth, as we shall see in the following chapter of the pope's bull. Nevertheless the casuists, when they come to treat of a perfect confession under the sacrament of penance, they unanimously say, that three things are absolutely necessary to a perfect confession, and to salvation too, viz.: *Oris confessio, cordis contritio,* and *operis satisfactio.* Though at the same time they say, except in case of pontifical dispensation with faculties, privileges, indulgences, and pardon of all sins committed by a man : But though they except this case, I am sure they do it out of obedience, and flattery, rather than their own belief. If they then believe, that without contrition of heart, the absolution is of no effect, why do they persuade the contrary to the penitent? Why do they take money for absolution? It is, then, a cheat, robbery, and sacrilege.

Secondly. I say, that the confessors [generally speaking] are the occasion of the ruin of many families, of many thefts, debaucheries, murders, and divisions among several families [for which they must answer before that dreadful tribunal of God, when and where all the secret practices and wickedness shall be disclosed]; add to this, that by auricular confession, they are acquainted with the tempers and inclinations of people, which contribute very much to heap up riches, and to make themselves commanding masters of all sorts of persons; for when a confessor is thoroughly acquainted with a man's temper and natural inclinations, it is the most easy thing in the world to bring him to his own opinion, and to be master over nim and his substance.

That the confessors, commonly speaking, are the occasion of all the aforesaid mischiefs, will appear by the following observations :

First, They get the best estates from the rich people, for the use and benefit of their communities, by which many and many private persons, and whole familes, are reduced and ruined   Observe now their practices as to the sick. If a

nobleman of a good estate be very ill, the confessor must be
by him night and day; and when he goes to sleep, his companion supplies his place, to direct, and exhort the sick to die
as a good christian, and to advise him how to make his last
will and testament. If the confessor is a down-right honest
man, he must betray his principles of honesty, or disoblige
his superior, and all the community, by getting nothing from
the sick; so he chargeth upon the poor man's conscience, to
leave his convent thousands of masses, for the speedy delivery
of his soul out of purgatory; and besides that, to settle a yearly
mass forever upon the convent, and to leave a voluntary gift,
that the friars may remember him in their public and private
prayers, as a benefactor of that community: And in these and
other legacies and charities, three parts of his estate go to
the church, or convents. But if the confessor have a large
conscience, then without any christian consideration for the
sick man's family and poor relations, he makes use of all the
means an inhuman, covetous man can invent, to get the whole
estate for his convent. And this is the reason why they are
so rich, and so many families so poor, reduced, and ruined.

From these we may infer thefts, murders, debaucheries,
and divisions of families. I say, the confessors are the original causes of all these ill consequences; for when they take
the best of estates for themselves, no wonder if private persons and whole families are left in such want, and necessity,
that they abandon themselves to all sorts of sins, and hazards
of losing both lives and honors, rather than to abate something
of their pride.

I might prove this by several instances, which I do not
question, are very well known by several curious people: and
though some malicious persons are apt to suspect that such
instances are mere dreams, or forgeries of envious people; for
my part I believe, that many confessors are the original cause
of the aforesaid evils, as may be seen by the following matter
of fact:

In the account of the jesuits and their practices, I said that
the reverend Navasques was the confessor of the countess of
Fuentes, who was left a widow at twenty-four years of age,
and never married again: for the reverend's care is to advise
them to live a single life. (Purity being the first step to
heaven.) The lady countess had no children, and had an
estate of her own, of 4000 pistoles a year, besides her jewels
and household goods, which, after her death, were valued at
15,000 pistoles. All these things and her personal estate

were left to the jesuits' college, though she had many near relations, among whom I knew two young gentlemen, second cousins of her ladyship, and two young ladies kept in the house as her cousins too. She had promised to give them a settlement suitable to their quality and merits: which promise the father confessor confirmed to them several times. But the lady died, and both the young ladies and the two gentlemen were left under the providence of God, for the countess had forgotten them in her last will; and the father confessor took no notice of them afterward. The two young ladies abandon ed themselves to all manner of private pleasures at first, and at last to public wickedness. As to the young gentlemen, in a few months after the lady's death, one left the city and went to serve the king, as a cadet: the other following a licentious life, was ready to finish his days with shame and dishonor upon a public scaffold, had not the goodness and compassion of the marquis of Camarrassa, then vice-roy of Aragon, prevented it. Now, whether the father confessor shall be answerable before God, for all the sins committed by the young ladies, and one of the gentlemen, for want of what they expected from the countess, or not? God only knows. .We may think and believe, that if the lady had provided for them according to their condition in the world, in all human probability they had not committed such sins. Or if the college, or the reverend father had been more charitable, and compassionate to the condition they were left in, they had put a timely stop to their wickedness.

Thirdly. I say that confessors and preachers are the occasion, that many thousands of young men and women choose a single, retired life, in a monastery or convent; and therefore are the cause of many families being extinguished, and their own treasure exceedingly increased.

If a gentleman have two or three sons, and as many daughters, the confessor of the family adviseth the father to keep the eldest son at home, and send the rest, both sons and daughters, into a convent or monastery; praising the monastical life, and saying, that to be retired from the world, is the safest way to heaven. There is a proverb which runs thus in English: *It is better to be alone, than in bad company.* And the confessors alter it thus: *It is better to be alone, than in good company,* which they pretend to prove with so many sophistical arguments, nay, with a passage from the scripture; and this not only in private conversation, but publicly in the pulpit. I remember, I heard my celebrated Mr. F. James Garcia preach a sermon upon the subject of a *retired life and solitude*, which sermon and others preached by him in Lent, in the cathedral church of St. Salvator, were printed afterwards. The book is in folio, and its title Quadragesima de Gracia. He was the first preacher I heard make use of the above proverb, and alter it in the aforesaid way ; and to prove the sense of his alteration he said : *Remember the woman in the apocalypsis that ran from heaven into the desert.* What! was not that woman in heaven, in the company of the stars and planets, by which are represented all the heavenly spirits ? Why, then, quits she that good company, and chooses to be alone in a desert place ? Because, said he, that woman is the holy soul, and for a soul that desireth to be holy, it is better to be alone than in good company. In the desert, in the convent, in the monastery, the soul is safe, free from sundry temptations of the world ; and so it belongs to a Christian soul, not only to run from bad company, but to quit the best company in the world and retire into the desert of a convent, or monastery, if that soul desire to be holy and pure ; this was his proof, and if he had not been my master, I would have been bold to make some reflections upon it. But the respect of a disciple, beloved by him, is enough to make me silent, and leave to the reader the satisfaction of reflecting in his own way, to which I heartily submit..

These, I say, are the advices the confessors give to the fathers of families, who, glad of lessening the expenses of the house, and of seeing their children provided for, send them into the desert place of a convent, which is really in the middle of the world. Now observe, that it is twenty to one, that their heir dies before he marries and has children : so the estate and everything else falls to the second, who is a professed friar or nun, and as they cannot use the expression of *meum* or *tuum*, all goes that way to the community. And this is the reason why many families are extinguished, and their names quite out of memory ; the convent so crowded, the kingdom so thin of people ; and the friars, nuns, and monasteries so rich.

Fourthly. I say that the confessors, priests, and especially friars, make good this saying among the common people : *Frayle o fraude es todo uno:* i. e., friar or fraud is the same thing ; for they not only defraud whole families, but make use of barbarous, inhuman means to get the estates of many rich persons.

The Marquis of Arino had one only daughter, and his sec-
G

ond brother was an Augustan friar, under whose care th
marquis left his daughter when he died. She was fifteen year
of age, ich and handsome. Her uncle and executor was a
that time doctor and professor of divinity in the university,
and prior of the convent, and could not personally take care
of his niece and her family; so he desired one of her aunts to
go and live with her, and sent another friar to be like a stew
ard and overseer of the house. The uncle was a good, honest
man and mighty religious. He minded more his office of prior,
his study and exercise of devotion, than the riches, pomp,
magnificence, and vanity of the world; so, seeing that the
discharge of his duty and that of an executor of his niece were
inconsistent together, he did resolve to marry her; which he
did to the baron Suelves, a young, handsome, healthy, rich
gentleman; but he died seven months after his marriage, so
the good uncle was again at the same trouble and care of his
niece, who was left a widow, but without children. After the
year of her mourning was expired, she was married to the
great president of the council, who was afterwards great
chancellor of the kingdom, but he died, leaving no children.
The first and second husband left all their estates to her; and
she was reckoned to have eighty thousand pistoles in yearly
rent and goods. A year after, Don Pedro Carillo, brigadier-
general, and general governor of the kingdom, married her,
but has no children by her. I left both the governor and the
lady alive, when I quitted the country. Now I come to the
point. It was specified in all the matches between the gentlemen and the lady, that if they had no issue by her, all the
estate and goods should fall to the uncle as a second brother
of her father; and so *ex necessitate* the convent should be for
ever the only enjoyer of it. It was found out, but too late,
that the friar steward, before she first married, had given her
a dose to make her a barren woman; and though nobody did
believe that the uncle had any hand in it, (so great an opinion the world and the lady's husband had of him,) everybody
did suspect at first the friar steward, and so it was confirmed
at last by his own confession; for, being at the point of
death, he owned the fact publicly and his design in it.

Another instance. A lady of the first rank, of eighteen
years of age, the only heiress of a considerable estate, was
kept by her parents at a distance from all sorts of company,
except only that of the confessor of the family, who was a learned and devout man: but as these reverends have always a
father companion to assist them at home and abroad, many

times the mischief is contrived and effected unknown to the confessor, by his wicked companion; so it happened in this instance. The fame of the wonderful beauty of this young lady was spread so far abroad, that the king and queen being in the city for eight months together, and not seeing the celebrated beauty at their court, her majesty asked her father one day, whether he had any children? And when he answered, that he had only one daughter, he was desired by the queen to bring her along with him to court the next day, for she had a great desire to see her beauty so much admired at home and abroad. The father could not refuse it, and so the next day the lady did appear at court, and was so much admired that a grandee (who had then the command of the army, though not of his own passions) said, this is the first time I see the sun among the stars. The grandee began to covet that inestimable jewel, and his heart burning in the agreeable flame of her eyes, he went to see her father, but could not see the daughter. At last, all his endeavors being in vain, for he was married, he sent for the confessor's companion, whose interest and mediation he got by money and fair promises of raising him to an ecclesiastical dignity; so, by that means, he sent a letter to the lady, who read it, and in a very few days he got her consent to disguise himself and come to see her along with the father companion; so one evening in the dark, putting on a friar's habit, he went to her chamber, where he was always in company with the companion friar, who by crafty persuasions made the lady understand, that if she did not consent to everything that the grandee should desire, her life and reputation were lost, &c. In the same disguise they saw one another several times, to the grandee's satisfaction, and her grief and vexation.

But the court being gone, the young lady began to suspect some public proof of her intrigue, till then secret, and consulting the father companion upon it, he did what he could to prevent it, but in vain. The misfortune was suspected, and owned by her to her parents. The father died of very grief in eight days' time; and the mother went into the country with her daughter, till she was free from her disease, and, afterwards, both ladies, mother and daughter, retired into a monastery, where I knew and conversed several times with them. The gentleman had made his will long before, by which the convent was to get the estate in case the lady should die without children; and as she had taken the habit of a nun, and professed the vows of religion, the prior was so ambitious that he asked the estate, alleging, that she, being a professed i. in, could have no children ; to which the lady replied, that she was obliged to obey her father's will, by which she was mis tress of the estate during her life ; adding, that it was bettei for the father prior not to insist on his demand ; for she was ruined in her reputation by the wickedness of one of his friars, and that she, if pressed, would show her own child, who was the only heir of her father's estate. But the prior, deaf to her threatenings, did carry on his pretensions, and, by an agreement, (not to make the thing more public than it was, for very few knew the true story,) the prior got the estate, obliging the convent to give the lady and her mother, during their lives, 400 pistoles every year, the whole estate being 5000 yearly rent.

I could give several more instances of this nature to con- vince that the confessors, priests, and friars are the fundamen- tal original cause of almost all the misdoings and mischiefs that happen in the families. By the instances already given every body may easily know the secret practices of some of the Romish priests, which are an abomination to the Lord, es- pecially in the holy tribunal of confession. So I may conclude and dismiss this first chapter, saying, that the confession is the mint of friars and priests, the sins of the penitent the metals, the absolution the coin of money, and the confessors the keepers of it. Now the reader may draw from these ac- counts as many inferences as he pleases, till, God willing, I furnish him with new arguments, and instances, of their evil practices in the second part of this work.

PART II.

This is a true copy of the Pope's Bull out of Spanish, in the translation of which into English, I am tied up to the letter, almost word for word, and this is to prevent (as to this point) all calumny and objection, which may be made against it, by some critic among the Roman-Catholics.

MDCCXVIII.

. Bull of the holy crusade, granted by the holiness of our most holy father Clement, the XIth, to the kingdoms of Spain, and the isles to them pertaining, in favor of all them, that should help and serve the king Dn. Philip V. our lord, in the war and expenses of it, which he doth make against the ene- mies of our catholic faith, with great indulgences and pardons, for the year one thousand seven hundred and eighteen.

The prophet Joel, sorry for the damages which the sons of Israel did endure by the invasion of the Chaldean armies, (zealous for and desirous of their defence, after having recom- mended to them the observance of the law) calling the sol- diers to the war, saith : That he saw, for the comfort of all, a mystical spring come out from God and his house, which did water and wash away the sins of that people. Chap. 3, v. 18.

Seeing then our most holy father, Clement XI, (who at this day doth rule and govern the holy apostolical see) for the zeal of the catholic king of the Spains, Dn. Philip, the Vth, for the defence of our holy faith, and for that purpose gathereth together, and maintaineth his armies against all the enemies of christianity, to help him in his holy enterprise, doth grant him this bull, by which his holiness openeth the springs of the blood of Christ, and the treasure of his inestimable merits; and with it encourageth all the christians to the assistance of this undertaking. For this purpose, and that they might enjoy this benefit, he orders to be published the following indulgen- ces, graces, and faculties, or privileges.

1. His holiness doth grant to all the true christians of the said kingdoms and dominions, dwellers, and settled, and inhab- itants in them, and to all comers to them, or should be found in them ; who, moved with the zeal of promoting the holy catho- lic faith, should go personally, and upon their own expenses,

to the war in the army, and with the forces which his majes'j
sendeth, for the time of one year, to fight against the Turks,
and other infidels, or to do any other service, as to help personally in the same army, continuing in it the whole year.   To
all these his holiness doth grant a free and full indulgence,
and pardon of all their sins, (if they have a perfect contrition,
or, if they confess them by mouth, and if they cannot, if they
have a hearty desire of it) which hath been used to be granted to them that go to the conquest of the holy land, and in
the year of Jubilee: and declares that all they that should
die before the end of the expedition, or in the way, as they
are going to the army before the expedition, should likewise
enjoy and obtain the said pardon and indulgence.

He granteth also the same to them, who, (though they do
not go personally) should send another upon their own expenses in this manner, viz.: If he that sends another is a cardinal, primate, patriarch, arch-bishop, bishop, son of a king,
prince, duke, marquis, or earl, then he must send as many as
he can possibly send, till ten ; and if he cannot send ten, he
must send at least four soldiers.   All other persons, of what
condition soever they may be, must send one ; in such a case,
two, or three, or four, may join and contribute, every one according to his abilities, and send one soldier.

2. *Item.*   The chapters, * all churches, monasteries of friars and nuns, without excepting mendicant orders, if ten, with
the consent of the chapter or community, do join to send one
soldier, they do enjoy the said indulgence ; and not they only,
but the person too, sent by them, if he be poor.

3. *Item.*   The secular priests, who, with the consent of
their diocesan, and the friars of their superiors, should preach
the word of God in the said army, or should perform any other
ecclesiastical and pious office (which is declared to be lawful
for them, without incurring irregularity) are empowered to
serve their benefices, by meet and fit tenants, having not the
cure of souls ; for if they have, they cannot without his holiness' consent.   And it is declared, that the soldiers employed
in this war are not obliged to fast the days appointed and commanded by the church, and which they should be obliged to
fast on, if they were not in the war.

4. *Item.*   His holiness grants (not only to the soldiers, but
to all them too, who, though they should not go, should encourage this holy work with the charity undermentioned) all
the indulgences, graces, and privileges in this bull contained,
and this for a whole year, reckoning from the publishing of it

m any place whatsoever, viz.: that (yet, in the time of apostolical, or ordinary *interdictum*, i. e., suspension of all ecclesiastical and divine service) they may hear mass either in the churches and monasteries, or in the private oratories marked and visited by the diocesan ; and, if they were priests, to say mass and other divine offices; or, if they were not, to make others to celebrate mass before them, their familiar friends and relations, to receive the holy sacrament of the Lord's supper and the other sacraments, except on Easter Sunday, provided that they have not given occasion for the said interdictum, nor hindered the taking of it: Provided, likewise, that every time they make use of such oratory, they should, according to their devotion, pray for union and concord among all Christian princes, the rooting out of heresies, and victory over the infidels.

5. *Item.* His holiness granteth, that in time of interdictum, their corpse may be buried in sacred ground, with a moderate funeral pomp.

6. *Item.* He grants to all, that should take this bull, that during the year, by the counsel of both spiritual and corporal physicians, they may eat flesh in Lent, and several other days in which it is prohibited : And likewise, that they may freely eat eggs and things with milk ; and that all these, who should eat no flesh, (keeping the form of the ecclesiastical fast,) do fulfil the precept of fasting : And in this privilege of eating eggs, &c., are not comprised the *patriarchs, primates, archbishops, bishops, nor other inferior prelates, nor any person whatsoever of the regulars, nor of the secular priests, (the days only of Lent,) notwithstanding from the mentioned persons, we except all those that are sixty years of age, and all the knights of the military orders, who freely may eat eggs, &c., and enjoy the said privilege.

7. *Item.* The abovenamed, that should not go, nor send any soldier to this holy war, out of their own substance, (if they should help to it, keeping a fast for devotion's sake, in some days, which are of no precept, and praying and imploring the help of God, for the victory against the infidels, and his grace, for the union among the Christian princes,) as many times as they should do it during the year, so many times it is granted them, and graciously forgiven fifteen years, and fifteen *quarantains* of pardon, and all the penances imposed on them, and in whatever manner due ; also that they be partakers of all the prayers, alms and pilgrimages of Jerusalem, and all the

good works which should be done in the universal militant church, and in each of its members.

8. *Item.* To all those, who, in the days of Lent and other days of the year, in which* estations are at Rome, should visit five churches, or five altars, and if there is not five churches, or five altars, five times should visit one church, or one altar, praying for the victory and union above mentioned, his holiness granteth that they should enjoy and obtain the indulgences and pardons, which all those do enjoy and obtain, that personally visit the churches of the city of Rome, and without the walls of it, as well as if they did visit personally the said churches.   •

9. *Item.* To the intent, that the same persons with more purity, and cleanness of their consciences, might pray, his holiness grants, that they might choose for their confessor any secular or regular priest licensed by the diocesan, to whom power is granted to absolve them of all sins and censures whatsoever, [though they be reserved to the apostolical see, and specified in the bull of the Lord's supper, except of the crime heresy,] and that they should enjoy free and full indulgence and pardon of them all. But of the sins not reserved to the apostolical see, they may be absolved *toties quoties*, i. e., as many times as they do confess them, and perform salutary penance: And if to be absolved, there be need of restitution, they might make it themselves, or by their heirs, if they have an impediment to make it themselves. Likewise the said confessor shall have power to communicate or change any vow whatsoever, though made with an oath, (excepting the vow of chastity, religion, and beyond seas) but this is, upon giving for charity what they should think fit, for the benefit of the holy crusade.

10. *Item.* That if, during the said year, they should happen, by sudden death, or by the absence of their confessor, to die without confessing their sins; if they die hearty penitents; and in the time appointed by the church, had confessed, and have not been negligent or careless in confidence of this grace, it is granted, that they should obtain the said free and full indulgence and pardon of all their sins; and their corpse might be buried in ecclesiastical burying place, (if they did not die excommunicated,) notwithstanding the interdictum.

11. Likewise his holiness hath granted by his particular brief, to all the faithful Christians, that take the bull twice a year, that they might once more, during their lives, and once more at the point of death, (besides what is said above,) be

absolved of all the sins, crimes, excesses of vhat nature soever, censures, sentences of excommunication, though comprised in the bull of the Lord's supper, and though the absolution of them be reserved to his holiness, (except the crime and offence of heresy,) and that they might twice more enjoy all the graces, indulgences, faculties and pardons granted in this bull.

12. And his holiness gives power and authority to us, Don Francis Anthony Ramirez de la Piscina, archdeacon of Alcarraz, prebendary and canon of the holy church at Toledo primate of the Spains, of his Majesty's council, apostolic, general commissary of the holy crusada, and all other graces in all the kingdoms and dominions of Spain, to suspend (during the year of the publishing of this bull) all the graces, indulgences, and faculties, granted to the said kingdoms, dominions, isles, provinces, to whatever churches, monasteries, hospitals, brotherhoods, pious places, and to particular persons, though the granting of them did contain words contrary to this suspension.

13. Likewise he gives us power to reinforce and make good again the same graces and faculties, and all others whatsoever; and he gives us and our deputies power to suspend the interdictum in whatever place this bull should be preached; and likewise to fix and determine the quantum of the contribution the people is to give for this bull, according to the abilities and quality of persons.

14. And we, the said apostolic general commissary of the holy crusada, (in favor of this holy bull, by the apostolical authority granted to us, and that so holy a work do not cease nor be hindered by any other indulgence,) do suspend, during the year, all the graces, indulgences and faculties, of this or any other kind, granted by his holiness, or by other popes his predecessors, or by the holy apostolical see, or by his authority, to all the kingdoms of his majesty, to all churches, monasteries, hospitals, and other pious places, universities, brotherhoods, and secular persons; though the said graces and faculties be in favor of the building of St. Peter's church at Rome, or of any crusada, though all and every one of them should contain words contrary to this suspension : So that, during the year, no person shall obtain, or enjoy, any other graces, indulgences or faculties whatsoever, nor can be published, except only the privileges granted to the superiors of the mendicant orders, as to their friars.

15. And in favor of this bull, and by the sa'? apostolical

authority we ded are, that all those that would take this bull
might obtain and enjoy all the graces, faculties and indulgen
ces, jubilees and pardons, which have been granted by our
holy fathers, Paul the 5th, and Urbannus the 8th, and by other
popes of happy memory, and by the holy apostolical see or by
its authority, mentioned and comprised in the said suspension,
and which, by the apostolical commission, we reinforce and
make good again ; and by the same authority do suspend the
interdictum for eight days before and after publishing this
bull, in any place whatsoever (as it is contained in his holiness' brief): And we command that everybody, that would
take this bull, be obliged to keep by him the same which is here
printed, signed and sealed with our name and seal, and that otherwise they cannot obtain nor enjoy the benefit of the said bull.

16. And whereas you (Peter de Zuloaga) have given two
reales de plata, which is the charity fixed by us, and have
taken this bull, and your name is written in it, we do declare,
that you have already obtained, and are granted the said indulgences, and that you may enjoy and make use of them in
the abovementioned form. Given at Madrid, the eighteenth
day of March, one thousand seven hundred and eighteen.

Form of absolution, which, by virtue of this bull, may be given to all those
that take the bull once in their life time, and once upon the point of
death.

Misereatur tui Omnipotens Deus, &c. By the authority of
God and his holy apostles St. Peter and St. Paul, and our most
holy father (N.) to you especially granted and to be committed,
I absolve you from all censure of the greater or lesser excommunication, suspension, interdictum, and from all other censures and pains, or punishments, which they have incurred
and deserved, though the absolution of them be reserved to the
apostolic see, (as by the same is granted to you.) And I
bring you again into the union and communion of the faithful
Christians: And also I absolve you from all the sins, crimes,
and excesses, which you have now here confessed, and from
those which you would confess, if you did remember them,
though they be so exceeding great, that the absolution of them
be reserved to the apostolical see ; and I do grant you free and
full indulgence, and pardon of all your sins now and whenever
confessed, forgotten, and out of your mind, and of all the pains
and punishments which you were obliged to endure for them
n ourgatory. In the name of the Father, of the Son, and of
the Holy Ghost.—Amen.

Brief, or sum of the estations and indulgences of Rome, which his holiness grants to all those that would take and fulfil the contents of this bull.

The first day in St. Sabine, free and full indulgence
    Thursday in St. George,   do.
    Friday in St. John and St. Paul,   do.
    Saturday in St. Criffon,   do.
    First Sunday in Lent, in St. John, St. Paul, do.
    Monday in St. Peter ad Vincula,   do.
    Tuesday in St. Anastasie,   do.
    *And this day everybody takes a soul out of purgatory.
Wednesday in St. Mary the greater, free and full indulgence.
    Thursday in St. Laurence Panispema, do.
    Friday in the saints apostles,   do.
    Saturday in St. Peter,   do.
Second Sunday in Lent, in St. Mary of Na-
    vicula, and St. Mary the greater, do.
    Monday in St. Clement,   do.
    Tuesday in St. Balbine,   do.
    Wednesday in St. Cicile,   do.
    Thursday in St. Mary transtiber,   do.
    Friday in St. Vidal,   do.
    Saturday in St. Peter and St. Marcelin, do.
    *And this day everybody takes one soul out of purgatory.
Third Sunday in Lent in St. Laurence,
    extra Muros, free and full indulgence.
    *And this day everybody takes one soul out of purgtory.
Monday in St. Mark, free and full indulgence.
    Tuesday in St. Potenciane,   do.
    Wednesday in St. Sixte,   do.
    Thursday in St. Cosme, and St. Damian,
    the image of our lady of Populi and
    Pacis, is shown.   do.
    Friday in St. Laurence in Lucina, do.
    Saturday in St. Susane, and St. Mary of the angels.
Fourth Sunday in Lent in St. Crosse of Jerusalem, do.
    *This day everybody takes one soul out of purgatory
Monday in the 4-crowned free and full indulgences.
    Tuesday in St. Laurence in Damascus, do.
    Wednesday in St. Peter,   do.
    Thursday in St. Silvastre and in St. Mary in
    the mountains,   do.
    Friday in St. Usebe,   do.
    Saturday in St. Nicholas in prison, do.
Fifth Sunday in Lent in St. Peter,   do.

Mond ay in St. Crissone, free and full indulgence
Tuesday in St. Quirce,   do.
Wednesday in St. Marcelle,   do.
Thursday in St. Appollinaris,   do.
Friday in St. Estephan,   do.
*This day everybody takes one soul out of purgatory.
Saturday in St. John ante Portam Latinam, free and full in-
   dulgence.
   *And this day every one takes a soul out of purgatory.
Sixth Sunday in Lent in St. John de Leteran, full and free in-
                                       [dulgence.
Monday in St. Praxedis,   do.
Tuesday in St. Priske,   do.
Wednesday in St. Mary the greater,   do.
Thursday in St. John de Leteran,   do.
Friday in St. Crosse of Jerusalem, and in St.
   Mary of the angels,   do.
Saturday in St. John de Leteran,   do.
Easter Sunday in St. Mary the greater,   do.
Monday in St. Peter,   do.
Tuesday in St. Paul,   do.
Wednesday in St. Laurence, extra muros,   do.
*This day everybody takes a soul out of purgatory.
Thursday in the saints apostles, free and full indulgence
Friday in St. Mary Rotunda,   do.
Saturday in St. John Deleteran,   do.
Sunday after Easter in St. Pancracy,   do.

ESTATIONS AFTER EASTER.

In the greater litanies : St. Mark's day ; in St.
   Peter,   do.
Ascension-day in St. Peter,   do.
Whitsunday in St. John de Leteran,   do
Monday in St. Peter,   do
Tuesday in St. Anastasie,   do.
Wednesday in St. Mary the greater,   do
Thursday in St. Laurence, extra muros,   do.
*This day everybody takes a soul out of purgatory.
Friday in the saints apostles, free and full indulgence
Saturday in St. Peter,   do.

ESTATIONS IN ADVENT

First Sunday in St. Mary the greater,   do.
   And in the same church all the holy days of
      our lady,   do

Second Sunday in St. Crosse of Jerusalem, free and full in-
   The same day in St. Mary of the angels,   do.   [dulgence.
Third Sunday in St. Peter,   do.
   Wednesday of the four rogations, in St. Mary the greater.
   Friday in the saints apostles,   do.
   Saturday in St. Peter,   do.
Fourth Sunday in the saints apostles,   do.
                CHRISTMAS NIGHT.
At the first mass in St. Mary the greater, in the
   Manger's chapel,   do.
.At the second mass St. Anastasie,   do.
                CHRISTMAS DAY.
At the third mass in St. Mary the greater,   do.
   Monday in St. Mary Rotunda,   do.
   Tuesday in St. Mary the greater,   do.
The innocent's day in St. Paul,   do.
The circumcision of Christ in St. Mary transtiber,
The Epiphany in St. Peter,   do.
Dominica in Septuag. in St. Laurence, extra muros.
   *This day everybody takes a soul out of purgatory.
Dominica in Sexag. in St. Paul, free and full indulgence.
Dominica in Quinquag. in St. Peter,   do.
   And because, every day of the year, there is estations at
Rome, with great indulgences, therefore it is granted to all
those that take this bull, the same indulgences and pardons
'very day which are granted at Rome.
   DON FRANCIS ANTHONY RAMIRET, DE LA PISOINA.

Explanation of this bull, and remark upon it.

BULL OF CRUSADE.

   A pope's brief, granting the sign of the cross to those that
take it. All that a foreigner can learn in the dictionaries, as
to this word, is the above account; therefore I ought to tell
you that are foreigners, that the word crusada was a grant of
the cross; i. e., that when the king of Spain makes war
against the Turks and infidels, his coat of arms, and the motto
of his colors, is the cross, by which all the soldiers understand such a war is an holy war, and that the army of the
king, having in its standard the sign of the cross, hath a great
advantage over the enemy; for, as they do believe, if they
die in such a war, their souls go straight to heaven; and to
confirm them in this opinion, the pope grants them this bull,
signed with the sign of the cross, so many indulgences as you
have read in it.
                        H

Again, crus, or cross, is the only distinguishing charater
of those that follow the colors of Jesus Christ, from whence
crusada is derived, that is to say, a brief of indulgences and
privileges of the cross granted to all those that serve in the
war for the defence of the Christian faith against all its enemies whatsoever.

This bull is granted by the pope every year to the king of
Spain, and all his subjects, by which the king increases his
treasure, and the pope takes no small share of it. The excessive sums of money, which the bull brings in to the king
and pope, everybody may easily know, by the account I am
going to give of it.

It is an inviolable custom in Spain, every year, after Christmas, to have this bull published in every city, town, and bor-
ough, which is always done in the following manner:

The general commissary of the holy crusade most commonly resides at Madrid, from whence he sends to his deputies,
in every kingdom or province, the printed bulls they want in
their respective jurisdictions. This bull being published at
Madrid by the general commissary or his deputy, which is
always done by a famous preacher, after the gospel is sung in
the high mass, and in a sermon which he preaches upon this
subject. After this is done at Madrid, (I say,) all the deputies
of the holy crusada send from the capital city, where they
reside, friars with a petit commissary to every town and village, to preach and publish the bull. Every preacher has his
own circuit, and a certain number of towns and villages, to
publish it in, and, making use of the privileges mentioned in
the bull, he in his sermon persuades the people that nobody
can be saved that year without it, which they do and say every
year again.

The petit commissary, for his trouble, has half a real of
eight, i. e., two and fourpence a day; and the preacher, according to the extent of the circuit, has twenty or thirty crowns
for the whole journey, and both are well entertained in every
place.

Every soul, from seven years of age and upwards, is obliged
to take a bull, and pay two reals of plate, i. e., thirteen pence
three farthings of this money; and one part out of three of the
living persons take two or three, according to their families
and abilities. The regular priests are obliged to take, three
times every year, the bull, for which they pay two reals of
plate: In the beginning of Lent another, which they call bull
of lactic nous, i. e, bull to eat eggs, and things of milk, with-

out which they cannot : And another in the holy week. For
the bull of lacticinous they pay four and ninepence, and the
same for the bull of the holy week ; the friars and nuns do
the same. Now, if you consider the number of ecclesiastics
and nuns and all the living souls from seven years of age and
upwards, you may easily know what vast sums of money the
king gets in his dominions by this yearly brief, of which the
third part or better goes to Rome one way or other.

Add to this the bull of the dead. This is another sort of
bull ; for the pope grants in it pardon of sins, and salvation to
them, who, before they die, or after their death their relations
for them, take this bull of defunctorum. The custom of taking this bull is become a law, and a very rigorous law, in
their church ; for nobody can be buried, either in the church
or in the church-yard, without having this bull upon their
breasts, which (as they say) is a token and signal that they
were Christians in their lives, and after death they are in the
way of salvation.

So many poor people, either beggars or strangers, or those
that die in the hospitals, could not be buried without the help
of the well-disposed people, who bestow their charities for
the use of taking bulls of the dead, that the poor destitute people might have the benefit of a consecrated burying-place.
The sum for this bull is two reals of plate, and whatever
money is gathered together in the whole year goes to the pope,
or (as they say) to the treasure of the church. Now I leave
to everybody's consideration, how many persons die in a year,
in so vast dominions as those of the king of Spain, by which,
in this point, the pope's benefit, or the treasure of the church,
may be nearly known.

O stupid, blind, ignorant people ! Of what use or benefit
is this bull after death ? Hear what St. John tells you : *Happy
are they that die in the Lord.* It is certain that all those that
die in the grace of the Lord, heartily penitent, and sorry for
their sins, go immediately to enjoy the ravishing pleasures of
eternal life ; and those that die in sin, go to suffer forever in
the dark place of torment. And this happens to our souls
the very instant of their separation from their bodies. Let
everybody make use of their natural reason, and read impar-
tially the scripture, and he will find it to be so, or else he will
believe it to be so. Then if it is so, they ought to consider,
that when they take this bull (which is commonly a little before they carry the corpse) into the church the judgment of
God, as to the soul, is over, (for in the twinkling of an eye he

may lay the charges and pass the sentence)—at that time the
soul is either in heaven or hell. What, then, doth the bull
signify to them?   But of this I shall speak in another place.
And now I come to the explanation of the bull, and the remarks upon it.

This bull I am speaking of was granted five years ago to
the faithful people of Spain, by the late pope, and which a
gentleman of the army took accidentally from a master of a
ship out of Biscay, whose name is Peter de Zoloaga, as it is
signed by himself in the same bull, and may be seen at the
publisher's.   I have said already that a bull is every year
granted to the king of Spain, by the pope in being, who, either
for the sake of money, or for fear, doth not scruple at all to
grant quite contrary bulls to two kings at the same time
reigning in Spain. Now I crave leave to vindicate my pres
ent saying.

When the present king of Spain, Philip the Vth, went there
and was crowned, both the arms spiritual and temporal, rep-
resentatives of the whole nation, (as in these kingdoms, the
house of lords and commons;) gave him the oath of fidelity
acknowledging him for their lawful sovereign: And when
this was done, pope Clement XIth did confirm it, nay, his holi
ness gave him the investiture of Naples, which is the sealing
up all the titles and rights belonging to a lawful king, and
after this he granted him the bull crusade, by which he acknowledged him king, and gave him help to defend himself
and his dominions against all the enemies of Christianity, and
all enemies whatsoever. Everybody knows that this pope
was for the interests of the house of *Bourbon*, rather than the
house of *Austria ;* and so no wonder, if he did not lose any
time in settling the crown and all the right upon Philip of
Bourbon, rather than upon Charles the IIId, the present emperor of Germany.

This last, thinking that the right to the crown of Spain belonged to him, of which I shall not talk, begun the war
against Philip, supported by the Heretics, (as the Spaniards
call the English,) and being proclaimed at Madrid, and at
Saragossa, he applied to the pope to be confirmed king, and to
get both the investiture of Naples, and the bull of the holy
crusade.   As to the investiture of Naples, I leave it to the history written upon the late war : But as to the bull, the pope
granted it to him, giving him all the titles he gave to Philip.
At the same time there were two kings, and two bulls, and one
pope, and one people. The divines met together to examine

this point, viz. : Whether the same people, having given their
oath of fidelity to Philip, and taken the bull granted to him,
were obliged to acknowledge Charles as a king, and take the
bull granted to him.

The divines for Philip were of opinion that the pope could
not annul the oath, nor dispense with the oath taken by the
whole nation, and that the people were obliged in conscience
not to take any other bull than that granted to Philip ; and their
reason was, that the pope was forced by the imperial army to
do it; and that his holiness did it out of fear, and to prevent
the ruin of the church, which then was threatened.

The divines for Charles did allege the pope's infallibility,
and that every Christian is obliged in conscience to follow the
st declaration of the pope, and blindly to obey it, without
quiring into the reasons that did move the pope to it. And
e same dispute was about the presentation of bishops, for
ere was at the same time a bishoprick vacant, and Charles
ving appointed one, and Philip another, the pope confirmed
hem both, and both of them were consecrated. From this it
appears that the pope makes no scruple at all in granting two
bulls to two kings at the same time, and to embroil with them
the whole nation ; which he did, not out of fear, nor to prevent
the ruin of the church, but of self-interest, and to secure his
revenue both ways, and on both sides.

But, reader, be not surprised at this ; for this pope I am
speaking of, was so ambitious, and of so haughty a temper,
that he did not care what means he made use of, either to
please his temper, or to quench the thirst of his ambition. I
say, he was of so haughty a temper, that he never suffered
his decrees to be contradicted or disputed, though they were
against both human and divine laws. To clear this, I will
give an account of an instance in a case which happened in
his pontificate :

I was in Lisbon ten years ago, and a Spanish gentleman,
whose surname was Gonzalez, came to lodge in the same
house where I was for a while before ; and as we, after supper,
were talking of the pope's supremacy and power, he told me
that he himself was a living witness of the pope's authority
on oath : and, asking him how, he gave the following account

I was born in Granada, said he, of honest and rich, though
not noble parents, who gave me the best education they could
in that city. I was not twenty years of age when my father
and mother died, both within the space of six months. They
left me all they had in the world, recommending to me, in their

testament, to take care of my sister Dorothea, and to provide
for her. She was the only sister I had, and at that time in the
eighteenth year of her age. From our youth we had tenderly
loved one another; and upon her account, quitting my studies,
I gave myself up to her company. This tender brotherly love
produced in my heart at last another sort of love for her; and
though I never showed her my passion, I was a sufferer by it.
I was ashamed within myself to see that I could not master
nor overcome this irregular inclination; and perceiving that
the persisting in it would prove the ruin of my soul, and my
sister's too, I finally resolved to quit the country for a while,
to see whether I could dissipate this passion, and banish out
of my heart this burning and consuming fire; and after having settled my affairs, and put my sister under the care of a
aunt, I took my leave of her, who, being surprised at this u
expected news, she upon her knees begged me to tell the re
son that moved me to quit the country; and, after telling h
that I had no reason, but only a mind and desire to travel tw
or three years, and that I begged of her not to marry any person in the world, until my return home, I left her and went to
Rome. By letters of recommendation, by money, and my
careful comportment, I got myself, in a little time, into the
favor and house of cardinal A. I. Two years I spent in his
service at my own expense, and his kindness to me was so
exceeding great, that I was not only his companion, but his
favorite and confidant. All this while, I was so raving and in
so deep a melancholy, that his eminence pressed upon me to
tell him the reason. I told him that my distemper had no
remedy: but he still insisted the more to know my distemper.
At last, I told him the love I had for my sister, and that it
being impossible she should be my wife, my distemper had no
remedy. To this he said nothing, but the day following went
to the sacred palace, and meeting in the pope's antechamber
cardinal P. I., he asked him whether the pope could dispense
with the natural and divine impediment between brother and
sister to be married; and, as cardinal P. I. said that the pope
could not, my protector began a loud and bitter dispute with
him, alleging reasons by which the pope could do it. The pope,
hearing the noise, came out of his chamber, and asked what
was the matter? He was told it, and, flying into an uncommon
passion, said the pope may do everything, I do dispense with it,
and left them with these words. The protector took testimony
of the Pope's declaration, and went to the datary and drew a
public instrument of the dispensation, and, coming home, gave

t to me, and said, though I shall be deprived of your good
services and company, I am very glad that I serve you in this
to your heart's desire and satisfaction. Take this dispensation, and go whenever you please to marry your sister   I left
Rome, and came home, and after I had rested from the fatigue
of so long a journey, I went to present the dispensation to the
bishop, and to get his license ; but he told me that he could not
receive the dispensation, nor give such a license; I acquainted my protector with this, and immediately an excommunication was despatched against the bishop, for having disobeyed
the pope, and commanding him to pay a thousand pistoles for
the treasure of the church, and to marry me himself; so, I was
married by the bishop, and at this time I have five children by
my wife and sister.

From these accounts, Christian reader, you may judge of
that pope's temper and ambition, and you may likewise think
of the rest as you may see it in the following discourse.

The title, head, or direction of this bull is, to all the faithful
Christians, in the kingdoms and dominions of Spain, who
should help, or serve in the war, which the king makes against
Turks, infidels, and all the enemies of the holy catholic faith ;
or to those that should contribute, and pray for the union
among the Christian princes, and for the victory over the enemies of Christianity.

The Roman Catholics, with the pope, say and firmly believe
(I speak of the generality) that no man can be saved out of
their communion ; and so they reckon enemies of their faith
all those that are of a different opinion ; and we may be sure
that the Protestants or heretics (as they call them) are their
irreconcilable enemies.

They pray publicly for the extirpation of the heretics,
Turks, and infidels in the mass; and they do really believe
they are bound in conscience to make use of all sorts of means,
let them be ever so base, inhuman, and barbarous, for the
murdering of them. This is the doctrine of the church of
Rome, which the priests and confessors do take care to sow in
the Roman Catholics; and by their advice, the hatred, malice,
and aversion is raised to a great height against the heretics,
as you shall know by the following instances.

First, in the last war between Charles the 3d, and Philip
the 5th, the Protestants confederate with Charles did suffer
very much by the country people. Those, encouraged by the
priests and confessors of Philip's part, thinking that if any
Christian could kill a heretic, he should do God service, did

murder in private many soldiers, both English and Dutch. I
saw, and I do speak now before God and the world, in a town
called Ficentes de Ebro, several arms and legs out of the
ground in the field, and inquiring the reason why those corpses
were buried in the field, (a thing indeed not unusual there,)
I was answered, that those were the corpses of some English
heretics, murdered by the patrons or landlords, who had killed
them to show their zeal for their religion, and an old maxim
among them: *De los Enemigos los menos:* let us have as
few enemies as we can.   Fourteen English private men were
killed the night before in their beds, and buried in the field,
and I myself reckoned all of them ; and I suppose many others
were murdered, whom I did not see, though I heard of it.

The murderers make no scruple of it, but, out of bravery,
and zeal for their religion, tell it to the father confessor, not as
a sin, but as a famous action done by them in favor of their
faith.   So great is the hatred and aversion the catholics have
against the protestants and all enemies of their religion.   We
could confirm the truth of this proposition with the cruelty of
the late king of France against the poor Huguenots, whom we
call now refugees.   This is well known to everybody, therefore I leave Lewis and his counsellors where they are in the
other world, where it is to be feared they endure more torments
than the banished refugees in this present one.   So, to conclude what I have to say upon the head or title of this bull, I
may positively affirm that the pope's design in granting it, is,
first, out of interest ; secondly, to encourage the common people to make war, and to root up all the people that are not of
his communion, or to increase, this way, if he can, his reve-
nues, or the treasure of the church.

I come now to the beginning of the bull, where the pope or
his sub-delegate, deputy, or general commissary, doth ground
the granting of it in that passage of the prophet Joel, chap.
iii. v. 18, expressed in these words : That *he saw for the comfort of all, a mystical fountain come out from God in his house,*
or (as it is in Spanish in the original bull,) *from God and from
the Lord's house, which did water and wash the sins of that
people.*

The reflections, which may be made upon this text, I leave
to our divines, whose learning I do equally covet and respect :
I only say that in the Latin Bible I have found the text thus :
*Et fons e domo Jehovæ prodibit, qui irrigabit vallem cedrorum
Lectissimarum.*   And in our English translation : *And a foun-
tain shall come forth of the house of the Lord, and shall water*

Half buried bodies of Englishmen murdered by Catholics.

he valley of Shittem. Now I leave the learned man to make
nis reflections, and I proceed to the application.

Seeing then our most holy father (so goes on) Clement the
XIth, for the zeal of the catholic king, for the defence of ou.
holy faith, to help him in this holy enterprise, doth grant him
this bull, by which his holiness openeth the springs of the blood
of Christ; and the treasure of his inestimable merits, and with
it encourageth all the Christians to the assistance of this undertaking.

I said before that the pope grants every year such a bull as
this for the same purpose: so every year he openeth the
springs of Christ's blood. O heaven! what is man that thou
shouldst magnify him? Or, rather, what is this man that he
should magnify himself, taking upon him the title of *most holy
father,* and that of *his holiness?* A man (really a man) for.
it is certain that this man and many others of his predecessors
had had several b——s. This man (I say) to take upon himself the power of opening the springs of Christ, and this every
year!! Who will not be surprised at his assurance, and at his
highest provocation of the Lord and his Christ?

For my part, I really believe that he openeth the springs of
the blood of Christ, and openeth afresh those wounds of our
Redeemer, not only every year, but every day without ceasing.
This I do believe, but not as they believe it; and if their
doctrine be true among themselves, by course they must agree
with me in this saying, that the pope doth crucify afresh our
Saviour Christ without ceasing. In the treatise of vices and
sins, the Romish divines propose a question : *utrum,* or whether
a man that takes upon himself one of God's attributes, be a
blasphemous man, and whether such a man by his sins can
kill God and Christ? As to the first part of the question, they all do agree that such a man is a blasphemous man.
As to the second part, some are of an opinion that such an expression, of *killing* God, has no room in the question. But the
greater part of scholastic and moral authors do admit the expression, and say such a man cannot kill God effectively, but
that he doth it affectively; that is to say, that willingly taking
upon himself an attribute of God, and acting against his laws,
he doth affront and offend, in the highest degree, that supreme
lawgiver; and by taking on himself the office of a high priest,
the power of forgiving sins, which only belong to our Saviour
Jesus, he affectively offends, and openeth afresh his wounds
and the springs of his blood: and if it were possible for us to
see him face to face, whom no man living hath seen yet; as

we see him through a glass now, we should find his high indig
nation against such a man. But he must appear before the
dreadful tribunal of our God, and be judged by him according
to his deeds : he shall have the same judgment with the antichrist, for though we cannot prove by the scriptures that he is
the antichrist, notwithstanding we may defy antichrist himself,
whoever he be, and whenever he comes, to do worse and more
wicked things than the pope doth.   O, what a fearful thing is
it to fall into the hands of a living God !   Now I come to the
articles of the bull ; and first of all,

   1. His holiness grants a free and full indulgence and par
don of all their sins to those who, upon their own expenses, go
to, or serve, personally, in the war against the enemies of the
Roman Catholic faith ; but this must be understood if they con
tinue in the army the whole year : so the next year they are
obliged to take this bull, and to continue in the same service,
if they will obtain the same indulgence and pardon, and so on
all their life time ; for if they quit the service, they cannot enjoy this benefit, therefore, for sake of this imaginary pardon,
they continue in it till they die, for otherwise there is no pardon of sins.

   Let us observe another thing in this article.   The same indulgence and pardon is granted to those that die in the army,
or going to the army before the expedition, or before the end
of the year ; but this must be understood also, if they die with
perfect contrition of their sins ; or if they do confess them by
mouth, or, if they cannot, if they have a hearty desire to confess
them.   As to the first condition, *if they die with perfect contrition*, no Roman or Protestant divine will deny that God will
forgive such a man's sins, and receive him into his everlasting
favor ; so to such a man, a free and full indulgence and pardon
is of no use ; for, without it, he is sure to obtain God's mercy
and forgiveness.

   As to the second condition, *or if they do confess them by
mouth, or have a hearty desire to do it ;* if a man want a hearty
repentance, or is not heartily penitent and contrite, what can
this condition of confessing by mouth, or having a hearty desire
for it, profit such a man's soul ?   It being certain that a man
by his open confession may deceive the confessor and his own
soul, but he cannot deceive God Almighty, who is the only
searcher of our hearts.   And if the Catholics will say to this,
that open confession is a sign of repentance, we may answer
them, that among the Protestants it is so, for being not obliged
to do it, nor by the laws of God, nor by those of the church.

when they do it, it is, in all human probability, a sure sign of
repentance; but among the Roman Catholics, this is no argument of repentance, for very often their lips are near the Lord,
but their hearts very far off.

How can we suppose that an habitual sinner, that, to fulfil
the precepts of their church, confesses once a year, and after
it, the very same day, falls again into the same course of life ,
how can we presume, I say, that the open confession of such a
man is a sign of repentance? And if the Roman Catholics
reply to this, that the case of this first article is quite different,
being only for those that die in the war with true contrition and
repentance, or open confession, or hearty desire of it; I say
that in this case it is the same as in others. For, whenever
and wherever a man dies truly penitent and heartily sorry for
his sins, such a man, without this bull and its indulgences and
pardons, is forgiven by God, who hath promised his Holy Spirit
to all those that ask it; and, on the other side, if a man dies
without repentance, though he confesseth his sins, he cannot
obtain pardon and forgiveness from God, and in such a case
the pope's indulgences and pardons cannot free that man from
the punishment his impenitent heart hath deserved.

Observe, likewise, that to all those warriors against the enemies of the Romish faith, the pope grants the same indulgences which he grants to those that go to the conquest of the
holy land, in the year of jubilee. The Roman Catholics ought
to consider, that the greatest favor we can expect from God
Almighty, is only the pardon of our sins, for his grace and
everlasting glory do follow after it. Then, if the pope grants
them free, full, and general pardon of their sins in this bull,
what need have they of the pardons and indulgences, granted
to those that go to the conquest of the holy land, and in the
year of jubilee?

But because few are acquainted with the nature of such indulgences and graces granted in the year of jubilee, I must
crave leave from the learned people to say what I know in this
matter. I will not trouble the public with the catalogue of the
pope's bulls, but I cannot pass by one article contained in one
of these bulls, which may be found in some libraries of curious
gent.emen and learned divines of our church, and especially
in the Earl of Sunderland's library, which is directed to the
Roman Catholics of England in these words: *Filii mei date
mihi corda vestra, et hoc sufficit vobis:* My children, give me
your hearts, and this is sufficient. So by this, they may swear
and curse, steal and murder, and commit most heinous crimes;

if they keep their hearts for the pope, that is enough to be saved. Observe this doctrine, and I leave it to you, reader, whether such an opinion is according to God's will, nay, to natural reason, or not?

The article of the bull, for the year of jubilee, doth contain these words : *If any Christian, and professor of our Catholic faith, going to the holy land, to the war against the Turks and Infidels, or in the year of jubilee to our city of Rome, should happen to die in the way, we declare that his soul goes straightway to heaven.*

The preachers of the holy crusade, in their circuits, are careful in specifying, in their sermons, all these graces and indulgences, to encourage the people, either to go to the war, or to make more bulls than one. With this crowd of litanies and pardons, the pope blinds the common people, and increases his treasure.

In this same first article of our present bull, it is said, that the same graces and indulgences are granted to all those, who, though they do not go personally, should send another upon their own expenses ; and that if he be a cardinal, primate, patriarch, archbishop, bishop, son of a king, prince, duke, marquis, or earl, he must send ten, or at least four soldiers, and the rest of the people one, or one between ten.

Observe now, that, according to the rules of their morality no man can merit, by any involuntary action ; because, as they say, he is compelled and forced to it. How can, then, this noble people merit or obtain such graces and indulgences, when they do not act voluntarily ? for, if we mind the pope's expression, he compels and forces them to send ten soldiers, or at least four. They have no liberty to the contrary, and consequently they cannot merit by it.

The Second Article of this Bull.

The pope compriseth in this command of sending one soldier, chapters, parish churches, convents of friars, and monasteries of nuns, without excepting the mendicant orders ; but the pope in this doth favor the ecclesiastical persons more than the laity ; for as to the laity, he says, that three or four may join together, and send one soldier ; and as to the ecclesiastical persons, he enlarges this to ten persons, that, if between them, ten do send one soldier, they all, and the person sent by them, obtain the said graces. I do believe there is a great injustice done to the laity ; for these have families to maintain, and the ecclesiastics have not, and the greatest part of the riches are in their hands. This I can aver, that I read in the chronicles of the Franciscan order, written by Fr. Anthony Perez, of the same order, where, extolling and praising the providence of God upon the Franciscan friars, he says, that the general of St. Francis's order doth rule and govern continually 600,000 friars in Christendom, who having nothing to live upon, God takes care of them, and all are well clothed and maintained. There are in the Roman Catholic religion 70 different orders, governed by 70 regular generals, who, after six years of command, are made either bishops or cardinals. I say this by the by, to let the public know the great number of priests and friars, idle and needless people in that religion; for if in one order only there are 600,000 friars, how many shall be found in 70 different orders; I am sure if the pope would command the 50th part of them to go to this holy war, the laity would be relieved, the king would have a great deal more powerful army, and his dominions would not be so much embroiled with divisions, nor so full of vice and debauchery, as they are now.

The Third Article.

It is lawful for the priests and friars to go to this war to preach the word of God in it, or serve, or help in it, without incurring irregularity. They do preach and encourage the soldiers to kill the enemies of their religion, and to make use of whatever means they can for it; for in so doing there is no sin, but a great service done to God.

Out of this war, if a priest strike another and there is mutilation, or if he encourage another to revenge or murder, he incurs irregularity, and he cannot perform any ecclesiastical or divine service, till he is absolved by the pope, or his deputy: But in the war against the enemies of their religion, nay, out of the war they advise them to murder them, as I have said before, and this without incurring irregularity. O blindness of heart! He endeth this article by excusing the soldiers from fasting when they are in the army, but not when they are out of it; a strange thing that a man should command more than God. Our Saviour Jesus Christ commands us to fast from sin, not from meat; but more of this in another article.

The Fourth Article.

In this article the pope compriseth all the people, and puts them upon double charges and expenses, for besides the contribution for a soldier, every body must take the bull if he will obtain the said graces, and must give two reals of plate, i. e

I

thirteen pence half-penny. This is a bitter and hard thing for
the people: but see how the pope sweetens it. I grant, besides
the said graces, to all those who should take this bull and give
the charity under mentioned, that even in the time of suspension of divine and ecclesiastical service, they may hear and
say mass, and other devotions, &c. Charity must be voluntary to be acceptable to God: How then can he call it charity,
when the people must pay for the bull, or some of their goods
shall be sold? And not only this, but that their corpse cannot
be buried in sacred ground without it, as is expressed in the
fifth article.

The Sixth Article.

The pope doth excuse all that take this bull not only from
fasting, but he gives them license to eat flesh in lent by the
consent of both physicians spiritual and temporal. This is,
if a man is sick, he must consult the physician, whether he
may eat flesh or not; and if the physician gives his consent,
he must ask his father-confessor's consent too, to eat flesh in
lent and other days of ecclesiastical prohibition. Only a stupid man will not find out the trick of this granting, for in the
first place, *necessitas caret lege;* necessity knows no law: If
a man is sick, he is excused by the law of God, nay, by the law
of nature from hurtful things, nay, he is obliged in conscience
to preserve his health by using all sorts of lawful means.
This is a maxim received among the Romans, as well as among
us. What occasion is there then of the pope's and both physicians' license to do such a thing? Or if there is such a power
in the bull, why doth not the pope grant them licence absolutely, without asking consent of both physicians? We may
conclude that such people must be blindly superstitious, or
deeply ignorant.

But this great privilege must be understood only for the
laity, not for the secular, nor regular priests, except the cardinals, who are not mentioned here, the knights of the military
order, and those that are sixty years of age and above. But
the priests and friars (notwithstanding this express prohibition)
if they have a mind, evade it on pretence of many light distempers, of the assiduity of their studies, or exercise of preaching the lent's sermons; and by these and other, as they think,
weighty reasons, they get a license to eat flesh in lent. So we
see, that they will preach to the people obedience to all the
commandments of the pope, and they do disobey them; they
preach so, because they have private ends and interests in so

doing, but they do not observe them themselves, because they
are against their inclinations, and without any profit, and so
advising the people to mind them, they do not mind them themselves

The Seventh and Eighth Articles.

To the same, the pope grants fifteen years, and fifteen
quarantains of pardon, and all the penances not yet performed
by them, &c. Observe the ignorance of that people: the pope
grants them fifteen years and fifteen quarantains of pardon
by this bull, and they are so infatuated that they take it every
year; indeed they cannot desire more than the free and general pardon of sins; and if they obtain it by one bull for fifteen
years, and fifteen quarantains, what need or occasion have
they for a yearly bull? Perhaps some are so stupid as to think
to heap up pardons during this life for the next world, or to
leave them to their children and relations: but observe, likewise, that to obtain this, they must fast for devotion's sake
some days not prohibited by the church. They really believe,
that keeping themselves within the rules of ecclesiastical fasting, they merit a great deal; but God knows, for as they say,
the merit is grounded in the mortification of the body, and by
this rule, I will convince them that they cannot merit at all.

For let us know how they fast, and what, and how they
eat? Now I will give a true account of their fasting in general; the rules which must be observed in a right fasting are
these—In the morning, it is allowed by all the casuistical authors, to drink whatever a body has a mind for, and eat an
ounce of bread, which they call *parva materia*, a small matter.
And as for the drink, they follow the pope's declaration concerning chocolate. Give me leave to acquaint you with the
case.

When the chocolate begun to be introduced, the jesuits'
opinion was, that being a great nourishment, it could not be
drunk without breaking fast; but the lovers of it proposing the
case to the pope, he ordered to be brought to him all the in-
gredients of which the chocolate is made, which being accordingly done, the pope drank a cup, and decided the dispute, saying, *potus non frangit jejunium:* Liquid doth not break fasting,
which declaration is a maxim put into all their *moral sums;* and
by it every body may lawfully drink as many cups as he
pleases and eat an ounce of bread, as a small matter in the
morning; and by the same rule any body may drink a bottle

of wine or two, without breaking his fasting, for liquid doth not break fasting.

At noon they may eat as much as they can of all sorts of things, except flesh; and at night, it is allowed not to sup, but to take something by way of collation: in this point of collation, the casuists do not agree together; for some say that nobody can lawfully eat but eight ounces of dry and cold things as bread, walnuts, raisins, cold fried fishes, and the like. Other authors say, that the quantity of this collation, must be measured with the constitution of the person who fasts; for if the person is of a strong constitution, tall, and of a good appetite, eight ounces are not enough, and twelve must be allowed to such a man, and so of the rest. This is the form of their fasting in general: though some few religious and devout persons eat but one meal a day; nay, some used to fast twenty-four hours without eating any thing; but this is once in a year, which they call a *fast with the bells*, that is, in the holy week, among other ceremonies, the Roman Catholics put the consecrated host or wafer in a rich *urna* or box, on Thursday, at twelve of the clock in the morning; and they take it out on Friday at the same time; these twenty-four hours every body is in mourning, nay, the altars are veiled, and the monument where they place the image of Jesus Christ upon the cross, is all covered with black. The bells are not heard all this while; and, as I said, many used to fast with the bells; and they make use of this expression to signify that they fast twenty-four hours without eating any thing at all.

From these we may easily know whether their bodies are mortified with fasting or not? For how can a man of sense say, that he mortifies his body with fasting, when he drinks two or three cups of chocolate, with a small toast in the morning, eats as much as he can at dinner, and eight ounces at night: Add to this, that he may sit in company and eat a crust of bread, and drink as many bottles of wine as he will. this is not accounted collation, because liquid doth not break fasting. This is the form of their fasting, and the rules they must observe in it, and this is reckoned a meritorious work; and therefore doing this, they obtain the said indulgences and pardons of this bull.

Observe likewise, that the Roman Catholics of Spain are allowed to eat, in some days, prohibited by the church, and especially Saturdays, the following things: The head and pluck of a sheep, a cheevelet of a fowl, and the like; nay, they may boil a leg of mutton, and drink the broth of it. This

toleration of eating such things was granted by the pope to
king Ferdinand, who being in a warm war against the Moors,
the soldiers suffered very much in the days of fasting for
want of fish, and other things eatable for such days; and for
this reason the pope granted him and his army license to eat
the abovementioned things on Saturdays, and other days of
fasting commanded by the church; and this was in the year
1479. But this toleration only to the army was introduced
among the country people, especially in both Old and New
Castilla, and this custom is become a law among them. But
this is not so in other provinces of Spain, where the common
people have not the liberty of eating such things; among the
quality only those that have a particular dispensation from
the pope for them and their families.

There is an order of friars, called *La orden de la victoria,*
the order of the victory, whose first founder was St. Francis
de Paula; and the Friars are prohibited by the rules, statutes
and constitution of the order, to eat flesh; nay, this prohibition stands in force during their lives, as it is among the Carthusians, who, though in great sickness, cannot eat any thing
of flesh; but this must be understood within the convent's
gate; for when they go abroad they may eat any thing without trangressing the statute of the order.

But the pleasantness of their practices will show the tricks
of that religion. As to the victorian friars, I knew in Saragossa, one father Conchillos, professor of divinity in his convent, learned in their way, but a pleasant companion. He
was, by his daily exercise of the public lecture, confined to
his convent every day in the afternoon; but as soon as the
lecture was over, his thought and care was to divert himself
with music, gaming, &c. One evening, having given me
an invitation to his room, I went accordingly, and there was
nothing wanting of all sorts of recreation, music, cards,
comedy, and very good merry company. We went to supper,
which was composed of nice, delicate, eatable things, both of
flesh and fish, and for the dessert the best sweatmeats. But
observing, at supper, that my good Conchillos used to take a
leg of partridge and go to the window, and come again and
take a wing of a fowl, and do the same, I asked him whether
he had some beggar in the street, to whom he threw the leg
and wing? No, said he to me. What then do you do with
them out of the window? What, said he; I cannot eat flesh
within the walls, but the statute of my order doth not forbid
me to eat it without the walls; and so, whenever we have a

I 2

fancy for it, we may eat flesh, putting our heads out of the window. Thus they give a turn to the law, but a turn agreeable to them: And so they do in all their fastings, and abstinences from flesh.

As to the Carthusians, and their abstinence and fasting, I could say a great deal, but am afraid I should swell this treatise beyond its designed length, if I should amuse you with an account of all their ridiculous ways. This I cannot pass by, for it conduces very much to clearing this point of abstinence and fasting. The order of this constitution is—

First: A continual abstinence from flesh; and this is observed so severely and strictly, that I knew a friar, who, being dangerously ill, the physicians ordered to apply, upon his head, a young pigeon, opened alive at the breast; which being proposed by the prior to the whole community, they were of opinion that such a remedy was against the constitution, and therefore not fit to be used any way: That these poor friars must die rather than touch any fleshly thing, though it be for the preserving their health.

Secondly. Perpetual silence and confinement is the next precept of St. Brune, their founder: That is, that the friars cannot go abroad out of the convent, or garden walls, only the prior and procurator may go upon business of the community. The rest of the friars' lives are thus: Each of them has an apartment with a room, bed-chamber, kitchen, cellar, closet to keep fruit in, a garden, with a well, and a place in it for firing. Next to the door of the apartment there is a wheel in the wall, which serves to put the victuals in at noon, and at night, and the friar turns the wheel, and takes his dinner and supper, and in the morning he puts in the wheel the plates, by which the servant, that carries the victuals, knows they are in good health; and if he finds the victuals again, he acquaints the father prior with it, who straight goes to visit them. The prior hath a master-key of all the rooms, for the friars are obliged to lock the door on the inside, and to keep the room always shut, except when they go to say mass in the morning, and to say the canonical hours in the day time; then if they meet one another, they can say no other words but these: One says, Brother, we must die; and the other answers, We know it. Only on Thursday, between three and four in the afternoon, they meet together for an hour's time, and if it be fair weather, they go to walk in the garden of the convent, and if not, in the common hall, where they cannot talk of other things, but of the lives of such or such a saint; and when the hour is over,

every one goes to his own chamber. So they obterve fasting
and silence continually, but except flesh, they eat the most exquisite and delicate things in the world; for commonly in one
convent there are but twenty friars, and there is not one convent of Carthusians, which hath not five, six, and many, twenty thousand pistoles of yearly rent.

Such is their fasting from flesh and conversation; but let us
know their fasting from sins.

Dr. Peter Bernes, secular priest, belonging to the parish
church of the blessed Mary Magdalene, (as they do call her,)
being 32 years of age, and dangerously ill, made a vow to the
glorious saint, that if he should recover from that sickness,
he would retire into a Carthusian convent. He recovered,
and accordingly, renouncing his benefice and the world, he
took the Carthusian habit, in the convent of the Conception,
three miles from Saragossa. For the space of three years he
gave proofs of virtue and singular conformity with the statutes
of the order. His strict life was so crowded with disciplines
and mortifications, that the prior gave out, in the city, that he
was a saint on earth. I went to see him with the father prior's
consent, and indeed I thought there was something extraordinary in his countenance, and in his words; and I had taken
him myself for a man ready to work miracles. Many people
went to see him, and among the crowd a young woman, acquainted with him before he took the habit, who unknown to
the strict friars got into his chamber, and there she was kept
by the pious father eighteen months. In that time the prior
used to visit the chamber, but the Senora was kept in the bed-
chamber, till at last the prior went one night to consult him
upon some business, and hearing a child cry, asked him what
was the matter; and though my friend Bernes endeavored to
conceal the case, the prior found it out; and she, owning the
thing, was turned out with the child, and the father was confined for ever: And this was his virtue, fasting and abstinence
from flesh, &c.

To those that either fast in the abovesaid manner, or keep
fasting for devotion's sake, his holiness grants, (taking this bull
of crusade) all the said graces, pardons and indulgences; and
really, if such graces were of some use or benefit, the people
thus doing, want them very much; or may be, the pope knowing these practices, doth this out of pity and compassion for
their souls, without thinking that this bull is a great encouragement and incitement to sin.

The Ninth Article.

This article contains, first, that to pray with more purity every body taking this bull may choose a confessor to his own fancy, who is empowered to absolve sins, except the crime of heresy, reserved to the pope, or apostolical see. You must know what they mean by the crime heresy. Salazar Irribarren and Corella, treating of the reserved sins, say, that the crime of heresy is, viz.: If I am all alone in my room, and the door being locked up, talking to myself; I say, I do not believe in God, or in the pope of Rome, this is heresy. They distinguish two sorts of heresies; one interna, and another externa, that is, public and secret. The public heresy, such as that I have now told you of, nobody can absolve, but the pope himself. The second being only in thought, every body can absolve, being licensed by the bishop, by the benefit of this bull. So, whoever pronounces the pope is not infallible: the English or protestants may be saved: The Virgin Mary is not to be prayed to: The priest hath not power to bring down from heaven J. C. with five words: Such an one is a public heretic, and he must go to Rome, if he desireth to get absolution.

Secondly. This article contains, that by the benefit of this bull, every body may be free from restitution, during his own life; and that he may make it by his heirs after his death. O what an unnatural thing is this! What, if I take away from my neighbor three hundred pounds, which is all he hath in the world to maintain his family, must I be free from this restitution, and leave it to my heir's will to make it after my death? Must I see my neighbor's family suffer by it; and can I be free before God, of a thing that God, nature and humanity, require of me to do? Indeed this is a diabolical doctrine. Add to this what I have said of the bull of composition, that is, if you take so many bulls to compound the matter with your confessor, you will be free forever from making restitution: But really you shall not be free from the eternal punishment.

Likewise, by the power of this bull, any confessor may commute any vow, except those of chastity, religion, and beyond seas: But this is upon condition that they should give something for the crusade. O God, what an expression is this! To commute any vow, except those of chastity, &c. So, if I make a vow to kill a man, if I promise upon oath to rob my neighbor, the confessor may commute me these vows, for sixpence: But if I vow to keep chastity, I must go to Rome, to the pope himself. What an expression is this! I say again, now many millions have vowed chastity? If I say two mil'

lions I shall not lie. And how many of these two millions
observe it? If I say five hundred, I shall not lie. And for all
this, we see nobody go to Rome for absolution.

The Roman Catholics will say, that by these words, *vow of
chastity*, must be only understood abstaining from marriage;
but I will leave it to any man of reason, whether the nature
of chastity compriseth only that? Or let me ask the Roman
Catholics, whether a priest, who has made a vow of chastity,
that is, never to marry, if he commits the sins of the flesh, will
be accounted chaste or not? They will, and must say, not.
Then, if so many thousands of priests live lewdly, breaking
the vow of chastity, why do they not go to the pope for absolution? To this they never can answer me; therefore the
pope, in this bull, doth blind them, and the priests do what
they please, and only the common people are imposed upon,
and suffer by it. God Almighty, by his infinite power, enlighten them all, that so the priests may be more sincere, and
the people less darkened.

The Tenth Article.

The pope grants the same indulgences to those that should
die suddenly, if they die heartily sorry for their sins. Of this
I have spoken already, and said, that if a man dies truly penitent he hath no occasion for the pope's pardon, for his true pen-
itence hath more interest (if I may thus express myself) with
God Almighty, than the pope with all his infallibility. So I
proceed to the next, which is

The Eleventh Article.

In this article the pope grants besides the said indulgences,
to those that take this bull, that they may twice more in the
same year be absolved of all their sins, of what nature soever
once more during their lives, and once more at the point of
death. This is a bold saying, and full of assurance, O poor
blind people! Where have you your eyes or understanding?
Mind, I pray, for the light of your consciences, this impudent
way of deceiving you, and go along with me. The pope has
granted you, in the aforesaid articles, all you can wish for, and
now again, he grants you a nonsensical privilege, viz. that
you may twice at the point of death, be absolved of all your
sins. Observe, passing by, that a simple priest, who hath not
been licensed by the ordinary to hear confessions, upon urgent
necessity, i. e. upon the point of death is allowed by all

the casuistical authors, nay, by the councils, to absolve all sins whatsoever, if there be not present another licensed priest. Again, nobody can get such an absolution, as is expressed in this bull, but at the point of his soul's departing from the body, i. e. when there is no hope of recovery; and the confessors are so careful in this point, that sometimes, they begin to pronounce the absolution, when a man is alive, and he is dead before they finish the words.

Now pray tell me how can a man be twice in such a point? And if he got once as much, as he cannot get the second time, vhat occasion hath he for the second full, free, and plenary indulgence, and absolution of all his sins? I must stop here, for if I was to tell freely my opinion upon this point, some will think I do it out of some private ends; which I never do upon delivering matters of fact.

The Twelfth Article.

Here the most holy father gives his power and authority to the general apostolical commissary of the crusade, and all other graces and faculties, to revoke and suspend all the graces and indulgences granted in this bull, by his holiness, during the year of publishing it; and not only to suspend them upon any restriction or limitation, but absolutely, though this, or any other bull, or brief of indulgences, granted by this or other popes, did contain words contrary to it, viz: Suppose if Clement, or another pope, should say, I grant to such an one such faculties, and I anathematize all those that should attempt to suspend the said faculties. This last expression would be of no force at all, because this bull specifies the contrary.

So it is a thing very remarkable, that the pope dispossesseth himself by this bull, of all his power and authority, and giveth it to the general apostolical commissary, insomuch that the apostolical commissary hath more power than the pope himself, during the year: and this power and authority is renewed and confirmed to him by his holiness. And not only he has this power over the pope, but over all the popes, and their briefs, in whatsoever time granted to any place, or person whatsoever. For it is in the apostolical commissary's power to suspend all graces and privileges whatsoever, granted since the first pope began to grant indulgences, which things are all inconsistent with the independency and supremacy of the holy father, nay, according to the principles and sentiments of their own authors, but we see they are consistent with their blindness and ignorance.

The Thirteenth Article.

This article showeth us plainly the reason, why the pope acts thus in granting of his power to the general apostolical commissary of the crusade, for he grants him authority to revoke and suspend all the indulgences here granted by himself and other popes, but he grants him the same authority to call again the very same indulgences, and to make them good again. And next to this power (observe this) he grants him and his deputies power to fix and settle the price or charity, the people ought to give for the bull. This is the whole matter, and we may use the English saying, *No cure, no pay,* quite reverse, *No pay, no cure,* no indulgence nor pardon of sins. The treasure of the church (being a spiritual gift) cannot be sold for money, without Simony. And if the Romans say that the pope has that power derived from Christ, or given gratis to him, let them mind the words: *Quod gratis accepistis, gratis date.* If the pope payeth nothing for having such power, if he has it gratis, why does he sell it to the faithful? Can a private man, or his deputy put a price on a spiritual thing? O blindness of heart!

The Fourteenth Article.

In this article the general apostolical commissary makes use of his power and authority, he says, *In favor of this holy bull, we do suspend, during the year, all the graces, indulgences, and faculties of this, or any other kind, &c. Though they be in favor of the building of St. Peter's church at Rome. Except only from this suspension the privileges granted to the superiors of the mendicant orders.* He excepts only from this suspension the privileges of the four mendicant orders, because the friars of those orders, being mendicants or beggars, they can be no great hindrance of this project. I ask my countrymen this question: If Dn. Francis Anthony Ramirez has such a power, to do and undo, in despite of the pope, whatever he pleases for a whole year; and this power is renewed to him every year, by a fresh bull; of what use is the pope in Spain? And if he has resigned his authority to Don Ramirez, why do they send every year to Rome for privileges, dispensations, faculties, bulls, &c., and throw their money away? If Ramirez has power to stop, and make void any concession by the pope, what need have they for so great trouble and expense? Is not this a great stupidity and infatuity? Observe the next article.

The Fifteenth Article.

All those prohibitions and suspensions aforementioned, are only to oblige the people to take the bull; for the general apostolical commissary says: *We declare that all those that take this bull, do obtain and enjoy all the graces, and faculties, &c. which have been granted by the popes Paul the 5th, and Urbanus the 8th, &c.* So if a poor man takes no bull, though he be heartily penitent, there is no pardon for him. I say, there is no pardon for him from the pope and his commissary, but there is surely pardon for him from God; and he is in a better way than all the bigots that take the bull, thinking to be free by it from all their sins.

Observe also the last words of this article: *We command that every body that takes this bull, be obliged to keep by him the same, which is here printed, signed and sealed with our name and seal; and that otherwise they cannot obtain, nor enjoy the benefit of the said bull.* This is a cheat, robbery, and roguery; for the design of the general apostolical commissary is, to oblige them to take another bull. The custom is, that when they take every year a new bull, they ought to show the old one, or else they must take two that year. Now let us suppose that all the contents of the bull are as efficacious as the bigots do believe them to be. A man takes the bull, pays for it, and performs and fulfilleth the contents of it. Is not this enough to enjoy all the graces, &c? What is the meaning then of commanding to keep the same bull by them, but a cheat, robbery, and roguery? I do not desire better proof of this than what the commissary affords me in his following words, by which he contradicts himself. He says, and *whereas you* (speaking with Peter Dezuloaga, who was the man that took the bull which was left at the publisher's shop) *have given two reals of plate, and have taken this bull, and your name is written in it, we declare that you have already obtained and are granted the said indulgences, &c. And that you may enjoy and make use of them, &c.*

If he has already obtained all, of what use may it be to keep the bull by him? How can the commissary make these expressions agree together? 1st. *If he doth not keep the bull by him, he cannot enjoy the benefit of the bull.* 2d. *As soon as he takes it, he has already obtained all the graces, &c., and enjoys the benefit of the bull.* These are two quite contrary _nings. Then the design in the first is robbery and roguery, and in the second, cheat, fraud, and deceit.

Reflec. again: *Whereas you have taken the bull and paid* *for it, you have already obtained all the indulgences and par* *don of sins.* By this declaration, infallible to the Romans, let a man come from committing murder, adultery, sacrilege, &c if he takes and pays for the bull, his sins are already pardoned. Is not this a scandalous presumption? If a man is in a, state of sin, and has no repentance in his heart, how can such a man be pardoned at so cheap a rate as two reals of plate? If this was sure and certain, the whole world would embrace their religion, for they then would be sure of their salvation. Again, if they believe this bull to be true, how can they doubt of their going to heaven immediately after death? For a man, whose sins are pardoned, goes straightway to heaven; so if the sins of all men and women (for every body takes the bull' are pardoned by it, and consequently go to heaven, why do they set up a purgatory? or why are they afraid of hell?

Let us say, that we may suspect, that this bull sends more people into hell, than it can save from it; for it is the greatest encouragement to sin in the world. A man says, I may satisfy my lusts and passions, I may commit all wickedness, and yet I am sure to be pardoned of all, by the taking of this bull for two reals of plate. By the same rule, their consciences cannot be under any remorse nor trouble, for if a man commits a great sin, he goes to confess, he gets absolution, he has by him this bull, or permission to sin, and his conscience is at perfect ease, insomuch that after he gets absolution, he may go and commit new sins, and go again for absolution.

If we press with these reflections and arguments the Roman catholic priests, especially those of good sense, they will answer that they do not believe any such thing; for if a man (say they) doth not repent truly of his sins, he is not pardoned by God, though he be absolved by the confessor. Well, if it be so, why does the pope, by his general apostolical commissary, say, *Whereas you have taken and paid for this bull,* *you have already obtained pardon for your sins, &c.* We must come then to say, that the cheat, fraud, and deceit is in the pope, and that Don Ramirez is the pope's instrument to impose so grossly upon the poor Spaniards. The confessor grants free and full indulgence and pardon of all sins, and of all the pains and punishments which the penitent was obliged to endure for them in purgatory. By virtue of this absolution then, we may say, no soul goes to purgatory especially out of the dominions of the king of Spain, for as I said, in the beginning of the explanation of the bull, every living soul, from seven

K

years of age and upwards, is obliged to take the bull, and con
sequently, if every soul obtains the grant of being pardoned of
all the pains which they were to endure and suffer in purgatory, all go to heaven. Why do the priests ask masses, and say
them for the relief of the souls in purgatory.

Let us from these proceed to the sum of the estations and
indulgences granted to the city of Rome, which the pope
grants likewise to all those that take the bull, and fulfil the
contents of it.

Estations, in this place, signify the going from one church
to another, in remembrance of Christ's being, or remaining so
long on Mount Calvary, so long in the garden, so long on the
cross, so long in the sepulchre.

We call also *estations,* or to walk the estations, to go from
the first cross to the mount Calvary, &c. This is a new thing
to many of this kingdom, therefore, a plain account of that custom among the Romans, will not be amiss in this place.

There is in every city, town and village, a mount Calvary
out of the gates, in remembrance of the Calvary where our
Saviour was crucified. There are fourteen crosses placed at
a distance one from another. The first cross is out of the
gates, and from the first to the second, the Romans reckon so
many steps or paces, more or less from the second to the third,
and so on from one to another of the remaining, till they come
to the twelfth cross, which is in the middle of two crosses, which
represent two crosses which the two malefactors were crucified
on each side of Christ. They walk these twelve estations in
remembrance of all the steps and paces our Saviour walked
from the gates of the city of Jerusalem to mount Calvary,
where he was crucified. In the first estation, you will see the
image of Jesus, with the cross on his shoulders, in the second,
falling down, &c. In the last cross, our last estation of the
three crosses, Jesus is represented crucified between two malefactors.

Every Friday in the year, the devout people walk the estations, and kneel down before every cross, and say so many
pater nosters, &c., and a prayer for the meditation of what
did happen to our Jesus at that distance. When the weather
hinders the people from going to the great Calvary, they have
another in every church, and in the cloisters of the convents,
and monasteries, and they walk the estations there, and especially in lent, there is such a crowd of people every Friday in
the afternoon, that there is scarcely room enough in the high
way for all to kneel down.

On good Friday in the evening, is the great procession, at which almost all the people assist with lanterns in their hands The people, both men and women, old and young, go to church in the afternoon. The parish minister, dressed in a surplice, and a sacerdotal cloak on, and a square black cap on his head, and the rest of the clergy in their surplices, and the reverend father preacher in his habit. This last begins a short exhortation to the people, recommending to them devotion, humility, and meditation of our Saviour's sufferings; after he has done, the prior of the fraternity of the blood of Christ, ordereth the procession in this manner: First of all, at the head of it, a man in a surplice, carrieth the cross of the parish, and two boys on each side, with two high lanterns, immediately after begins the first estation of our Saviour, painted in a standard, which one of the fraternity carrieth, and the brethren of that estation follow him in two lines: and the twelve estations ordered in the same manner, follow one another. After the estations, there is a man representing Jesus Christ, dressed in a Tunica or a Nazarine's gown, with a crown of thorns on his head, that carrieth on his shoulders a long, heavy cross, and another man, representing Simon, of Cirene, behind helps the Nazarine to carry the Cross. After him the preacher, clergy, and parish minister, and after them all the people, without keeping any form or order. Thus the procession goes out of the church, singing a proper song of the passion of Jesus; and when they come to the first cross of the estations of Calvary, the procession stops there, and the preacher makes an exhortation, and tells what our Saviour did suffer till that first step, and making the same exhortations in each of the eleven crosses; when they come at the twelfth, the preacher, on the foot of the cross which is placed between the two crosses of the malefactors, begins the sermon of the passion and sufferings of Christ, and when he has done, the procession comes back again to the church, and there the preacher dismisses the people with an act of contrition, which the people repeat after him.

These are the estations of the holy Calvary; but besides these the estations of the holy sepulchre; that is, to visit seven churches, or seven times one church, on holy Thursday, when Jesus is in the monument;—but of these things I shall treat in another place.

Now, by these foregoing indulgences, and full pardon of sins, the pope does not grant to all those that take the bull, and fulfil the contents of it (which are only to pay for it) any body may easily know a list of the days in which any one that visits the churches mentioned in it enjoys at Rome all the aforesaid faculties, pardon of sins, and indulgences, and as you may observe, at the end of the *summario*, that every day of the year, there are, at Rome, many indulgences and pardons granted in some church or other to all those that go to visit them. So by the grant of the pope, in the bull of Crusade, the same indulgences and pardons are given, and in the same day) that is every day of the year) to all those that take the bull. From this any body may draw the same consequence as before, that a man cannot be afraid in the Romish church, to go to hell; he may commit every day all villanies in the world, and yet every day, having the bull, is sure of getting free and full pardon of his sins, and this without the trouble of going to confess: for if they will take the pains to read the contents of the bull, with a serious mind, they will find the truth of what I say, That without the trouble of confessing sins, any body obtains full pardon of all the crimes he has committed.

For the general apostolical commissary, (who has the pope's power and authority) says, that he that takes the bull, payeth for it, and writes his name in it, *ipso facto*, i. e. already obtains all the indulgences and pardon of sins, &c. mentioned in the bull; and he does not say, *If he confess*, or, *if he be a hearty penitent;* but already, without any limitation or reservation, *already he enjoys all*, and *may make use of all the graces, &c.* So, by these expressions, it appears, that a man, taking the bull, paying for it, and writing his name in it, may commit murder and robbery, &c. and yet obtain every day free and full pardon of his sins, without the trouble of confessing them to a priest, who, if covetous, will ask money for absolution, or money for masses, for the relief of the souls in purgatory.

This I must own of my country people, that they are kept in so great ignorance by the priests, that I might dare to say, that not one of a thousand that takes the bull, reads it, but blindly submits to what the minister of the parish tells him, without further inquiry. This is a surprising thing to all the protestants; and it is now to me, but I can give no other reasons for their ignorance in point of religion, as for the generality, but their bigotry, and blind faith in what the preachers and priests tell them; and, next to this, that it is not allowed to them to read the scripture, nor books of controversy about religion.

I come now to the days in which every body takes a soul out of purgatory. Observe those marked with a star, and besides them, there is in every convent and parish church, at least, one privileged altar, i. e. any body that says five times *Pater Noster*, &c., and five times, *Ave Maria*, with *Gloria Patria*, &c., takes a soul out of purgatory, and this at any time and in any day of the year, and not only in Spain, by the virtue of the bull, but in France, Germany, Italy, and in all the Roman Catholic countries where they have no bull of Crusade. From this, I say, that if there is a purgatory, it must be an empty place, or that it is impossible to find there any soul at all, and that the Roman Catholics take every year more souls out of it. than can go into it; which I shall endeavor to prove by evident arguments, grounded on their principles and belief.

For, first of all, there is in the bull nine days in the year in which every living person takes a soul out of purgatory, and by this undeniable truth among themselves, it appears that every living person, man, woman, or child, from seven years of age and upwards, takes every year nine souls out of purgatory.

Secondly. Every body knows the Roman Catholic's opinion, that nobody can be saved out of their communion; and by this infallible (as they believe) principle, they do not allow any place in purgatory to the souls of protestants, and other people of other professions; and so only Roman Catholic souls are the proprietors of that place of torment.

Thirdly. It is undeniable, by the Romans, that ever since the place of purgatory was built up by the popes and councils, the Roman catholics have enjoyed the granting of a privileged altar in every church, that, by their prayers, the souls of their parents or friends may be relieved and delivered out of that place.

Fourthly. That to this granting, the popes have been so generous, that they have granted, in such days, special privileges to some churches, for all those that should visit them, to take souls out of purgatory.

Fifthly. That all the prayers said before such altars for such a soul in purgatory, if the soul is out of it when the person says the prayers, those prayers go to the treasure of the church; and by this opinion, undeniable by them, the treasury of the church is well stocked with prayers, and when the pope has a mind to grant, at once, a million of prayers, he may take a million of souls out of purgatory.

These five principles and observations are incontestable by any of the Roman catholics. Now let us compute the number of Roman catholics that are alive, and the number of the dead every year. I say, compute, that is, suppose a certain number of the living and of the dead every year. And I begin with the kingdom of Spain, and its dominions, as the only par takers of the privileges granted in the bull of Crusade.

First. Let us suppose, that in the whole dominions of Spain, there are about six millions of living persons; I speak of the Roman catholics: and that three millions of those catholics die every year· and that all their souls go to purgatory; for though the supposition is disadvantageous to my purpose, I will allow them more than they can expect. In the first place, by reasonable computation, half of the living persons do not die every year: but I suppose this, to make my argument so much the stronger. Secondly. In their opinion, very many of the souls of those that die, go to heaven, and some to hell, which is contrary to the bull. By this computation, the three millions of people that remain alive, by the bull, take out of purgatory, seven and twenty millions of souls that very year. For there are nine days, in the bull fixed, on which every living person takes one soul out of purgatory; if then, only three millions of people die annually, how can the three remaining alive take out twenty-seven millions, it being impossible that there should be more than three millions of souls in purgatory that year. And besides this plain demonstration, and besides the nine days appointed in the bull, according to their belief, and every day in the year, and, *toties quoties*, they pray at a privileged altar, they take out of purgatory that soul for which they pray, or if that soul is not in purgatory, any other which they have a mind for, or else the prayer goes to the treasure of the church: and so, by this addition, we may say, that if, out of three millions of living persons, only half a million of people pray every day; this half million take out of purgatory, yearly, one hundred and eighty-two millions and a half of souls. If they scruple this number, let them fix any other living persons, and then multiply nine times more the number of souls delivered out of purgatory every year, by virtue of the nine days mentioned in the bull; or by the privileged altars, multiply one to three hundred sixty-five souls delivered out of the flames every year, by every living person, as I shall demonstrate more plainly hereafter.

As for France, Germany, Italy, Portugal, and other Roman catholic countries, as I said before, they have their privileged altars to take a soul out of purgatory, *toties quoties*, a Roman says so many *pater nosters*, and *ave·marias* before them. And so use the same multiplication to convince them, that there cannot be so many souls in purgatory as they deliver out of it every year, or that purgatory of course, must be an empty place, &c.

If they answer to this strong reason, that we must suppose for certain, that the souls of many millions of people, for many years past, are in purgatory, and that there is stock enough taken out of it every year, if there were ten times more living persons than there are now in the Roman Catholic countries; I say, that the supposition has no room at all, and that it is impossible; for let us begin at the time when purgatory was first found out by the pope, and let us suppose, *gratis*, that there is such a place, which we deny.

The first year that that imaginary place was settled among the Romans, the very same year the privileged altars were in fashion. The people that were left alive that year took out all the souls of the persons dead the same year, and more too, for as the new privilege was granted them, every body was more charitable in taking the souls of his relations and friends out of sufferings at so cheap a rate as five *pater nosters*, &c The next year the same, and so on, year by year, till this present time, so that it is impossible to believe that there are a greater number of souls than of persons dead.

I say again, that by these principles, sure among the Romans, the catholics only of Spain, and all the dominions belonging to it, are enough to deliver out of purgatory all the souls of all the catholics dead, from the begining of the world in Christendom. If what they believe were certain, it should be certain too, that since the bull is granted to the catholic kings and their dominions, which is since the reign of king Ferdinand, the catholic, only the Spaniards have delivered out of purgatory more souls than persons have died since the universal flood: for every living person, from that time till this present day, has taken out of purgatory, every year, 365 souls by the privileged altars, and nine more by virtue of the bull. Now I leave to the curious reader to make use of the rule of multiplication, and he will find clear demonstrations of my saying. I do not talk now of those innumerable souls that are freed from this place every day of the year by the masses, leaving this for another place.

Indeed I have searched among the sophistries of the Roman catholics, to see whether I could find some reason or answer to this: and I protest, I could not find any; for as I am sure, they will endeavor to cloud this work with groundless subterfuges and sophistries, I was willing to prevent all sorts of objections, which may be made by them. Only one answer,

which I may believe they will give me, comes now into my
head, and it is this, that as the Romans cannot answer any
thing contrary to my demonstration, it is to be feared that they
will say, that I reason and argue as an ignorant, because I do
not know that the souls in purgatory are fruitful beings, that
one produces a great many little ones every year, I say, it is
to be feared, that being pressed, they must come at last to such
nonsensical, fantastical, dreaming reasons, to answer to this
urgent argument. So we may safely conclude, and with a
Christian confidence say, that if there is such a place as purgatory, it must be an empty place, or that it is impossible to
find there any souls, or that the Roman catholics take every
year more souls out of it, than can go into it: all which, being
against the evidence of natural reason, and computation made,
it is a dream, fiction, or to say the truth, roguery, robbery, and
a cheat of the pope and priests. As for the pope, (if the report in the public news be true,) I must beg leave to except
for a while this present pope, who, in his behaviour, makes
himself the *exception of the rule.* I say, for a *while,* for by
several instances, (as I shall speak of in the third part,) many popes have had a good beginning, and a very bad end.
God enlighten him with his holy spirit, that he may bring in all
papist countries to our reformation. And I pray God Almighty, from the bottom of my heart, to give to all the Romans
such a light as his infinite goodness has been pleased to grant
me; and that all my country people, and all those that call
themselves Roman catholics, would make the same use of
that light which I have endeavored to make use of myself, to
know the corruptions of their church, and to renounce them
with as firm and hearty resolution as I have done myself:
And I pray God, who is to be my judge, to continue in me
the same light, and his grace, that I may live and die in the
religion I have embraced, and to give me the desired comfort
of my heart, which is to see many of my beloved country
people come and enjoy the quietness of mind and conscience
which I enjoy, as to this point of religion, and way of salvation; and I wish I could prevail with them to read the bull,
which, they believe, is the *sancto sanctorum,* the passport to
heaven; and I am sure they would find the contrary, and see
that it is only a dream, a dose of opium to lull them asleep,
and keep them always ignorant. That Almighty God may
grant them and me *too* all these things, is my constant prayer
to Him.

PART III.

A practical account of their Masses, Privileged Altars, Transubstantiation, and Purgatory.

comprise all the four heads in one chapter, because there is a near relation between nem al, though I shall speak of them separately, and as distinct articles

ARTICLE I.

Of their Masses.

THE Mass for priests and friars is better, and has greater power and virtue than the loadstone, for this only draws iron, but that allures and gets to them silver, gold, precious stones, and all sorts of fruits of the earth; therefore it is proper to give a description of every thing the priests make use of to render the mass the most magnificent and respectful thing in the world, in the eyes of the people.

The priest every morning, after he has examined his conscience, and confessed his sins, (which they call reconciliation,) goes to the vestry and washes his hands; afterwards, he kneels down before an image of the crucifix, which is placed on the draws, where the ornaments are kept, and says several prayers and psalms, written in a book, called *preparaterium*. When the priest has done, he gets up, and goes to dress himself, all the ornaments being ready upon the draws, which are like the table of an altar; then he takes the *Ambito*, which is like an Holland handkerchief, and kissing the middle of it, puts it round about his neck, and says a short prayer. After he takes the *Alva*, which is a long surplice with narrow sleeves, laced round about with fine lace, and says another prayer while he puts it on. The clerk is always behind to help him. Then he takes the *Cingulum*, i e. the *girdle*, and says a prayer; after he takes the *Stola*, which is a long list of silk, with a cross in the middle, and two crosses at the ends of it, and says another prayer while he puts it on his neck, and crosses it before his breast, and ties it with the ends of the girdle. After he takes the *Manipulum*, i. e. a short list of the same silk, with as many crosses in it, and ties it on

117

the left arm, saying a short prayer. Then he takes the *Casulla*, i. e. a sort of a dress made of three yards of silk stuff, a yard wide behind, and something narrower before, with a hole in the middle, to put his head through it. After he is thus dressed, he goes to the corner of the table, and taking the *chalice*, cleans it with a little Holland towel, with which the *chalice's* mouth is covered; after he puts a large host on the *patena*, i. e. a small silver plate gilt, which serves to cover the *chalice*, and puts on the host a neat piece of fine holland laced all over. Then he covers all with a piece of silk, three quarters of a yard in square. After he examines the *corporales*, i. e. two pieces of fine, well-starched holland, with lace round about; the first is three quarters of a yard square, and the second half a yard; and folding them both, puts them in a flat cover, which he puts on the *chalice*, and taking a squared cap, if he is a secular priest, puts it on his head, and having the *chalice* in his hands, makes a great bow to the crucifix, says a prayer, and goes out of the vestry to the altar, where he designs to say mass. This is, as to the private mass. Now before I proceed to the great mass, which is always sung, it is fit to talk of the riches of their ornaments.

As in the Romish church are several festivals, viz. those of our Saviour Christ, Christmas, Circumcision, Epiphany, Easter, Ascension, Pentecostes, and Transfiguration: Those of the Holy Cross; those of the blessed Virgin Mary; those of the angels, apostles, martyrs, confessors, virgins, &c. So there are several sorts of ornaments, and of divers colors; white for all the festivals of Jesus Christ, except pentecostes, in which the ornaments are red; white also for the festivals of the Virgin Mary, confessors, and virgins; red for martyrs; violet color for advent and lent; and black for the masses of the dead.

The same rule is observed in the front of the altar's table, or *ara altaris*, which are always adorned with hangings the color of the day's festivals. In every parish church and convent, there are many ornaments of each of the said colors, all of the richest silks, with silver, gold and embroidery. There are many long cloaks or *palia* of all sorts of colors, several dozens of *alvas*, or surplices of the finest holland, with the finest laces round about them, *chalice* of silver, the inside of the cup gilt, many of gold, and many of gold set with diamonds and precious stones. There is one in the cathedral of St. Salvator, in the city of Saragossa, which weighs five pounds of gold, set all over with diamonds, and is valued at 15,000 crowns, and this is not accounted an extraordinary one.

A possenet of silver, gilt all over, to keep the holy water and hysop, with a silver handle, to be used in holy days at church, is an indispensable thing almost in every church; as also two big candlesticks four feet high, for the two *accolits* or *assistants* to the great mass. In several churches there are two *ciriales*, i. e. big candlesticks five feet high all of silver, which weigh two hundred pounds in some churches, and another bigger than these for the blessed candle on candlemas day. Six other middle silver candlesticks, which serve on the *ara* or altar's table, silver, and (in many churches) gold bottles and plate to keep the water and wine that is used in the mass, a small silver bell for the same use, an incensary, and stand for the missal or mass-book, and another stand of silver two feet high, for the deacon and sub-deacon to read on it the epistle and gospel.

There is also in the great altar, the *custodia*, i. e. a figure of the sun and beams made of gold, and many of them set with precious stones to keep in the centre of it the great consecrated host, in the middle of two crystals: The foot of the *custodia* is made of the same metal; it is kept in a gilt tabernacle, and shown to the people on several occasions, as I will mention in another place.

Besides this rich custodia, there is a large silver or gold cup kept in the same, or another tabernacle on another altar, which is to keep the small consecrated wafers for the communicants. Before those tabernacles a silver lamp is burning night and day. The altars are adorned on several festivals with the silver bodies of several saints, some as large as a man, some half bodies with crowns or mitres set with precious stones.

I could name several churches and convents, where I saw many rarities and abundance of rich ornaments, but this being a thing generally known by the private accounts of many travellers, I shall only give a description of the rarities and riches of the church of the lady del Pilar, and that of St. Salvator, in the city of Saragossa; because I never met with any book which did mention them, and the reason, as I believe, is, because foreigners do not travel much in Spain, for want of good conveniences on the roads, and for the dismal journey in which they cannot see a house, sometimes in twenty miles, and sometimes in thirty.

In the Cathedral church of St. Salvator, there are forty-five

prebendaries, besides the dean, arch-deacon, chanter, and sixty-six beneficiates, six priests and a master, and twelve boys
for the music, and sixty clerks and under clerks, and sextons
The church contains thirty chapels, large and small, and the
great altar, thirty feet high and ten broad, all of marble stone,
with many bodies of saints of the same, and in the middle of
it the transfiguration of our Saviour in the mount Tabor, with
the apostles all represented in marble figures.   The front of
the altar's table is made of solid silver, the frame gilt, and
adorned with precious stones.   In the treasure of the church
they keep sixteen bodies of saints of pure silver, among which,
that of St. Peter Argues, (who was a prebendary in the same
church, and was murdered by the Saracens,) is adorned with
rich stones of a great value.   Besides these they keep twelve
half silver bodies of other saints, and many relics set with gold
and diamonds.   Forty-eight silver candlesticks for the altar's
table, two large ones, and the third for the blessed candle, 300
pound weight each: thirty-six small silver candlesticks; and
six made of solid gold for the great festivals.   Four possenets
of silver, two of solid gold, with the handles of hysops of the
same.   Two large crosses, one of silver, the other of gold, ten
feet high, to carry before the processions.   Ten thousand ounces of silver in plate, part of gilt, to adorn the two corners of
the altar on great festivals, and when the archbishop officiates,
and says the great mass.   Thirty-three silver lamps, of which
the smallest is an hundred and fifty pounds weight, and the
largest, which is before the great altar, gilt all over, is six
hundred and thirty pounds weight.   Abundance of rich ornaments for priests, of inexpressible value.   Eighty-four chali-
ces, twenty of pure gold, and sixty-four of silver, gilt on the
inside of the cup; and the rich chalice, which only the archbishop makes use of in his pontifical dress.

All these things are but trifles in comparison with the great
custodia they make use of to carry the great host through the
streets on the festival of *Corpus Christi:* This was a present
made to the cathedral by the Archbishop of Sevil, who had
been prebendary of that church before.   The circumference
of the sun and beams is as big as the wheel of a coach; at the
end of each beam there is a star.   The centre of the sun,
where the great host is placed between two crystals, set with
large diamonds; the beams are all of solid gold set with several precious stones, and in the middle of each star, a rich em-
erald set in gold.   The crystal with the great host is fixed in
the mouth of the rich chalice, on a pedestal of silver, all gilt

over which is three feet high. The whole custodia is five
hundred pounds weight, and this is placed on a gilt base,
which is carried by twelve priests, as I shall tell you in another
article. Several goldsmiths have endeavored to value this
piece, but nobody could set a certain sum upon it. One said
that a million of pistoles was too little. And how the archbishop could gather together so many precious stones, every
body was surprised at, till we heard that a brother of his grace
died in Peru, and left him great sums of money, and a vast
quantity of diamonds and precious stones.

I come now to speak of the treasure and rarities of the Lady *del Pilar*. In the church of this lady is the same number
of prebendaries and beneficiates, musicians, clerks, and sextons, as in the catholic Church of St. Salvator, and as to the
ornaments and silver plate, they are very much the same, except only that of the great custodia, which is not so rich.
But as to the chapel of the blessed Virgin, there is, without
comparison, more in it than in the cathedral. I shall treat of
the image in another chapter   Now as to her riches, I will
give you an account as far as I remember, for it is impossible
for every thing to be kept in the memory of man.

In the little chapel, where the image is on a pillar, are four
angels, as large and tall as a man, with a big candlestick,
each of which is made wholly of silver gilt. The front of two
altars is solid silver, with gilt frames, set with rich stones. Before the image there is a lamp, (as they call it,) a spider of
crystal, in which twelve wax candles burn night and day: The
several parts of the spider are set with gold and diamonds,
which was a present made to the Virgin by Don John, of Austria, who also left her in his last will, his own heart, which accordingly was brought to her, and is kept in a gold box set
with large diamonds, and which hangs before the image.
There is a thick grate round about the little chapel, of solid
silver: Next to this is another chapel to say mass in before
the image; and the altar-piece of it is all made of silver, from
the top to the altar's table, which is of jasper stone, and the
front of silver, with the frame gilt, set with precious stones.
The rich crown of the Virgin is twenty-five pounds weight, set
all over with large diamonds. Besides this rich one, she has
six pounds more of pure gold, set with rich diamonds and emeralds, the smallest of which is worth half a million.

The roses of diamonds and other precious stones she has
to adorn her mantle, are innumerable; for though she is dressed every day in the color of the church's festival, and never

L

uses twice the same mantle, which is of the best stuff, em broidered with gold; she has new roses of precious stones, every day for three years together; she has three hundred and sixty-five necklaces of pearls and diamonds, and six chains of gold set with diamonds, which are put on her mantle on the great festivals of Christ.

In the room of her treasure are innumerable heads, arms, legs, eyes, and hands, made of gold and silver, presented to her by the people, which have been cured as they believe, by miracle, through the Virgin's divine power and intercessions. In this second chapel are one hundred and ninety-five silver lamps, in three lines, one over the other. The lamps of the lowest rank are bigger than those of the second, and these are bigger than those of the third. The five lamps facing the image are about five hundred pounds weight each, the sixty of the same line four hundred pounds weight, and those of the third line, one hundred pounds weight. Those of the second line are two hundred pounds weight. There is the image of the Virgin in the treasure, made in the shape of a woman five feet high, all of pure silver, set with precious stones, and a crown of gold set with diamonds, and this image is to be carried in a public procession the days appointed. I will speak of the miraculous image in the following chapter

I remember that when the Rt. Hon. Lord Stanhope, then General of the English forces, was in Saragossa, after the battle, he went to see the treasure of the lady of Pilar, which was shown to him, and I heard him say these words: *If all the kings of Europe should gather together all their treasures and precious stones, they could not buy half of the riches of this treasury.* And by this expression of so wise and experienced a man, every body may judge of the value.

After this short account of the ornaments to be used at mass, and the incomparable treasures of the Romish church, I proceed to a description of the great or high masses, their ceremonies, and of all the motions and gestures the priests make in the celebration of a mass.

Besides the priest, there must be a deacon, subdeacon, two *acoliti,* i. e. two to carry the large candlesticks before the priest, and one to carry the incensary. The incenser helps the priest when he dresses himself in the vestry, and the two *acoliti* help the deacon and subdeacon. When all three are dressed, the incenser and the two acoliti in their surplices, and large collars round about their necks, made of the same stuff as that of the priest's *casulla,* and deacon and subdeacon's *al-*

matices, i. e. a sort of carulla, with open sleeves, I say, the incenser puts fire in the incensary, and the acoliti takes the candlesticks with the wax candles lighted, and the subdeacon takes the chalice and corporals, and so making a bow to the crucifix in the vestry, they go out into the church to the great altar. There are commonly three steps to go up to the altar, and the priest and five assistants kneel down at the first step, then leaving the incense and acoliti to stay there, the priest, deacon and subdeacon go up to the altar's table, and all knee. down there again. The subdeacon leaves the chalice on a little table next to the altar's table at the right hand, and then they turn back again to the highest step, and kneeling down again, the priest, deacon, and subdeacon get up, leaving the incenser and acoliti on their knees, and begin the mass by a psalm, and after it the priest says the general confession of sins, to which the deacon and subdeacon answer, *Misereatur tui, &c.* Then they say the general confession themselves, and after it the priest absolves them, and saying another psalm, they go up again to the altar's table, which the priest kisses, and he and the two assistants kneel down, and rise again. Then the incenser brings the incensary and incense, and the priest puts in three spoonsfull of it, and taking the incensary from the deacon's hands, he incenses three times the tabernacle of the *Eucharistia,* and goes twice to each side of it, he kneels down then, and the deacon takes up the hem of the priest's casulla, and so goes from the middle of the altar to the right corner, incensing the table, and returning from the corner to the middle, then kneels down and gets up, and goes to the left corner, and from the left goes again to the right corner, and giving the incensary to the deacon, he incenses three times the priest, and gives the incensary to the incenser, and this incenses twice the deacon. The assistants always follow the priest, making the motions that he does.

The incenser has the *missal* or mass-book ready on the altar's table at the right corner, and so the priest begins the psalm of the mass: all this while the musicians are singing the beginning of the mass till *kyrie eleijon;* and when they have finished, the priest sings these three words: *Gloria in excelsis deo.* And the musicians sing the rest. While they are singing, the priest, deacon, and subdeacon, making a bow to the tabernacle, go to sit on three rich chairs at the right hand of the *ara* or altar's table; and as soon as the music has ended the gloria, they go to the middle of the table, kneel down, and get up, and the priest kissing the table turns to the people, opening his arms, and says, in Latin, The *Lord be with you*, to which, and all other expressions the music and the people answer; then turns again his face to the altar, kneels down gets up, and the assistants doing the same, the priest goes to the right corner, and says the collect for the day, and two, or sometimes five or six prayers in commemoration of the saints, and last of all, a prayer for the pope, king and bishop of the diocess, against heretics, infidels and enemies of their religion, or the holy catholic faith.

Then the subdeacon, taking the book of the epistles and gospels, goes down to the lowest step, and sings the epistle, which ended, he goes up to the priest, kisses his hand, leaves the book of the gospels on the little table, takes the *missal* or mass-book, and carries it to the left corner. Then the priest goes to the middle, kneels down, kisses the altar, says a prayer, and goes to say the gospel, while the music is singing a psalm, which they call *Tractus gradualis.* The gospel ended, the priest goes again to the middle, kneels down, rises and kisses the table, and turns half to the altar, and half to the people, and the deacon, giving him the incense-box, he puts in three spoonsfull of it, and blesses the incense: The incenser takes it from the deacon, who taking the book of the gospel, kneels down before the priest and asks his blessing. The priest gives the blessing, and the deacon kisses his hand, and then he goes to the left corner and sings the gospel, viz: the left corner, as to the people of the church, but as to the altar, it is the right. While the deacon sings the gospel, the priest goes to the opposite corner and there stands till the gospel is ended: Then the deacon carrieth to him the book open, and the priest kissing it, goes to the middle of the table, and kneeling, rising, kissing the table, the assistants doing the same, he turns his face to the people, openeth his arms, and says again, *The Lord be with you.* Then he turns again before the altar, and says, *Let us pray.* The music begins the *offertory,* when there is no creed to be sung, for there is no creed in all their festivals.

While the musicians sing the offertory, the deacon prepares the chalice, that is, he puts the wine in it, and after him, the subdeacon pours in three drops of water, and cleaning nicely the mouth of the cup, the deacon gives it to the priest, who takes it in his hands, and offering it to the Eternal, sets it on the clean *corporales,* and covers it with a small piece of fine holland: then he says a prayer, and putting incense in the incensary as before, kneels, and then rising, incenses the table, as is said, which done, the subdeacon pours water on the priest's fore-fingers, which he washes and wipes with a clean towel, and after returns to the middle of the table, and after some prayers, he begins to sing the preface, which ended, he says some other prayers. Before the consecration, he joins his two hands, and puts them before his face, shuts his eyes, and examines his conscience for two or three minutes; then opening his eyes and arms, says a prayer, and begins the consecration. At this time every body is silent, to hear the words, and when the priest comes to pronounce them, he says with a loud voice, in Latin, *Hoc est enim corpus meum.* Then he leaves the consecrated Host on the *ara*, kneels down, and getting up, takes again the host with his two thumbs and two foremost fingers, and lifts it up as high as he can, that every body may see it, and leaving it again on the same *ara*, kneels down, and then rising up, takes the chalice, and after he has consecrated the wine, leaves it on the *ara*, and making the same motions and bows, he lifts it up as he did the host, and placing it on the ara, covers it, and with the same gestures, he says a prayer in remembrance of all the saints, all parents, relations, friends, and of all the souls in purgatory, but especially of that soul for whom the sacrifice of that mass is offered to God by Jesus Christ himself. I say, by Jesus Christ himself, for as Chrysostom and Amb.* say, the priest, not only representing Christ, but in the act of celebrating and consecrating is the very same Christ himself. Thus it is in the catechism published by decree of the council of Trent.†

Between this and the sumption, or the taking of the host, and drinking of the cup, the priest says some prayers, and sings *Our Father*, in Latin, kneeling down several times.— When he comes to the communion, he breaks the host by the middle, leaves one part on the table, and breaks off the other half, a little piece, and puts it into the cup; this done, he eats the two half hosts, and drinks the wine; and for fear any small fragments should remain in the cup, the deacon puts in more wine, and the priest drinks it up, and going to the corner with the chalice, the subdeacon pours water upon the priest's two thumbs and foremost fingers, and being well washed, goes

* Hom. 2. in 2d Timoth. and Hom. de prod, Judæ Amb. lib. 4, de sacram, C. 4.

† Sed unus etiam, atque idem Sacerdos est Christus Dominus:—Nam Ministri qui Sacrificium faciunt, non suam sed Christi personam accipiunt, cum ejus Corpus et Sanguinem conficiunt, id quod et ipsius Consecrationis Verbis ostenditur, Sacerdos inquit: Hoc est Corpus meum, personam videlicet Christi Domini gerens, panis et vini Substantiam in veram ejus Corporis et Sanguinis Substantiam convertit.

L 2

to the middle of the table, and drinks up the water. Then
the deacon takes the cup and wipes it, and putting on every
thing, as when they came to the altar, gives it to the subdeacon, who leaves it on the little table near the altar. After
this is done, the priest, kneeling and getting up, and turning
to the people and opening his arms, says, *The Lord be with
you*, and two or more prayers; and last of all, the gospel of St.
John, with which he ends the mass; so in the same order they
went out of the vestry, they return into it again, saying a prayer for the souls in purgatory. After the priest is undrest, the
incensor and acoliti kneel down before him, and kiss his right
hand: Then they undress themselves, and the priest goes to
the humiliatory to give God thanks for all his benefits.

The same ceremonies, motions and gestures the priest
makes in a private mass, but not so many in a mass for the
dead. They have proper masses for the holy Trinity, for
Christ, the Virgin Mary, angels, apostles, martyrs, confessors,
virgins, and for the dead; the ornaments for this last are always black. This is a true description of the ceremonies of
the mass: Now let us give an account of the means the priests
make use of for the promoting of this sacrifice, and increasing
their profit.

The custom, or rule for public masses, which are always
sung, is this: the person that goes to the clerk and asks a mass
to be sung, carries at least six wax candles, which burn upon
the altar's table, while the mass lasts, and a good offering for
the priest, and besides that, must give the charity, which is a
crown, and the same for a mass sung for the dead; but if a
person have a mind to have a mass sung, such or such a day
forever, he must give, or settle upon the chapter or community, a pistole every year, and these are called settled masses,
and there are of these masses in every parish, church and
convent, more than the priests and friars can say in a year
for ever since the comedy of the mass began to be acted on
the stage of the church, the bigots of it successively have
settled masses every year; the priests and friars then cannot
discharge their conscience, while they keep the people ignorant of the truth of the matter.

Thus they blind the people: Suppose to be in a convent or a
hundred friars and priests, and that in that convent are two
hundred private and public masses settled every day, the
charity of one hundred is a manifest fraud and robbery, for
they receive it, and cannot say the masses. And nevertheless, they accept every day new foundations and settlements

of masses; for if the people ask the dean, or prior, whether there is a vacancy for a mass, they will never answer no; and this way they increase the yearly rents continually.

This is to be understood of the chapter or community, and I must say, that the chapters, and parish churches, are not so hard upon the people as the convents of friars are, though they are not so rich as the communities: The reason is, because a parish priest has, during his life, his tithes and book-money. But a prior of a convent commands that community only three years; therefore, while the office lasts, they endeavor to make money of every thing. I knew several priors very rich after their priorship; and how did they get riches, but by blinding and cheating the people, exacting money for masses which never were said, nor sung, nor ever will be?

As to the private priests and friars, and their cheating ways, there is so much to be said on them that I cannot, in so small a book as this is, give a full account of all; so I shall only tell the most usual methods they have to heap up riches by gathering thousands of masses every year.

Observe first of all, that if a priest is a parish minister, or vicar, he has every day of the year certain families, for whose souls, or the souls of their ancestors, he is to celebrate and offer the sacrifice of the mass. And if he is a friar, he has but one mass every week left to him, for six days he is obliged to say mass for the community: So by this certain rule, a parish minister cannot in conscience receive any money for masses, when he knows he cannot say more masses than those settled for every day in the year; and by the same rule, a friar cannot in conscience receive more money than for fifty-two masses every year, and consequently those that receive more are deceivers of the poor ignorant people, robbers of their money, and commit sacrilege in so doing.

And that they take more than they in justice can, shall appear in several instances.

First: I never saw either secular or regular priests refuse the charity for a mass, when a christian soul asked them to say it; and I knew hundreds of priests mighty officious in asking masses from all sorts of people.

Secondly: In all families whatsoever, if any one is dangerously sick, there are continually friars and priests waiting till the person dies, and troubling the chief of the family with petitions for masses for the soul of the deceased; and if he is rich, the custom is, to distribute among all the convents and parishes one thousand, or more masses to be said the day of

burial. When the Marquis of St. Martin died, his lady dis
tributed a hundred thousand masses, for which she paid the
very same day five thousand pounds sterling, besides one thousand masses, which she settled upon all the convents and parish churches, to be said every year forever, which amounts
to a thousand pistoles a year forever.

Thirdly: The friars, most commonly, are rich, and have
nothing of their own (as they say); some are assisted by their
parents, but these are very few. They give two thirds of
whatever they get to the community; and in some strict orders
the friars ought to give all to the convent; nevertheless, they
are never without money in their pockets, for all sorts of diversions; and it is a general observation, that a friar at cards is a
resolute man; for as he does not work to get money, or is sure
of getting more if he lose, he does not care to put all on one
card; therefore gentlemen do not venture to play with them,
so they are obliged to play with one another.

, I saw several friars who had nothing in the world but the
allowance of their community, and the charity of 52 masses a
year, venture on the card 50 pistoles; another lose 200 pistoles
in half an hour's time, and the next day have money enough
to play. And this is a thing so well known, that many of our
officers that have been in Spain, can certify the truth of it, as
eye-witnesses.

Now, as to the method they have to pick up money for so
many masses, they do not tell it; but as I never was bound not
to discover it, and the discovery of it, I hope, will be very useful to the Roman Catholics, though disadvantageous to priests
and friars, I think myself obliged, in conscience, to reveal this
never-revealed secret, for it is for the public good, not only of
protestants, who by this shall know thoroughly the cheats of
the *Romish* priests, but of the Roman Catholics too, who bestow their money for nothing to a people that make use of it to
ruin their souls and bodies.

The thing is this, that the friars are said to have a privilege
from the pope (I never saw such a privilege myself, though I
did all my endeavors to search and find it out) of a *centenaria
missa*, i. e. a brief, where the pope grants them the privilege
of saying one mass for a hundred; which privilege is divulged
among priests and friars, who keep it a secret among themselves: so that, as they say, one mass is equivalent to a hundred masses. I did not question when I was in the communion, that the pope could do that and more, but I was suspicious of the truth of such a grant. Now observe that by this

brief, every friar, having for himself 52 masses free every year, and one mass being as good as a hundred, he may get the charity of 5200 masses, and the least charity for every mass being two reals of plate, i. e. fourteen pence of our money, he may get near 300 pounds a year.

The secular priests, by this brief of *centenaria missa*, have more masses than the private friars; for though they have 365 settled masses to say in a year, they have, and may get the charity of 99 masses every day, which comes to 3,006,135 masses every year. In the convents that have 120 friars, and some 400, the prior, having 6 masses every week from each of his friars, by the same rule, the prior may have millions of millions of masses.

Hear now, how they do amuse the credulous people: If a gentleman, or gentlewoman, or any other person goes to church, and desires one mass to be said for such or such a soul, and to be present at it, there is always a friar ready, from six in the morning, till one, to say mass. He takes the charity for it, and he goes to say it, which he says for that soul, as I say now: For till such time, as he gets the charity of a hundred masses, which is above five pounds sterling, he will not say his own mass, or the mass for him. And so the rest of the friars do, and many priests too. The person that has given the charity, and has heard the mass, goes home fully satisfied that the mass has been said for him, or to his intention.

As to the communities: If somebody dieth, and the executors of the testament go to a father prior, and beg of him to say a thousand masses, he gives them a receipt, whereby the masses are said already; for he makes them believe that he has more masses said already by his friars to his own intention, and that out of the number he applies 1000 for the soul of the dead person; so the executors upon his word take the receipt of the masses, which they want to show to the Vicar General, who is to visit the testament, and see every spiritual thing ordered in it, accomplished accordingly.

This custom of asking money for masses is not only among the friars, but among the *beatas*, nuns, and whores too, for a *beata*, with an affected air of sanctity goes up and down to visit the sick, and asks beforehand many masses from the heads of families, alleging that by her prayers and so many masses, the sick may be recovered and restored to his former health; but these, if they get money for masses, they give it to their spiritual confessors, who say them as the beata order-eth. And according to their custom and belief, there is no

harm at all in so doing. The evil is in the nuns, who get every where abundance of masses, on pretence they have priests
and friars of their relations, who want the charity of masses.
And what do they with the money? Every nun having a
Devoto, or gallant to serve her, desireth him to say so many
masses for her, and to give her a receipt; he promises to do
it, but he never doth say the masses, though he giveth a receipt: so the nun keeps the money, the friar is paid by her in
an unlawful way, the people are cheated, and the souls in
purgatory (if there was such a place) shall remain there forever, for want of relief.

But the worst of all is, that a public, scandalous woman
will gather together a number of masses, on pretence that she
has a cousin in such a convent, who wants masses, i. e. the
charity for them. And what use do they make of them?—
This is an abomination to the Lord. They have many friars
who visit them unlawfully, and pay for it in masses; so the
woman keeps the money in payment of her own and their sins,
gets a receipt from the friars, and these never say the masses;
for how can we believe that such men can offer the holy sacrifice (as they call the mass) for such a use? And if they do it,
which is, in all human probability, impossible, who would not
be surprised at these proceedings? Every body indeed.

There is another custom in the church of Rome, which
brings a great deal of profit to the priests and friars, viz. the
great masses of brotherhoods, or fraternities. In every parish
church, and especially in every convent of friars and nuns,
there is a number of these fraternities, i. e. corporations of
tradesmen; and every corporation has a saint for their advocate or patron, viz. the corporation of shoe-makers has for an
advocate St. Chrispin and Chrispinia: the Butchers St. Bartholomew, &c. and so of the rest. There is a prior of the
corporation, who celebrates the day of their advocate with a
solemn mass, music, candles, and after all, an entertainment
for the members of the fraternity, and all the friars of the
community. To this the corporation gives eight dozen of
white wax candles to illuminate the altar of their patron,
when the solemn mass is sung, and whatever remains of the
candles goes to the convent. The prior payeth to the community 20 crowns for the solemn mass, and 10 crowns to the
musicians. The day following the corporation gives 3 dozen
yellow candles, and celebrates an anniversary, and have many
masses sung for the relief of their brethren's souls in purga
ory; for every mass they pay a crown. And besides all

these, the corporation has a mass settled every Friday, which is to be sung for the relief of the brethren's souls, for which and candles, the convent receiveth 6 crowns every Friday. There is not one church nor convent without two or three of these corporations every week: for there are saints enough in the church for it, and by these advocates of the friars, rather than of the members of the corporation, every body may form a right judgment of the riches the priests and friars get by these means.

One thing I cannot pass by, though it has no relation with the main subject of the mass; and this is, that after the solemn mass is finished, the prior of the corporation, with his brethren, and the prior of the convent, with his friars, go all together to the refectory or common hall, to dinner, there they make rare demonstrations of joy, in honor of the advocate of that corporation. The prior of the convent makes a short speech before dinner, recommending to them to eat and drink heartily, for after they have paid all the honor and reverence to their advocate that is due, they ought to eat, and drink, and be merry; so they drink till they are happy, though not drunk.

I heard a pleasant story, reported in town, from a faithful person, who assured me he saw, himself, a friar come out of the refectory, at 8 at night, and as he came out of the convent's gate, the moon shining that night, and the shadow of the house being in the middle of the street, the merry friar thinking that the light of the moon, in the other half part of the street, was water, he took off his shoes and stockings, and so walked till he reached the shadow; and being asked by my friend the meaning of such extravagant folly, the friar cried out, *a miracle, a miracle!* The gentleman thought that the friar was mad: but he cried the more, *a miracle! a miracle!*— *Where is the miracle?* (the people that came to the windows asked him;) *I came this minute through this river,* (said he) *and I did not wet the soles of my feet;* and then he desired the neighbors to come and be witnesses of the miracle. In such a condition the honor of the advocate of that day did put the reverend friars; and this and the like effects such festivals occasion, both in the members of the convents and corporation.

Now I come to the means and persuasions the friars make use of for the extolling and praising this inestimable sacrifice of the mass, and the great ignorance of the people in believing them. First of all, as the people know the debaucheries and lewd lives of many friars and priests, sometimes they are loth

to desire a sinful friar to say mass f ; r them , thinking that his
mass cannot be so acceptable to God Almighty as that which is
said by a priest of good morals: So far the people are illumi-
nated by nature; but to this, priests and friars make them believe, that though a priest be the greatest sinner in the world,
the sacrifice is of the same efficacy with God, since it is the
sacrifice made by Christ on the Cross for all sinners; and that
it was so declared by the pope, and the council of Trent.

Put it together with what the same council declares, that the
priest doth not only represent Christ when he offereth the sacrifice, but that he is the very person of Christ at that time, and
that therefore David calls them Christs by these words : *Nolite
tangere Christos meos.* O execrable thing! If the priest is
the very Christ in the celebration of the mass, how can he at
the same time be a sinner? It being certain that Christ knew
no sin: and if that Christ Priest, offering the sacrifice, is in
any actual moral sin, how can the sacrifice of the mass, which
is (as to them) the same sacrifice Christ did offer to his eternal Father on the cross, be efficacious to the expiation of the
sins of all people? For, in the first place, that sacrifice offered by a Priest-Christ, in an actual mortal sin, cannot be an expiation of the sin by which the priest is spiritually dead. Secondly, if the Christ-Priest is spiritually dead by that mortal
sin, how can such a priest offer a lively spiritual sacrifice?—
We must conclude then, that the priests, by such blasphemous
expressions, not only deceive the people, but rob them of
their money, and commit a high crime, but that the sacrifice
he offers is really of no effect or efficacy, to the relief of the
souls in the pretended purgatory.

From what has been said, it appears that the priests and
friars make use of whatever means they can to cheat the people, to gratify their passions, and increase their treasure.
For what cheat, fraud, and roguery, can be greater than this
of the *centenaria missa* with which they suck up the money
of poor and rich, without performing what they promise?

If the pope's privilege for that *hundred mass* was really true,
natural reason shews, it was against the public good, and therefore ought not to be made use of: for by it, friars and priests
will never quench their thirst of money and ambition, till they
draw to them the riches of Christendom, and by these means,
they will wrong the supposed souls in purgatory, and ruin their
own too. Decency in the sacerdotal ornaments is agreeable
to God our Lord, but vanity and profaneness is an abomination before him. Of what use can all the riches of their churches

and ornaments be? To make the sacrifice of the mass more efficacious, it cannot be for; the efficacy of it proceeds from Christ himself, who made use of different ornaments than those the priests make use of. Nor is it to satisfy their own ambition, for they could get more by saying them; it is only to make Mistress Mass the more admired, and gain the whole people to be her followers and courtiers.

O that the Roman laity would consider the weight of these Christian observations, and if they will not believe them because they are mine, I heartily beg of them all, to make pious and serious reflections upon themselves, to examine the designs of the priests and friars, to mind their lives and conversations; to observe their works; to cast up accounts every year, and see how much of their substance goes to the clergy and church for masses. Sure I am, they will find out the ill and ambitious designs of their spiritual guides. They will experience their lives not at all (most commonly,) answerable to their characters, and sacerdotal functions; and more, their own substances and estates diminished every year. Many of their families corrupted by the wantonness, their understandings blinded by the craft, their souls in the way to hell, by the wicked doctrines, and their bodies under suffering by the needless impositions of priests and friars.

They will find also, that the pomp and brightness of a solemn mass, is only vanity to amuse the eyes, and a cheat to rob the purse. That the *centenaria missa* never known to them before, is a trick and invention of priests and friars, to delude and deceive them, and by that means impoverish and weaken them, and make themselves masters of all.

They will come at last to consider and believe, that the Roman Catholic Congregations, ruled and governed by priests and friars, do sin against the Lord, i. e. the spiritual heads do commit abomination before the Lord, and that they cannot prosper here, nor hereafter, if they do not leave off their wicked ways. Pray read the fifth chapter, the seventeenth verse, and the following, of Judith, and you shall find the case and the truth of my last proposition. *While* (says he) *these people sinned not before their God, they prospered, because the God that hateth iniquity was with them. But when they departed from the way that he appointed them, they were destroyed.* This was spoken of the Jews, but we may understand it of all nations, and especially of the Romans, who are very much of a piece with the Jews of old, or no better. We see the priests departed from the way that he appointed them. What can they

M

expect but destruction, if they do not leave off their wickedness, and turn unto the Lord? And the worst is, tha the innocent laity will suffer with them, for God punishes, as we see
in the old testament, a whole nation for the sins of their rulers.
And it is to be feared the same will happen to the Roman
church, for the sins of their priests. May God enlighten them.
—Amen.

. ARTICLE II.

Of the privileged altar.

A privileged altar is the altar to which (or to some image on
it) the pope has granted a privilege of such a nature, that whosoever says before it, or before the image, so many *pater nosters,* &c.; and so many *ave maria's,* with *gloria patri,* &c.
obtains remission of his sins, or relieveth a soul out of purgatory. Or whoever ordereth a mass to be said on the *ara* ot
such an altar, and before the image, has the privilege (as they
believe) to take out of purgatory that soul for which the sacrifice of the mass is offered.

The Cardinals, Patriarchs, Primates, Archbishops and Bishops, can grant to any image forty days of full and free indulgence, and fifteen *quarantains* of pardon, for those that visit
the said image, and say such a prayer before it as they have
appointed at the granting of such graces: So not only the images of the altars in the church, but several images in the corners of the streets, and on the highway, have those graces
granted to them by the bishop of the diocess: nay, the beads,
or rosary of the Virgin Mary, of some considerable persons,
have the same grants. And what is yet more surprising, the
picture of St. Anthony's pig, which is placed at the saint's feet,
has the granting of fifteen quarantains of pardon of sins for
those that visit and pray before him. What the people do on
St. Martin's day, I shall tell in another chapter.

I will not dispute now, whether the popes and bishops have
authority to grant such privileges; but I only say, that I do not
believe such a dream: for the pope has usurped the supremacy and infallibility, and his ambition being so great, he never
will dispossess himself of a thing by which he makes himself
more supreme, infallible, and rich; by keeping all those graces in his own hands, he would oblige all the bigots o seek
after him and pay him for them, and have him in more veneration than otherwise he would be in.

These privileges are a great furtherance to carry on the
ecclesiastical interests, and to bring the people to offer their

prayers and money, and to be blinded and deceived by those papal inventions. But because I have already treated of these privileges, I proceed to the third article.

ARTICLE III.

Of Transubstantiation, or the Eucharist.

I shall say nothing touching the scholastic opinions of the Romish church, about the sacrament of the Eucharist, or the real presence of Jesus Christ in it; for these are well known by our learned and well instructed laity: so I will confine myself wholly to their practices in the administration of this sacrament, and the worship paid to it by the priests and laity; and what strange notions the preachers put in the people's heads about it.

First, as to the administration of this sacrament, actual or habitual intention being necessary in a priest, to the validity and efficacy of the sacrament, open confession and repentance of his sins. He goes to consecrate the bread and wine, and, (as they say, believe, and make the people believe) with five words they oblige Jesus Christ to descend from heaven to the host with his body, soul and divinity, and that so he remains there as high and almighty as he is in heaven; which they endeavor to confirm with pretended miracles, saying, that many priests of pure lives have seen a little boy instead of a wafer, in the consecrated host, &c.

In winter, twice every month, and in summer, every week, the priest is to consecrate one great host, and a quantity of small ones, which they do in the following manner:—After the priest has consecrated the great and small, besides the host which he is to receive himself, the priests of the parish, or friars of the convent, come in two lines, with wax candles lighted in their hands, and kneel down before the altar, and begin to sing an hymn and anthem to the sacrament of the altar (so it is called by them); then the priest openeth the tabernacle where the old great host is kept between two crystals, and takes out of the tabernacle the *custodia*, and a cup of small consecrated wafers, and puts them on the table of the altar; then he takes the great old host, eats it, and so he does the small ones; then he puts the new great consecrated host between the two crystals of the *custodia*, and the new small ones into the communion cup, because the small ones serve the common people. Then he incenses the great host on his knees, and having a white, neat towel round his neck, with

:he ends of it he takes the *custodia*, and turns to the people and makes the figure of a cross before the people, and turning to the altar, puts the *custodia* and the cup of the small wafers in the tabernacle, and locketh the door, and the priests go away.

The reason why the great host and the small ones are renewed twice a month in winter, and every week in summer (as they say), is (mind this reason, for the same is against them) because in summer, by the excessive heat, the host may be corrupted and putrified, and produce worms, which many times has happened to the great host, as I myself have seen. So to prevent this, they consecrate every week in summer time; but in winter, which is a more favorable time to preserve the host from corruption, only once in a fortnight. If Christ is then in the host with the body, soul and divinity, and David says, that the *holy one* (i. e. Christ who is God blessed forevermore) *never shall see corruption,* how comes it, that that host, that holy one, that Christ, is sometimes corrupted and putrified? The substance of bread being only subject to corruption, being vanished, and the body of Jesus Christ substituted in its place this body by a just inference is corrupted; which is against the scripture, and against the divinity of Jesus Christ.

Again: I ask, whether the worms engendered in that host, come out of the real body of Christ, or out of the material substance of the host? If out of the body of Christ, every body may infer from this the consequences his own fancy suggests. And if they say that the worms are engendered in the material substance of the bread, then the substance of the bread remains after the consecration, and not (as they say) the real substance of the body of Christ.

Again: It is a rule given by all the casuists, that that host must be eaten by the priest. I do ask the priest that eats the host with the worms, whether he believeth that host and worms to be the real body of Christ or not? If he says no, why doth he eat it to the prejudice of his own health? And if he believeth it to be the real body of Christ, I do ask again, whether the worms are Christ, with body, soul, and divinity, or not? If they are not, I give the said instance: And if they answer in the affirmative; then I say, that a priest did not eat the host and worms, (as I saw myself,) on pretence of the loathing of his stomach, and after the mass was ended, he carried the host, (two priests accompanying him with two candles,) and threw it into a place which they call Piscina; a place where they throw the dirty water after they wash their hands, which runs out of the church into the street. What can we say now? If the worms and corrupted host is the real body of Christ, see what a value they have for him, when they throw it away like dirty water; and if that host comes out of the running *piscina* into the street, the first dog or pig passing by (which is very common in Spain) may eat it. And if they are not, besides the said instance of eating it to the prejudice of their health, we may add this, namely: Why do the priests and two more carry the host in form of procession, and with so great veneration, with lights and psalms, as if it was the real body of Christ?

Now, as to the way of administering the sacrament to the people, they do it in the following manner, which is also against the fantastical transubstantiation. I said that the priest or friar consecrates small hosts once a week, to give them to the people when they go to receive. The priest in his surplice, and with the *stola* on, goes to the altar, says the prayer of the sacrament, opens the tabernacle, and taking out of it the cup, opens it, and turning to the communicants, takes one of the wafers with his thumb and the foremost finger of his right hand, lifts it up, and says, *See the lamb of God that taketh away the sins of the world,* which he repeats three times; and after goes straightway to the communicants, and puts a wafer into each of their mouths. When all have received, he puts the cup again into the tabernacle, and goes to the vestry. This is when the people receive before or after mass; but when they receive at mass, the priest consecrates for himself a great host, and after he has eaten it, he takes the cup out of the tabernacle and gives the small wafers, consecrated before by another priest, to the communicants, and putting again the cup into the tabernacle, or *sacrarium,* (as they call it,) drinks the consecrated wine himself.

I will not spend my time in proving, that the denying of the chalice to the laity is a manifest error, and that it is only to extol and raise the ecclesiastical dignity to the highest pitch: But I come to their ridiculous, nonsensical practices in several accidental cases, viz: First, I myself gave the sacrament to a lady, who had on that day a new suit of clothes, but she did not open her mouth wide enough to let the wafer on her tongue, and by my carelessness it fell upon one of her sleeves, and from thence to the ground; I ordered her not to quit the place till I had done; so, after the communion was over, I went to her again, and cutting a piece of the sleeve, where the wafer had

m 2

touched, and scratching the ground, I took both the piece and dust, and carried them to the *piscina;* but I was suspended *ab officio* and *beneficio* for eight days, as a punishment for my distraction, and not minding well my business. But this rule and custom of throwing into the *piscina,* among the dirty water, every thing that the host had touched, they ought to throw the fingers of the priest, or at least the tongues of men and women into the same place; and thus, their tricks and superstitious ceremonies never would be discovered nor spread abroad. How inconsistent this custom is with right sense and reason, every body may see.

Secondly. In the Dominican's convent it happened, that a lady who had a lap-dog, which she always used to carry along with her, went to receive the sacrement with the dog under her arm, and the dog looking up and beginning to bark when the friar went to put the wafer in the lady's mouth, he let the wafer fall, which happened to drop into the dog's mouth. Both the friar and the lady were in a deep amazement and confusion, and knew not what to do; so they sent for the reverend father prior, who resolved this nice point upon the spot, and ordered to call two friars and the clerk, and to bring the cross, and two candlesticks with two candles lighted, and to carry the dog in from the procession into the vestry, and keep the poor little creature there with illuminations, as if he was the host itself, till the digestion of the wafer was over, and then to kill the dog and throw it into the piscina. Another friar said, it was better to open the dog immediately, and take out the fragments of the host; and a third was of opinion, that the dog should be burnt on the spot. The lady, who loved dearly her Cupid, (this was the dog's name,) entreated the father prior to save the dog's life, if possible, and that she would give any thing to make amends for it. Then the prior and friars retired to consult what to do in this case; and it was resolved, that the dog should be called for the future, *El perillo del sacramento,* i. e. The sacrament's dog. 2. That if the dog should happen to die, the lady was to give him a burying in consecrated ground. 3. That the lady should take care not to let the dog play with other dogs. 4. That she was to give a silver dog, which was to be placed upon the tabernacle where the hosts are kept. And, 5. That she should give twenty pistoles to the convent. Every article was performed accordingly, and the dog was kept with a great deal of care and veneration. The case was printed, and so came to the ears of the inquisitors, and Don Pedro Guerrero, first inquisi-

.or, thinking the thing very scandalous, sent for the poor dog, and kept him in the inquisition to the great grief of the lady. What became of the dog nobody can tell. This case is worthy to be reflected on by serious, learned men, who may draw consequences to convince the Romans of the follies, covetousness, and superstitions of the priests.

This I aver, that after this case was published, it was disputed on in all the moral academies; but as I cannot tell all the sentiments and resolutions of them, I will confine myself to those of the academy of the holy trinity, wherein I was present when the case was proposed by the president, in the following terms:

Most reverend and learned brethren—the case of the dog (blasphemously called the sacrament's dog) deserves your application and searching, which ought to be carried on with a wise, christian, and solid way of arguing, both in this case, or any other like it. For my part, I am surprised when I think of the irregular, unchristian method, the priors and friars took in the case, and both the case and their resolution call for our mature consideration. Thanks be to God, that our people give full obedience to our mother the church, and that they inquire no further into the matter, after some of our teachers have advised them; otherwise the honor and reputation of our brethren would be quite ruined. For my part, (*salva fide*,) I think, that upon the same case, the priest ought to let the thing drop there, and take no further notice, rather than to give occasion to some critics to scandalize, and to laugh at the whole clergy. Besides, that it is to abate the incomparable value of the *Eucharistia*, and to make it ridiculous before good, sensible men.

Thus the president spoke; and fifteen members of the academy were of his opinion. One of the members said, that being certain that the dog had eaten the real body and blood of Jesus Christ, the priest, after the communion was over, was obliged to call the lady in private, and give a vomit to the dog, and to cast into the *piscina* what he should throw up. Another said, that the sacrament being a spiritual nourishment to the soul, he was obliged to ask a question, and it was, whether the sensitive soul of the dog was nourished by the sacrament or not? All agreed in the affirmative, upon which the questionist formed the following argument: The soul nourished by the sacrament of the body and blood of Christ, who is eternal life, is immortal; but the sensitive soul of the dog was nourished by Christ, according to your opinions: *Ergo*, the soul of the dog

is immortal; then, if immortal, where is the soul to go after
death; to heaven, to hell, or to purgatory? We must answer,
to neither of these places: So we disown that the dog did eat
the body of Christ; and there is more in the sacrament than
we can comprehend; and (*salva fide*, and in the way in argument) I say, that the dog ate what we see in the host, and not
what we believe. Thus the member ended his discourse.

After all these disputes, the case was thus resolved: that
the priest should ask the inquisitors' advice, who being the
judges in matters of faith, may safely determine what is to be
done in such a case, and the like.

Thirdly. I have already said in another place, that the
reverend father friar James Garcia was reputed among the
learned, the only man for divinity in this present age; and that
he was my master, and by his repeated kindness to me, I may
say, that I was his well-beloved disciple. I was to defend a
public thesis of divinity in the university, and he was to be
president or moderator. The thesis contained the following at treises: *De Essentia et Attributis Dei: De Visione Be-
atifica: De Gratia Justificante et Auxiliante: De Providentia:
De Actu Libero: De Trinitate:* and *De Sacramentis in gen-
ere.* All which I had learned from him. The shortest
treatise, of all he taught publicly in the university, was the
Eucharistia. The proofs of his opinion were short, and the
objections against them very succinct and dark. I must confess, that I was full of confusion, and uneasy for fear that some
doctor of divinity would make an argument against our opinion, touching the sacrament of Eucharistia. And I endeavored
to ask my master to instruct me, and furnish me with answers
suitable to the most difficult objections that could be proposed;
but though he desired me to be easy about it, and that, upon
necessity, he would answer for me; I replied with the following objection: God will never punish any man for not believing
what is against the evidence of our senses, but the real presence in Eucharistia is so: *Ergo,* (*salva fide,*) God will not
punish any man for not believing the real presence of Christ
there. To this he told me that none of the doctors would propose such an argument to me, and he advised me not to make
such an objection in public, but to keep it in my heart. But
father, (said I,) I ask your answer. My answer is (said he)
aliud Lingua doceo, aliud Corde credo; i. e. I teach one thing,
and I believe another. By these instances, I have given now,
every body may easily know the corruptions of the Romish
church, and the nonsensical opinions of their priests and fri-

ars, as also, that the learned do not believe in their hearts, that there is such a monster as *transubstantiation*, though for some worldly ends, they do not discover their true sentiments about it.

Now I proceed to the worship, and adoration, both the clergy and laity pay to the holy host or sacrament.

I shall not say any thing of what the people do, when the priests in a procession under a canopy carried the sacrament to the sick, for this custom and the pomp of it, and the idolatrous worship and adoration offered to it, is well known by our travellers and officers of the army.

Philip the IVth, king of Spain, as he was a hunting, met in the way a crowd of people following a priest, and asking the reason, he was told that the priest carried the consecrated wafer in his bosom to a sick person; the priest walked, and the king, leaving his horse, desired the priest to mount and ride on it, and holding the stirrup, bareheaded, he followed the priest all the way to the house, and gave him the horse for a present. From the king to the shepherd, all the people pay the same adoration to the holy host, which shall be better known by the pomp and magnificence they carry the great host with, in the solemn festival of corpus Christi, or of Christ's body. I shall describe only the general procession made on that day in Saragossa, of which I was an eye-witness.

Though the festival of corpus Christi be a moveable feast, it always falls on a Thursday. That day is made the great general procession of corpus Christi, and the Sunday following, every congregation through the streets of the parish, and every convent of friars and nuns through the cloisters of the convent go with great pomp to the private procession of Christ's body. As to the general great one, the festival is ordered in the following manner:

The Dean of the cathedral church of St. Salvator sends an officer to summon all the communities of friars, all the clergy of the parish churches, the Viceroy, governor and magistrates, the judges of the civil and criminal council, with the lord chancellor of the kingdom, and all the fraternities, brotherhoods, or corporations of the city, to meet together on the Thursday following, in the metropolitan cathedral church of St. Salvator, with all the standards, trumpets, giants,* both of

* Three big giant men, and three giant women, and six little ones, drest in men and women's clothes, made of thin wood, and carried by a man hid under the clothes. The big ones are fifteen feet high, which

the greater or lesser size in their respective habits of office or dignity, and all the clergy of the parish churches, and friars of convents, to bring along with them in a procession, with due reverence, all the silver bodies of saints on a base or pedestal, which are in their churches and convents. *Item:* Orders are published in every street, that the inhabitants or house-keepers are to clean the streets which the sacrament is to go through, and cover the ground with greens, and flowers, and to put the best hangings in the fronts of the balconies, and windows: All which is done accordingly; or else he that does not obey and perform such orders, is to pay 20 pistoles without any excuse whatsoever.

At three in the afternoon, the viceroy goes in state with the governor, judges, magistrates and officers, to meet the archbishop in his palace, and to accompany his grace to church, where all the communities of friars, clergy and corporations, are waiting for them. The dean and chapter receive them at the great porch, and after the archbishop has made a prayer before the great altar, the music begins to sing, *Pange lingua gloriosa,* while the archbishop takes out of the tabernacle the host upon the rich chalice, and placeth it on the great *custodia,* on the altar's table. Then the quire begins the evening songs, in which the archbishop in his pontifical habit officiateth, and when all is over, his grace giveth the blessing to the people with the sacrament in his hands. Then the archbishop, with the help of the dean, archdeacon and chanter, placeth the *custodia* on a gilt pedestal, which is adorned with flowers and the jewels of several ladies of quality, and which is carried on the shoulders of twelve priests, drest in the same ornaments they say mass in. This being done, the procession begins to go out of the church in the following order:

First of all the bagpipe, and the great and small giants, dancing all along the streets. 2. The big silver cross of the cathedral, carried by a clerk-priest, and two young assistants, with silver candlesticks and lighted candles. 3. From the cross to the piper, a man with a high hook goes and comes back again while the procession lasts. The hook is called St. Paul's hook, because it belongs to St. Paul's church. That hook is very sharp, and they make use of it in that procession, to cut down the signs of taverns and shops, for fear that the holy custodia should be spoiled. 4. The standard and sign of the youngest corporation, and all the members of it, with a wax

are kept in the hall of the city, for the magnificence and splendor of that day.

candle in their hands, forming two lines, whom all the corporations follow one after another in the same order. There are thirty corporations, and the smallest is composed of thirty members. 5. The boys and girls of the blue hospital with their master, mistress, and chaplain in his *alva stola*, and long sacerdotal cloak. 6. The youngest religion (the order of St. Francis is called St. Francis' religion, and so are all orders, which they reckon 70, and which we may really, in the phrase of a satirical gentleman, call 70 *religions without religion* with their reverend and two friars more at the end of each order, drest in the ornaments they use at the altar: and so all the orders go one after another in the same manner. There are 20 convents of friars, and on this solemn festival, every one being obliged to go to the procession, we reckon there may be about two thousand present on this occasion; and 16 convents of nuns, the number of them by regular computation is 1500. 7. The clergy of the youngest parish, with the parish cross before, and the minister of it behind them in sacred ornaments. And so the clergy of other parishes follow one another in the . same order, every friar and priest having a white wax candle lighted in his hand.

The number of secular priests, constantly residing in Saragossa, is 1200 in that one town: So by the said account, we find all the ecclesiastical persons to amount to 4700, when the whole of the inhabitants come to 15000 families.

8. The clergy of the cathedrals of St. Salvator, and the lady of Pilar, with all their sacerdotal ornaments, as also the musicians of both cathedrals which go before the *custodia* or sacrament, singing all the way. Then the 12 priests more, that carry the canopy under which the sacrament goes, and under the end of it the dean, and two prebends, as deacon and subdeacon. The archbishop in his pontifical habit goes at the subdeacon's right hand, the viceroy at the archbishop's, and the deacon and subdeacon, one at the right and the other at the left, all under the canopy. Six priests, with incense and incensaries on both sides of the *custodia*, go incensing the sacrament without intermission; for while one kneels down before the great host, and incenses it three times, the other puts incense in his incensary, and goes to relieve the other, and thus they do, from the coming out of the church, till they return back again to it.

9. The great chancellor, presidents, and councils, follow after, and after all, the nobility, men and women, with lighted candles. This procession lasts four hours from the time it goes

out, till it comes into the church again. All the bells of the convents and parishes ring all this time; and if there were not so many idolatrous ceremonies in that procession, it would be a great pleasure to see the streets so richly adorned with the best hangings, and the variety of persons in the procession.

The riches of that procession are incredible to a foreigner; but matters of fact (the truth of which may be inquired into) must be received by all serious people. I have spoken already of the rich *custodia* which the archbishop of Sevil gave to the cathedral, and of the rich chalice set in diamonds. Now be sides these two things, we reckon 33 silver crosses belonging to convents, and parish churches, ten feet high, and about the thickness of the pole of a coach; thirty-three small crosses which the priests and friars, who officiate that day, carry in their hands; these crosses, though small, are richer than the big one, because in the middle of the cross there is a relic, which is a piece of wood (as they say) of the cross on which our Saviour was crucified, and which they call *holy wood.* This relic is set in precious stones, and many of them set in diamonds. Thirty-three sacerdotal cloaks to officiate in, made of Tusy d'or, edged with pearls, emeralds, rubies, and other rich stones. Sixty-six silver candlesticks, four feet high. A large gold possenet, and a gold handle for the hysop; six incen saries, four of them silver, and two of gold; four silver incense boxes, and two gold ones. Three hundred and eighty silver bodies of saints on their rich gilt pedestals, of which two hun dred are whole bodies, and the rest half, but many are gilt, and several wear mitres on their heads, embroidered with pre cious stones.

The image of St. Michael, with the devil under his feet, and the image with wings, are of solid silver, gilt all over.

With this magnificence they carry the sacrament through the principal streets of the city, and all the people that are in the balconies and lattice windows throw roses and other flow ers upon the canopy of the sacrament as it goes by. When the procession is over, and the sacrament placed in the taber nacle, there is a stage before the altar to act a sacramental or divine comedy, which lasts about an hour, and this custom is practised also on Christmas eve. By these, every body may know their bigotries, superstitions and idolatries.

Now I come to say something of the strange notions the priests and friars, confessors and preachers, put in the people's heads, concerning the host. First, they preach and charge the people to adore the sacrament, but never to touch the consecrated host or wafer, this being a crime against the catholic faith, and that all such as dare to touch it, must be burned in the inquisition. Secondly, to believe that the real flesh and blood of Jesus Christ is in the Eucharist; and that, though they cannot see it, they ought to submit their understanding to the catholic faith. Thirdly, that if any body could lawfully touch the host, or wafer, and prick it with a pin, blood would come out immediately, which they pretend to prove with many miracles, as that of the *corporales* of Daroca, which, as it comes *a propos*, I cannot pass by without giving an account of it.

Daroca is an ancient city of the kingdom of Aragon, which bordereth on Castilla. It is famous among the Spaniards for its situation and strength, and for the mine that is in the neighboring mountain to it. For the floods coming with impetuosity against the walls, and putting the city in great danger, the inhabitants dug three hundred yards from one end of the mount to the other, and made a subterranean passage, and the floods going that way, the city is ever since free from danger. But it is yet more famous for what they call *corporales*. The story is this:—When the Moors invaded Spain, a curate near Daroca took all imaginable care to save the consecrated wafers that were in the tabernacle, and not to see them profaned by the infidels, and open enemies of their faith. There were but five small hosts in all, which he put with the fine holland on which the priest puts the great host when he says mass; and this piece of holland is called corporales. The Moors were at that time near, and nobody could make an escape; and the priest, ready to lose his own life, rather than to see the host profaned, tied the corporales with the five wafers in it, on a blind mule, and whipped the beast out of town, said, Speed you well, for I am sure that the sacrament on your back will guide you to some place free from the enemies of our religion. The mule journeyed on, and the next day arrived at Daroca, and some people observed the corporales tied with the holy stola to the mule's belly, were surprised at so rare and unexpected a thing, and called a priest of the great parish church; he came to the mule, and examining the thing, found the five wafers converted into blood, and stamped on the holland cloth; which spots of blood (or painting) of the bigness of a tenpenny piece, are preserved till this present time. Then the priest cried out, *a miracle*, the clergy in great devotion and procession came with candles and a canopy, and taking the mule

N

under it, went to the great church; and when the minister of
the parish had taken the stola and corporales from off the mule,
he went to place the corporales on the ara altaris, or the altar's table, but the mule not well pleased with it, left the company, and went up to the steeple or belfry: then the parish
minister (though not so wise as the mule) followed the mule
up stairs, and seeing the beast mark a place there with its
mouth, he soon understood that the mule being blind, could
neither go up, nor mark that place without being inspired
from above; and having persuaded the people of the same, all
agreed that there should be a little chapel built to keep the holy corporales. When this resolution was approved by the
clergy and laity, the mule died on the steeple. At the same
time the curate having made his escape, and by divine inspiration followed the mule's steps, came to Daroca, and telling
the whole cause of his putting the sacrament on the mule to
save it from profanation, both clergy and laity began to cry
out, *a miracle from Heaven;* and immediately further agreed,
that the mule should be embalmed and kept before the
holy corporales in the steeple, *ad perpetuam Rei Memoriam: Item,* to make a mule of the best stone could be found,
in honor of the mule, and that for the future his name
should be the *holy mule.* All things being done accordingly, and the city never having been mastered by the Moors,
(as the inhabitants say,) they instituted a solemn festival, to
which ever since the neighbors, even fourteen leagues distant, come every year. Those that go up to the steeple to
see the holy miracle of the wafers converted into blood, and
the holy mule, must pay four reals of plate. The people
of Daroca call it sometimes, *the holy mystery,* another time
the holy miracle; the sacrament of the mule by some ignorants;
the holy sacrament on a mule by the wise, &c. I myself took a
journey to see this wonder of Daroca, and paying the fees,
went up to have a full view of every thing: and really, I
saw a mule of stone, and a coffin wherein the embalmed mule
was kept, (as the clerk told me,) but he did not open it, for the
key is kept always at the bishop's palace: I saw likewise the
linen with five red spots in a little box of gilt silver, two can
dles always burning before it; and a glass lamp before the
mule's coffin. At that time I believed every part of the story
All sorts of people believe, as an infallible truth, that every
body's sight is preserved during life in the same degree of
strength and clearness it is in at the time they see these bloody
spots, which is proved by many instances of old women, who

by that means have excellent eyes to the last. *Item:* They give out that no blind person ever came before the corporales, without his sight being restored to him; which I firmly believe, for no blind person ever was up in the steeple. I cannot swear this, but I have very good reason to affirm it; for in the first place, there is a small book printed, called "Directions for the faithful people," teaching them how to prepare themselves before they go up to see the holy mystery of the corporales of Daroca. One of the advices to the blind is, that they must confess and receive the sacrament, and have the soul as clean as crystal, and to endeavor to go up to the steeple from the altar's table without any guide; and that if some cannot go as far as the chapel of the belfry, it is a sign that man is not well prepared. The distance between the altar and the steeple's door is about forty yards, and there are nine strong pillars in the body of the church; so the poor blind people, before they can reach the belfry's door, commonly break their noses, some their heads, &c. And some, more cautious and careful, and happy in finding out the door, when they are in the middle of the stairs, find a snare or stock, and break their legs; for I remember very well, when I went up myself, I saw a sort of a window in the middle of one of the steps, and asking the use of it, the clerk told me, it was to let down through it the rope of the great bell. Then I inquired no farther; but now, being sure that there was but that small window shut up in the whole pair of winding stairs, I conclude, that it could not be there for the said use, and in all probability that window was the snare to catch the poor blind people in. Therefore, the clerk being not sure of the miracle, by this prevents the discovery of the want of virtue in the holy corporales, to cure all diseases, and at the same time gives out a miracle, and the miracle is, that the blind man has broke his leg, and that it is a just punishment for daring to go up either unprepared, or with little faith; so no blind man has recovered sight by the virtue of the corporales.

By means of this same direction, no sick person dareth to go up; but if they recover, it must be a miracle of the holy mystery. And if a mule happen to be sick, the master of it goes and makes the beast give three turns around the steeple, thinking that its brother mule hath power to cure it. Many will be apt to suspect the truth of this story; nay, some will think it a mere forgery; but I appeal to several officers of the army that went through Daroca, to be witnesses for me. It may be they were not told all the circumstances of it, because

the people there having strange notions of an heretic; but the
mule and corporales being the most remarkable thing in the
city, I am sure many did hear of it, though nobody of the heretics could see the holy mystery, being a thing forbidden by
their church.

With this, and the like pretended miracles, priests and friars, confessors and preachers, make the people believe the
real presence of Christ's body in the host, and the ineffable virtue of this sacrament to cure all bodily distempers: nay, what
is more than all these, they persuade, and make the people
believe, that if a man or a woman has the consecrated wafer
by them, they cannot die suddenly; nay, nor be killed by
violent hands. So great is the power of the host (they say,)
that if you show it to the enraged sea, the storm immediately
ceaseth; if you carry it with you, you cannot die, especially
a sudden death. And really, they may venture to give out
this doctrine as an infallible point, for they are sure no body
will dare to touch the host, and much less to carry it with them,
it being so high a crime, that if any body was found out
with the consecrated wafer on his body, the sentence is
already passed by the inquisitors, that such a person is to be
burnt alive.

A parish priest carrying the consecrated host to a sick person out of the town, was killed by a flash of lightning, which
accident being clearly against this pretended infallible power
of the host, the people took the liberty to talk about it; but the
clergy ordered a funeral sermon, to which the nobility and
common people were invited by the common cryer. Every
body expected a funeral sermon: but the preacher, taking for
his text *Judicium sibi mouducat*, proved, that the priest killed
by a flash of lightning, was certainly damned, and that his
sudden death, while he had the consecrated host in his hands,
was the reward of his wickedness; and that his death was to
be looked upon as a miracle of the holy host, rather than an
instance against the infinite power of it; for, said he, we have
carefully searched and examined every thing, and have found
that he was not a priest, and therefore had no authority to
touch the host, nor administer the sacrament of the eucharist.
And with this the murmur of the people ceased, and every body
afterwards thought, that the sudden death of the priest was
a manifest miracle wrought by the host, and a visible punishment from heaven for his sacrilegious crimes.

The truth is, that the priest was ordained by the bishop of
Tarasona, in Aragon. The thing happened in the city of

Calatayed, in the same kingdom; his name was Mossen Pedro Aquilar; he was buried in the church called the *Sepulchre of our Lord.* The reverend father Fombuena was the preacher, and I was one of the hearers, and one that believed the thing as the preacher told us, till after a while, some members of the academy having examined the case, and found that he was really a priest, proposed it to the assembly, that every body might give his opinion about it. The president said that such a case was not to be brought into question, but the doctrine of the church touching eucharistia to be believed without any scruples.

Again, That the host has no virtue nor power to calm the raging sea, I know myself by experience; and as the relation of the thing may prove effectual to convince other Roman Catholics of their erroneous belief, as well as the passage itself did me, it seems fit in this place to give an account of it, and I pray God Almighty, that it may please him to give all the Roman Catholics the same conviction, some way or other, his infinite goodness was pleased to give me, that they may take as firm a resolution as I have taken, to espouse the safest way to salvation: for if we take our measures concerning the truths of religion from the rules of holy scriptures, and the platform of the primitive churches; nay, if the religion of Jesus Christ as it is delivered in the New Testament, be the true religion, (as I am certain it is) and the best and safest way to salvation; then certainly the protestant religion is the purest, that is, at this day, in the world; the most orthodox in faith, and the freest on the one hand from idolatry and superstition, and on the other, from whimsical novelties and enthusiasms, of any now extant; and not only a safe way to salvation, but the safest of any I know of in the world. Now I come to my story.

After I left my country, making use of several stratagems and disguises, I went to France, dressed in officer's clothes, and so I was known by some at Paris, under the name of the Spanish officer. My design was to come to England, but the treaty of Utretcht not being concluded, I could not attempt to come from Calais to Dover without a pass. I was perfectly a stranger in Paris, and without any acquaintance, only one French priest, who had studied in Spain, and could speak Spanish perfectly well, which was a great satisfaction to me, for at that time I could not speak French. The priest (to whom I made some presents,) was interpreter of the Spanish letters to the king's confessor, father le Telier, to whom he introduc-

ed me; I spoke to him in Latin, and told him I had got a grea:
fortune by the death of an uncle in London, and that I should
be very much obliged to his reverence, if by his influence I
could obtain a pass.   The priest had told him that I was a Captain, which the father believed; and my brother having been
a captain, (though at that time he was dead,) it was an easy
thing to pass for him.   The first visit was favorable to me, for
the father confessor promised to get me a pass, and bid me call
for it two or three days after, which I did; but I found the rev
erend very inquisitive, asking me several questions in divinity: I answered to all, that I had studied only a little Latin.—
He then told me there was no possibility of obtaining a pass
for England, and that if I had committed any irregular thing
in the army, he would give me a letter for the king of Spain
to obtain my pardon, and make my peace with him again.   I
confess this speech made me very uneasy, and I began to suspect some danger; so I thanked him for his kind offer to me,
and told him I had committed nothing against my king or
country, which I would convince him of, by refusing his favor,
and by returning back into Spain that very week.   So I took
my leave of him, and the day following I left Paris, and went
back to St. Sebastian, where I kept my lodgings till I got the
opportunity of a ship for Lisbon.   The merchants of Saragossa trade to St. Sebastian, where I was afraid of being known,
and discovered by some of them, and for this reason I kept
close in my room, giving out that I was not well.   How to get
a ship was the only difficulty; but I was freed from this by
sending for the father rector of the Jesuits, on pretence that I
was very ill, and was willing to confess my sins.   Accordingly
he came to me that very day, and I began my confession, in
which I only told him, that as I was an officer in the army, and
had killed another officer, for which the king had ordered me
to be taken up, so that my life being in danger, and my conscience in trouble on account of the murder, I put both life
and soul into his hands.   He asked me all the usual questions.
but I confessing no other sin, the father thought I was a good
christian, and something great in the world; so he bade me he
easy and mind nothing but keep myself in readiness for my
voyage, and that he would send a captain of a ship to me
that very night, who should take me along with him into the
ship, and sail out the next morning.   And so all was performed accordingly, and I went that night to embark.   What directions the father rector gave the captain I know not; this I
know, that I was treated as if I were the son of a grandee,

and served by the captain himself. This was the first time of
my life being at sea, and I was very sick the two first days;
the third day a great storm began, which put me in fear of
losing my life. But then calling to my memory that the divine power was said to be in a consecrated host, to calm the
raging sea, and knowing that a priest had power to consecrate
at any time, and every where, upon urgent necessity, I went
into the captain's cabin, and took one of the white wafers he
made use of for sealing letters, and being alone, I made this
promise before God Almighty, from the bottom of my heart,
that if he would graciously condescend to remove my scruples
at once, by manifesting the real presence of his body in the
host, and its infinite power, by calming the raging tempest at
the sight of the one I was now going to consecrate, then I
would return back again into my church and country, and live
and die in the Romish communion; but if the effect did not
answer to the doctrine preached of the host, then I would live
and die in the church that knoweth no such errors, nor obey-
eth the pope. After this promise, I said my prayers of preparation to consecrate; and after I had consecrated one wafer
(which I was sure in my conscience was duly consecrated,
for the want of ornaments and a decent place, is no hindrance
to the validity of the priest's consecration,) I went up, and hi-
ding the wafer from the captain and the crew of the ship, I
shewed it to the sea, and trembling all over, stood in that condition for half an hour. But the storm at that time increased
so violently, that we lost the mast of the ship, and the captain
desired me to go down. I was willing to wait a little longer
for the efficacy of the host, but finding none at all, I went
down, and kneeling, I began to pray to God, and thinking I
was obliged to eat the consecrated host for reverence sake, I
did eat it, but without any faith of the efficacy and power of
it. Then I vowed before God, never to believe any doctrine
of the Romish church, but those that were taught by Jesus
Christ and his apostles, and to live and die in that only. After
this vow, though the storm did continue for a day and a night,
my heart was calmed, all my fears vanished, and though with
manifest danger of our lives, we got into Vigo's harbor, and
safe from the storm.

I left the ship there, and by land I went to Portugal, having
an inward joy and easiness in my heart; but having stopped
at Porto-Porto, to take a little rest, I fell sick of an intermitting
fever, which brought me to the very point of death three times,
in three months and nine days. The minister of the parish be-

ing told by my landlord, the condition I was in, past hopes of recovery, came to visit me, and desired me to confess and receive as a good christian ought to do; but I thanking him for his good advice, told him, that I was not so sick as he believed, and that I would send for him if I had any occasion, and really, I never believed that I was to die of that distemper, and by this thought, I was freed from priests and confessors.

When I was out of danger, and well recovered, I went to Lisbon, where I had the opportunity of talking with some English merchants, who explained to me some points of the protestant religion, and my heart was in such a disposition, that their words affected me more than all the sermons and moral sums of the Romish church had ever done before.

I knew a captain in the Spanish army, Don Alonzo Corsega by name, who was killed at the siege of Lerida, in whose bosom was found (in a little purse,) the consecrated wafer, for which his body was burnt to ashes. It is very likely that the poor man thinking to escape from death by that means, he took it out of his mouth when he went to receive, and kept it as an amulet against the martial instruments, which paid no respect to its fancied divinity.

Now by these instances I have given you already, it appears that the practices of the Romish priests, in the administration of the Eucharist, either to healthy or sick people, are only observed for interest's sake, as the worship and adoration given to the consecrated wafer, tends only to the increase of their treasure. And lastly, the doctrine of transubstantiation and real presence of Christ, which they endeavor to make the people believe by supposed miracles, is only to cheat and blind the poor laity, and raise in them a great reverence and admiration of their persons and office.

O Lord God, who receivest into thy favor those that fear thee, and do work righteousness, suffer not so many thousands of innocent people to be led in the way of error, but enlighten them with thy spirit, put the light of the Gospel upon the candlestick, that all those who are in darkness may by that means come to the safe way of salvation, and live and die in the profession of thy truth, and the purity of that perfect religion taught by thine only son, our Saviour Jesus Christ our Lord. Amen.

ARTICLE IV.

Of Purgatory.

I cannot give a real account of Purgatory, but I will tell all
I know of the practices and doctrines of the Romish priests and
friars, in relation to that imaginary place, which indeed
must be of vast extent and almost infinite capacity, if, as
the priests give out, there are as many apartments in it as
conditions and ranks of people in the world among Roman-
Catholics.

The intenseness of the fire in Purgatory is calculated by
them, which they say is eight degrees, and that of hell only
four degrees. But there is a great difference between these
two fires, in this, viz. that of purgatory (though more intense,
active, consuming and devouring) is but for a time, of which
the souls may be freed by the suffrages of masses; but that of
hell is forever. In both places, they say, the souls are tormented, and deprived of the glorious sight of God, but the
souls in purgatory (though they endure a great deal more than
those in hell) have certain hopes of seeing God sometime or
other, and that hope is enough to make them to be called *the
blessed souls.*

Pope Adrian the Third, confessed, that there was no mention of purgatory in scripture, or in the writings of the holy
fathers; but notwithstanding this, the council of Trent has settled the doctrine of purgatory without alleging any one passage of the holy scripture, and gave so much liberty to priests
and friars by it, that they build in that fiery palace, apartments
for kings, princes, grandees, noblemen, merchants and tradesmen, for ladies of quality, for gentlemen and tradesmen's wives,
and for poor common people. These are the eight apartments
which answer to the eight degrees of *intensus ignis,* i. e. intense fire; and they make the people believe, that the poor
people only endure the least degree; the second being greater,
is for gentlewomen and tradesmen's wives, and so on to the
eighth degree, which being the greatest of all, is reserved for
kings. By this wicked doctrine they get gradually masses
from all sorts and conditions of people, in proportion to their
greatness. But as the poor cannot give so many masses as
the great, the lowest chamber of purgatory is always crowded
with the reduced souls of those unfortunately fortunate people,
for they say to them, that the providence of God has ordered
every thing to the ease of his creatures, and that foreseeing

that the poor people could not afford the same number of mas
ses that the rich could, his infinite goodness had placed tnem
in a place of less sufferings in purgatory.

But it is a remarkable thing, that many poor, silly tradesmen's wives, desirous of honor in the next world, ask the friars whether the souls of their fathers, mothers, or sisters, can be
removed from the second apartment (reckoning from the lowest) to the third, thinking by it, that though the third degree of
fire is greater than the second, yet the soul would be better
pleased in the company of ladies of quality; but the worst is,
that the friar makes such women believe, that he may do it
very easily, if they give the same price for a mass the ladies of
quality give. I knew a shoemaker's wife, very ignorant, proud,
and full of punctilios of honor, who went to a Franciscan friar, and told him that she desired to know whether her own
father's soul was in purgatory or not, and in what apartment.
The friar asked her how many masses she could spare for it;
she said two; and the friar answered, your father's soul is
among the beggars. Upon hearing this, the poor woman began to cry, and desired the friar to put him, if possible, in the
fourth apartment, and she would pay him for it; and the *quantum* being settled, the friar promised to place him there the
next day; so the poor woman ever since gives out that her
father was a rich merchant, for it was revealed to her, that his
soul is among the merchants in purgatory.

Now what can we say, but that the pope is the chief Governor of that vast place, and priests and friars the quarter-masters that billet the souls according to their own fancies, and
have the power, and give for money the king's apartments to
the soul of a shoemaker, and that of a lady of quality to her
washer-woman.

But mind reader, how chaste the friars are in procuring a
separate place for ladies in purgatory; they suit this doctrine
to the temper of a people whom they believe to be extremely
jealous, and really not without ground of them, and so no soul
of a woman can be placed among men. Many serious people
are well pleased with this christian caution; but those that are
given to pleasure do not like it at all; and I knew a pleasant
young collegian, who went to a friar and told him: father, I
own I love the fair sex; and I believe my soul will always retain that inclination. I am told that no man's soul can be in
company with ladies, and it is a dismal thing for me to think,
that I must go there, (but as for hell, I am in no danger of it,
thanks to the pope,) where I shall never see any more women,

which will prove the greatest of torments to my soul: so I have resolved to agree with your reverence beforehand, upon this point. I have a bill of ten pistoles upon Peter la Vinna Ban quer, and if you can assure me, either to send me straight to heaven when I die, or to the ladies apartment in purgatory, you shall have the bill; and if you cannot, I must submit to the will of God, like a good christian. The friar seeing the bill, which he thought ready money, told him that he could do either of the two, and that he himself might choose which of the two places ne pleased. But father (said the collegian,) the case is, that I love Donna Teresa Spinola, but she does not love me, and I do not believe that I can expect any favor from her in this world, so I would know whether she is to go before me to purgatory or not. O! that is very certain (said the friar.) I choose then (said the collegian,) the ladies apartment, and here is the bill, if you give me a certificate under your hand, that the thing shall be so; but the friar refusing to give him any authentic certificate, the collegian laughed at him, and made satirical verses upon him, which were printed, and which I read. I knew the friar too, who being mocked publicly, was obliged to remove from his convent to another in the country.

Notwithstanding all these railleries, of which the inquisitors cannot take notice, being not against the catholic faith; priests and friars do daily endeavor to prove, that purgatory is a real existent place, and that by masses, the souls detained in it are daily delivered out of it. And this they prove by many revelations made to devout, pious people; and by many apparitions.

They not only preach them publicly, but books are printed of such revelations and apparitions. I remember many of them, but I shall not trouble the reader with them; only I will tell some of the most remarkable ones of my time.

In the latter end of King Charles the Second's reign, a nun of Guadalarajara wrote a letter to his majesty, acquainting him, that it was revealed to her by an angel, that the soul of his father, Philip the IV. was still in purgatory, (all alone in the royal apartments) and likewise in the lowest chamber, the said king Philip's shoemaker, and that upon saying so many masses, both should be delivered out of it, and should go to enjoy the ravishing pleasures of an eternal life. The nun was reputed a saint upon earth, and the simple king gave orders to his confessor to say, or order so many masses to be said, for that purpose; after which, the said nun wrote again to his majesty,

congratulating and wishing him joy, for the arrival of his father to heaven; but that the shoemaker, who was seven degrees lower than Philip in purgatory, was then seven degrees
higher than his majesty in heaven, because of his better life
on earth, who never had committed any sin with women, as
Philip had done all his life time, but that all was forgiven to
him on account of the masses.

Again, they give out in the pulpit, that the pope has an absolute power to make the mass efficacious to deliver the soul,
for which it is said, out of that place; and that his holiness can
take at once all the souls out of it; as Pious the Vth did, (as
they report) who, when he was cardinal, was mighty devout,
and a great procurer of the relief of souls, and who had promised them with a solemn oath, that if, by their prayers in purgatory, he should be chosen Pope, then he would empty purgatory of all the souls at once. At last, by the intercession of
the souls with God Almighty, he was elected pope, and immediately he delivered all the souls out of that place; but that
Jesus Christ was so angry with the new pope, that he appeared
to him, and bade him not to do any such thing again, for it was
prejudicial to the whole clergy and friarship. That pope delivered all the souls out of purgatory, by opening the treasure
of the church, in which were kept millions of masses, which
the popes make use of for the augmenting the riches of the
holy see. But he took care not to do it again; for though *quod-
cunque solveritis in Terra, erit solutum et in Cœlis*, there is
not specified the same power in purgatory, therefore, ever
since, the popes take no authority, nor liberty to sweep purgatory at once, for it would prove their ruin, and reduce the
clergy to poverty.

When some ignorant people pay for a mass, and are willing
to know whether the soul for which the mass is said, is, after
the mass, delivered out of purgatory; the friar makes them believe, that the soul will appear in the figure of a mouse within
the tabernacle of the altar, if it is not out of it, and then it is a
sign that the soul wants more masses; and if the mouse does
not appear, the soul is in heaven. So when the mass is over,
he goes to the tabernacle backwards, where is a little door with
a crystal, and lets the people look through it: But O pitiful
thing! They see a mouse which the friars keep, (perhaps for
this purpose) and so the poor sots give more money for more
masses, till they see the mouse no more. They have a revelation ready at hand, to say, that such a devout person was
told by an angel, that the soul for which the mass is said, was

to appear in the figure of a mouse in the *sacrario* or tabernacle.

Many other priests and friars do positively affirm, and we see many instances of it forged by them in printed books, that when they consecrate the host, the little boy Jesus doth appear to them in the host, and that is a sign that the soul is out of purgatory. There is a fine picture of St. Anthony de Paula, with the host in his hand, and the little Jesus is in the host, because that divine boy frequently appeared to him when he said mass, as the history of his life gives an account. But at the same time, they say, that no layman can see the boy Jesus, because it is not permitted to any man but to priests to see so heavenly a sight: and by that means they give out what sort of stories they please, without any fear of ever being found out in a lie.

As to the second day of November, which is the day of the souls of purgatory, in which every priest and friar sayeth three masses for the delivery of so many souls out of the pains of it, they generally say, that from three of the clock, of the first day of November (all-saints' day) till three in the afternoon, the next day, all the souls are out of purgatory, and entirely free from the pains of it; (those four and twenty hours being granted by his holiness for a refreshment to them) and that all that while they are in the air diverting themselves, and expecting the relief of so many masses, to get by them the desired end, viz. The celestial habitations. On these twenty-four hours, they ring the bells of all the churches and convents, which (as they say) is a great suffrage and help to the souls, and on that day only, priests and friars get more money than they get in two months time beside; for every family, and private persons too, give yellow wax candles to the church, and money for masses and responsá, i. e. a prayer for the dead, and all these twenty-four hours the churches are crowded with people, and the priests and friars continually singing prayers for the dead, and this they call the priests and friars fair day; which they solemnize with the continual ringing of bells, though they give out, that it is a suffrage for the souls of purgatory.

And on the same pretence, there is a man in every parish that goes in the dark of the evening through all the streets with a bell, praying for the souls, and asking charity for them in every house, always ringing the bell as a suffrage. The duke of Ossuna made a witty repartee to pope Innocent the XIth, on this subject. The duke was ambassador for the king of Spain at Rome, and he had a large bell on the top of his house, to gather his domestics when he was going out. Many cardinals lived by his palace, and complained to the pope, tha. the ambassador's bell disturbed them; (for the duke used to order to ring the bell when he knew the cardinals were at home) and the pope spoke immediately to the duke, and asked his Excellency the reason of keeping so big a bell? To which the duke answered, that he was a very good christian, and a good friend to the souls of purgatory, to whom the ringing of the bell was a suffrage. The pope took in good part this raillery, and desired him to make use of some other signal to call his servants; for that of the bell was very noisy, and a great disturbance to the cardinals, his neighbors; and that if he was so good a friend to the souls of purgatory, he would do them more service by selling the bell, and giving the money for masses.

To tell the truth the duke did not care for the souls, but all his design was to vex the cardinals: So the next day he ordered to bring down the bell, and to put in the same place a cannon, or a great piece of ordnance, and to give twelve shots every morning and twelve at midnight, which was the time the cardinals were at home. So they made a second complaint to the pope; upon this, he spoke to the duke again, and he answered to his holiness, that the bell was to be sold, and the money to be delivered to the priests for masses; but that he had ordered the cannon as a suffrage for the souls of the poor soldiers that had died in the defence of the holy see. The pope was very much affronted by this answer, and as he was caressing a little lap-dog he had in his arms, got up, and said, —Duke, I take more care of the souls of the poor soldiers than you of your own soul; at which, the duke taking out of the pope's arms the lap-dog, and throwing him through the window, said, And, I take care to shew the pope how he ought to speak with the king of Spain, to whom more respect is due. Then the pope, knowing the resoluteness of the duke, and that his holiness could get nothing by an angry method, chose to let the thing drop there, rather than to make more noise; so the duke kept his cannon piece, and the cardinals were obliged to remove their families into a more quiet place.

A mendicant friar one day asked some charity from the same duke, for the souls of purgatory, and said, My lord, if you put a pistole in this plate, you shall take out of purgatory that soul for which you design it. The duke gave the pistole, and asked whether the soul of his brother was already out of it? And when the friar said, Yea; the duke took again his pistole, and told the friar, Now you cannot put his soul into purgatory again. And it is to be wished that every one was like that duke, and had the same resolution to speak the truth to the pope himself and all his quarter-masters.

I have told in the first article of this chapter, that every Friday is appointed to say masses for the souls in purgatory, which did belong to corporations of fraternities, and what great profit priests, and especially friars, get by it. Now by this infallible custom and practice, we may say, that purgatory contains as many corporations of souls, as there are corporations of tradesmen here below, which fraternities are more profitable to all sorts of communities of friars, than the living members of them upon earth. But some of these people, either out of pleasantry, or out of curiosity, ask sometimes in what part of the world, or of the air, is that place of purgatory? To which the friars answer, that it is between the centre of the earth and this earthly superfices; which they pretend to prove, and make them believe by revelations, and especially by a story from a jesuit father, who in his travels saw the earth open by an earthquake, and in the deep a great many people of a flaming red color, from which nonsensical account they conclude, to blind the poor people, that those were the souls of purgatory, red as the very flame of fire. But observe, that no priest or friar would dare to tell such frivolous stories to people of good sense, but to the ignorant, of which there are great numbers in those parts of the world.

When they preach a sermon of the souls, they make use of brimstone, and burn it in the pulpit, saying, that such flames are like those of the fire in purgatory. They make use of many pictures of the souls that are in the middle of devouring fire, lifting up their hands to heaven, as if they were crying for help and assistance. They prove their propositions with revelations and apparitions, for they cannot find in the scripture any passage to ground their audacious thoughts on, and such sermons are to the people of sense better diversion than a comedy; for besides the wretchedness of style and method, they tell so many sottish stories, that they have enough to laugh at afterwards for a long while.

I went to hear an old friar, who had the name of an excellent preacher, upon the subject of the souls in purgatory, and he took his text out of the twenty-first chapter of the Apoc. 27th verse: *And there shall in no wise enter into it any thing that defileth, neither whatsoever worketh abomination; by* which he settled the belief of a purgatory, proving by some romantic authority that such a passage ought to be understood of purgatory, and his chief authority was, because a famous interpreter, or expositor, renders the text thus. There shall not enter into it (meaning heaven) any thing which is not proved by the fire, as silver is purified by it. When he had proved this text, he came to divide it, which he did in these three heads: *First,* that the souls suffer in purgatory three sorts of torments, of which the first was fire, and that greater than the fire of hell. *Secondly,* to be deprived of the face of God: And *Thirdly,* which was the greatest of all torments, to see their relations and friends here on earth diverting themselves, and taking so little care to relieve them out of those terrible pains. The preacher spoke very little of the two first points, but he insisted upon the third a long hour, taxing the people of ingratitude and inhumanity; and that if it was possible for any of the living to experience, only for a moment, that devouring flame of purgatory, certainly he would come again, and sell whatever he had in the world, and give it for masses: And what pity it is (said he) to know that there are the souls of many of my hearers' relations there, and none of them endeavor to relieve them out of that place. He went on and said: I have a catalogue of the souls, which, by revelation and apparition, we are sure are in purgatory; for in the first place, the soul of such a one (naming the soul of a rich merchant's father) appeared the other night to a godly person, in the figure of a pig, and the devout person, knowing that the door of his chamber was locked up, began to sprinkle the pig with holy water, and conjuring him, bade him speak, and tell him what he wanted? And the pig said, I am the soul of such an one, and I have been in purgatory these ten years for want of help. When I left the world, I forgot to tell my confessor where I left 1000 pistoles, which I had reserved for masses. My son found them out, and he is such an unnatural child, that he doth not remember my pitiful condition; and now by the permission of heaven, I come to you, and command you to discover this case to the first preacher you meet, that he may publish it, and tell my son, that if he doth not give that money for masses for my relief, I shall be for ever in purgatory, and his soul shall certainly go to hell.

The credulous merchant, terrified with this story, believing every tittle of it, got up before all the people, and went into the vestry, and when the friar had finished, he begged of him to go along with him to his house, where he should receive the money, which he did accordingly, for fear of a second thought; and the merchant gave freely the 1000 pistoles, for fear that his father's soul should be kept in purgatory, and he himself go to hell.

And besides these cheats and tricks, they make use of themselves to exact money, they have their solicitors and agents that go from one house to another, telling stories of apparitions and revelations, and these are they which we call *beatas* and *devotas;* for as their modesty in paparel, their hypocritical air, and daily exercises of confessing and receiving is well known in the world, the common people have so good an opinion of them, that they believe, as an article of faith, whatever stories they tell, without further inquiry into the matter: So those cunning, disguised devils (or worse) instructed by the friar their confessor, go and spread abroad many of these apparitions, by which they get a great deal of money for masses, which they give to the father confessor.

Nay, of late, the old nuns, those that, to their grief, the world despises, have undertaken the trade of publishing revelations and apparitions of souls in purgatory, and give out that such a soul is, and shall be in it, until the father, mother, or sister, go to such a friar, and give him so many masses, which he is to say himself, and no other. And the case is, that by agreement between the old skeleton, and the covetous father, he is to give her one third of all the masses that he receives by her means and application. So you see the nature of this place of purgatory, the apartments in it, the degrees of the fire of it, the means the priests and the friars make use of to keep in repair that profitable palace; and above all, the stupidity, sottishness and blindness of the people, to believe such dreams as matters of fact. What now can the Roman Catholics say for themselves? I am aware that they will say that I am a deceiver and impostor. The Jews said of our Saviour, (John vii., v. 12.) some, that he was a good man; others said, nay but he deceiveth the people, when he was telling the truth. So I shall not be surprised at any calumny or injury dispersed by them; for I am sure in my conscience, before God and the world, that I write the truth. And let nobody mind the method in this account, for now I look upon the prac·tices and cheats of the priests and friars in this point of purgatory, as the most ridiculous, nonsensical, and roguish of all their tricks; so how can a man that has been among them, and is now in the right way, write moderately, without ridiculing them?

o 2

I must dismiss this article with my address to the papist
priests of England and Ireland. Some of them (immediately
after my book was published and read by them) did command
their parishioners in their respective mass houses (as I was
told by a faithful friend) not to read my book, *sub pena excom-
municationis.* Others made frivolous remarks on some of my
observations and matters of fact; nay, a zealous protestant
having lent one of my books to a Roman catholic lady, she
gave it to her priest, and desired his opinion about it. The
priest read it over, and corrected only five passages with his
hand in the same book, of which I shall speak in my second
part. Above all, this article of purgatory is the hardest thing
to them; but they ought to consider, that I speak only of my
country people, and if they complain I must crave leave to say
that by that, they make us believe that the Spanish contagion
has reached to them, and want of the same remedy with the
Spaniards, namely, a narrow searching into the matter, &c

PART IV.

Of the Inquisitors and their Practices.

In the time of King Ferdinand the fifth, and Queen Isabella, the mixture of Jews, Moors, and Christians was so great, the relapses of the new converts so frequent, and the corruptions in matters of religion so bare-faced in all sorts and conditions of people, that the cardinal of Spain thought the introducing the inquisition could be the only way of stopping the course of wickedness and vice; so as the sole remedy to cure the irreligious practices of those times, the inquisition was established in the year 1471, in the court, and many other dominions of Spain.

The cardinal's design in giving birth to this tribunal, was only to suppress heresies, and chastise many horrible crimes committed against religion, viz; Blasphemy, sodomy, polygamy, sorcery, sacrilege, and many others, which are also punished in these kingdoms by the prerogative court, but not by making use of so barbarous means as the inquisition doth. The design of the cardinal was not blamable, being in itself good, and approved by all the serious and devout people of that time, but the performance of it was not so, as will appear by and by.

I can only speak of the inquisition of Saragossa, for as I am treating of matters of fact, I may tell with confidence what I knew of it, as an eye-witness of several things done there. This tribunal is composed of three inquisitors, who are absolute judges; for, from their judgment there is no appeal, not even to the pope himself, nor to a general council; as doth appear from what happened in the time of king Philip the second, when the inquisitors having censured the cardinal of Toleda, the pope sent for the process and sentence, but the inquisitors did not obey him, and though the council of Trent discharged the cardinal, notwithstanding, they insisted on the performance and execution of their sentence.

The first inquisitor is a divine, the second, a casuist, and the third, a civilian; the first and second are always priests and promoted from prebends to the high dignity of being holy inquisitors. The third sometimes is not a priest, though he is dressed in a clerical habit. The three inquisitors of my time were, first, Don Pedro Guerrero; second, Don Francisco Torrejon; third, Don Antonio Aliaga. This tribunal hath a high sheriff, and God knows how many constables and under officers, besides the officers that belong to the house, and that live in it; they have likewise an executioner; or we may say, there are as many executioners, as officers and judges, &c.; besides these, there are many qualificators and familiares, of which I will give an account by themselves.

The inquisitors have a despotic power to command every living soul; and no excuse is to be given, nor contradiction to be made, to their orders; nay, the people have not liberty to speak nor complain in their misfortunes, and therefore there is a proverb which says, *Con la inquisition chiton.* Do not meddle with the inquisition; or, as to the inquisition say nothing. This will be better understood by the following account of the method they make use of for the taking up and arresting the people: which is thus:

When the inquisitors receive an information against any body, which is always in private, and with such secrecy that none can know who the informer is (for all the informations are given in at night) they send their officers to the house of the accused, most commonly at midnight, and in a coach,— they knock at the door, (and then all the family are in bed) and when some body asks from the windows who is there; the officers say, *the holy inquisition.* At this word, he that answered, without any delay, or noise, or even the liberty of giving timely notice to the master of the house, comes down to open the door. I say, without the liberty of giving timely notice, for when the inquisitors send the officers, they are sure, by the spies, that the person is within, and if they do not find the accused, they take up the whole family, and carry them to the inquisition: so the answerer is with good reason afraid of making any delay in opening the street door. Then they go up stairs and arrest the accused without telling a word, or hearing a word from any of the family, and with great silence putting him into the coach, they drive to the holy prison. If the neighbors by chance hear the noise of the coach, they dare not go to the window, for it is well known that no other coach but that of the inquisition is abroad at that time of the night; nay, they are so much afraid, that they dare not even to ask the next morning their neighbors any thing about it, for those that talk of any thing that the inquisition does, are liable to undergo the same punishment, and this, may be, the night following. So if the accused be the daughter, son, or father, &c., and some friends or relations go in the morning to see the family, and ask the occasion of their tears and grief, they answer that their daughter was stolen away the night before, or the son, or father or mother, (whoever the prisoner be) did not come home the night before, and that they suspect he was murdered, &c. This answer they give, because they cannot tell the truth without exposing themselves to the same misfortune; and not only this, but they cannot go to the inquisition to inquire for the prisoner, for they would be confined for that alone. So all the comfor the family can have in such a case, is to imagine that the prisoner is in China, or in the remotest part of the world, or in hell, where in *nullus ordo sed sempiternus horror inhabitat.* This is the reason why nobody knows the persons that are in the inquisition till the sentence is published and executed, except those priests and friars summoned to hear the trial.

The qualificators and familiares which are in the city and country, upon necessity, have full power to secure any person suspected with the same secrecy, and commit him to the nearest commissary of the holy office of the inquisition, and he is to take care to send them safely to prison; which is all done by night, and without any fear that the people should deliver the prisoner, nay, or even talk of it.

Qualificators,

Are those, who, by order from the inquisitors, examine the crimes committed by the prisoners against the catholic faith, and give their opinions or censures about it: they are obliged to secrecy as well as other people; but as the number of them is great, the inquisitors must commonly make use of ten or twelve of the most learned that are in the city, in difficult cases; but this is only a formality, for their opinions and censures are not regarded, the inquisitors themselves being the absolute decisive judges. The distinguishing mark of a qualificator is the cross of the holy office, which is a medal of pure gold as big as a thirteen, with a cross in the middle, half white and half black, which they wear before their breast; but in public functions or processions, the priests and friars wear another bigger cross of embroidery on their cloak or habits. To be qualificator is a great honor to his whole fami

ly and relations, for this is a public testimony of the old christianity and pure blood (as they call it) of the family.

No nobleman covets the honor of being qualificator, for they
are all ambitious of the cross of St. James, of Alcantara,
of Calatravia, of Malta, and the golden fleece, which are the
five orders of the nobility; so the honor of a qualificator is for
those people, who, though their families being not well known,
are desirous to boast of their antiquity and christianism,
though to obtain such honor, they pay a great sum of money:
for, in the first place, he that desireth to be a qualificator, is
to appear before the holy tribunal, to make a public profession
of the catholic faith, and to acknowledge the holy tribunal
for the supreme of all others, and the inquisitors for his own
judges. This is the first step. After, he is to lay down on
the table the certificate of his baptism, and the names of his
parents for four generations; the towns and places of their
former habitations; and two hundred pistoles for the expenses
in taking informations.

This done, he goes home till the inquisitors send for him,
and if they do not send for him in six months time he loseth
the money and all hopes of getting the cross of qualificator;
and this happens very often for the reasons I shall give by
and by.

The inquisitors send their commissaries into all the places
of the new proponent's ancestors, where they may get some
account of their lives and conversations, and of the purity of
their blood, and that they never were mixed with Jewish fam
ilies, nor heretics, and that they were old Christians. These
examinations are performed in the most rigorous and severe
manner that can be; for if some of the informers and witnesses
are in a falsity, they are put into the inquisition; so every body
gives the report concerning the family in question, with great
caution, to the best of his knowledge and memory. When
the commissaries have taken the necessary informations with
witnesses of a good name, they examine the parish book, and
take a copy of the ancestors' names, the year and day of their
marriages, and the year, day, and place of their burials. The
commissaries then return to the inquisitors with all the examinations, witnesses, proofs, and convictions of the purity and
ancient christianity of the proponent's families, for four generations; and being again examined by the three inquisitors,
if they find them real and faithful, then they send the same
commissaries to inquire into the character, life, and conversa
tion of the *postulant*, or demanding person, but in this point

the commissaries pass by many personal failings, so when the report is given to the holy inquisitors, they send for the *postulant* and examine him concerning matters of faith, the holy scriptures, the knowledge of the ancient fathers of the church, moral cases, all which is but mere formality, for the generality of the holy fathers themselves do not take much pains in the study of those things, and therefore the postulant is not afraid of their nice questions, nor very solicitous how to resolve them.

When the examination is over, they order the secretary to draw the patent of the grant of the holy cross to such an one in regard to his families' old purity of blood and christianity, and to his personal parts and religious conversation, certifying in the patent, that for four generations past, none of his father's or mother's relations were at all suspected in points concerning the holy Roman catholic faith, or mixed with Jewish or heretical blood.

The day following, the postulant appears before the assembly of qualificators in the hall of the inquisition, and the first inquisitor celebrates the mass, assisted by the two qualificators, as deacon and subdeacon. One of the oldest brethren preacheth a sermon on that occasion, and when the mass is over, they make a sort of procession in the same hall, and after it, the inquisitor gives the book of the gospel to the postulant, and makes him swear the usual oaths; which done, the postulant, on his knees, receiveth the cross or medal, from the hands of the inquisitor, who, with a black ribbon, puts it on the postulant's neck, and begins to sing *te deum*, and the collect of thanks, which is the end of the ceremonies. Then all the assistant qualificators congratulate the new brother, and all go up to the inquisitor's apartment to drink chocolate, and after that, every one to his own dwelling place.

The new qualificator dineth with the inquisitors that day, and after dinner the secretary brings in a bill of all the fees and expenses of the informations; which he must clear before he leaves the inquisition. Most commonly the whole comes to four hundred pistoles, including the two hundred he gave in the beginning; but sometimes it comes to a thousand pistoles, to those whose ancestors families were out of the kingdom, for then the commissaries expend a great deal more: and if it happen they find the least spot of Jewdaism, or Heresy, in some relation of the family, the commissaries do not proceed any further in the examinations, but come back again to the inquisition immediately, and then the postulant is never

sent for by the inquisitors, who keep the two hundred pistoles
for pious uses.

Familiares,

Are always laymen, but of good sense and education. These
wear the same cross, and for the granting of it, the inquisitors
make the same informations and proofs as they make for qualificators. The honor and privileges are the same; for they
are not subject but to the tribunal of the inquisition. Their
businesses are not the same; for they are only employed in
gathering together, and inquiring after all books against the
catholic faith, and to watch the actions of suspected people.
They take a turn sometimes into the country, but then they do
not wear their cross openly till occasion requires it. They
insinuate themselves into all companies, and they will even
speak against the inquisition, and against religion, to try whether the people are of that sentiment; in short they are spies
of the inquisitors. They do not pay so much as the qualificators, for the honor of the cross, but they are obliged to take a
turn now and then in the country at their own expense. They
are not so many in number as the qualificators, for in a trial
of the inquisition, where all ought to be present, I once reckoned 160, and twice as many qualificators. I saw the list of
them both, i. e. of the whole kingdom of Aragon, wherein are
qualificators, of the secular priests, 243; and of the regular
406; familiares, 208.

The royal castle, formerly the palace of the king of Ara
gon, called Aljafeira, was given to the inquisitors to hold thei
tribunal there, and prison too. It is a musket shot distant from
the city, on the river side. But after the battle of Almanza,
when the duke of Orleans came as generalissimo of the Spanish and French army, he thought that place necessary to put a
strong garrison in; so he made the marquis de Torsey governor
of the fort of Aljafeira, and turned out the inquisitors; who
being obliged, by force, to quit their apartments, took a large
nouse near the Carmelites' convent: but two months after,
finding that the place was not safe enough to keep the prisoners in, they removed to the palace of the earl of Fuents, in
the great street called Coso, out of which they were turned
by Monsieur de Legal, as I shall tell by and by.

A form of their public trial.

If the trial is to be made publicly, in the hall of the holy
office, the inquisitors summon two priests out of every parish

church, and two regular priests out of every convent, all the qualificators and familiares that are in the city; the sheriff, and all the under officers; the secretary, and three inquisitors. All the aforesaid meet at the common hall on the day appointed for the trial at ten in the morning. The hall is hung in black, without any windows, or light, but what comes in through the door. At the front there is an image of our Saviour on the cross, under a black velvet canopy, and six candlesticks with six thick yellow wax candles on the altar's table: On one side there is a pulpit, with another candle, where the secretary reads the crimes; three chairs for the three inquisitors, and round about the hall, seats and chairs for the summoned priests, friars, familiares, and other officers.

When the inquisitors are come in, an under officer crieth out, Silence, silence, silence, the holy fathers are coming;— and from that very time, till all is over, nobody speaks nor spits; and the thought of the place puts every body under respect, fear, and attention. The holy fathers, with their hats on their heads, and serious countenances, go, and kneeling down before the altar, the first inquisitor begins to give out, *Veni Creator Spiritus, Mentos tuorum visita,* &c. And the congregation sing the rest, and the collect being said by him also, every body sits down. The secretary then goes up to the pulpit, and the holy father rings a small silver bell, which is the signal for bringing in the criminal. What is done afterwards will be known by the following trial and instances, at which I was present, being one of the youngest priests of the cathedral, and therefore obliged to go to those dismal tragedies; in which, the first thing, after the criminal comes in, and kneels down before the inquisitors, who receives a severe, bitter correction from the inquisitor, who measures it according to the nature of the crimes committed by the criminal; of all which, to the best of my memory, I will give an account in the first trial.

Trial I.

Of the reverend father Joseph Silvestre, Franciscan friar; and the mother Mary of Jesus, abbess of the monastery of Epila, of Franciscan nuns. Father Joseph was a tall, lusty man, 40 years of age, and had been 12 years professor of philosophy and divinity in the great convent of St. Francis. *Sor

---

*Sor is a title given to the nuns, which answers to Sister, as coming from the Latin Sorror.

P

Mary was 32 years old, mighty witty, and of an agreeable countenance. These two criminals were drest in brown gowns, painted all over with flames of fire, representing hell, a thick rope tied about their necks, and yellow wax candles in their hands. Both, in this dull appearance, came and prostrated themselves at the inquisitor's feet, and the first holy father began to correct them in the following words:

Unworthy creatures, how can our catholic Roman faith be preserved pure, if those who, by their office and ministry, ought to recommend its observance in the most earnest manner, are not only the first, but the greatest transgressors of it? Thou that teachest another not to steal, not to commit fornication, 'dost thou steal and commit sacrilege, which is worse than fornication? In these things we could show you pity and compassion; but as to the transgressions of the express commandments of our church, and the respect due to us the judges of the holy tribunal, we cannot; therefore your sentence is pronounced by these holy fathers of pity and compassion, lord inquisitors, as you shall hear now, and afterwards undergo.

Sor Mary was in a flood of tears; but father Joseph, who was a learned man, with great boldness and assurance, said, What, do you call yourselves holy fathers of pity and compassion? I say unto you, that you are three devils on earth, fathers of all manner of mischief, barbarity and lewdness.

No inquisitors were ever treated at such a rate before, and we were thinking that friar Joseph was to suffer fire, for this high affront to them. But Don Pedro Guerrero, first judge, though a severe, haughty, passionate man, ordered only a gag, or bit of a bridle to be put into his mouth; but friar Joseph flying into a fury, said, I despise all your torments, for my crimes are not against you, but against God, who is the only judge of my conscience, and you do yet worse things, &c.

The inquisitors ordered to carry him to prison, while the crimes and sentence were reading. So he was carried in, and the nun with great humility heard the accusation and sentence.

The secretary, by order, began to read, 1st. That friar Joseph was made father confessor, and sor Mary mother abbess. That in the beginning they showed a great example of humility and virtue to the nuns; but afterwards all this zeal of theirs appeared to be mere hypocrisy, and a cover for their wicked actions: for as she had a grate in the wall of friar Joseph's room, they both did eat in private, and fast in public: That the said friar Joseph was found in bed with sor Mary by such a nun; and that she was found with child, and took a remedy to prevent the public proof of it: That both friar Joseph and sor Mary had robbed the treasure of the convent; and that one day they were contriving how to go away into another country, and that they had spoken in an irreverent manner of the pope and inquisitors.

This was the whole accusation against them, which friar Joseph and sor Mary had denied before, saying, it was only hatred and malice of the informers against them, and desired the witnesses to be produced before them; and this being against the custom of the holy office, the holy fathers had pronounced the sentence, viz: That friar Joseph should be deprived of all the honors of his order, and of active and passive voice, and be removed to a country convent, and be whipped three times a week for the space of six weeks. That sor Mary should be deprived of her abbacy, and removed into another monastery: this punishment being only for their audacious and unrespectful manner of talking against the pope and inquisitors.

Indeed, by this sentence we did believe, that the crimes they were charged with were only an invention of the malicious nuns; but poor friar Joseph suffered for his indiscretion; for though the next day the inquisitors gave out that he escaped out of prison, we really believe he had been strangled in the inquisition.

This was the first trial I was present at, and the second was that of Mary Guerrero and friar Michael Navarro, of which I have given an account in the chapter of auricular confessions. After these two trials the inquisitors were turned out by monsieur de Legal, and for eight months we had no inquisition. How this thing happened, is worthy of observation; therefore I shall give a particular account of it, that I may not deprive the public of so pleasant a story.

In 1706, after the battle of Almanza, the Spanish army being divided into two bodies, one through the kingdom of Valencia, to the frontiers of Catalonia, commanded by the duke of Berwick; the other composed of the French auxiliary troops, 14,000 in number, went to the conquest of Arragon, whose inhabitants had declared themselves for king Charles III. The body of French troops was commanded by his highness the duke of Orleans, who was the generalissimo of the whole army. Before he came near the city, the magistrates

went to meet him, and offered the keys of the city, but he re
fused them, saying, he was to enter it through a breach; and
so he did, treating the people as rebels to their lawful king.
And when he had ordered all the civil and military affairs of
the city, he went down to the frontiers of Catalonia, leaving
his lieutenant-general, monsieur de Jofreville, governor of the
town.   But this governor being a mild tempered man, was
loth to follow the orders left him as to the contribution money:
So he was called to the army, and the lieutenant-general, monsieur de Legal, came in his place.   The city was to pay 1,000
crowns a month, for the duke's table, and every house a pistole, which by computation made the sum of 18,000 pistoles a
month, which were paid eight months together; besides this,
the convents were to pay a donative, or gift, proportionable to
their rents.   The college of Jesuits were charged 2,000 pistoles, the Dominicans 1,000, Augustins 1,000, Carmelites
1,000, &c.   Monsieur de Legal sent first to the Jesuits, who
refused to pay, saying, it was against the ecclesiastical immu-
nity: But Legal, not acquainted with these sort of excuses,
sent four companies of grenadiers to quarter in their college
at discretion: The father sent immediately an express to the
king's father confessor, who was a jesuit, with complaints
about the case: But the grenadiers did make more expedition
in their plundering and mischiefs, than the courier did in his
journey. So the fathers, seeing the damage all their goods
had already received, and fearing some violence upon their
treasure, went to pay monsieur Legal the 2,000 pistoles as a
donative.

Next to this he sent to the Dominicans.   The friars of this
order are all familiares of the holy office, and depending upon
it, they did excuse themselves in a civil manner, saying, they
had no money, and if monsieur de Legal had a mind to insist
upon the demand of the 1000 pistoles, they could not pay
them, without sending to him the silver bodies of the saints.
The friars thought by this to frighten monsieur de Legal, and
if he was so resolute as to accept the offer, to send the saints
in a procession, and raise the people, crying out *Heresy, Heresy*.   De Legal answered to the friars, that he was obliged to
obey the duke's orders, and so he would receive the silver
saints: So the friars all in a solemn procession, and with
lighted candles in their hands, carried the saints to the governor Legal: And as soon as he heard of this public devotion
of the friars, he ordered immediately four companies of grenadiers to line the streets on both sides, before his house, and to

keep their fuzees in one hand, and a lighted candle in the other, to receive the saints with the same devotion and veneration. And though the friars endeavored to raise the people, nobody was so bold as to expose themselves to the army, there being left eight regiments to keep the mob under fear and subjection. Legal received the saints, and sent them to the mint, promising to the father prior to give him what remained above the 1,00ʊ pistoles. The friars being disappointed in the project of raising the people, went to the inquisitors to desire them to release immediately their saints out of the mint, by excommunicating monsieur de Legal, which the inquisitors did upon the spot; and the excommunication being drawn and signed, they gave strict orders to their secretary to go and read it before monsieur de Legal, which he did accordingly: And monsieur the governor, far from flying into a passion, with a mild countenance took the paper from the secretary, and said, Pray, tell your masters, the inquisitors, that I will answer them to-morrow morning. The secretary went away fully satisfied with Legal's civil behaviour. The same minute, as if he was inspired by the holy spirit, without reflecting upon any consequence, he called his own secretary, he bid him draw a copy of the excommunication, putting out the name of Legal, and inserting in its place *the holy Inquisitors.* The next morning he gave orders for four regiments to be ready, and sent them along with his secretary to the inquisition, with command to read the excommunication to the inquisitors themselves, and if they made the least noise, to turn them out, open all the prisons, and quarter two regiments there. He was not afraid of the people, for the duke took away all the arms from every individual person, and on pain of death commanded that nobody should keep but a short sword; and besides, four regiments were under arms, to prevent all sorts of tumult and disturbance: So his secretary went and performed the governor's orders. The inquisitors were never more sur-
·prised than to see themselves excommunicated by a man that had no authority for it, and resenting it, they began to cry out, *War against the heretic de Legal;* this is a public insult against our catholic faith. To which the secretary answered, *Holy Inquisitors,* the king wants this house to quarter his troops in, so walk out immediately: And as they continued in their exclamations, he took the inquisitors, with a strong guard, and carried them to a private house destined for them; but when they saw the laws of military discipline, they begged leave to take their goods along with them, which was immedi-

ately granted; and the next day they set out for Madrid, to complain to the king, who gave them this slight answer I am very sorry for it, but I cannot help it; my crown is in danger, and my grandfather defends it, and this is done by his troops, if it had been done by my troops, I should apply a speedy remedy: But you must have patience till things take another turn. So the inquisitors were obliged to have patience for eight months.

The secretary of monsieur de Legal, according to his orders, opened the doors of all the prisons, and then the wickednesses of the inquisitors were detected, for four hundred prisoners got liberty that day, and among them sixty young women were found very well drest, who were, in all human appearance, the number of the three inquisitors' *Seraglio*, as some of them did own afterwards. But this discovery, so dangerous to the holy tribunal, was in some measure prevented by the archbishop, who went to desire monsieur de Legal to send those women to his palace, and that his grace would take care of them; and that in the mean time, he ordered an ecclesiastical censure to be published against those that should defame, by groundless reports, the holy office of the inquisition. The governor answered to his grace, he would give him all the assistance for it he could; but as to the young women, it was not in his power, the officers having hurried them away: And indeed it was not; for it is not to be supposed that the inquisitors, having the absolute power to confine in their *Seraglio* whomsoever they had a fancy for, would choose ordinary girls, but the best and handsomest of the city: So the French officers were all so glad of getting such fine mistresses, that they immediately took them away, knowing very well they would follow them to the end of the world for fear of being confined again. In my travels in France afterwards, I met with one of those women at Rotchfort, in the same inn I went to lodge in that night, who had been brought there by the son of the master of the inn, formerly lieutenant in the French service in Spain, who had married her for her extraordinary beauty and good parts. She was the daughter of counsellor Ballabriga, and I knew her before she was taken up by the inquisitors' orders: but we thought she was stolen by some officer; for this was given out by her father, who died of grief and vexation, without the comfort of opening his trouble, nay, even to his confessors, so great is the fear of the inquisitors there.

I was very glad to meet one of my country-women in my

travels; and as she did not remember me, and especially in
my then disguise, I was taken for nothing but an officer. I
resolved to stay there the next day, to have the satisfaction of
conversing with her, and have a plain account of what we
could not know in Saragossa, for fear of incurring the ecclesiastical censure, published by the archbishop.   Now my conversation with her being *a propos*, and necessary to discover
the roguery of the inquisitors, it seems proper to divert the reader with it.

Mr. Faulcaut, my country-woman's husband, was then at
Paris, upon some pretensions; and though her father and
mother-in-law were continually at home, they did not mistrust
me, I being a countryman of their daughter-in-law, who freely
came to my room at any time; and as I was desiring her not
to expose herself to any uneasiness on my account, she answered me, Captain, we are now in France, not in Saragossa,
and we enjoy here all manner of freedom, without going beyond the limits of sobriety; so you may be easy in that point,
for my father and mother-in-law have ordered me to be obliging to you, nay, and to beg the favor of you to take your repose here this week, if your business permit it, and to be
pleased to accept this their small entertainment on free-cost,
as a token of their esteem to me, and my country-gentleman.
If it had not been for my continual fear of being discovered, I
would have accepted the proposition; so I thanked her, and
begged her to return my hearty acknowledgment to the gen
tleman and lady of the house, and that I was very sorry, that
my pressing business, at Paris, would prevent and hinder me
to enjoy so agreeable company: but if my business was soon
despatched at Paris, then, at my return, I would make a halt
there, may-be for a fortnight.   Mrs. Faulcaut was very much
concerned at my haste to go away: but she did make me promise to come back again that way.   So amidst these compliments from one to another, supper came in, and we went to it,
the old man and woman, their daughter and I: none but Mrs.
Faulcaut could speak Spanish, so she was my interpreter, for
I could not speak French.   After supper, the landlord and
landlady left us alone, and I began to beg of her the favor to
tell me the accident of her prison, of her sufferings in the inquisition, and of every thing relating to the holy office; and
fear not, (said I,) for we are in France, and not in Saragossa;
here is no inquisition, so you may safely open your heart to a
countryman of yours.   I will, with all my heart, (said she,)

and to satisfy your curiosity, I shall begin with the occasion of my imprisonment, which was as follows.

I went one day with my mother to visit the countess of Attarass, and I met there Don Francisco Torrejon, her confessor, and second inquisitor of the holy office. After we had drunk chocolate, he asked my age, and my confessor's name, and so many intricate questions about religion, that I could not answer him. His serious countenance did frighten me, and as he perceived my fear, he desired the countess to tell me, that he was not so severe as I took him to be: after which he caressed me in the most obliging manner in the world; he gave me his hand, which I kissed with great respect and modesty; and when he went away, he told me, My dear child, I shall remember you till the next time. I did not mind the sense of the words; for I was unexperienced in matters of gallantry, being only fifteen years old at that time. Indeed he did remember me, for the very night following, while in bed, hearing a hard knocking at the door, the maid went to the window, and asking, Who is there? I heard say, The holy inquisition. I could not forbear crying out, Father, father, I am ruined for ever. My dear father got up, and inquiring what the matter was, I answered him, with tears, The inquisition; and he, for fear that the maid should not open the door as quick as such a case required, went himself, as another Abraham, to open the door, and to offer his dear daughter to the fire of the inquisitors, and as I did not cease to cry out, as if I was a mad girl, my dear father, all in tears, did put in my mouth a bit of a bridle, to show his obedience to the holy office, and his zeal for the catholic faith, for he thought I had committed some crime against religion; so the officers gave me but time to put on my clothes, took me down into the coach, and without giving me the satisfaction of embracing my dear father and mother, they carried me into the inquisition. I did expect to die that very night; but when they carried me into a noble room, well furnished, and an excellent bed in it, I was quite surprised. The officers left me there, and immediately a maid came in with a salver of sweetmeats and cinnamon water, desiring me to take some refreshment before I went to bed: I told her that I could not; but that I should be obliged to her, if she could tell me whether I was to die that night or not? Die, (said she,) you do not come here to die, but to live like a princess, and you shall want nothing in the world but the liberty of going out; and now pray mind nothing, but to go to bed, and sleep easy, for to-morrow you shall see wonders in this house, and as I am chosen to be your waiting maid, I hope you will be very kind to me. I was going to ask her some questions, but she told me, Madam, I have not leave to tell you any thing else till to-morrow, only that nobody shall come to disturb you; and now I am going about some business, and I will come back presently, for my bed is in the closet near your bed: So she left me there for a quarter of an hour. The great amazement I was in, took away all my senses, or the free exercise of them, for I had not liberty to think of my parents, nor of grief, nor of the danger that was so near me: So in this suspension of thought, the waiting-maid came and locked the chamber door after her, and told me, Madam, let us go to bed, and only tell me at what time in the morning you will have the chocolate ready? I asked her name, and she told me it was Mary. Mary, for God's sake, (said I,) tell me whether I come to die or not? I have told you, madam, that you came (she said) to live as one of the happiest creatures in the world. And as I observed her reservedness, I did not ask her any more questions: So recommending myself to God Almighty, and to our lady of Pilar, and preparing myself to die, I went to bed, but could not sleep one minute. I was up with the day, but Mary slept till six of the clock: Then she got up, and wondering to see me up, she said to me, Pray, madam, will you drink chocolate now? Do what you please (said I): then she left me half an hour alone, and she came back with a silver plate with two cups of chocolate, and some biscuit on it. I drank one cup, and desired her to drink the other, which she did. Well, Mary, (said I,) can you give me any account of the reason of my being here? Not yet, madam, (said she,) but only have patience for a little while. With this answer she left me; and an hour after came again with two baskets, with a fine holland shift, a holland under petticoat, with fine lace round it; two silk petticoats and a little Spanish waistcoat, with a gold fringe all over it; with combs and ribbons, and every thing suitable to a lady of higher quality than I: But my greatest surprise was to see a gold snuff-box, with a picture of Don Francisco Torrejon in it. Then I soon understood the meaning of my confinement. So I considered with myself, that to refuse the present would be the occasion of my immediate death; and to accept of it, was to give to him, even on the first day, too great encouragement against my honor. But I found, as I thought then, a medium in the case; so I said, Mary, pray give my service to Don Francisco Torrejon, and tell him, that as I could not bring my clothes with me last night, honesty permits me to accept of these clothes, which are necessary to keep me decent; but since I take no snuff, I beg his lordship to excuse me, if I do not accept this box. Mary went to him with this answer, and came again with a picture nicely set in gold, with four diamonds at the four corners of it, and told me, that his lordship was mistaken, and that he desired me to accept that picture, which would be a great favor to him: and while I was thinking with myself what to do, Mary said to me, Pray, madam, take my poor advice, accept the picture, and every thing that he sends to you; for consider, that if you do not consent and comply with every thing he has a mind for, you will soon be put to death, and no body will defend you; but if you are obliging and kind to him, he is a very complaisant and agreeable gentleman, and will be a charming lover, and you will be here like a queen, and he will give you another apartment, with a fine garden, and many young ladies shall come to visit you: So I advise you to send a civil answer to him, and desire a visit from him, or else you will soon begin to repent yourself. O dear God, (said I,) must I abandon my honor without any remedy! If I oppose his desire, he by force will obtain it. So, full of confusion, I bid Mary to give him what answer she thought fit. She was very glad of my humble submission, and went to give Don Francisco my answer. She came back a few minutes after, all overjoyed, to tell me, that his lordship would honor me with his company at supper, and that he could not come sooner on account of some business that called him abroad; but in the mean time desired me to mind nothing, but how to divert myself, and to give to Mary my measure for a suit of clothes, and order her to bring me every thing I could wish for. Mary added to this, Madam, I may call you now my mistress, and must tell you, that I have been in the holy office these fourteen years, and I know the customs of it very well; but because silence is imposed upon me under pain of death, I cannot tell you any thing but what concerns your person: So, in the first place, do not oppose the holy father's will and pleasure: Secondly, if you see some young ladies here, never ask them the occasion of their being here, nor any thing of their business, neither will they ask you any thing of this nature, and take care not to tell them any thing of your being here you may come and divert yourself with them at such hours as are appointed; you shall have music, and all sorts of recreations; three days hence you shall dine with them: they are all ladies of quality, young and merry. and this is the best of lives; you will not long for going abroad, you will be so well diverted at home; and when your time is expired, then the holy fathers will send you out of this country, and marry you to some nobleman. Never mention the name of Don Francisco, nor your name to any. If you see here some young ladies of your acquaintance in the city, they will never take notice of your formerly knowing each other, though they will talk with you of indifferent matters; so take care not to speak any thing of your family.

All these things together made me astonished, or rather stupified, and the whole seemed to me a piece of enchantment; so that I could not imagine what to think of it. With this lesson she left me, and told me she was going to order my dinner; and every time she went out, she locked the door after her. There were but two high windows in my chamber, and I could see nothing through them; but examining the room all over, I found a closet with all sorts of historical and profane books, and every thing necessary for writing. So I spent my time till the dinner came in, reading some diverting amorous stories, which was a great satisfaction to me. When Mary came with the things for the table, I told her that I was inclined to sleep, and that I would rather sleep than go to dinner; so she asked me whether she should awaken me or not, and at what time? Two hours hence (said I,) so I lay down and fell asleep, which was a great refreshment to me. At the time fixed she wakened me, and I went to dinner, at which was every thing that could satisfy the most nice appetite. After dinner she left me alone, and told me, if I wanted any thing, I might ring the bell and call: So I went to the closet again, and spent three hours in reading. I think really I was under some enchantment, for I was in a perfect suspension of thought, so as to remember neither father nor mother, for this run least in my mind, and what was at that time most in it, I do not know. Mary came and told me, that Don Francisco was come home, and that she thought he would come to see me very soon, and begged of me to prepare myself to receive him with all manner of kindness. At seven in the evening Don Francisco came, in his night-gown and night-cap, not with the gravity of an inquisitor, but with the gaiety of an officer. He saluted me with great respect and civility, and told me that he had designed to keep my company at supper, but could not that night, having some business of consequence to finish in his closet; and that his coming to see me was only out of the respect he had for my family, and to

tell me at the same time, that some of my lovers had procured
my ruin forever, accusing me in matters of religion; that the
informations were taken, and the sentence pronounced against
me, to be burnt alive, in a dry pan, with a gradual fire, but
that he, out of pity and love to my family, had stopped the ex
ecution of it.　Each of these words was a mortal stroke on my
heart, and knowing not what I was doing, I threw myself at
his feet, and said, Seignor, have you stopped the execution
for ever?　That only belongs to you to stop it, or not (said he);
and with this he wished me a good night.　As soon as he went
away, I fell a crying; but Mary came and asked me what
obliged me to cry so bitterly?　Ah! good Mary, (said I,) pray
tell me what is the meaning of the dry pan and gradual fire?
For I am in expectation of nothing but death, and that by it.
O, pray never fear, you will see another day the pan and gradual fire; but they are made for those that oppose the holy fathers' will, not for you, who are so ready to obey them.　But,
pray, was Don Francisco very civil and obliging?　I do not
know, (said I,) for his discourse has put me out of my wits;
that I know that he saluted me with respect and civility, but
he has left me abruptly.　Well, (said Mary,) you do not know
him; he is the most obliging man in the world, if people are
civil with him, and if not, he is as unmerciful as Nero; and so
for your own preservation, take care to oblige him in all respects; now, pray go to supper, and be easy.　I was so much
troubled in mind with the thoughts of the dry pan and gradual
fire, that I could neither eat nor sleep that night.　Early in
the morning Mary got up, and told me, that nobody was yet
up in the house, and that she would show me the dry pan and
gradual fire, on condition, that I should keep it a secret for her
sake, and my own too; which I having promised her, she took
me along with her and showed me a dark room with a thick
iron door, and within it an oven, and a large brass pan upon
it, with a cover of the same, and a lock to it; the oven was
burning at that time, and I asked Mary for what use the pan
was there? And she, without giving me any answer, took me
by the hand, out of that place, and carried me into a large room,
where she showed me a thick wheel, covered on both sides
with thick boards, and opening a little window, in the centre
of it, desired me to look with a candle on the inside of it, and
I saw all the circumference of the wheel set with sharp razors.
After that she showed me a pit full of serpents and toads. Then
she said to me, Now, my good mistress, I'll tell you the use of
these three things. The dry pan and gradual fire are for her-

etics, and those th\t oppose the holy father's will and pleasure for they are put all naked and alive into the pan, and the cover of .t being locked up, the executioner begins to put in the oven a small fire, and by degrees he augmenteth it till the body is burnt to ashes. The second is designed for those that speak against the pope, and the holy fathers; and they are put within the wheel, and the door being locked, the executioner turns the wheel till the person is dead. And the third is for those that contemn the images, and refuse to give the due respect and veneration to ecclesiastical persons, for they are thrown into the pit, and there they become the food of serpents and toads.

Then Mary said to me, that another day she would shew me torments for public sinners, and transgressors of the five commandments of our holy mother the church; so I, in a deep amazement, desired Mary to shew me no more places, for the very thoughts of those three, which I had seen, were enough to terrify me to the heart. So we went to my room, and she charged me again to be very obedient to all the commands Don Francisco should give me, or to be assured, if I did not, I was to undergo the torment of the dry pan. Indeed I conceived such an horror for the gradual fire, that I was not mistress of my senses, nay, nor of my thoughts: so I told Mary that I would follow her advice. If you are in that disposition (said she) leave off all fears and apprehensions, and expect nothing but pleasure and satisfaction, and all manner of recreation, and you shall begin to experience some of these things this very day. Now let me dress you, for you must go to wish a good morrow to Don Francisco, and to breakfast with him. I thought really this was a great honor to me, and some comfort to my troubled mind; so I made all the haste I could, and Mary conveyed me through a gallery into Don Francisco's apartment. He was still in bed, and desired me to sit down by him, and ordered Mary to bring the chocolate two hours after, and with this she left me alone with Don Francisco. Mary came with the chocolate, and kneeling down, paid me homage as if I was a queen; and served me first with a cup of chocolate, still on her knees, and bade me give another cup to Don Francisco myself, which he received mighty graciously, and having drunk up the chocolate, she went out. So at ten of the clock, Mary came again, and dressing me, she desired me to go along with her, and leaving Don Francisco in bed, she carried me into another chamber very delightful, and better furnished than the first; for the windows of it were lower, and I

Q

had the pleasure of seeing the river and the gardens on the
other side out of it. Then Mary told me, Madam, the young
ladies of this house will come before dinner to welcome you,
and make themse'ves happy in the honor of your company,
and I will take you to dine with them. Pray remember the advices I have given you already, and do not make yourself unhappy by asking useless questions. She had not finished these
words, when I saw entering my apartment, (which consisted
of a large anti-chamber and a bed-chamber with two large
closets) a troop of young beautiful ladies, finely dressed, who
all, one after another, came to embrace me, and to wish me
joy. My senses were in a perfect suspension, and I could not
speak a word, nor answer their kind compliments. But one
of them seeing me so silent, said to me, Madam, the solitude
of this place will affect you in the beginning, but when you
begin to be in our company, and feel the pleasure of our
amusements and recreations, you will quit your pensive
thoughts. Now we beg of you the honor to come and dine
with us to-day, and henceforth three days in a week. I thanked
them, and we went to dinner. That day we had all sorts of
exquisite meats, and were served with delicate fruits and
sweet-meats. The room was very long, with two tables on
each side, another at the front of it, and I reckoned in it that
day, 52 young ladies, the oldest of them not exceeding 24
years of age; six maids served the whole number of us, but
my Mary waited on me alone at dinner. After dinner we
went up stairs into a long gallery, all round about with lattice
windows; where, some of us playing on instruments of music,
others playing at cards, and others walking about, we spent
three hours together. At last, Mary came up, ringing a small
bell, which was the signal to retire into our rooms, as they
told me; but Mary said to the whole company, Ladies, to-day
is a day of recreation, so you may go into what room you
please, until eight o'clock, and then you are to go into your
own chambers: so they all desired leave to go with me to my
apartment, to spend the time there, and I was very glad that
they preferred my chamber to another; so all going down together, we found in my anti-chamber a table, with all sorts of
sweet-meats upon it, iced cinnamon water, and almonds milk,
and the like, every one ate and drank, but nobody spoke a
word, touching the sumptuousness of the table, nor mentioned
any thing concerning the inquisition of the holy fathers. So
we spent our time in merry, indifferent conversation. till eight
t'clock Then every one retired into their own room, and

Mary told me that Don Francisco did wait for me, so we went
to his apartment, and supper being ready, we both alone sat at
table, attended by my maid only. After supper Mary went
away, and next morning she served us with chocolate, which
we drank, and then slept till ten o'clock. Then we got up,
and my waiting maid carried me into my chamber, where I
found ready, two suits of clothes, of a rich brocade, and every
thing else, suitable to a lady of the first rank. I put on one,
and when I was quite dressed, the young ladies came to wish
me a good morrow, all dressed in different clothes, and better
than the day before, and we spent the second and third days in
the same recreation. But the third morning after drinking
chocolate, as the custom was, Mary told me, that a lady was
waiting for me in the other room, and desired me to get up,
with a haughty look. I thought that it was to give me some
new comfort and diversion; but I was very much mistaken, for
Mary conveyed me into a young lady's room, not eight feet
long, which was a perfect prison, and there, before the lady,
told me, Madam, this is your room, and this young lady your
bedfellow and comrade, and left me there with this unkind
command. O heavens! thought I, what is this that has happened to me? I fancied myself out of grief, and I perceived
now the beginning of my vexation. What is this, dear lady,
(said I) is this an enchanted palace, or a hell upon earth? I
have lost father and mother, and what is worse, I have lost my
honor and my soul forever. My new companion, seeing me
like a mad woman, took me by the hands, and said to me,
Dear sister, (for this is the name I will give you henceforth)
leave off your crying, leave off your grief and vexation for
you can do nothing by such extravagant complaints, but heap
coals of fire on your head, or rather under your body. Your
misfortunes and ours are exactly of a piece: you suffer nothing that we have not suffered before you; but we are not allowed to show our grief, for fear of greater evils. Pray, take
good courage, and hope in God; for he will find some way or
other to deliver us out of this hellish place; but above all things,
take care not to shew any uneasiness before Mary, who is the
only instrument of our torments, or comfort, and have patience
till we go to bed, and then without any fear, I will tell you
more of the matter. We do not dine with the other ladies to-
day, and may be, we shall have an opportunity of talking before night, which I hope will be of some comfort to you. I was
in a most desperate condition, but my new sister Leonora
(this was her name) prevailed so much upon me, that I over-

came my vexation before Mary came again, to bring our din·
ner, whici was very different from that I had three days before.   After dinner, another maid came to take away the plat-
ter and knife, for we had but one for us both, so locked the
door.

   Now, my sister, said she, we need not fear being disturbed
all this night: so I may safely instruct you, if you will promise me, upon the hopes of salvation, not to reveal the secret,
while you are in this place, of the things I shall tell you.   I
threw myself down at her feet, and promised secrecy.   Ther
she begun to say: My dear sister, you think it a hard ̀case
that has happened to you, I assure you all the ladies in this
house have already gone through the same, and in time you
shall know all their stories, as they hope to know yours.   I
suppose that Mary has been the chief instrument of your
fright, as she has been of ours, and I warrant you she has
shown to you some horrible places, though not all, and that at
the only thought of them, you were so much troubled in your
mind, that you have chosen the same way we did to get some
ease in our heart.   By what has happened to us, we know
that Don Francisco has been your *Nero;* for the three colors
of our clothes are the distinguishing tokens of the three holy
fathers: The red silk belongs to Francisco, the blue to Guerrero, and the green to Aliaga.   For they used to give, the
three first days, these colors to those ladies that they bring for
their use.   We are strictly commanded to make all demonstrations of joy, and to be very merry three days, when a young
lady comes here, as we did with you, and you must do with
othe s.   But after it we live like prisoners, without seeing any
living soul but the six maids, and Mary, who is the house-keep-
er.   We dine all of us, in the hall, three days a week, and
three days in our rooms.   When any of the holy fathers have
a mind for one of his slaves, Mary comes for her at nine of
the clock, and conveyeth her to his apartment: but as they
have so many, the turn comes, may-be once in a month, except for those who have the honor to give them more satisfaction than ordinary, those are sent for often.   Some nights Mary leaves the door of our rooms open, and that is a sign that
some of the fathers have a mind to come that night, but he
comes in so silent that we do not know whether he is our own
patron or not.   If one of us happen to be with child, she is removed to a better chamber, and she sees no person but the
maid till she is delivered.   The child is sent away, and we do
not know where it is gone.   Mary does not suffer quarrels

between us, for if one happens to be troublesome she is bitterly chastised for it: So we are always under a continual fear. I have been in this house these six years, and I was not fourteen years of age, when the officers took me from my father's house, and I have been brought to bed but once. We are at present fifty-two young ladies, and we loose every year six or eight, but we do not know, where they are sent; but at the same time we get new ones, and sometimes I have seen here seventy-three ladies. All our continual torment is to think, and with great reason, that when the holy fathers are tired of one, they put her to death; for they will never run the hazard of being discovered in these misdemeanors: So, though we cannot oppose their commands, and therefore we commit these enormities, yet we still fervently pray God and blessed mother, to forgive us them, since it is against our wills we do them, and to preserve us from death in this house. So my dear sister, arm yourself with patience, and put your trust in God, who will be our only defender and deliverer.

This discourse of Leonora did ease me in some measure, and I found every thing as she had told me. And so we lived together eighteen months, in which time we lost eleven ladies, and we got nineteen new ones. I knew all their stories, which I cannot tell you to night, but if you will be so kind as to stay here this week, you will not think your time lost when you come to know them all. I did promise her to stay that week, with a great deal of pleasure and satisfaction; but though it was very late, and the people of the house were retired, I begged her to make an end of the story concerning herself, which she did in the following manner:

After the eighteen months, one night, Mary came and ordered us to follow her, and going down stairs, she bade us go into a coach, and this we thought the last day of our lives We went out of the house, but where, we did not know, and were put into another house, which was worse than the first where we were confined several months, without seeing any of the Inquisitors, or Mary, or any of our companions: And in the same manner we were removed from that house to another, where we continued till we were miraculously delivered by the French officers. Mr. Faulcaut, happily for me, did open the door of my room, and as soon as he saw me, he began to show me much civility, and took me and Leonora along with him to his lodgings, and after he heard my whole story, and fearing that things would turn to our disadvantage, he ordered the next day to send us to his father. We were drest in men's

Q 2

clothes, to go the more safely, and so we came to this house, where I was kept for two years as the daughter of the old man, till Mr. Faulcaut's regiment being broke, he came home, and two months after, married me. Leonora was married to another officer, and they live in Orleans, which being in your way to Paris, I do not question but you will pay her a visit. Now my husband is at court, soliciting a new commission, and he will be very glad of your acquaintance, if he has not left Paris before you go to it. Thus ended our first entertainment the first night.

I stayed there afterwards twelve days, in which she told me the stories of all the young ladies, which Leonora did repeat to me without any alteration, as to the substantial points of them. But these diverting accounts, containing more particular circumstances touching the horrible procedure of the tribunal, but more especially, being full of amorous intrigues, I think fit not to insert them here, but to give them in a separate book, to the public if desired; for as I have many other things to say touching the corruptions of the Romish priests, these accounts may be inserted there, to shew the ill practices and corruptions of the inquisitors. So I proceed to speak of the new quarters of the French troops in the inquisition, and of the restoration of the holy fathers into it, and afterwards I will go on with the instances of the public trials.

When the Marquis de Taurcey was chosen Governor of the fort of Aljaferia, where formerly the holy office was kept, he put a strong garrison into it; the holy fathers were obliged to remove, and take away their prisoners; but they did wall all the doors of their secret prisons, where they used to keep the hellish engines, so we could not then know any thing of their barbarity in the punishment of innocents, and I think, that as they did consider themselves as unsettled, and being in hopes to recover again the former place, they did not remove their inhuman instruments of torment, so there were none found in the last house when they were turned out: nay, among so great a number of prisoners delivered out of it, we could converse with none of them, for as soon as they got out, for fear of a new order from the king or pope, they made their escape out of the country, and they were much in the right of it, for the inquisition is a place to be very much feared, and not to be tried a second time, if one can help it.

At last, after eight months reprieve, the same inquisitors came again with more power than before, for Don Pedro Guerrero, first Inquisitor, was chosen by the Pope, at King Philip's request, ecclesiastical judge, for priests, friars, and nuns, to examine and punish crimes of disaffection to his majesty: So, for a while, he was Pope, King, and Tyrant. The first thing he did was to give the public an account of the crimes for which all the prisoners that had been delivered, were confined in the inquisition, to vindicate this way the honor of the three Inquisitors, commanding at the same time, all sorts of persons to discover and secure any of the said prisoners, under pain of death. This proclamation was a thing never before heard of, and we may say, that *satisfactio non petita, generat suspicionem:* for really, by this, they did declare themselves guilty of what was charged on them, in relation to the Seraglio, in the opinion of serious, sensible people. But every body was terrified by the said proclamation, and none dared to say any thing about it.

The unmerciful Guerrero, like a roaring lion, began to devour all sorts of people, showing, by this, his great affection to the king, and fervent zeal for the pope; for, under pretence of their being disaffected to his majesty, he confined, and that publicly, near three hundred friars, and one hundred and fifty priests, and a great number of the laity. Next to this, he made himself master of their estates, which were sold publicly, being bought by the good loyal subjects. He did suspend, *ab officio et beneficio,* many secular priests, and banished them out of the dominions of Spain; whipt others publicly, banished and whipt friars, and took the liberty insolently to go into the monastery of the nuns of St. Lucia, and whipt six of them for being affected to Charles the IIId, and he imprisoned Donna Catherina Cavero, only for being the head of the imperial faction. But observe, that this whipping of the nuns is only giving them a discipline, i. e. so many strokes with a rod on the shoulders; but Guerrero was so impudent and barefaced a *Nero,* that commanding the poor nuns to turn their habits backwards, and discover their shoulders, he himself was the executioner of this unparalleled punishment.

As to the laity that were put into the inquisition, and whose estates were seized, we did not hear any thing of them, but I am sure they did end their miserable lives in that horrid place. Many of them left a great family behind them, who all were reduced to beggary; for when the heads of them were confined, all the families must suffer with them: And this is the reason, why more than two thousand families left the city, and every thing they had, rather than undergo the miseries of that time, and the cruel persecution of Guerrero. So we may believe, that having so great authority as he had, he soon could recruit his Seraglio.

Though Guerrero was so busy in the affairs of the king, he did not forget the other business concerning the catholic faith; so, to make the people sensible of his indefatigable zeal, he began again to summons priests and friars to new trials, of which I am going to speak.

The trial of a Friar of St. Jerome, organist of the convent in Saragossa.

All the summoned persons being together in the hall, the prisoner and a young boy were brought out; and after the first inquisitor had finished his bitter correction, the secretary read the examinations and sentence, as follows:

Whereas, informations were made, and by evidences proved, that Fr. Joseph Peralta has committed the crime of Sodomy, with the present John Romeo, his disciple, which the said Romeo himself, owned upon interrogatories of the holy inquisitors: they having an unfeigned regard for the order of St. Jerome, do declare and condemn the said Fr. Joseph Peralta, to a year's confinement in his own convent, but that he may assist at the divine service, and celebrate mass. *Item*, for an example to other like sinners, the holy fathers declare that the said John is to be whipped through the public streets of the town, and receive at every corner, as it is a custom, five lashes; and that he shall wear a coroza, i. e. a sort of a mitre on his head, feathered all over, as a mark of his crime. Which sentence is to be executed on Friday next, without any appeal.

After the secretary had done, Don Pedro Guerrero did ask Fr. Joseph, whether he had any thing to say against the sentence or not? And he answering, no, the prisoners were carried back to their prisons, and the company were dismissed. Observe the equity of the inquisitors in this case: the boy was but fourteen years of age, under the power of Fr. Joseph, and he was charged with the penalty and punishment Fr. Joseph did deserve. The poor boy was whipped according to the sentence, and died the next day.

The Trial of Father Pueyo, Confessor of the Nuns at St. Munica.

This criminal had been but six days in the inquisition, before he was brought to hear his sentence, and every thing being performed as before, the secretary read.

. Whereas father Pueyo has committed fornication with five spiritual daughters, (so the nuns which confess to the same confessor continually, are called) which is, besides fornication, sacrilege and transgression of our commands, and he himself having owned the fact, we therefore declare that he shall keep his cell for three weeks, and lose his employment, &c.

The inquisitor asked him whether he had any thing to say against it: and father Pueyo said, holy father, I remember that when I was chosen father confessor of the nuns of our mother St. Monica, you had a great value for five young ladies of the monastery, and you sent for me, and begged of me to take care of them: so I have done, as a faithful servant, and may say unto you, *Domine quinque talenta tradidisti me, ecce alia quinque super lucratus sum.* The inquisitors could not forbear laughing at this application of the scripture; and Don Pedro Guerrero was so well pleased with this answer, that he told him, *you said well:* Therefore, *Peccata tua remittuntur tibi, nunc vade in pace, et noli amplius peccare.* This was a pleasant trial, and Pueyo was excused from the performance of his penance by this impious jest.

The trial and sentence of the Licentiate Lizondo.

The secretary read the examinations, evidence and convictions, and the said Lizondo (who was a licentiate, or Master o Arts) himself did own the fact, which was as follows:

The said Lizondo, though an ingenious man, and fit for the sacerdotal function, would not be ordained, giving out that he thought himself unworthy of so high dignity, as to have every day the Saviour of the world in his hands, after the consecration. And by this feigned humility he began to insinuate himself into the people's opinion, and pass for a religious, godly man, among them. He studied physic, and practised it only with the poor, in the beginning; but being called afterwards by the rich and especially by the Nuns, at last he was found out in his wickedness; for he used to give something to make the young ladies sleep, and this way he obtained his lascivious desires. But one of the evidences swore that he had done these things by the help of magic, and that he had used only an incantation, with which he made every body fall asleep:— But this he absolutely denied, as an imposition and falsity.— We did expect a severe sentence, but it was only that the licentiate was to discover to the inquisitors, on a day appointed by them, the receipt for making the people sleep; and that the punishment to be inflicted on him, was to be referred to the

discretion of the holy fathers.   We saw him afterwards every
day, walking in the streets; and this was all his punishment
We must surely believe that such crimes are reckoned but a
trifle among them, for very seldom they show any great displeasure or severity to those that are found guilty of them.

Of the Order of the Inquisitors to arrest an Horse, and to bring him to the Holy Office.

The case well deserves my trouble in giving a full account
of it; so I will explain it from the beginning to the end.   The
rector of the university of Saragossa has his own officers to ar
rest the scholars, and punish them if they commit any crime.
Among their officers there was one called Guadalaxara, who
was mighty officious and troublesome to the collegians or stu
dents; for upon the least thing in the world he arrested them
The scholars did not love him at all, and contrived how they
should punish him, or to play some comical tricks upon him.
At last, some of the strongest agreed to be at the bottom of the
steeple of the university in the evening, and six of them in the
belfry, who were to let down a lusty young scholar, tied with
a strong rope, at the hearing of the word *war*.   So the scholars that were in the yard, and at the bottom of the steeple,
picked a quarrel purposely to bring Guadalaxara there, and
when he was already among them, arresting one, they cried
out *war*.   At which sign the six in the steeple let down the
tied scholar, who taking in his arms Guadalaxara, and being
pulled up by the six, he carried him almost 20 feet high, and
let him fall down.   The poor man was crying out, O Jesus!
the Devil has taken me up.   The students that were at the
bottom had instruments of music, and put off their cloaks to
receive him in, and as he cried out, *the Devil, the Devil*, the
musicians answered him with the instruments, repeating the
same words he pronounced himself, and with this, gathering
together great numbers of scholars, they took him in the middle, continuing always the music and songs, to prevent, by this,
the people's taking notice of it, and every body believed that it
was only a mere scholastic diversion: So, with this melody
and rejoicings, they carried the troublesome Guadalaxara out
of the gates of the city into the field, called the *Burnt Place*,
because formerly the heretics were burnt in that field.   There
was a dead horse, and opening his belly, they tied the poor
officer by the hands and legs, and placed him within the horse's
belly, which they sewed, leaving the head of Guadalaxara
out, under the tail of the horse, and so they went back into

the city. How dismal that night was to the poor man, any
body may imagine; but yet it was very sweet to him, in comparison to what he suffered in the morning; for the dogs going
to eat of the dead horse's flesh, he, for fear they should eat off
his head, continually cried out, ho! ho! *perros,* i. e. dogs, and
that day he found that not only the scholars, but even the very
dogs were afraid of him, for dogs did not dare approach the
dead horse. The laborers of the city, who were a most ignorant sort of people, but very pleasant in their rustic expressions, going out to the field, by break of the day, saw the dogs
near the horse, and heard the voice, ho! ho! *perros.* They
looked up and down, and seeing nobody, drew near the horse,
and hearing the same voice, frightened out of their senses,
went into the city again, and gave out that a dead horse was
speaking in the *burnt field;* and as they affirmed and swore
the thing to be true, crowds of people went to see and hear
the wonder, or, as many others said, the miracle of a dead
horse speaking. A public notary was among the mob, but no
one dared to go near the horse. The notary went to the inquisitors to make affidavit of this case, and added that no one
having courage enough to approach the horse, it was proper
to send some of the friars, with holy water and stola, to exorcise
the horse, and find out the cause of his speaking. But the
inquisitors who think to command beasts, as well as reasonable
creatures, sent six of their officers, with strict orders, to carry
the horse to the holy office. The officers having an opinion
that the devil must submit to them, went, and approaching the
horse, they saw the head under the tail, and the poor man crying out, help, take me out of this putrified grave; for God's
sake, good people, make haste, for I am not the devil, nor ghost,
nor apparition, but the real body and soul of Guadalaxara,
the constable of the university; and I do renounce, in this place,
the office of arresting scholars forever; and I do forgive them
this wrong done to me, and thanks be to God, and to the Virgin of Pilar, who has preserved my body from being converted into a dead horse, that I am alive still.

These plain demonstrations of the nature of the thing did not
convince, in the least, the officers of the inquisition, who are
always very strict in the performance of the orders given
them, so they took the dead horse and carried it to the inqui
sition. Never were more people seen in the streets and win
dows than on that day, besides the great crowd that followed
the corpse, which I saw myself; the inquisitors having notice
beforehand, went to the hall to receive the informations from

the horse; and after they had asked him many questions, the
poor man pushed up the tail with his nose to speak, to see, and
to be seen, still answering them; the wise holy fathers trusting not to his information, gave orders to the officers to carry
the speaking horse to the torture, which being done accordingly, as they began to turn the ropes through the horse's belly,
at the third turning of them the skin of the belly broke, and
the real body of Guadalaxara appeared in all his dimensions,
and by the horse's torture, he saved his life. The poor man
died three weeks after, and he forgave the scholars who contrived this mischief, and an elegy was made on his death.

*Thesis defended by F. James Garcia, in the hall of the
Inquisition.*

The case of the Rev. father F. James Garcia, made a great
noise in Spain, which was thus:

This same James Garcia is the learned man of whom I have
spoken several times in my book. His father, though a shoemaker by trade, was very honest and well beloved, and as
God had bestowed on him riches enough, and having but one
child, he gave him the best education he could, in the college
of Jesuits, where, in the study of grammar, he signalized himself for his vivacity and uncommon wit. After going to the
university, he went through philosophy and divinity, to the
admiration of his masters; he entered St. Augustin's order,
and after his noviciate was ended, desired to obtain the degree
of master of arts; he defended public thesis of philosophy,
and after, other thesis of divinity, without any moderator to
answer for him in case of necessity. The thesis and some
propositions were quite new to the learned people; for among
other propositions, one was *Innocentium esse verum pontificem,
non est de fide,* i. e. it is not an article of faith that Innocent is the
true pope. And next to this proposition, this other: *Non cre-
dere quod non video, non est contra fidem.* It is not against
the Catholic faith not to believe what I do not see.

Upon account of these two propositions, he was summoned
by the inquisitors, and ordered to defend the said propositions
separately, in the hall of the inquisition, and answer for six
days together, to all the arguments of the learned Qualificators, which he did, and kept his ground, that instead of
being punished for it, he was honored with the cross of the
Qualificator, after the examinations were made of the purity
of his blood.

Sentence given against Lawrence Castro, goldsmith of Saragossa.

Lawrence Castro was the most famous and wealthy goldsmith in the city, and as he went one day to carry a piece of plate to Don Pedro Guerrero, before he paid him, he bade him go and see the house along with one of his domestic servants, which he did, and seeing nothing but doors of iron, and hearing nothing but lamentations of the people within; having returned to the inquisitor's apartment, Don Pedro asked him, Lawrence, how do you like this place? To which Lawrence said, I do not like it at all, for it seems to me the very hell upon earth. This innocent, but true answer, was the only occasion of his misfortune; for he was immediately sent into one of the hellish prisons, and at the same time many officers went to his house to seize upon every thing, and that day he appeared at the bar, and his sentence was read: he was condemned to be whipped through the public streets, to be marked on his shoulders with a burning iron, and to be sent forever to the gallies: but the good, honest, unfortunate man died that very day; all his crime being only to say, that the holy office did seem to him hell on earth.

. At the same time, a lady of good fortune was whipped, because she said in company, I do not know whether the pope is a man or a woman, and I hear wonderful things of him every day, and I imagine he must be an animal very rare. For these words she lost honor, fortune and life, for she died six days after the execution of her sentence: and thus the holy fathers punish trifling things, and leave unpunished horrible crimes.

The following instance will be a demonstration of this truth, and show how the inquisitors favor the ecclesiastics more than the laity, and the reason why they are more severe upon one than the other.

In the diocess of Murcia was a parish priest in a village in the mountains. The people of it were almost all of them shepherds, and were obliged to be always abroad with their flocks: so the priest being the commander of the shepherdesses, began to preach every Friday in the afternoon, all the congregation being composed of the women of the town. His constant subject was, the indispensable duty of paying the tithes to him, and this not only of the fruits of the earth, but of the seventh of their sacraments too, which is matrimony, and he had such great eloquence to persuade them to secrecy,

R

as to their husbands, and a ready submission to him, that he
began to reap the fruit of his doctrine in a few days, and by
this wicked example, he brought into the list of the tithes all
the married women of the town, and he received from them
the tenth for six years together; but his infernal doctrine and
practice was discovered by a young woman who was to be
married, of whom the priest asked the tithe before hand; but
she telling it to her sweet-heart, he went to discover the case
to the next commissary of the inquisition, who having examined the matter, and found it true, he took the priest and sent
him to the inquisition; he was found guilty of so abominable a
sin, and he himself confessed it; and what was the punishment
inflicted on him? Only to confine him in a friar's cell for six
months. The priest being confined, made a virtue of necessity, and so composed a small book, entitled, *The True Penitent*, which was universally approved by all sorts of people, for
solid doctrine and morality. He dedicated the work to the holy inquisitors, who, for a reward of his pains, gave him another parish a great deal better than the first. But hardened
wretch! There he fell again to the same trade of receiving
the tithes; upon which the people of the parish complained to
the governor, who acquainted the king with the case, and his
majesty ordered the inquisitors to apply a speedy remedy to
it; so the holy fathers sent him to the pope's gallies for five
years time.

I must own, it is quite against my inclination to give this
and the like accounts, for it will seem very much out of the
way of a clergyman; but if the reader will make reflections on
them, and consider that my design is only to shew how unjust-
ly the inquisitors act in this and other cases, he will certainly
excuse me; for they really deserve to be ridiculed more than
argued against, reasoning being of no force with them, but a
discovery of their infamous actions and laws, may-be will pro
duce, if not in them, in some people at least, a good effect.

The Roman Catholics believe there is a purgatory, and that
the souls suffer more pains in it than in hell. But I think the
inquisition is the only purgatory on earth, and the holy fathers
are the judges and executioners in it. The reader may form
a dreadful idea of the barbarity of that tribunal, by what I
have already said, but I am sure it will never come up to what
it is in reality, for it passeth all understanding, not as the
peace of God, but as the war of the devil.

So that we may easily know by this, and the aforesaid account, that they leave off all observance of the first precepts

of the holy office, and chastise only those that speak either against the pope, clergy, or the holy inquisition.

The only reason of settling that tribunal in Spain, was to examine and chastise sinners, or those that publicly contemned the faith. But now a man may blaspheme and commit the most heinous crimes, if he says nothing against the three mentioned articles, is free from the hellish tribunal.

Let us except from this rule the rich Jews, for the poor are in no fear of being confined there; they are the rich alone that suffer in that place, not for the crime of Jewdaism, (though this is the color and pretence,) but the crime of having riches. Francisco Alfaro, a Jew, and a very rich one, was kept in the inquisition of Seville four years, and after he had lost all he had in the world, was discharged out of it with a small correction: this was to encourage him to trade again and get more riches, which he did in four years time. Then he was put again in the holy office, with the loss of his goods and money. And after three years imprisonment he was discharged, and ordered to wear for six months, the mark of *San-Benito*, i. e. a picture of a man in the middle of the fire of hell, which he was to wear before his breast publicly.— But Alfaro a few days after, left the city of Seville, and seeing a pig without the gate, he hung the *San-Benito* on the pig's neck, and made his escape. I saw this Jew in Lisbon, and he told me the story himself, adding, Now I am a poor Jew, I tell every body so, and though the inquisition is more severe here than in Spain, nobody takes notice of me. I am sure they would confine me forever, if I had as much riches as I had in Seville. Really, the holy office is more cruel and inhuman in Portugal than in Spain, for I never saw any publicly burnt in my own country, and I saw in Lisbon seven at once, four young women and three men; two young women were burnt alive and an old man, and the others were strangled first.

But being obliged to dismiss this chapter, and leave out many curious histories, I promise to relate them in the second part of this work. Now let me entreat all true protestants to join with me in hearty prayer to God almighty.

O eternal God, who dost rule the hearts of kings, and orderest every thing to the glory of the true religion, pour thy holy spirit upon the heart of Louis the first, that he may see the barbarous, unchristian practices of the inquisitors, and with a firm resolution abolish all laws contrary to those given us by thy only son, our Saviour, Jesus Christ our Lord. *Amen.*

PART IV.

Of their Prayers, Adoration of Images, and Relics.

ARTICLE I.

Of their Prayers.

THE prayers sung ör said, in the church, are seven canonical hours, or the *seven services,* viz: *Tertia, Sexta, Nona, Vesperæ, Matutina,* and *Completæ.*—*Prima* is composed of the general confession, three psalms, and many other prayers, with the *Martyrologio Sanctorum,* i. e. with a commemoration of all the saints of that day. *Tertia* is a prayer or service of three psalms, anthem, and the collect of the day, &c. *Sexta* and *Nona* are the same. *Vesperæ,* or evening songs contain five anthems, five psalms, an hymn, *Magnificat,* or msoul doth magnify, &c., with an anthem, collect of the day and commemorations of some saints. *Matutina,* or matins is the longest service of the seven, for it contains, 1st. The psalm. *O come let us sing:* 2d. An hymn: 3d. Three anthems three psalms, and three lessons of the Old Testament: 4th Three anthems, three psalms, and three lessons of the day. i. e. of the life of the saint of that day, or the mystery of it 5th. Three anthems, three psalms, three lessons, of which the first beginneth with the gospel of the day, and two or three lines of it, and the rest is an homily, or exposition of the gospel: 6th. *Te Deum:* 7th. Five anthems, five psalms, an hymn, anthem of the day, the psalm, *Blessed be the Lords of Israel,* &c., the collect of the day, and some commemorations.—*Completæ,* or complices, is the last service, which contains the general confession, an anthem, three or four psalms, and *Lord now lettest thou,* &c., and some other adherent prayers for the Virgin, the holy cross, saints, &c. All these seven services are said, or sung, in Latin, every day in the cathedral churches, but not in all the parish churches.

In the cathedral churches on the festivals of the first class, or the greatest festivals, as those of Christ and the Virgin

196

Maiy, all the seven canonical hours are sung, *Prima* at six in the morning, and a mass after it. *Tertia* at ten, the great mass after, and after the mass, *Sexta* and *Nona*. At two, or three in the afternoon, the *evening song;* at seven, *complices;* and half an hour after midnight, the *matins*. In the festivals of the second class, as those of the apostles, and some saints placed in that class by the popes, *Tertia,* evening songs and matins are all that are sung, and likewise every day, though not with organ, nor music.

In the parish churches the priests sing only *Tertia,* and *evening songs* on Sundays and festivals of the first class; except where there are some foundations, or settlements for singing *evening songs* on other private days. But the great mass is always sung in every parish church, besides the masses for the dead, which are settled to be sung.

In the convents of the friars, they observe the method of the cathedral, except some days of the week granted to them by the prior, as recreation days, and then they say the service, and go to divert themselves all the day after. As to the nuns, I have given an account in the first chapter of their lives and conversation.

The priests and friars that do not say, or sing the service with the community, are obliged in conscience to say those seven canonical hours every day, and if they do not, they commit a mortal sin, and ought to confess it among the sins of *omission*. Besides these seven services, they have, not by precept, but by devotion, the service, or small office of the Virgin Mary, the seven penitential psalms, and other prayers of saints, which are by long custom become services of precept, for they never will dare to omit them, either for devotion's sake, or for fear that the laity would tax them with coldness and negligence in matters of exemplary devotion.

As to the public prayers of the laity, they all are contained in the beads or rosary of the Virgin Mary, and to give them some small comfort, there is a fixed time in the evening in every church for the rosary. The sexton rings the bell, and when the parishioners, both men and women, are gathered together, the minister of the parish, or any other priest, comes out of the vestry, in his surplice, and goes to the altar of the Virgin Mary, and lighting two or more candles on the altar's table, he kneels down before the altar, makes the sign of the cross, and begins the rosary with a prayer to the Virgin: and after he has said half of the *Ave Maria,* &c., the people say the other half, which he repeats ten times, the people doing

R 2

the same. Then he says *Gloria Patri,* &c.; and the people answer, *As it was in the beginning,* &c. Then, in the same manner, the priest says half of *Our Father,* and ten times half *Ave Maria,* and so he and the people do, till they have said them fifty times. This done, the priest says another prayer to the Virgin, and begins her litany, and after every one of her titles, or encomiums, the people answer *Ora pro nobis,* pray for us. The litany ended, the priest and people visit five altars, saying before each of them one *Pater Noster,* and ʻone *Ave Maria,* with *Gloria Patri;* and lastly, the priest, kneeling down before the great altar, says an act of contrition, and endeth with *Lighten our darkness, we beseech thee,* &c. All the prayers of the rosary are in the vulgar tongue, except, *Gloria Patri* and *Ora pro nobis,* i. e. *Glory be to thee,* &c., and *Pray for us.*

After the rosary, in some churches, there is *Oratio Mentalis,* i. e. a prayer of meditation, and for this purpose the priest of the rosary, or some other of devout life and conversation, readeth a chapter in some devout book, as *Thomas à Kempis,* or *Francis de Sales,* or *Father Eusebio,* of the difference between temporal and eternal things; and when he has ended the chapter, every one on their knees, begin to meditate on the contents of the chapter, with great devotion and silence. They continue in that prayer half an hour or more, and after it, the priests say a prayer of thanksgiving to God Almighty, for the benefits received from him by all there present, &c.

I said *public prayers of the laity;* for when they assist at the divine service, or hear mass, they only hear what the priest says in *Latin,* and answer Amen. Generally speaking, they do not understand Latin, especially in towns of 300 houses, and villages, there can scarcely be found one *Latinist,* except the curate, and even he very often doth not understand perfectly well what he reads in *Latin.* By this universal ignorance we may say, that they do not know what they pray for; nay, if a priest was so wicked in heart, as to curse the people in church, and damn them all in *Latin,* the poor idiots must answer *Amen,* knowing not what the priest says. I do not blame the common people in this point, but I blame the pope and priests that forbid them to read the scripture, and by this prohibition they cannot know what St. Paul says about praying in the vulgar tongue: So the pope and priests, and those that plead ignorance, must answer for the people before the dreadful tribunal of God.

Besides this public prayer of the rosary, they have private prayers at home, as the *crea, the Lord's prayer, a prayer to the Virgin, the act of contrition,* and other prayers to saints, angels, and for souls in purgatory. But this prayer of the rosary is not only said in church, but is sung in the streets, and the custom was introduced by the *Dominican* friars, who, in some parts of Spain, are called *The Fathers of the holy rosary.* Sundays and holy days, after *evening songs,* the prior of the Dominicans, with all his friars and corporation, or fraternity of the holy rosary, begins the Virgin's *evening songs,* all the while ringing the bells, which is to call for the procession, and when the evening songs are over, the clerk of the convent, drest in his *Alva* or surplice, taking the standard where the picture of the Virgin Mary is drawn with a frame of roses, and two novices in surplices, with candlesticks, walking on each side of the standard, the procession beginneth. First, all the brethren of the corporation go out of the church, each with a wax candle in his hand; the standard followeth after, and all the friars, in two lines, follow the standard. In this order the procession goes through the streets, all singing *Ave Maria,* and the laity answering as before. They stop in some public street, where a friar, upon a table, preacheth a sermon of the excellency and power of the rosary, and gathering the people, they go back again into the church, where the rosary being over, another friar preacheth upon the same subject another sermon, exhorting the people to practise this devotion of the rosary; and they have carried so far this extravagant folly, that if a man is found dead, and has not the beads or rosary of the Virgin in his pocket, that man is not reckoned a christian, and he is not to be buried in consecrated ground till somebody knoweth him, and certifieth that such a man was a christian, and passeth his word for him. So every body takes care to have always the beads or rosary in his pocket, as the characteristic of a christian. But this devotion of the rosary is made so common among bigots, that they are always with the beads in their hands, and at night round about their necks. There is nothing more usual in Spain and Portugal, than to see people in the markets, and in the shops, praying with their beads, and selling and buying at the same time; nay, the procurers in the great Piazza are praying with their beads, and at the same time contriving and agreeing with a man for wicked intrigues. So all sorts of persons having it as a law to say the rosary every day: some say it walking, others in company, (keeping silent for a while) but the rest talking

or laughing: so great is their attention and devotion in this
indispensable prayer of the holy rosary.

But this is not the worst of their practices; for if a man or
priest neglects one day to say the rosary, he doth not commit
a mortal sin, though this is a great fault among them; but the
divine service, or seven canonical hours, every priest, friar,
and nun, is obliged to say every day, or else they commit a
mortal sin, by the statutes of the church and popes. This service, which is to be said in private, and with christian devotion,
is as much profaned among ecclesiastics and nuns, as the rosary among the laity; for I have seen many ecclesiastics (and
I have done it myself several times) play at cards, and have
the breviary on the table, to say the divine service at the
same time. Others walking in company, and others doing
still worse things than these, have the breviary in their hands,
and reading the service, when they at the same time are *in
occasione proxima peccati;* and, notwithstanding they believe
they have performed exactly that part of the ecclesiastical
duty.

I know that modesty obligeth me to be more cautious in this
account, and if it was not for this reason, I could detect the
most horrible things of friars and nuns that ever were seen
or heard in the world; but leaving this unpleasant subject, I
come to say something of the profit the priests and friars get
by their irreligious prayers, and by what means they recommend them to the laity.

The profits priest and friars get by their prayers, are not so
great as that they get by absolution and masses; for it is by an
accident, if sometimes they are desired to pray for money.—
There is a custom, that if one in a family is sick, the head of
the family sends immediately to some devout, religious friar
or nun, to pray for the sick, so by this custom, not all priests
and friars are employed, but only those that are known to live
a regular life. But because the people are very much mista
ken in this, I crave leave to explain the nature of those whom
the people believe religious friars, or in Spanish, *Gazmonnos.*
In every convent there are eight or ten of those *Gazmonnos,* or
devout men, who, at the examination for confessors and preachers, were found quite incapable of the performance of the
great duties, and so were not approved by the examiners of the
convent. And though they scarcely understand *Latin,* they
are permitted to say mass, that by that means the convent
might not be at any expense with them. These poor idiots,
being not able to get any thing by selling absolutions, nor by

preaching, undertake the life of a *Gazmonnos*, and live a mighty retired life, keeping themselves in their cells, or chambers, and not conversing with the rest of the community: so their brethren *Gazmonnos* visit them, and among themselves, there is nothing spared for their diversion, and the carrying on their private designs.

When they go out of the convent it must be with one of the same *farandula*, or trade.   Their faces look pale; their eyes are fixed on the ground, their discourse all of heavenly things, their visits in public, and their meat and drink but very little before the world, though in great abundance between themselves, or, as they say, *Inter privatos parietes*.   By this mortifying appearance, the people believe them to be godly men, and in such a case as sickness, they rather send to one of these to pray for the sick, than to other friars of less public fame.— But those hypocrites, after the apprenticeship of this trade is over, are very expert in it, for if any body sends for one of them, either without money, or some substantial present, they say they cannot go, for they have so many sick persons to visit and pray for, that it is impossible for them to spare any time. But if money or a present is sent to him, he is ready to go and pray every where.

So these ignorant, hypocritical friars, are always followed by the ignorant people, who furnish them with money and presents, for the sake of their prayers, and they live more comfortable than many rich people, and have one hundred pistoles in their pockets oftener than many of the laity who have good estates.

Some people will be apt to blame me for giving so bad a character of those devout men in appearance, when I cannot be a judge of their hearts.   But I answer, that I do not judge thus of all of them, but only of those that I knew to be great hypocrites and sinners; for I saw seven of them taken up by the inquisitors, and I was at their public trial, as I have given an account in the former chapter.   So, by these seven we may give a near guess of the others, and say, that their outward mortifying appearance is only a cloak of their private designs.

There are some nuns likewise, who follow the same trade as I have given one instance in the chapter of the inquisition, and though the ignorant people see every day some of these *Gazmonnos* taken up by the inquisitors, they are so blinded, that they always look for one of them to pray.   These hypocrites do persuade the heads of families, that they are obliged in conscience to mind their own business, rather than to pray, and that the providence of God has ordered every thing for the best for his creatures, and that he, (foreseeing that the heads of families would have no time to spare for prayers) has chosen such religious men to pray for them, so they are well recompensed for their prayers, and God only knoweth whether they pray or not. Most commonly, when they are wanted, they are at the club, with their brethren *Gazmonnos*, eating and drinking, afterwards painting their faces with some yellow drug, to make themselves look pale and mortified. O good God! how great is thy patience in tolerating such wicked men.

As to the means the priests and friars make use of, and the doctrine 'hey preach to recommend this exercise of praying to the people, I can give one instance of them as matter of fact. Being desired to preach upon the subject of prayer, by the mother abbess of the nuns of St. Clara, who told me in private, that many of her nuns did neglect their prayers, and were most commonly at the grate with their devotees, and the good mother, out of pure zeal, told me that such nuns were the devils of the monastery; so to oblige her, I went to preach, and took my text out of the gospel of St. Mathew, chap. xvii. 5. 21. *Howbeit, this kind goeth not out but by prayer and fasting*, but in our vulgar, the text is thus, *Howbeit this kind of devils, &c.* And after I had explained the text, confining myself wholly to the learned Silveria's commentaries, I did endeavor to prove, that the persons devoted to God by a public profession of monastical life, were bound in conscience to pray without ceasing, as St. Paul tells us, and that if they neglected this indispensable duty, they were worse than devils: and after this proposition, I did point out the way and method to tame such devils, which was by prayer and fasting. And lastly, the great obligation laid upon us by Jesus Christ and his apostles, to make use of this exercise of prayer, which I did recommend as a *medium* to attain the highest degree of glory in heaven, and to exceed even angels, prophets, patriarchs, apostles, and all the saints of the heavenly court.

I do not intend to give a copy of the sermon, but I cannot pass by the proof I gave to confirm my proposition, to show by it, the trifling method of preaching most generally used among the Roman Catholic preachers.

The historiographers and chronologers of St. Augustine's order, say, (said I) that the great father Augustine is actually in heaven, before the throne of the holy Trinity, as a reward for the unparalleled zeal and devotion he had upon earth, for that holy mystery, and because he spent all his free time on earth in praying, which makes him now in heaven greater than all sorts of saints. They say more, viz. that in the heaven of the holy trinity, there are only the Father, the Son, the Holy Ghost, the Virgin Mary, St. Joseph, and, the last of all, St. Augustine. Thus father Garcia, in his Santoral, printed in Saragossa, in 1707 *vide* sermon on St. Augustine.

To this, I knew would be objected the 11th verse of the xi. chap. of St. Matthew, *Among them that are born of women, there hath not risen a greater than* John *the Baptist.* To which I did answer, that there was no rule without an exception, and that St. Augustine was excepted from it: and this I proved by a maxim received among divines, viz. *Infimum supremi excedit supremum infimi,* the least of a superior order exceeds the greatest of an inferior. There are three heavens, as St. Paul says, and, as other expositors, three orders. They place in the first heaven, the three divine persons, the Virgin Mary, St. Joseph, and St. Augustine; in the second, the spiritual intelligences; and in the third, St. John Baptist, at the head of all the celestial army of saints. Then, if St. Augustine is the last in the highest heaven, though St. John is the first in the lowest, we must conclude, by the aforementioned maxim, that the great Father Augustine exceeds in glory all the saints of the heavenly court, as a due reward for his fervent zeal in praying, while he was here below among men.

The more I remember this and the like nonsensical proofs and methods of preaching, the more I thank God for his goodness in bringing me out of that communion into another, where, by application, I learn how to make use of the scripture, to the spiritual good of souls, and not to amusements which are prejudicial to our salvation.

Thus I have given you an account of the public and private prayers of priests, friars, nuns, and laity; of the profits they have by it, and of the methods they take to recommend this exercise of praying, to all sorts and conditions of people. Sure I am, that after a mature consideration of their way of praying, and of that we make use of in our reformed congregations, every body may easily know the great difference between them both, and that the form and practice of prayers among Protestants, are more agreeable to God, than those of the Romish priests and friars can be.

ARTICLE II.

Of the adoration of Images.

The adoration of images was commanded by several gene al councils, and many popes, whose commands and decrees are obeyed as articles of our christian faith, and every one that breaketh them, or, in his outward practice, doth not conform to them, is punished by the inquisitors as an heretic—therefore, it is not to be wondered at, if people, educated in such a belief, without any knowledge of the sin of such idolatrous practices, do adore the images of the saints with the same, and sometimes more devotion of heart than they do God Almighty in Spirit.

I begin, therefore, this article with myself, and my own forgetfulness of God. When I was in the college of Jesuits to learn grammar, the teachers were so careful in recommending to their scholars devotion to the Virgin Mary of Pilar, of Saragossa, that this doctrine, by long custom, was so deeply impressed in our hearts, that every body, after the school was over, used to go to visit the blessed image, this being a rule and a law for us all, which was observed with so great strictness, that if any student by accident missed that exercise of devotion, he was the next day severely whipped for it. For my part, I can aver, that during the three years I went to the college, I never was punished for want of devotion to the Virgin. In the beginning of our exercises, we were bidden to write the following words, *Dirige in calamum Virgo Maria, meum;* Govern my pen, O Virgin Mary! And this was my constant practice in the beginning of all my scholastical and moral writings, for the space of ten years, in which, I do protest, before my eternal Judge, I do not remember whether I did invoke God, or call on his sacred name or not. This I remember, that in all my distempers and sudden afflictions, my daily exclamation was, *O Virgin del Pilar!* Help me, O Virgin! &c. so great was my devotion to her, and so great my forgetfulness of our God and Saviour Jesus Christ. And indeed a man that does not inquire into the matter, hath more reason, according to the doctrine taught in those places, to trust in the Virgin Mary, than in Jesus Christ: for these are common expressions in their sermons, *That neither God nor Jesus Christ can do any thing in Heaven, but what is approved by the blessed Mary, that she is the door of glory, and that nobody can enter into it, but by her influence,* &c. And the preachers give out these propositions as principles of our faith, insomuch, that if any body dares to believe the contrary, he is reputed an heretic, and punished as such.

But because this article requireth a full explanation, and an account to be given of the smallest circumstances belonging to it, I shall keep the class and order of Saints, and of the adoration they are worshipped with, by most people of the Roman Catholic countries. And first of all, the image of Jesus Christ is adored as if the very image of wood was the very Christ of flesh and bones. To clear this, I will give an instance or two of what I saw myself.

In the cathedral church of St. Salvator, there was an old image of Jesus Christ, crucified, behind the choir, in a small unminded chapel; nobody took notice of that crucifix, except a devout prebend, or cannon of the church, who did use every day to kneel down before that image, and pray heartily to it. The prebend (though a religious man in the outward appearance) was ambitious in his heart of advancement in the church; so, one day, as he was on his knees before the old image, he was begging that, by its power and influence, he might be made a bishop, and after a cardinal, and lastly, pope; to which earnest request the image made him this answer: *Et tu que me ves a qui, que hazes pormi?* i. e. *And thou seest me here, what dost thou do for me?* These very words are written, at this present day, in gilt letters upon the crown of thorns of the crucifix: To which the prebend answered, *Domine peccavi, et malum coram te feci;* i. e. *Lord I have sinned, and done evil before thee.* To this humble request, the image said, *Thou shalt be a bishop;* and accordingly he was made a bishop soon after. These words, spoken by the crucifix of the cathedral church, made such a noise, that crowds of well disposed, credulous people used to come every day to offer their gifts to the miraculous image of our Saviour; and the image, which was not minded at all before, after it spoke, was, and has been ever since, so much reverenced, that the offerings of the first six years were reckoned worth near a million of crowns. The history of the miracle reports, that the thing did happen in the year 1562, and that the chapter did intend to build a chapel in one corner of the church, to put the crucifix in with more veneration and decency; but the image spoke again to the prebend, and said, *My pleasure is to continue where I am till the end of the world:* So the crucifix is kept in the same chapel, but richly adorned, and nobody ever since dare touch any thing belonging to the image, for fear of disobliging the crucifix. It has an

S

old wig on its head, the very sight of which is enough to make every one laugh; its face looks so black and disfigured, that nobody can guess whether it is the face of a man or woman, but every body believes that it is a crucifix, by the other circumstances of the cross, and crown of thorns.

The image is so much adored, and believed to have such a power of working miracles, that if they ever carry it out in a procession, it must be on an urgent necessity: For example, if there is a want of rain in such a degree that the harvest is almost lost, then, by the common consent of the archbishop and chapter, a day is fixed to take the crucifix out of its chapel in a public procession, at which all the priests and friars are to assist without any excuse, and the devout people too, with marks of repentance, and public penances. Likewise the archbishop, viceroy, and magistrates, ought to assist in robes of mourning; so when the day comes, which is most commonly very cloudy, and disposed to rain, all the communities meet together in the cathedral church: And in the year 1706, I saw, upon such an occasion as this, 600 disciplinants, whose blood ran from their shoulders to the ground, many others with long heavy crosses, others with a heavy bar of iron, or chains of the same, hanging at their necks; with such dismal objects in the middle of the procession, 12 priests drest in black ornaments, take the crucifix on their shoulders, and with great veneration carry it through the streets, the eunuchs singing the litany.

I said, that this image is never carried out but when there is great want of rain, and when there is sure appearance of plenteous rain; so they never are disappointed in having a miracle published after such a procession: Nay, sometimes it begins to rain before the crucifix is out of its place, and then the people are almost certain of the power of the image: So that year the chapter is sure to receive double tithes: For every body vows and promises two out of ten to the church for the recovery of the harvest.

But what is more than this, is, that in the last wars between king Philip and king Charles, as the people were divided into two factions, they did give out by the revelation of an ignorant, silly *beata*, that the crucifix was a *butiflero*, i. e. affectionate to king Philip; and at the same time there was another revelation, that his mother, the Virgin of Pilær, was an *imperialist*, i. e. for king Charles; and the minds of the people were so much prejudiced with their opinions, that the partizans of Philip did go to the crucifix, and those of king Charles to the

Virgin of Pilar. Songs were made upon this subject: one said, *When Charles the Third mounts on his horse, the Virgin of Pilar holds the stirrup.* The other said, *When Philip comes to our land, the Crucifix of St Salvator guides him by his hand.* By these two factions, both the Virgin and her son's image began to lose the presents of one of the parties, and the chapter, having made bitter complaint to the inqusitors, these did put a stop to their sacrilegious practices. So high is the people's opinion of the image of the crucifix, and so blind their faith, that all the world would not be able to persuade them that that image did not speak to the canon or prebendary, and that it cannot work miracles at any time. Therefore our custom was, after school, to go first to visit the crucifix, touch its feet with our hands, and kiss it, and from thence go to visit the image of the Virgin of Pilar, of which I am going to speak, as the next image to that of Jesus Christ, though, in truth, the first as to the people's devotion.

And because the story, or history of the image, is not well known, (at least, I never saw any foreign book treat of it,) it seems proper to give a full account of it here, to satisfy the curiosity of many that love to read and hear; and this, I think, is worth every body's observation.

The book, called *The History of our Lady of Pilar, and her Miracles,* contains, to the best of my memory, the following account:

The apostle St. James came, with seven new converts, to preach the gospel in Saragossa, (a city famous for its antiquity, and for its founder Cæsar Augustus; but more famous for the heavenly image of our lady,) and as they were sleeping on the river Ebro's side, a celestial music awakened them at midnight, and they saw an army of angels, melodiously singing, come down from heaven, with an image on a pillar, which they placed on the ground, forty yards distant from the river, and the commanding angel spoke to St. James and said, This image of our queen shall be the defence of this city, where you come to plant the Christian religion; take therefore good courage, for, by her help and assistance, you shall not leave this city without reducing all the inhabitants of it to your Master's religion; and as she is to protect you, you also must signalize yourself in building a decent chapel for her. The angels leaving the image on the earth, with the same melody and songs, went up to heaven, and St. James and his seven converts, on their knees began to pray, and thank God for this

inestimable tıeasure sent to them; and the next day they began to build a chapel with their own hands.

I have already given an account of the chapel, and the
riches of it; now I ought to say something of the idolatrous
adoration given to that image, by all the Roman catholics of
that kingdom, and of all that go to visit her.

The image has her own chaplain, besides the chapter of the
prebends and other priests, as I have told before. The Virgin
-chaplain has more privilege and power than any king, archbishop, or any ecclesiastical person, excepting the pope; for
his business is only to dress the image every morning, which
he doth in private, and without any help: I say in private,
that is drawing the four curtains of the Virgin's canopy, that
nobody may see the image naked. Nobody has liberty, but
this chaplain, to approach so near the image, for as the author
of the book says, *An archbishop (who had so great assurance
as to attempt to say mass on the altar table of the Virgin,) died
upon the spot, before he began mass.* I saw king Philip and
king Charles, when they went to visit the image, stand at a
distance from it. With these cautions it is very easy to give
out, that nobody can know of what matter the image is made,
that being a thing referred to the angels only; so all the favor
the Christians can obtain from the Virgin, is only to kiss her
pillar, for it is contrived, that by having broke the wall backwards, a piece of pillar, as big as two crown pieces is shown,
which is set out in gold round about, and there kings, and
other people, kneel down to adore and kiss that part of the
stone. The stones and lime that were taken, when the wall
was broke, are kept for relics, and it is a singular favor,
if any can get some small stone, by paying a great sum
of money.

There is always so great a crowd of people, that many times
they cannot kiss the pillar; but touch it with one of their
fingers, and kiss afterwards the part of the finger that touched
the pillar. The large chapel of the lamp is always, night and
day, crowded with people; for, as they say, that chapel was
never empty of Christians, since St. James built it; so the
people of the city, that work all day, go out at night to visit
the image, and this blind devotion is not only among pious
people, but among the profligate and debauched too, insomuch
that a lewd woman will not go to bed without visiting the
image; for they certainly believe, that nobody can be saved,
if they do not pay this tribute of devotion to the sacred image.

And to prove this erroneous belief, the chaplain, who dresses the image (as he is reckoned to be a heavenly man) may easily give out what stories he pleases, and make the people believe any revelation from the Virgin to him, as many of them are written in the book of the Virgin of Pilar, viz: Dr. Augustine Ramirez, chaplain to the image, in 1542, as he was dressing it, it talked with him for half a quarter of an hour, and said,

My faithful and well beloved Augustine, I am very angry with the inhabitants of this my city for their ingratitude. Now, I·tell you as my own chaplain, that it is my will, and I command you to publish it, and say the following words, which is my speech to all the people of Saragossa:—Ungrateful people, remember that after my son died for the redemption of the world, but more especially for you the inhabitants of this my chosen city, I was pleased, two years after I went up to heaven, in body and soul, to pitch upon this select city for my dwelling place; therefore I commanded the angels to make an image perfectly like my body, and another of my son Jesus, on my arms, and to set them both on a pillar, whose matter nobody can know, and when both were finished, I ordered them to be carried in a procession, round about the heavens, by the principal angels, the heavenly host following, and after them the Trinity, who took me in the middle; and when this procession was over in heaven, I sent them down with illuminations and music to awake my beloved James, who was asleep on the river side, commanding him by my ambassador Gabriel, to build with his own hands a chapel for my image, which he did accordingly; and ever since I have been the defence of this city against the Saracen army, when by my mighty power, I killed in one night at the breach, 50,000 of them, putting the rest to a precipitate flight. After this visible miracle, (for many saw me in the air fighting,) I have delivered them from the oppression of the Moors, and preserved the faith and religion unpolluted for many years, in this my city. How many times have I succored them with rain in time of need? How many sick have I healed? How much riches are they masters of, by my unshaken affection to them all? And what is the recompense they give me for all these benefits? Nothing but ingratitude. I have been ashamed these fifteen years, to speak before the eternal Father, who made me queen of this city: many and many times I am at court, with the three persons, to give my consent for pardoning several sinners; and when the Father asketh me about my city, I am so bashful that I cannot lift up my eyes to him. He

s 2

knoweth very well their ingratitude, and blameth me for suffering so long their covetousness: and this very morning, being called to the council of the Trinity for passing the divine decree, under our hands and seal for the bishoprick of Saragossa, the Holy Spirit has affronted me, saying I was not worthy to be of the private council of heaven, because I did not know how to govern and punish the criminals of my chosen city; and I have vowed not to go again to the heavenly court, until I get satisfaction from my offenders. So I thunder out this sentence, against the inhabitants of Saragossa, that I have resolved to take away my image from them, and resign my government to Lucifer, if they do not come, for the space of fifteen days, every day with gifts, tears and penances, to make due submission to my image, for the faults committed by them these fifteen years. And if they come with prodigal hands, and true hearts, to appease my wrath, which I am pleased with, they shall see the rainbow for a signal, that I receive them again into my favor. But, if not, they may be sure that the Prince of Darkness shall come to rule and reign over them; and further, I do declare, that they shall have no appeal, from this my sentence, to the tribunal of the Father, for this is my will and pleasure.

After this revelation was published, all the inhabitants of the city were under such a concern, that the magistrates, by the Archbishop's order, published an ordinance for all sorts of people to fast three days every week, and not to let the cattle go out those days, and to make the cattle fast as well as the reasonable creatures; and as for the infants, not to suckle them but once a day. All sorts of work were forbidden for fifteen days time, in which the people went to confess and make public penances, and offer whatever money and rich jewels they had, to the Virgin.

Observe now, that the publishing of the revelation was in the month of May, and it is a customary thing for that country to see almost every day the rainbow at that time: so there was by all probability, certain hopes that the rainbow would not fail to shew its many colored faces to the inhabitants of Saragossa, as did happen the eleventh day; but it was too late for them, for they had bestowed all their treasures on the image of the Virgin. Then the rejoicings began, and the people were almost mad for joy, reckoning themselves the most happy, blessed people in the universe.

By these and the like revelations, given out every day by

the Virgin's chaplain, the people are so much infatuated, that they certainly believe there is no salvation for any soul without the consent of the Virgin of Pilar; so they never fail to visit her image every day, and to pay her due homage, for fear that if she is angry again, Lucifer should come to reign over them. And this is done by the Virgin's crafty chaplain, to increase her treasure and his own too. As to him, I may aver, that the late chaplain, Don Pedro Valenzula was but five years in the Virgin's service; yearly rent is 1000 pistoles, and when he died, he left in his testament, 20,000 pistoles to the Virgin, and 10,000 to his relations; now how he got 30,000 pistoles clear in six years, every body may imagine.

As to the miracles wrought by this image, I could begin to give an account, but never make an end; and this subject requiring a whole book to itself, I will not trouble the reader with it, hoping in God that if he is pleased to spare my life some years, I shall print a book of their miracles and revelations, that the world may, by it, know the inconsistent grounds and reasons of the Romish communion.

Now, coming again to the adoration of images, I cannot pass by one or two instances more of the image of Jesus Christ, adored by the Roman Catholics.

The first is that of the crucifix in the monument, both on Thursday and Friday of the holy week. The Roman Catholics have a custom on holy Thursday, to put the consecrated host in the monument till Friday morning at eleven of the clock, as I have already said, treating of the estation of the holy Calvary.

Now I will confine myself wholly to the adoration paid to the crucifix, and all the material instruments of our Saviour's passion, by priests, friars, and magistrates. In every parish church and convent of friars and nuns, the priests form a monument, which is of the breadth of the great altar's front, consisting of ten or twelve steps, that go gradually up to the Ara, or altar's table, on which lies a box, gilt, and adorned with jewels, wherein they keep for twenty-four hours, the great host, which the priest that officiates, has consecrated on Thursday, between eleven and twelve. In this monument, you may see as many wax candles as parishioners belonging to that church, and which burn twenty-four hours continually. At the bottom of the monument there is a crucifix laid down on a black velvet pillow, and two silver dishes on each side. At three of the clock, in the afternoon, there is a sermon preached by the Lent preachers, whose constant text is, *Mandatum novum do*

vobis, ut diligatis invicem, sicut dilexi vos. Expressing in it,
the excessive love of our Saviour towards us. After it the prelate washes the feet of twelve poor people, and all this while
the people that go from one church to another, to visit the
monuments, kneel down before the crucifix, kiss its feet, and
put a piece of money into one of the dishes. The next day, in
the morning, there is another sermon of the passion of our
Saviour, wherein the preacher recommends the adoration of the
cross according to the solemn ceremony of the church. That
day, i. e. Good Friday, there is no Mass in the Romish church,
for the host which was consecrated the day before, is received
by the minister, or prelate, that officiates, and when the passion is sung, then they begin the adoration of the crucifix,
which is at the bottom of the monument, which is performed
in the following manner: First of all, the priest that officiates,
or the bishop, when he is present, pulling off his shoes, goes
and kneels down three times before the crucifix, kisses its feet,
and in the same manner comes back again to his own place.
All the priests do the same, but without putting any thing into
the dish, this being only a tribute to be paid by the magistrates
and laity. This being done by all the magistrates, the priest
bids them to come at four in the afternoon, to the descent of
Jesus Christ, from the cross, and this is another idolatrous ceremony and adoration.

The same crucifix that was at the bottom of the monument,
is put on the great altar's table, veiled or covered with two curtains, and when the people are gathered together in the
church, the chapter or community comes out of the vestry, and
kneeling down before the altar, begins in a doleful manner to
sing the psalm, *Miserere,* and when they come to the verse,
Tibi soli peccavi, &c., they draw the curtains, and shew the
image of Christ crucified to the people. Then the preacher
goes up to the pulpit, to preach of the pains and afflictions of
the Virgin Mary, (whose image shedding tears is placed before the image of her son.) I once preached upon this occasion in the convent of St. Augustine, in the city of Huesca,
and my text was, *Animam meam pertransivit gladius.* After
the preacher has exaggerated the unparalleled pains of the
Virgin Mary, seeing her son suffer death in so ignominious a
manner, he orders Satellites (so they call those that stand
with the nails, hammer and other instruments used in their
crucifixion) to go up to the cross, and take the crown of thorns
off the crucifix's head, and then he preaches on that action,
representing to the people his sufferings as movingly as possi-

ble.   After the Satellites have taken the nails out of the hands
and feet, they bring down the body of Jesus, and lay him in the
coffin, and when the sermon is over, the procession begins,
all in black, which is called the burying of Christ.   In that
procession, which is always in the dark of the evening, there
are vast numbers of disciplinants that go along with it, whipping themselves, and shedding their blood, till the body of Jesus is put into the sepulchre.   Then every body goes to adore
the sepulchre, and after the adoration of it, begins the procession of the estations of the holy Calvary, of which I have spoken already in the second chapter of this book.

I will not deprive the public of another superstitious ceremony of the Romish Priests, which is very diverting, and by
which their ignorance will be more exposed to the world; and
this is practised on the Sunday before Easter, which is called
Dominica Palmarum, in which the church commemorates the
triumphant entry of Jesus Christ in Jerusalem, sitting on an
ass, the people spreading their clothes and branches of olive
trees on the ground: so, in imitation of this triumph, they do
the same in some churches and convents.

The circumstance of one being representative of Jesus, on
an ass, I never saw practised in Saragossa, and I was quite
unacquainted with it till I went to Alvalate, a town that belongs to the archbishop in temporalibus and spiritualibus,
whither I was obliged to retire with his Grace, in his precipitate flight from King Charles's army, for fear of being taken
prisoner of state.   We were there at the Franciscan convent
on that Sunday, and the archbishop being invited to the ceremony of the religious triumph, I went with him to see it, which
was performed in the following manner.

All the friars being in the body of the church, the guardian
placing his Grace at the right hand, the procession began, every friar having a branch of olive trees in his hand, which
was blessed by the Rev. Father Guardian; so the cross going
before, the procession went out of the church to a large yard
before it: But, what did we see at the door of the church, but
a fat friar, dressed like a Nazareen, on a clever ass, two friars
holding the stirrups, and another pulling the ass by the bridle.
The representative of Jesus Christ took place before the
archbishop.   The ass was an he one, though not so fat as the
friar, but the ceremony of throwing branches and clothes before him, being quite strange to him, he began to start and ca-
per, and at last threw down the heavy load of the friar.—The
ass ran away, leaving the reverend on the ground, with one

arm broken. This unusual ceremony was so pleasing to us all, that his Grace, notwithstanding his deep melancholy, laughed heartily at it. The ass was brought back, and another friar, making the representative, put an end to this ass-ike ceremony.

But the ignorance and superstition begins now; when the ceremony was over, a novice took the ass by the bridle, and began to walk in the cloister, and every friar made a reverence, passing by, and the people kneeling down before him, said, O happy ass! But his Grace displeased at so great a superstition, spoke to the guardian, and desired him not to suffer his friars to give such an example to the ignorant people, as to adore the ass. The guardian was a pleasant man, and seeing the archbishop so melancholy, only to make him laugh, told his Grace that it was impossible for him to obey his Grace, without removing all his friars to another convent, and bring a new community. Why so? said his Grace. Because (replied the guardian) all my friars are he asses. And you the guardian of them (answered his Grace.) Thus priests and friars excite the people, to adore images.

But because this article of images, and that of relics, contribute very much to the discovery of the idolatries, and of the bigotries and superstitions of all those of that communion, I shall not leave this subject, without giving an account of some remarkable images which are worshipped and adored by them all.

They have innumerable images of Christ, the Virgin Mary, the angels and saints in the streets, in small chapels built within the thickness of the walls, and most commonly in the corners of the streets, which the people adore, kneel down before, and make prayers and supplications to. They say, that many of those images have spoken to some devout persons, as that of St. Philip Nery did to a certain ambitious priest, who, walking through the street where the image was, was talking within himself, and saying, Now I am a priest, next year I hope to be a dean, after bishop, then cardinal, and after all, summus pontifex. To which soliloquy the image of St. Philip answered, And after all these honors comes death, and after death, hell and damnation forever. The priest, being surprised at this answer, so much apropos, and looking up and down, he saw the mouth of the image open, by which he concluded that the image had given him the answer; and so taking a firm resolution to leave all the thoughts of this deceitful world, with his own money he purchased the house where the image was, and built a decent chapel in honor of St. Philip, which now, by the gifts of pious people, is so much enlarged, that we reckon St. Philip's church and parish to be the third in the city for riches, the number of beneficiate priests being 46, besides the rector.

In St. Philip's church there is a miraculous crucifix, called El santo Christo de las peridas; The holy Christ of child-bed women; which is much frequented by all people, but chiefly by the ladies, who go there to be churched, and leave the purification offering mentioned in the ceremonial law of Moses. And as there is this image which is an advocate of women delivered of child, there are also two images, who are advocates of barren women, one of the Virgin in the convent of Recolet friars of St. Augustine, and another of St. Antonio del Paula: The first is called the barren women, the second, the intercessor of the barren ladies. This second image is in the convent of Victorian friars, and is kept in a gilt box in a chapel within the cloister, and the door is always locked up, and the key kept by the father corrector, i. e. the superior of the convent.

Another practice, of paying worship and adoration to the Virgin Mother, and her child Jesus in a manger, is observed on Christmas, and eight days after: But especially the nuns do signalize themselves on this festival, and that on which Jesus was lost and found again in the temple; for they hide the child in some secret place under the altar's table, and after evening songs they run up and down through the garden, cloisters and church, to see whether they can find the innocent child, and the nun that finds him out, is excused, for that year, from all the painful offices of the convent; but she is to give, for three days together, a good dinner to all the nuns and father confessor; and that year she may go to the grate at any time, without any leave or fear, for she doth not assist at the public service of prayers: in short, she has liberty of conscience that year, for finding the lost child, and she is often lost too at the end of the year, by following a licentious sort of a life.

These are, in some measure, voluntary devotions and adorations, but there are many others by precept of the church, and ordinances of several popes, who have granted prope services to several images, with which priests and friars do serve and adore them, or else they commit a mortal sin, as well as if they neglected the divine and ecclesiastical service and the due observance of the ten commandments of the law of God. I will give a few instances of these adorations by precept, and with them I shall conclude.

There are in the church of Rome, proper services granted by the popes for the invention or finding out of the cross, and for the exaltation of it, and every priest, friar, and nun, is obliged in conscience, to say these services in honor of the cross; and after the great mass they adore the cross, and this is properly adoration, for they say in the hymn, Let us come and adore the holy cross, &c., and the people do the same af- ter them. They carry the cross on the 3d of May, and on the great Litany-days, in a solemn procession, to some high place out of the town, and after the officiating priest has lifted up the cross towards the south, north, west, and east, blessing the four parts of the world, and singing the Litany, the pro- cession comes back to the church. These festivals are cele- brated with more devotion and veneration, as to the outward appearance, than pomp and magnificence, except in the churches dedicated to the holy cross, where this being the tit- ular festival, is constantly performed with all manner of cere monies, as the days of the first class.

There are proper services granted to the Virgin Mary, un- der the following names: The Virgin of the rose of St. Dom- inick, of the girdle of St. Augustine, or the rope of St. Fran- cis, and of the scapulary of Mount carmel. All these distin- guishing signs of the Virgin Mary, are celebrated by the church and fraternities of devout people, and adored by all christians, being all images and relics to be worshiped by the command of the pope. Now, by what has been said, where can we find expressions fit to explain the wickedness of the Romish priests, the ignorance of the people, committed to their charge, and the idolatrous, nonsensical, ridiculous ceremonies with which they serve, not God, but saints, giving them more tribute of adoration than to the Almighty? I must own, that the poor people who are easily persuaded of every thing, are not so much to be blamed, but the covetous, barbarous clergy; for these (though many of them are very blind) are not to be supposed ignorant of what sins they do commit, and advise the people to commit: so, acting against the dictates of their own consciences, they, I believe, must answer for their ill- guided flock, before the tribunal of the living God.

THE

INQUISITION OF GOA

[FROM DR BUCHANAN'S RESEARCHES IN ASIA.]

"Goa, Convent of the Augustinians, Jan. 23, 1808.

"On my arrival at Goa, I was received into the house of Captain Schuyler, the British Resident. The British force here is commanded by Col. Adams, of his Majesty's 78th regiment, with whom I was formerly well acquainted in Bengal.* Next day I was introduced by these gentlemen to the Viceroy of Goa, the Count de Cabral. I intimated to his excellency my wish to sail up the river to Old Goa,† (where the Inquisition is,) to which he politely acceded. Major Pareira, of the Portuguese establishment, who was present, and to whom I had letters of introduction from Bengal, offered to accompany me to the city, and to introduce me to the archbishop of Goa, the Primate of the Orient.

"I had communicated to Col. Adams, and to the British Resident, my purpose of inquiring into the state of the Inquisition. These gentlemen informed me, that I should not be able to accomplish my design without difficulty; since every thing relating to the Inquisition was conducted in a very secret manner, the most respectable of the lay Portuguese themselves being ignorant of its proceedings; and that, if the priests were to discover my object, their excessive jealousy and alarm would prevent their communicating with me, or satisfying my inquiries on any subject.

* The forts in the harbor of Goa were then occupied by British troops, (two King's regiments, and two regiments of native infantry,) to prevent its falling into the hands of the French.

† There is Old and New Goa. The old city is about eight miles up the river. The Viceroy and the chief Portuguese inhabitants reside at New Goa, which is at the mouth of the river, within the forts of the harbor. The old city, where the Inquisition and the Churches are, is now almost entirely deserted by the secular Portuguese, and is inhabited by the priests alone. The unhealthiness of the place, and the ascendency of the priests, are the causes assigned for abandoning the ancient city.

T

217

"On receiving this intelligence, I perceived that it would be necessary to proceed with caution. I was, in fact, about to visit a republic of priests; whose dominion had existed for nearly three centuries; whose province it was to prosecute heretics, and particularly the teachers of heresy; and from whose authority and sentence there was no appeal in India.

"It happened that Lieutenant Kempthorne, Commander of His Majesty's brig Diana, a distant connexion of my own, was at this time in the harbor. On his learning that I meant to visit Old Goa, he offered to accompany me, as did Captain Stirling, of His Majesty's 84th regiment, which is now sta tioned at the forts.

"We proceeded up the river in the British Resident's barge, accompanied by Major Pareira, who was well qualified by a thirty years' residence, to give information concerning local circumstances. From him I learned that there were upwards of two hundred Churches and Chapels in the province of Goa and upwards of two thousand priests.

"On our arrival at the city, it was past twelve o'clock; all the churches were shut, and we were told that they would not be opened again till two o'clock. I mentioned to Major Pareira, that I intended to stay at Old Goa some days; and that I should be obliged to him to find me a place to sleep in. He seemed surprised at this intimation, and observed that it would be difficult for me to obtain a reception in any of the Churches or Convents, and that there were no private houses into which I could be admitted. I said I could sleep any where; I had two servants with me, and a travelling bed. When he perceived that I was serious in my purpose, he gave directions to a civil officer in that place, to clear out a room in a building which had long been uninhabited, and which was then used as a warehouse for goods. Matters at this time presented a very gloomy appearance: and I had thoughts of returning with my companions from this inhospitable place. In the mean time we sat down in the room I have just mentioned, to take some refreshment, while Major Pareira went to call on some of his friends. During this interval, I communicated to Lieut. Kempthorne the object of my visit. I had in my pocket 'Dellon's Account of the Inquisition at Goa;' * and I mentioned some

* Monsieur Dellon, a physician, was imprisoned in a dungeon of the Inqui-sition at Goa for two years, and witnessed an Auto da Fe, when some here-tics were burned; at which time he walked barefoot. After his release he wrote the history of his confinement. His descriptions are in general very accurate.

particulars. While we were conversing on the subject the great bell of the Cathedral began to toll; the same which Dellon observes, always tolls before day-light, on the morning of the Auto da Fe. I did not myself ask any questions of the people concerning the Inquisition; but Mr. Kempthorne made inquiries for me and he soon found out that the Santa Casa, or Holy Office was close to the house where we were then sitting. The gentlemen went to the window to view the horrid mansion; and I could see the indignation of free and enlightened men arise in the countenances of the two British officers, while they contemplated a place where formerly their own countrymen were condemned to the flames, and into which they themselves might now suddenly be thrown, without the possibility of rescue.

"At two o'clock we went out to view the churches, which were now open for the afternoon service; for there are regular daily masses; and the bells began to assail the ear in every quarter.

"The magnificence of the churches of Goa, far exceeded any idea I had formed from the previous description. Goa is properly a city of Churches; and the wealth of provinces seems to have been expended in their erection. The ancient specimens of architecture at this place, far excel any thing that has been attempted in modern times, in any other part of the East, both in grandeur and in taste. The chapel of the palace is built after the plan of St. Peter's at Rome, and is said to be an accurate model of that paragon of architecture. The church of St. Dominic, the founder of the Inquisition, is decorated with paintings of Italian masters. St. Francis Yaver lies enshrined in a monument of exquisite art, and his coffin is enchased with silver and precious stones. The cathedral of Goa is worthy of one of the principal cities of Europe; and the church and convent of the Augustinians (in which I now reside) is a noble pile of building, situated on an eminence, and has a magnificent appearance from afar.

"But what a contrast to all this grandeur of the churches is the worship offered in them! I have been present at the chapels every day since I arrived; and I seldom see a single worshipper, but the ecclesiastics. Two rows of native priests, kneeling in order before the altar, clothed in coarse black garments, of sickly appearance and vacant countenances, perform here, from day to day, their laborious masses, seemingly unconscious of any other duty or obligation of life.

"The day was now far spent, and my companions were about to leave me. While I was considering whether I should return with them, Major Pareira said he would first introduce me to a priest, high in office, and one of the most learned men in the place. We accordingly walked to the convent of the Augustinians, where I was presented to Josephus à Doloribus, a man well advanced in life, of pale visage, and penetrating eye, rather of a reverend appearance, and possessing great fluency of speech and urbanity of manners. At first sight he presented the aspect of one of those acute and prudent men of the world, the learned and respectable Italian Jesuits, some of whom are yet found, since the demolition of their order, reposing in tranquil obscurity, in different parts of the East. After half an hour's conversation in the Latin language, during which he adverted rapidly to a variety of subjects, and inquired concerning some learned men of his own church, whom I had visited in my tour, he politely invited me to take up my residence with him during my stay at Old Goa. I was highly gratified by this unexpected invitation; but Lieutenant Kempthorne did not approve of leaving me in the hands of the Inquisitor: For judge our surprise, when we discovered that my learned host was one of the Inquisitors of the holy office, the second member of that august tribunal in rank, but the first and most active agent in the business of the department. Apartments were assigned to me in the college adjoining the convent, next to the rooms of the Inquisitor himself; and here I have been four days at the very fountain-head of information, in regard to those subjects which I wished to investigate. I breakfast and dine with the Inquisitor almost every day, and he generally passes his evenings in my apartment. As he considers my inquiries to be chiefly of a literary nature, he is perfectly candid and communicative on all subjects.

"Next day after my arrival, I was introduced by my learned conductor to the Archbishop of Goa. We found him reading the Latin Letters of St. Francis Xavier. On my adverting to the long duration of the city of Goa, while other cities of Europeans in India had suffered from war or revolution, the Archbishop observed that the preservation of Goa was 'owing to the prayers of St. Francis Xavier.' The Inquisitor looked at me to see what I thought of this sentiment. I acknowledged that Xavier was considered by the learned among the English to have been a great man. What he wrote himself bespeaks him a man of learning, of original genius, and great fortitude of mind; but what others have written for

him and of him, has tarnished his fame, by making him the
inventor of fables. The Archbishop signified his assent. He
afterwards conducted me into his private chapel, which is decorated with images of silver, and then into the Archiepiscopal Library, which possesses a valuable collection of books.
As I passed through our convént, in returning from the Arch
bishop's, I observed among the paintings in the cloisters a
portrait of the famous Alexis de Menezes, Archbishop of Goa,
who held the Synod of Diamper near Cochin in 1599, and
burned the books of the Syrian Christians. From the inscription underneath, I learned that he was the founder
of the magnificent church and convent in which I am now
residing."

"On the same day I received an invitation to dine with the
chief Inquisitor, at his house in the country. The second
Inquisitor accompanied me, and we found a respectable company of priests, and a sumptuous entertainment. In the library of the chief Inquisitor, I saw a register containing the
present establishment of the Inquisition at Goa, and the
names of all the officers. On my asking the chief Inquisitor
whether the establishment was as extensive as formerly, he
said it was nearly the same. I had hitherto said little to any
person concerning the Inquisition, but I had indirectly gleaned
much information concerning it, not only from the Inquisitors
themselves, but from certain priests, whom I visited at their
respective convents; particularly from a Father in the Franciscan Convent, who had himself repeatedly witnessed an
Auto da Fe."

"*Goa, Augustinian Convent,* 26th Jan. 1808.
"On Sunday, after Divine Service, which I attended, we
looked over together the prayers and portions of Scripture for
the day, which led to a discussion concerning some of the
doctrines of Christianity. We then read the third chapter of
St. John's Gospel, in the Latin Vulgate. I asked the Inquisitor whether he believed in the influence of the Spirit there
spoken of. He distinctly admitted it; conjointly however he
thought in some obscure sense with water. I observed that
water was merely an emblem of the purifying effects of the
Spirit, and could be but an emblem. We next adverted to
the expression of St. John in his first epistle, 'This is he that
came by water and blood: even Jesus Christ; not by water
only, but by water and blood:'—blood to atone for sin, and
water to purify the heart; justification and sanctification,

T 2

both of which were expressed at the same moment on the
cross. The inquisitor was pleased with the subject. I referred to the evangelical doctrines of Augustin (we were now in
the Augustinian convent) plainly asserted by that father in a
thousand places, and he acknowledged their truth. I then
asked him in what important doctrine he differed from the
protestant church? He confessed that he never had had a theological discussion with a protestant before. By an easy tran-
sition we passed to the importance of the Bible itself, to
illuminate the priests and people. I noticed to him, that after
looking through the colleges and schools, there appeared to
me to be a total eclipse of Scriptural light. He acknowledged that religion and learning were truly in a degraded
state. I had visited the theological schools, and at every
place I expressed my surprise to the tutors, in presence of
the pupils, at the absence of the Bible and almost total want
of reference to it. They pleaded the custom of the place,
and the scarcity of copies of the book itself. Some of the
younger priests came to me afterwards, desiring to know
by what means they might procure copies. This inquiry for
Bibles was like a ray of hope beaming on the walls of the
Inquisition.

"I pass an hour sometimes in the spacious library of the
Augustinian convent. There are many rare volumes, but
they are chiefly theological, and almost all of the sixteenth
century. There are few classics; and I have not yet seen
one copy of the original Scriptures in Hebrew or Greek."

Goa, Augustinian Convent, 27th, Jan. 1808.

"On the second morning after my arrival, I was surprised
by my host, the Inquisitor, coming into my apartment clothed
in black robes from head to foot; for the usual dress of his
order is white. He said he was going to sit on the tribunal
of the Holy Office. 'I presume, Father, your august office
does not occupy much of your time.' 'Yes,' answered he,
'much. I sit on the tribunal three or four days every week.'

"I had thought, for some days, of putting Dellon's book
into the Inquisitor's hands; for if I could get him to advert
to the facts stated in that book, I should be able to learn, by
comparison, the exact state of the Inquisition at the present
time. In the evening he came in, as usual, to pass an hour
in my apartment. After some conversation, I took the pen
in my hand to write a few notes in my journal; and, as if to
amuse him, while I was writing, I took up Dellon's book,

which was lying with some others on the table, and handling
it across to him, asked him whether he had ever seen it. It
was in the French language, which he understood well.—
'Relation de l'Inquisition de Goa,' pronounced he, with a
slow articulate voice. He had never seen it before, and began
to read with eagerness. He had not proceeded far, before he
betrayed evident symptoms of uneasiness. He turned hastily
to the middle of the book, and then to the end, and then ran
over the table of contents at the beginning, as if to ascertain
the full extent of the evil. He then composed himself to read,
while I continued to write. He turned over the pages with ra-
pidity, and when he came to a certain place, he exclaimed in
the broad Italian accent 'Mendacium, Mendacium.' I requested he would mark those passages which were untrue,
and we should discuss them afterwards, for that I had other
books on the subject. 'Other books,' said he, and he looked
with an enquiring eye on those on the table. He continued
reading till it was time to retire to rest, and then begged to
take the book with him.

It was on this night that a circumstance happened which
caused my first alarm at Goa. My servants slept every night
at my chamber door, in the long gallery which is common to
all the apartments, and not far distant from the servants of
the convent. About midnight I was awaked by loud shrieks
and expressions of terror, from some person in the gallery.
In the first moment of surprise, I concluded it must be the
Alguazils of the holy office, seizing my servants to carry them
to the Inquisition. But, on going out, I saw my own servants
standing at the door, and the person who had caused the
alarm (a boy of about fourteen) at a little distance, surrounded by some of the priests, who had come out of their cells on
hearing the noise. The boy said he had seen a spectre,
and it was a considerable time before the agitation of his
body and voice subsided. Next morning at breakfast the Inquisitor apologized for the disturbance, and said the boy's
alarm proceeded from a phantasma animi,' a phantasm of the
imagination.

"After breakfast we resumed the subject of the Inquisition.
The Inquisitor admitted that Dellon's descriptions of the dungeons, of the torture, of the mode of trial, and of the Auto
da Fé, were, in general, just; but he said the writer judged
untruly of the motives of the Inquisitors, and very uncharita-
bly of the character of the Holy Church; and I admitted that,
under the pressure of his peculiar suffering, this might possi-

bly be the case. The Inquisitor was now anxious to know to
what extent Dellon's book had been circulated in Europe. I
told him that Picart had published to the world extracts from
it, in his celebrated work called 'Religious Ceremonies;' together with plates of the system of torture and burnings at
the Auto da Fe. I added that it was now generally believed
in Europe, that these enormities no longer existed, and that
the Inquisition itself had been totally suppressed; but that I
was concerned to find that this was not the case. He now
began a grave narration to show that the inquisition had un-
dergone a change in some respects, and that its terrors were
mitigated."*

*The following were the passages in Mr. Dellon's narrative, to which I
wished particularly to draw the attention of the Inquisitor. Mr. D had been
thrown into the Inquisition at Goa, and confined in a dungeon, ten feet square,
where he remained upwards of two years, without seeing any person, but the
gaoler who brought him his victuals, except when he was brought to his trial,
expecting daily to be brought to the stake. His alleged crime was, charging
the Inquisition with cruelty, in a conversation he had with a Priest at *Daman*,
another part of India.

" During the months of November and December, I heard every morning,
the shrieks of the unfortunate victims, who were undergoing the *Question.* I
remembered to have heard, before I was cast into prison, that the Auto da Fe
was generally celebrated on the first Sunday in Advent, because on that day
is read in the Churches that part of the Gospel in which mention is made of
the LAST JUDGMENT; and the Inquisitors pretend by this ceremony to exhibit
a living emblem of that awful event. I was likewise convinced that there
were a great number of prisoners, besides myself; the profound silence, which
reigned within the walls of the building, having enabled me to count the number of doors which were opened at the hours of meals. However, the first
and second Sundays of Advent passed by without my hearing of any thing,
and I prepared to undergo another year of melancholy captivity, when I was
aroused from my despair on the 11th of January, by the noise of the guards
removing the bars from the doors of my prison. The *Alcaide* presented me
with a habit, which he ordered me to put on, and make myself ready to attend him when he should come again. Thus saying, he left a lighted lamp
in my dungeon. The guards returned, about two o'clock in the morning, and
led me out into a long gallery, where I found a number of the companions of
my fate, drawn up in a rank against a wall: I placed myself among the rest,
and several more soon joined the melancholy band. The profound silence
and stillness caused them to resemble statues more than the animated bodies of
human creatures. The women, who were clothed in a similar manner, were
placed in a neighboring gallery, where we could not see them; but I remarked
that a number of persons stood by themselves at some distance, attended by
others who wore long black dresses, and who walked backwards and forward;
occasionally. I did not then know who these were: but I was afterwards informed that the former were the victims who were condemned to be burnt
and the others were their confessors.

" After we were all ranged against the wall of this gallery, we received eac .
large wax taper. They then brought us a number of dresses made of yea

"I had already discovered, from written or printed documents, that the Inquisition at Goa was suppressed by Royal Edict in the year 1775, and established again in 1779. The Franciscan Father before mentioned, witnessed the annual Auto da Fe, from 1770 to 1775. 'It was the humanity and tender mercy of a good King,' said the old Father, which abolished the Inquisition.' But immediately on his death, the power of the priests acquired the ascendant, under the Queen Dowager, and the tribunal was re-established, after a bloodless interval of five years. It has continued in operation ever since. It was restored in 1779, subject to certain restrictions, the chief of which are the two following: 'That a greater number of

low cloth, with the cross of St. Andrew painted before and behind. This is called the San Benito. The relapsed heretics wear another species of robe, called the Samarra, the ground of which is grey. The portrait of the sufferer is painted upon it, placed upon burning torches with flames and demons all round. Caps were then produced, called Carrochas; made of pasteboard, pointed like sugar-loaves, all covered over with devils and flames of fire.

"The great bell of the Cathedral began to ring a little before sunrise, which served as a signal to warn the people of God to come and behold the august ceremony of the Auto da Fe; and then they made us proceed from the gallery one by one. I remarked as we passed into the great hall, that the Inquisitor was sitting at the door with his secretary by him, and that he delivered every prisoner into the hands of a particular person, who is to be his guard to the place of burning. These persons are called Parrains, or *Godfathers* My Godfather was the commander of a ship. I went forth with him, and as soon as we were in the street, I saw that the procession was commenced by the Dominican Friars, who have this honor, because St. Dominic founded the Inquisition. These are followed by the prisoners, who walk one after the other, each having his Godfather by his side, and a lighted taper in his hand. The least guilty go foremost; and as I did not pass for one of them, there were many who took precedence of me. The women were mixed promiscuously with the men. We all walked barefoot, and the sharp stones of the streets of Goa wounded my tender feet, and caused the blood to stream; for they made us march through the chief streets of the city; and we were regarded every where by an innumerable crowd of people, who had assembled from all parts of India to behold this spectacle; for the Inquisition takes pains to announce it long before, in the most remote parishes. At length we arrived at the church of St. Francis, which was, for this time, destined for the celebration of the Act of Faith. On one side of the Altar, was the Grand Inquisitor and his Counsellors, and on the other the Viceroy of Goa and his Court. All the prisoners are seated to hear a sermon. I observed that those prisoners who wore the *horrible Carrochas* came in last in the procession. One of the Augustan Monks ascended the pulpit, and preached for a quarter of an hour. The sermon being concluded, two readers went up to the pulpit, one after the other, and read the sentences of the prisoners. My joy was extreme, when I heard that my sentence was not to be burnt, but to be a galley slave for five years. After the sentences were read, they summoned forth those miserable victims who were destined to be immolated by the Holy Inquisition The images of the heretics who had died in prison were brought witnesses should be required to convict a crimina. than weie before necessary;' and, 'That the Auto da Fe should not be held publicly as before; but that the sentences of the Tribunal should be executed privately, within ʼhe walls óf the Inquisition.'

"In this particular, the constitution cf the new Inquisition is more reprehensible than that of the old one; for, as the old Father expressed it, 'Nunc sigillum non reve.at Inquisitio.' Formerly the friends of those unfortunate persons who were thrown into its prison, had the melancholy satisfaction of seeing them once a year walking in the procession of the Auto da Fe; or, if they were condemned to die, they witnessed their death, and mourned for the dead. But now they have no means of learning for years whether they be dead or alive. The policy of this new code of concealment appears to be this, to preserve the power of the Inquisition, and at the same time to lessen the public odium of its proceedings, in the presence of British dominion and civilization. I asked the Father his opinion concerning the nature and frequency of the punishment within the walls. He said he possessed no certain means of giving a satisfactory answer; that every thing transacted there was declared to be 'sacrum et secretum.' But this he knew to be true, that there were constantly captives in the dungeons; that some of them are liberated after long confinement, but that they never speak afterwards of what passed within the place. He added that, of all the persons he had known, who had been liberated, he never knew one who did not carry about with him what might be called, 'the mark of the Inquisition;' that is to say, who did not show, in the solemnity of his countenance, or in his peculiar demeanor, or his terror of the priests, that he had been in that dreadful place.

up at the same time, their bones being contained in small chests, covered with flames and demons. An officer of the secular tribunal now came forward, and seized these unhappy people, after they had each received a *slight blow upon the breast*, from the Alcaide, to intimate that they were *abandoned*. They were then led away to the bank of the river, where the Viceroy and his Court were assembled, and where the faggots had been prepared the preceding day. As soon as they arrive at this place, the condemned persons are asked in what religion they choose to die; and the moment they have replied to this question, the executioner seizes them, and t hds them to a stake in the midst of the faggots. The day after the execution, the portraits of the dead are carried to the Church of Dominicans. The heads only are represented (which are generally very accurately drawn; for the Inquisition keeps 'excellent limners for the purpose,) surrounded by flames and demons; and underneath is the name and crime of the person who had been burned."—*Relation ce l'Inquisition de Goa*, chap. **xx**iv.

"The chief argument of the Inquisitor, to prove the melioration of the Inquisition, was the superior *humanity* of the Inquisitors. I remarked that I did not doubt the humanity of the existing officers; but what availed humanity in an Inquisitor? he must pronounce sentence according to the laws of the Tribunal, which are notorious enough; and a *relapsed Heretic* must be burned in the flames, or confined for life in a dungeon, whether the Inquisitor be humane or not. But if, said I, you would satisfy my mind completely on this subject, 'show me the Inquisition.' He said it was not permitted to any person to see the Inquisition. I observed that mine might be considered a peculiar case; that the character of the Inquisition, and the expediency of its long continuance, had been called in question; that I myself had written on the civilization of India, and might possibly publish something more on the subject, and that it could not be expected that I should pass over the Inquisition without notice, knowing what I did of its proceedings; at the same time I should not wish to state a single fact without his authority, or at least his admission of its truth. I added, that he himself had been pleased to communicate with me very fully on the subject, and that in all our discussions we had both been actuated, I hoped, by a good purpose. The countenance of the Inquisitor evidently altered on receiving this intimation, nor did it ever after wholly regain its wonted frankness and placidity. After some hesitation, however, he said, he would take me with him to the Inquisition the next day. I was a good deal surprised at this acquiescence of the Inquisitor, but I did not know what was in his mind.

"Next morning, after breakfast, my host went to dress for the Holy Office, and soon returned in his inquisitorial robes. He said he would go half an hour before the usual time, for he purpose of showing me the Inquisition. The buildings are about a quarter of a mile distant from the convent, and we proceeded thither in our *Manjeels.** On our arrival at the place, the inquisitor said to me, as we were ascending the steps of the outer stair, that he hoped I should be satisfied with a transient view of the inquisition, and that I would retire whenever he should desire it. I took this as a good omen, and followed my conductor with tolerable confidence.

* The Manjeel is a kind of Palankeen common at Goa. It is merely a sea cot suspended from a bamboo, which is borne on the *heads* of four men. Sometimes a footman runs before, having a staff in his hand, to which are attached little bells or rings, which he jingles as he runs, keeping time with the motion of the bearers.

"He led me first to the great hall of the Ir juisition. We were met at the door by a number of well-dressed persons, who, I afterwards understood, were the familiars, and attendants of the Holy Office: They bowed very low to the inquisitor, and looked with surprise at me. The great hall is the place in which the prisoners are marshalled for the procession of the Auto da Fe. At the procession described by Dellon, in which he himself walked barefoot, clothed with the painted garment, there were upwards of one hundred and fifty prison ers. I traversed this hall for sometime, with a slow step, re flecting on its former scenes; the inquisitor walked by my side, in silence. I thought of the fate of the multitude of my fellow-creatures who had passed through this place, condemned by a tribunal of their fellow-sinners, their bodies devoted to the flames, and their souls to perdition. And I could not help saying to him, ' Would not the holy church wish, in her mercy, to have those souls back again, that she might allow them a little further probation?' The inquisitor answered nothing, but beckoned me to go with him to a door at one end of the hall. By this door he conducted me to some small rooms, and thence to the spacious apartments of the chief inquisitor. Having surveyed these, he brought me back again to the great hall; and I thought he seemed now desirous that I should depart. ' Now, Father,' said I, ' lead me to the dungeons below, I want to see the captives.' ' No,' said he, ' that cannot be.' I now began to suspect that it had been in the mind of the inquisitor, from the beginning, to show me only a certain part of the inquisition, in the hope of satisfying my inquiries in a general way. I urged him with earnestness, but he steadily resisted, and seemed to be offended, or rather agitated, by my importunity. I intimated to him plainly, that the only way to do justice to his own assertions and arguments, regarding the present state of the Inquisition, was to shew me the prisons and captives. I should then describe only what I saw; but now the subject was left in awful obscurity. ' Lead me down,' said I, ' to the inner building, and let me pass through the two hundred dungeons, ten feet square, described by your former captives. Let me count the number of your present captives and converse with them. I want to see if there are any subjects of the British government, to whom we owe protection. I want to ask how long they have been here, how long it is since they beheld the light of the sun, and whether they ever expect to see it again. Show me the chamber of Torture; and declare what modes of execution or of punishment, are now pract sed within the walls of the Inquisition in lieu of the public Auto da Fe. If, after all that has passed, Father, you resist this reasonable request, I shall be j.stified in believing that you are afraid of exposing the real state of the Inquisition in India.' To these observations the inquisitor made no reply; but seemed impatient that I should withdraw. 'My good Father,' said I, 'I am about to take my leave of you, and thank you for your hospitable attentions, (it had been before understood that I should take my final leave at the door of the Inquisition, after having seen the interior,) and I wish always to preserve on my mind a favorable sentiment of your kindness and candor. You cannot, you say, show me the captives and the dungeons; be pleased then merely to answer this question, for I shall believe your word: How many prisoners are there now below, in the cells of the Inquisition?" The inquisitor replied, 'That is a question which I cannot answer.' On his pronouncing these words, I retired hastily towards the door, and wished him farewell.' We shook hands with as much cordiality as we could at the moment assume; and both of us, I believe, were sorry that our parting took place with a clouded countenance.

"From the Inquisition I went to the place of burning in the *Campo Santo Lazaro*, on the river side, where the victims were brought to the stake at the Auto da Fe. It is close to the palace, that the Viceroy and his court may witness the execution; for it has ever been the policy of the inquisition to make these spiritual executions appear to be the executions of the state. An old priest accompanied me, who pointed out the place, and described the scene. As I passed over this melancholy plain, I thought of the difference between the pure and benign doctrine, which was first preached to India in the Apostolic age, and that bloody code, which after a long night of darkness, was announced to it under the same name! And I pondered on the mysterious dispensation, which permitted the ministers of the inquisition, with their racks and flames, to visit these lands, before the heralds of the Gospel of Peace. But the most painful reflection was, that this tribunal should yet exist, unawed by the vicinity of British humanity and dominion. I was not satisfied with what I had seen or said at the Inquisition, and I determined to go back again. The inquisitors were now sitting on the tribunal, and I had some excuse for returning; for I was to receive from the chief inquisitor a letter which he said he would give me, before I left he

U

place, for the British Resident in Travancore, being an answer to a letter from that officer.

"When I arrived at the Inquisition, and had ascended the outer stairs. the door-keepers surveyed me doubtingly, but suffered me to pass, supposing that I had returned by permission and appointment of the inquisitor. I entered the great hall, and went up directly towards the tribunal of the Inquisition, described by Dellon, in which is the lofty crucifix. I sat down on a form and wrote some notes; and then desired one of the attendants to carry in my name to the inquisitor. As I walked up the hall, I saw a poor woman sitting by herself, on a bench by the wall, apparently in a disconsolate state of mind. She clasped her hands as I passed, and gave me a look expressive of her distress. This sight chilled my spirits. The familiars told me she was waiting there to be called up before the tribunal of the Inquisition. While I was asking questions concerning her crime, the second inquisitor came out in evident trepidation, and was about to complain of the intrusion, when I informed him that I had come back for the letter from the chief inquisitor. He said it should be sent after me to Goa; and he conducted me with a quick step towards the door. As we passed the poor woman, I pointed to her, and said, with some emphasis, 'Behold, Father, another victim of the holy Inquisition!' He answered nothing When we arrived at the head of the great stair, he bowed, and I took my last leave of Josephus à Doloribus, without uttering a word.

Note.—The Inquisition of Goa was abolished in the month of October, 1812.

THE

INQUISITION AT MACERATA,

IN ITALY

Narrative of Mr. Bower, who gives an account of this Court of Inquisition, and of secrets hitherto unknown, relative to their proceedings against heretics.

[Meth. Mag 3d Vol.]

" I never (says Mr. Bower,) pretended that it was for the sake of religion alone, that I left Italy; but on the contrary, have often declared, as all my friends can attest, that, had I never belonged to the Inquisition, I should have gone on, as most Roman Catholics do, without ever questioning the truth of the religion I was brought up in, or thinking of any other. But the unheard of cruelties of that hellish tribunal shocked me beyond all expression, and rendered me, as I was obliged, by my office of Counsellor, to be accessary to them, one of the most unhappy men upon earth. I therefore began to think of resigning my office; but as I had on several occasions, betrayed some weakness, as they termed it, that is, some compassion and humanity, and had upon that account been reprimanded by the Inquisitor, I was well apprized, that my resignation would be ascribed by him to my disapproving the proceedings of the holy tribunal. And indeed, to nothing else could he have ascribed it, as a place at that board was a sure way to preferment, and attended with great privileges, and a considerable salary. Being, therefore, sensible how dangerous a thing it would be to give the least ground to any suspicion of that nature, and no longer able to bear the sight of the many barbarities practised almost daily within those walls, nor the reproaches of my conscience in being accessary to them, I determined, after many restless nights, and much deliberation with myself, to withdraw at the same time from the Inquisitor, and from Italy. In this mind, and in the most unhappy and tormenting situation that can possibly be imagined, I continued near a twelvemonth, not able to prevail upon myself to execute the resolution I had taken on account of the many dangers which I foresaw would inevitably attend it, and the dreadful consequences of my failing in the attempt. But, being in the mean time, ordered by the Inquisitor to apprehend a person, with whom I lived in the greatest intimacy and friendship, the part I was obliged to act on that occasion, left so deep an impression in my mind as soon prevailed over all my fears, and made me determine to put into execution, at all events, and without further delay, the design I had formed. Of that remarkable transaction, therefore, I shall give here a particular account, the rather as it will shew in a very strong light, the nature of the proceedings in that horrid court.

The person whom the inquisitor appointed me to apprehend, was Count Vicenzo della Torre, descended from an illustrious family in Germany, and possessed of a very considerable estate in the territory of Macerata. He was one of my very particular friends, and had lately married the daughter of Signior Constantini, of Fermo, a lady no less famous for her good sense than her beauty. With her family too, I had contracted an intimate acquaintance, while Professor of Rhetoric in Fermo, and had often attended the Count during his courtship, from Macerata to Fermo, but fifteen miles distant. I therefore lived with both in the greatest friendship and intimacy; and the count was the only person that lived with me, after I was made Counsellor of the Inquisition, upon the same free footing as he had done till that time: my other friends being grown shy of me, and giving me plainly to understand, that they no longer cared for my company.

As this unhappy young gentleman was one day walking with another, he met two Capuchin friars; and turning to his companion, when they were passed, 'What fools,' said he, 'are these, to think they shall gain heaven by wearing sackcloth and going bare-foot! Fools indeed, if they think so, or that there is any merit in tormenting one's self: they might as well live as we do, and they would get to heaven quite as soon.' Who informed against him, whether the friars, his companion, or somebody else, I knew not; for the Inquisitors never tell the names of the informers to the Counsellors, nor the names of the witnesses, lest they should except against them. It is to be observed, that all who hear any proposition, that appears to them repugnant to, or inconsistent with the doctrine of the holy mother church, is bound to reveal it to the Inquisitor, and likewise to discover the person by whom it was uttered; and, in this affair, no regard is to be had to any ties, however sacred; the brother being bound to accuse the brother, the father to accuse the son, the son the father, the wife her husband, and the husband his wife; and all bound on pain of eternal damnation, and of being deemed and treated as accomplices, if they do not denounce in a certain time; and no confessor can absolve a person who has heard any thing said, in jest or in earnest, against the belief or practice of the church, till that person has informed the Inquisitor of it, and given him all the intelligence he can concerning the person by whom it was said.

Whoever it was that informed against my unhappy friend, whether the friars, his companion, or somebody else who might have overheard him, the Inquisitor acquainted the board one night (for to be less observed, they commonly meet, out of Rome, in the night) that the abovementioned propositions had been advanced, and advanced gravely, at the sight of two poor Capuchins: that the evidence was unexceptionable; and that they were therefore met to determine the quality of the proposition, and proceed against the delinquent agreeably to that determination. There are in each Inquisition twelve counsellors, viz. four Divines, four Canonists, and four Civilians. It is chiefly the province of the divines to determine the quality of the proposition, viz. Whether it is heretical, or only savors of heresy; whether it is blasphemous and injurious to God and his saints, or only erroneous, rash, schismatical, or offensive to pious ears.

That part of the proposition, ' Fools, if they think that there is any merit in tormenting one's self,' was judged and declared heretical, as openly contradicting the doctrine and practice of holy mother church, recommending austerities as highly meritorious. The Inquisitor observed, on this occasion, that by the proposition, ' Fools, indeed,' &c. were taxing with folly not only the holy fathers, who had all to a man practised great austerities, but St. Paul himself, who ' chastised his body,' that is, whipped himself, as the Inquisitor understood it, adding, that the practice of whipping one's self, so much recommended by all the founders of religious orders, was borrowed of that great apostle of the gentiles.

The proposition being declared heretical, it was unanimously agreed by the board, that the person who had uttered it should be apprehended and proceeded against agreeably to the laws of the Inquisition. And now the person was named; for, till it is determined whether the accused person should or should not be apprehended, his name is kept concealed from the counsellors, lest they should be biased, says the Directory

in his favor or against him. For, in many instances, they
keep up to an appearance of justice and equity, at the same
time that, in truth, they act in direct opposition to all the known
laws of justice and equity.   No words can express the concern
and astonishment it gave me to hear, on such an occasion, the
name of a friend for whom I had the greatest esteem and regard.   The Inquisitor was apprized of it; and, to give me an
opportunity of practising what he had so often recommended
to me, viz. of conquering nature with the assistance of grace,
he appointed me to apprehend the criminal, as he styled him,
and to lodge him safe, before day-light, in the prison of the ho
ly Inquisition.   I offered to excuse myself, but with the greatest submission, from being any ways concerned in the execution of that order; an order, I said, which I entirely approved
of, and only wished it might be put in execution by some
other person; for your lordship knows, I said, the connexion.
But the Inquisitor shocked at the word, 'What?' said he, with
a stern look and angry tone of voice, 'talk of connexions where
the faith is concerned? there is your guard, (pointing to the
Sbirri or baliffs, in waiting,) let the criminal be secured in St.
Luke's cell (one of the worst) before three in the morning.'—
He then withdrew with the rest of the counsellors, and as he
passed me, ' Thus,' he said, ' nature is conquered.'   I had betrayed some weakness, or sense of humanity, not long before,
in fainting away while I attended the torture of one who was
racked with the utmost barbarity; and I had, on that occasion,
been reprimanded by the Inquisitor for suffering nature to get
the better of grace; it being an inexcusable weakness, as he
observed, to be any way affected with the suffering of the
body, however great, when afflicted, as they ever are in the Holy
Inquisition, for the good of the soul.   And it was, I presume,
to make trial of the effect this reprimand had upon me, that
the execution of this cruel order was committed to me.   As I
could by no possible means decline it, I summoned all my resolution, after passing an hour by myself, I may say in the ag-
onies of death, and set out a little after two in the morning, for
my unhappy friend's house, attended by a notary of the Inquisition, and six armed Sbirri.
   We arrived at the house by different ways, and knocking at
the door, a maid-servant looked out of the window, and inqui
ring who knocked, was answered the Holy Inquisition, and at
the same time, ordered to awake nobody, but to come down
directly and open the door, on pain of excommunication.   At
these words, the servant hastened down, half naked as she

was, and having with much ado, in her great fright, at last opened the door, she conducted us, as she was ordered, pale and trembling, to her master's bed-chamber. She often looked very earnestly at me, as she knew me, and shewed a great desire of speaking to me; but of her I durst take no kind of notice. I entered the bed-chamber with the notary, followed by the Sbirri, when the lady awakening at the noise, and seeing the bed surrounded by armed men, screamed out aloud, and continued screaming, as out of her senses, till one of the Sbirri, provoked at the noise, gave her a blow on the forehead, that made the blood run down her face, and she swooned away. I rebuked the fellow very severely, and ordered him to be whipped as soon as I returned to the Inquisition.

In the meantime the husband awakening, and seeing me with my attendants, cried out in the utmost surprise, 'Mr. Bower!' He said then no more; nor could I for some time, utter a single word; and it was with much ado that, in the end, I mastered my grief so far as to be able to let my unfortunate friend know that he was a prisoner of the Holy Inquisition. 'Of the Holy Inquisition!' he replied, 'alas! what have I done? My dear friend, be my friend now.' He said many affecting things; but as I knew it was not in my power to befriend him, I had not the courage to look him in the face, but turning my back to him, withdrew, while he dressed, to a corner of the room, to give vent to my grief there. The notary stood by him while he dressed, and as I observed, quite unaffected. Indeed, to be void of all humanity, to be able to behold one's fellow-creatures groaning and ready to expire in the most exquisite torments cruelty can invent, without being in the least affected with their sufferings, is one of the chief qualifications of an inquisitor, and what all who belong to the Inquisition must strive to attain to. It often happens, at that infernal tribunal, that while an unhappy, and probably an innocent person is crying out in their presence on the rack, and begging by all that is sacred for one moment's relief, in a manner one would think no human heart could withstand; it often happens, I say, that the Inquisitor and the rest of that inhuman crew, quite unaffected with his complaints, and deaf to his groans, to his tears and entreaties, are entertaining one another with the news of the town; nay, sometimes they even insult, with unheard of barbarity, the unhappy wretches in the height of their torment.

To return to my unhappy prisoner; he was no sooner dressed, than I ordered the Bargello, or head of the Sbirri, to tie his

hands with a cord behind his back, as is practised on such oc
casions, without distinction of persons; no more regard being
shewn by the Inquisition to men of the first rank, when charged with heresy, than to the meanest artificers. Heresy dis-
solves all friendship; so that I durst no longer look upon the
man with whom I had lived in the greatest friendship and intimacy as my friend, or shew him, on that account, the least
regard or indulgence.   .

As we left the chamber, the countess, who had been conveyed out of the room, met us, and screaming out in a most
pitiful manner, upon seeing her husband with his hands tied
behind his back, like a thief or robber, flew to embrace him,
and hanging on his neck, begged, with a flood of tears, we
would be so merciful as to put an end to her life, that she
might have the satisfaction, the only satisfaction she wished
for in this world, of dying in the bosom of the man whom she
had vowed never to part with. The count, overwhelmed with
grief, did not utter a single word. I could not find in my heart,
nor was I in a condition to interpose; and indeed, a scene of
greater distress was never beheld by human eyes. However,
I gave signal to the notary to part them, which he did accordingly, quite unconcerned; but the countess fell into a swoon,
and the count was, in the meantime, carried down stairs, and
out of the house, amidst the loud lamentations and sighs
of his servants, on all sides; for he was a man remarkable
for the sweetness of his temper, and his kindness to all about
him.

Being arrived at the Inquisition, I consigned my prisoner
into the hands of the goaler, a lay brother of St. Dominic, who
shut him up in the dungeon mentioned above, and delivered
the key to me. I lay that night in the palace of the Inquisition, where every counsellor has a room, and returned next
morning the key to the inquisitor, telling him that his order
had been punctually complied with. The inquisitor had been
already informed of my whole conduct by the notary; and
therefore, upon my delivering the key to him, 'You have acted
(said he,) like one who is desirous at least to overcome with
the assistance of grace, the inclinations of nature;' that is, like
one who is desirous, with the assistance of grace, to meta-
morphose himself from a human creature, into a brute or a
devil.

In the Inquisition, every prisoner is kept the first week of his
imprisonment, in a dark narrow dungeon, so low that he cannot stand upright in it, without seeing any body but the gaoler,

Arrest of Count della Torre by Inquisitors.

whc brings him, every other day, his portion of bread and wa
ter, he only food that is allowed him. This is done, they say,
to tame him, and render him, thus weakened, more sensible
of the torture, and less able to bear it. At the end of the
week, he is brought in the night before the board to be examined; and on that occasion, my poor friend appeared so altered,
in a week's time that, had it not been for his dress, I should not
have known him; and indeed no wonder, a change of condition so sudden and unexpected; the unworthy and barbarous
treatment he had already met with; the apprehension of what
he might, and probably should suffer; and perhaps, more than
any thing else, the distressed and forlorn condition of his once
happy wife, whom he tenderly loved, whose company he had
enjoyed only six months, could be attended with no other effect
Being asked, according to custom, whether he had any enemies, and desired to name them; he answered, that he bore
enmity to no man, and hoped that no man bore enmity to him.
For as, in the Inquisition, the person accused is not told of the
charge brought against him, nor of the person by whom it is
brought; the Inquisitor asks him whether he has any enemies,
and desires him to name them. If he names the informer, all
further proceedings are stopped till the informer is examined
anew; and if the information is found to proceed from ill-will,
and no collateral proof can be produced, the prisoner is discharged. Of this piece of justice they frequently boast, at
the same time that they admit, both as informers and witnesses, persons of the most infamous characters, and such as are
excluded by all other courts. In the next place, the prisoner
is ordered to swear that he will declare the truth, and conceal
nothing from the holy tribunal, concerning himself or others,
that he knows, and the holy tribunal is desirous to know. He
is then interrogated for what crime he has been apprehended
and imprisoned by the Holy Court of the Inquisition, of all
courts the most equitable, the most cautious, the most merciful. To that interrogatory the count answered, with a faint
and trembling voice, that he was not conscious to himself of
any crime, cognizable by that Holy Court, nor indeed by any
other; that he believed, and ever had believed whatever holy
mother church believed, or required him to believe. He had,
it seems, quite forgot what he had unthinkingly said at the
sight of the two friars. The Inquisitor, therefore, finding he
did not remember, or would not own his crime, after many deceitful interrogatories, and promises which he never intended
to fulfil, ordered him back to his dungeon, and allowing him

anothɛr week, as is customary in such cases, to recol ect him
self, told him, that if he could not in that time prevail upon
himself to declare the truth, agreeable to his oath, means
would be found of forcing it from him; and he must expect no
mercy.

At the end of the week he was brought again before the in
fernal tribunal, and being asked the same questions, returned
the same answers, adding, that if he had done or said any
thing amiss, unwittingly or ignorantly, he was ready to own
it, provided the least hint of it were given him by any there
present, which he entreated them most earnestly to do. He
often looked at me, and seemed to expect, which gave me such
concern as no words can express, that I should say something
in his favor. But I was not allowed to speak on this occasion,
nor was any of the counsellors; and had I been allowed to
speak, I durst not have said any thing in his favor; the advocate appointed by the Inquisition, and commonly styled, 'The
Devil's Advocate,' being the only person that is suffered to
speak for the prisoner. This advocate belongs to the Inquisition, receives a salary of the Inquisition, and is bound by an
oath to abandon the defence of the prisoner if he undertakes
it, or not to undertake it, if he finds it cannot be defended
agreeably to the laws of the Holy Inquisition; so that the whole
is mere sham and imposition. I have heard this advocate, on
other occasions, allege something in favor of the person accused; but on this occasion he declared that he had nothing to
offer in defence of the criminal.

In the Inquisition, the person accused is always supposed
guilty, unless he has named the accuser among his enemies
and he is put to the torture if he does not plead guilty, and own
the crime that is laid to his charge, without being so much as
told what it is; whereas, in all other courts, where tortures are
used, the charge is declared to the party accused before he is
tortured; nor are they ever inflicted without a credible evidence brought of his guilt. But in the Inquisition, a man is
frequently tortured upon the deposition of a person whose evidence would be admitted in no other court, and in all cases
without hearing his charge. As my unfortunate friend continued to maintain his innocence, not recollecting what he had
said, he was, agreeably to the laws of the Inquisition, put to
the torture. He had scarce borne it twenty minutes, crying
out the whole time, 'Jesus Maria,' when his voice failed him
at once, and he fainted away. He was then supported, as he
nung by his arms, by two of the Sbirri, whose province it is to

manage the torture, till he returned to himself. He stil continued to declare that he could not recollect his having said or done any thing contrary to the Catholic faith, and earnestly begged they would let him know with what he was charged, being ready to own it, if it was true. The Inquisitor was then so gracious as to put him in mind of what he had said on seeing the two Capuchins. The reason why they so long conceal from the party accused, the crime he is charged with, is, that if he should be conscious to himself of his having ever said or done any thing contrary to the faith, which he is not charged with, he may discover that too, imagining it to be the very crime he is accused of. After a short pause, the poor gentleman owned that he had said something to that purpose; but, as he had said it with no evil intention, he had never more thought of it from that time to the present. He added, but with so faint a voice as scarce could be heard, that for his rashness, he was willing to undergo what punishment soever the holy tribunal should think fit to impose on him; and he again fainted away. Being eased for a while of his torment, and returned to himself, he was interrogated by the promoter fiscal (wnose business it is to accuse and to prosecute, as neither the informer nor the witnesses are ever to appear) concerning his intention. For, in the Inquisition, it is not enough for the party accused to confess the fact, he must likewise declare whether his intention was heretical or not; and many, to redeem themselves from the torments they can no longer endure, own their intention was heretical, though it really was not. My poor friend often told us he was ready to say whatever he pleased; but, as he never directly acknowledged his intention to have been heretical, as is required by the rules of that court, he was kept on the torture till, quite overcome with the violence of the anguish, he was ready to expire; and being then taken down, he was carried quite senseless, back to his dungeon; and there, on the third day, death put an end to his sufferings. The inquisitor wrote a note to his widow, to desire her to pray for the soul of her late husband, and warn her not to complain of the holy Inquisition, as capable of any injustice or cruelty. The estate was confiscated to the Inquisition, and a small jointure allowed out of it to the widow. As they had only been married six months, and some part of the fortune was not yet paid, the Inquisitor sent an order to the Constantini family, at Fermo, to pay to the holy office, and witnout delay, what they owed to the late count della Torre. For the effects of heretics are all ipso facto confiscated to the

Inquisition, and confiscated from the very day, not of their con
viction, but of their crime; so that all donations made after that
time are void; and whatever they have given, is claimed by
the Inquisition, into whatsoever hands it may have passed;
even the fortunes they have given to their daughters in marriage, have been declared to belong to, and are claimed by
the Inquisition; nor can it be doubted, that the desire of those
confiscations is one great cause of the injustice and cruelty of
that court.

The death of the unhappy count della Torre was soon pub
licly known; but no man cared to speak of it, not even his
nearest relations, nor so much as to mention his name, lest
any thing should inadvertently escape them that might be construed into a disapprobation of the proceedings of the most holy tribunal; so great is the awe all men live in of that jealous
and merciless court.

The other instance of the cruelty of the Inquisition, related
in the spurious account of my escape published by Mr. Baron,
happened some years before I belonged to the Inquisition; and
I do not relate it as happening in my time, but only as happening in the Inquisition of Macerata. It is related at length in
the annals of that Inquisition, and the substance of the relation is as follows: An order was sent from the high tribunal at
Rome, to all the inquisitors throughout Italy, enjoining them
to apprehend a clergyman minutely described in that order.
One answering the description in many particulars being discovered in the diocese of Osimo, at a small distance from
Macerata, and subject to that inquisition, he was there decoy-
ed into the Inquisition, and by an order from Rome, so racked
as to lose the use of his senses. In the mean time the true
person being apprehended, the unhappy wretch was dismissed
by a second order from Rome; but he never recovered the use
of his senses, nor was any care taken of him by the Inquisition. Father Piazza, who was then Vicar at Osimo to Father
Montecuccoli, Inquisitor at Macerata, and died some years ago
a good Protestant, at Cambridge, published an account of this
affair, that entirely agrees with the account I read of it in the
records of the Inquisition.

The deep impression that the death of my unhappy friend,
the most barbarous and inhuman treatment he had met with,
and the part I had been obliged to act in so affecting a tragedy,
made on my mind, got at once the better of my fears; so that
forgetting in a manner the dangers I had till then so much apprehended, I resolved, without further delay, to put in execu-

tion the design I had formed of quitting the Inquisition, and bidding forever adieu to Italy. To execute that design with some safety, I proposed to beg leave of the Inquisitor to visit the Virgin of Loretto, but thirteen miles distant, and to pass a week there; but in the mean time, to make the best of my way to the country of the Grisons, the nearest country to Macerata, out of the reach o.` the Inquisition. Having therefore, after many conflicts with myself, asked leave to visit the neighboring sanctuary, and obtained it, I set out on horseback the very next morning, leaving, as I proposed to keep the horse, his full value with the owner. I took the road to Loretto, but turned out of it at a small distance from Recanati, after a most violent struggle with myself, the attempt appearing to me, at that juncture, quite desperate and impracticable; and the dreadful doom reserved for me, should I miscarry, presented itself to my mind in the strongest light. But the reflection that I had it in my power to avoid being taken alive, and a persuasion that a man in my situation might lawfully avoid it, when every other means failed him, at the expense of his life, revived my staggered resolution; and all my fears ceasing at once, I steered my course, leaving Loretto behind me, to Rocca Contrada, to Fossonbrone, to Calvi in the dukedom of Urbino, and from thence through the Romagna into the Bolognese, keeping the by-roads, and at a good distance from the cities of Fano, Pesaro, Rimini, Forli, Faenza, and Imola, through which the high road passed. Thus I advanced very slowly, travelling, generally speaking, in very bad roads, and often in places where there was no road at all, to avoid, not only the cities and towns, but even the villages. In the mean time, I seldom had any other support but some coarse provisions, and a very small quantity even of them, that the poor shepherds, the countrymen, or wood cleavers, I met in those unfrequented by-places, could spare me. My horse fared not much better than myself; but, in choosing my sleeping place, I consulted his convenience as much as my own, passing the night where I found most shelter for myself, and most grass for him. In Italy there are a very few solitary farm houses or cottages, the country people there all live together in villages; and I thought it far safer to lie where I could be any way sheltered, than to venture into any of them. Thus I spent seventeen days before I got out of the ecclesiastical state; and I very narrowly escaped being taken or murdered, on the very borders of that state; it happened thus:

I had passed two whole days without any kind of subsis-

X

tence whatsoever, meeting with nobody in the by-roads that
would supply me with any, and fearing to come near any
house, as I was not far from the borders of the dominions of
the Pope. I thought I should be able to hold it till I got into
the Modanese, where I believed I should be in less danger
than while I remained in the papal dominions; but finding myself, about noon of the third day, extremely weak and ready
to faint away, I came into the high road that leads from Bo-
logna to Florence, a few miles distant from the former city,
and alighted at a post house, that stood quite by itself. Having asked the woman of the house whether she had any victuals
ready, and being told that she had, I went to open the door of
the only room in the house, (that being a place where gentlemen only stop to change horses,) and saw to my great surprise, a placard pasted on it, with a most minute description
of my whole person, and the promise of a reward of 800
crowns (about £200 English money) for delivering me up
alive to the Inquisition, being a fugitive from the holy tribunal,
and of 600 crowns for my head. By the same placard, all
persons were forbidden, on the pain of the greater excommuni
cation, to receive, harbor, or entertain me, to conceal, or screen
me, or to be any way aiding and assisting to me in making
my escape. This greatly alarmed me, as the reader may
well imagine; but I was still more affrighted, when entering
the room, I saw two fellows drinking there, who, fixing their
eyes upon me as soon as I came in, continued looking at me
very steadfastly. I strove, by wiping my face, by blowing
my nose, by looking out of the window, to prevent their having a full view of me. But, one of them saying, ' The gentleman seems afraid to be seen,' ' I put up my handkerchief,
and turning to the fellow, said boldly, ' What do you mean,
you rascal? Look at me—am I afraid to be seen? He said
nothing, but looking again steadfastly at me, and nodding his
head, went out, and his companion immediately followed him
I watched them, and seeing them, with two or three more, in
close conference, and no doubt consulting whether they should
apprehend me or not, I walked that moment into the stable,
mounted my horse unobserved by them, and while they were
deliberating in an orchard, behind the house, rode off full
speed, and in a few hours got into the Modanese, where I refreshed both with food and with rest, as I was there in no immediate danger, my horse and myself. I was indeed surprised
to find that those fellows did not pursue me: nor can I any
other way account for it, but by supposing, what is not im

probable, that, as they were strangers, as well as myself, and had all the appearance of banditti or ruffians flying out of the dominions of the Pope, the woman of the house did not care to trust them with her horses. From the Modanese I continued my journey, more leisurely through the Parmesan, the Milanese, and part of the Venetian territory, to Chiavenna, subject, with its district, to the Grisons, who abhor the very name of the Inquisition, and are ever ready to receive and protect all who, flying from it, take refuge, as many Italians do, in their dominions. However, as I proposed getting as soon as I could to the city of Bern, the metropolis of that great Protestant canton, and was informed that my best way was through the cantons of Ury and Underwald, and part of the canton of Lucern, all three popish cantons, I carefully concealed who I was, and from whence I came. For, though no Inquisition prevails among the Swiss, yet the Pope's nuncio, who resides at Lucern, might have persuaded the magistrates of those popish cantons to stop me, as an apostate and deserter from the order.

Having rested a few days at Chiavenna, I resumed my journey quite refreshed, continuing it through the country of the Grisons, and the two small cantons of Ury and Underwald, to the canton of Lucern. There I missed my way, as I was quite unacquainted with the country, and discovering a city at a distance, was advancing to it, but very slowly, as I knew not where I was; when a countryman, whom I met, informed me that the city before me was Lucern. Upon that intelligence, I turned out of the road as soon as the countryman was out of sight; and that night I passed with a good-natured shepherd in his cottage, who supplied me with sheep's milk, and my horse with plenty of grass. I set out very early next morning, making the best of my way westward, as I knew that Bern lay west of Lucern. But, after a few miles, the country proved very mountainous, and, having travelled the whole day over mountains, I was overtaken among them by night. As I was looking out for a place where I might shelter myself during the night, against the snow and the rain, (for it both snowed and rained,) I perceived a light at a distance, and making towards it, got into a kind of a foot-path, but so narrow and rugged that I was obliged to lead my horse, and feel my way with one foot, (having no light to direct me,) before I durst move the other. Thus, with much difficulty, I reached the place where the light was, a poor little cottage, and knocking at the door, was asked by a man within, who I

was, and what I wanted? I answered that I was a stranger
and had lost my way. 'Lost your way?' replied the man,
'there is no way here to lose.' I then asked him in what canton I was, and upon his answering, that I was in the canton of
Bern, 'I thank God,' I cried out, transported with joy, 'that I
am.' The good man answered, 'And so do I.' I then told
him who I was, and that I was going to Bern, but had quite
lost myself, by keeping out of all the high roads, to avoid falling into the hands of those who sought my destruction. He
thereupon opened the door; received and entertained me with
all the hospitality his poverty would admit of; regaled me
with sour crout and some new laid eggs, the only provisions
he had, and clean straw with a kind of rug for my bed, he having no other for himself and his wife. The good woman expressed as much satisfaction and good nature in her countenance, as her husband, and said many kind things in the
Swiss language, which her husband interpreted to me in the
Italian; for that language he well understood, and spoke so as
to be understood, having learned it, as he told me, in his
youth, while servant in a public house on the borders of Italy,
where both languages are spoken. I never passed a more
comfortable night; and no sooner did I begin to stir in the
morning, than the good man and his wife came both to know
how I had rested; and, wishing they had been able to accom-
modate me better, obliged me to breakfast on two eggs, which
providence, they said, had supplied them with for that purpose.
I then took leave of the wife, who, with her eyes lifted up to
heaven, seemed most sincerely to wish me a good journey.
As for the husband, he would by all means attend me to the
high road leading to Bern; which road, he said, was but two
miles distant from that place. But he insisted on my first going back with him, to see the way I had come the night before;
the only way, he said, I could have possibly come from the
neighboring canton of Lucern. I saw it, and shuddered at me
danger I had escaped; for I found that I had walked and led
my horse a good way along a very narrow path on the brink
of a very dangerous precipice. The man made so many pious
and pertinent remarks on the occasion, as both charmed and
surprised me. I no less admired his disinterestedness than
his piety; for, upon our parting, after he had attended me till
I was out of all danger of losing my way, I could by no means
prevail upon him to accept of any reward for his trouble. He
had the satisfaction, he said, of having relieved me in the

greatest distress, which was in itself a sufficient reward, and he cared for no other.

I reached Bern that night, and proposed staying some time there; but being informed by the principal minister of the place, to whom I discovered myself, that boats were frequently down the Rhine, at that time of the year, with goods and passengers from Basil to Holland, and advised by him to avail myself of that opportunity, I set out accordingly the next day, and crossing the popish canton of Soleurre in the night, but very carefully avoiding the town of that name, I got early the next morning to Basil. There I met with a most friendly reception from one of the ministers of the place, having been warmly recommended to him by a letter I brought with me from his brother at Bern. As a boat was to sail in two days, he entertained me very elegantly during that time at his house, and I embarked the third day, leaving my horse to my host, in return for his kindness.

The company in the boat consisted of a few traders, of a great many vagabonds, the very refuse of the neighboring nations, and some criminals flying from justice. But I was not long with them; for the boat striking against a rock not far from Strasburgh, I resolved not to wait till it was refitted, (as it was not my design to go to Holland) but to pursue my journey partly in the common diligence or stage-coach, and partly on post horses, through France into Flanders.

Having got safe into French Flanders, I there repaired to the college of the Scotch Jesuits at Douay, and discovering myself to the rector, I acquainted him with the cause of my sudden departure from Italy, and begged him to give immediate notice of my arrival, as well as of the motives of my flight to Michael Angelo Tambuvini, general of the order, and my very particular friend.

The rector wrote, as I had desired him, to the general, and the general, taking no notice of my flight, in his answer, (for he could not disapprove it, and did not think it safe to approve it,) ordered me to continue where I was till further orders. I arrived at Douay early in May; and continued there till the latter end of June, or the beginning of July, when the rector received a second letter from the general, acquainting him, that he had been commanded by the congregation of the Inquisition, to order me, wherever I was, back to Italy; to promise me, in their name, full pardon and forgiveness, if I obeyed· but if I did not obey, to treat me as an apostate. He added, that the same order had been transmitted, soon after my flight, to the nuncios at the different Roman Catholic courts, and he, therefore, advised me to consult my own safety with out further delay.

Upon the receipt of the general's kind letter, the rector was of opinion that I should repair by all means, and without loss of time, to England, not only as the safest asylum I could fly to, in my present situation, but as a place where I should soon recover my native language, and be usefully employed, as soon as I recovered it, either there or in Scotland. I readily closed with the rector's opinion, being very uneasy in my mind, as my old doubts, in point of religion, daily gained ground, and new ones arose upon my reading (which was my only employment) the books of controversy I found in the library of the college. The place being thus agreed on, and its being at the same time settled between the rector and me, that I should set out on the very next morning, I solemnly promised, at his request and desire, to take no kind of notice, after my arrival in England, of his having been any ways privy to my flight, or of the general's letter to him. This promise I have faithfully and honorably observed; and should have thought myself guilty of the blackest ingratitude if I had not observed it, being sensible that, had it been known at Rome, that either the rector or general had been accessary to my flight, the Inquisition would have resented it severely in both. For, although a Jesuit in France, in Flanders, or in Germany, is out of the reach of the Inquisition, the general is not; and the high tribunal not only have it in their power to punish the general himself, who resides constantly at Rome, but may oblige him to inflict what punishment they please on any of the order noxious to them.

The rector went that very night out of town; and in his absence, but not without his privity, I took one of the horses of the college, early next morning, as if I were going for change of air, being somewhat indisposed, to pass a few days at Lisle; but steering a different course, I reached Aire that night, and Calais the next day. I was there in no danger of being stopped and seized at the prosecution of the Inquisition, a tribunal no less abhorred in France than in England. But, being informed by the general, that the nuncios at the different courts had been ordered, soon after my flight, to cause me to be apprehended in Roman Catholic countries, through which I might pass, as an apostate or deserter from the order, I was under no small apprehension of being discovered and apprehended as such, even at Calais. No sooner, therefore, did I alight at the inn, than I went down to the quay; and there, as I was very little acquainted with the sea, and thought the passage much shorter than it is, I endeavored to engage some fishermen to carry me that very night, in one of their small vessels, over to England. This alarmed the guards of the harbor; and I should have been certainly apprehended, as a person guilty, or suspected of some great crime, fleeing from justice, had not Lord Baltimore, whom I had the good luck to meet in the'inn, informed me of my danger, and pitying my condition, attended me that moment, with all his company, to the port, and conveyed me immediately on board of his yacht. There I lay that night, leaving every thing I had, but the clothes on my back, in the inn; and the next day his lordship set me ashore at Dover, from whence I came in the common stage to London.

A SUMMARY

OF THE

ROMAN CATHOLIC FAITH.

When Romanists are charged with worshipping images, saints, the Virgin Mary, &c. and believing that their priests can forgive sins; opposing the reading of the scriptures; and with other errors, it is not uncommon for them to deny the truth of the accusation, and treat it as an unfounded slander. We have thought, therefore, that a short but comprehensive view of their faith, as epitomized by themselves, and supported by extracts from their standard writings, while it comported with the objects of this volume, would prove highly instructive and interesting to its readers.

The following summary, it will be perceived, is in the form of an oath. It was set forth by Pope Pius IV, and comprises the substance of the decrees of the council of Trent. Our readers will here discover, that one grand difference between Protestants and Catholics is, that while the former receive the Bible as the only divine rule of faith, the latter acknowledge the acts of Councils, the traditions of the Church, &c. as of inspired authority. And as those acts and traditions are not unfrequently opposed to the word of God,—yea, are most monstrously erroneous and wicked—some may account for the fact, that the Romish priesthood, where they have the power to prevent it, will never suffer the people to possess or read the Bible. It requires nothing under the divine blessing, but a universal knowledge of the Holy Scriptures, to overthrow every fabric of superstition, idolatry, and tyranny.

SUMMARY, &c

After reciting the Nicene creed, the oath proceeds—

"I most firmly admit and embrace the apostolical and ecclesiastical TRADITIONS, and all other observances and constitutions of the same church, (i. e. the Romish church) Also, I

248

ad.nit sacred scripture, according to the sense which has been held and is held by HOLY MOTHER CHURCH, to whom it belongs to judge of the true sense and interpretation of the sacred scriptures: nor will I ever receive or interpret it (scripture) except according to the unanimous consent of the Fathers.

I also profess that there are truly and properly, seven sacraments of the new law, instituted by our Lord Jesus Christ, and necessary, though not for each singly, yet for the whole human race, viz. Baptism, Confirmation, the Eucharist, Penance, Extreme Unction, Orders and Matrimony; and that they confer grace; and that, of these, baptism, confirmation and orders cannot be reiterated without sacrilege. I also receive and admit the received and approved rites of the Catholic Church, in the solemn administration of all the above mentioned sacraments.

I embrace and receive all and each of those things, which, in the *Holy Council of Trent,* have been defined and declared concerning original sin and justification.

I, in like manner, profess, that in the Mass is offered to God a true, proper, and propitiatory *sacrifice for the living and the dead;* and that, in the most holy sacrament of the Eucharist, there is truly, really and substantially, the BODY AND BLOOD, TOGETHER WITH THE SOUL AND DIVINITY OF OUR LORD JESUS CHRIST; and that there is made the change of the whole substance of the bread into the body, and the whole substance of the wine into the blood, which change the Catholic Church calls Transubstantiation: I confess, also, that under each kind alone, the whole and entire Christ and the true sacrament is taken.

I firmly hold that there is a Purgatory, and that the souls there detained, are helped by the suffrages of the faithful:— Likewise, the Saints reigning together with Christ, are to be venerated and invoked, and that they offer prayers to God for us; and that their RELIQUES are to be venerated. I most firmly assert that the IMAGES of Christ, and of the Mother of God, ever virgin; and also of the other saints, are to be held and retained, and a due honor and veneration is to be granted them.

I affirm also, that the power of indulgences was left by Christ in his church, and that the use of them is in the highest degree salutary to christian people.

I acknowledge the holy catholic and apostolical Romish church, to be mother and MISTRESS OF ALL CHURCHES; and I promise and swear true obedience to the Roman Pontiff, successor of the blessed Peter, Prince of the Apostles, and Vicar of Jesus Christ.

Also, all other things, handed down, defined, and declared by the sacred canons and general councils, and chiefly by the most holy of Trent, I undoubtingly receive and profess: and, at the same time, all things contrary, and all heresies whatever condemned, rejected, and anathematized, I, in like manner, condemn, reject, and anathematize. And this true catholic faith, OUT OF WHICH NO ONE CAN HAVE SALVATION, which at present I voluntarily profess and truly hold, I, the said A. B. promise, vow, and swear, that I will hold and confess the same entire and inviolate, to the last breath of my life, most constantly, God being my helper: and that I will take care as far as lies in me, that the same shall be held, taught, and preached by my subjects, or by those, the care of whom pertains to me by my office. So God help me and these holy gospels of God."

We would now call the attention of our readers to some remarks on the more important and distinguishing articles of the preceding summary of Roman Catholic Faith, and to some illustrations of these articles, drawn from standard writings of that denomination.

THE BIBLE AND TRADITIONS.

Traditions, it will be seen, are placed before the Bible in his epitome of faith. Indeed, the Word of God, as a rule of belief and conduct is, in effect, done away; and the interpretations of the church are put in its place. So that in every case, the inquiry of the faithful Romanist must be—not what saith the scripture—but, *what saith "Mother Church?"* Not to follow the church, however opposed she may be to the Bible, would be a violation of his oath.

The celebrated Council of Trent, which was called by a Bull of Pope Paul III. in the year 1542, decreed that the Roman Catholic-church received and venerated with equal affection of piety and reverence, the Bible and traditions. "Omnes libros tam veteris quam novi Testamenti,—nec non Traditiones—*pari pietatis affectu* ac *reverentia suscipit, et veneratur.*" When, however, tradition was not in accordance with the Word of God, it would be manifestly impossible to conform to this decree, unless a man could conscientiously receive and reverence a truth and its opposite error at the same time. And therefore, to relieve the conscience of the Romanist, it was necessary that the right of interpreting the Bible should be given exclusively to Mother Church, who is also the keeper of Tradition. Hence the Papist has, in fact and strictly speaking, only one standard of faith, and that is neither the Bible nor Tradition, but the Church. He professes, indeed, to acknowledge both the scriptures and tradition; but he is really bound to receive and obey whatever Mother Church declares to be the truth as contained in the Bible and Tradition. She must decide for him in every case, and from her judgment there can be no appeal. What her judgment is concerning the reading of the scriptures by the people, let us now see. It is to be found in the fourth of the *"Ten Rules concerning prohibited Books,"* established by the Fathers of the Council of Trent, and Pope Pius Fourth.

"Since, by experiment, it is manifest that if the holy bible in the common tongue be universally and indiscriminately permitted, more harm than utility will thence arise, on account of the temerity of men—in this particular let it be determined by the judgment of the Bishop or Inquisitor,—so that, with his counsel, the parish ministers or confessors, can grant the reading of the bible in the common tongue, translated by Catholic authors, to those who they shall have understood, can, from reading of this kind, receive not loss, but increase of faith and piety,—which license let them have in writing. But he who shall presume, without such license, to read or have the bible, unless it first be given up to the ordinary, cannot receive absolution of sins. Moreover, let Booksellers, who shall sell, or in any other way grant the bible written in the common dialect, to a person not having the aforesaid license, lose the price of the book, to be converted by the Bishop to pious uses, and let them be subjected to other punishments, according to the quality of their offence, at the will of the same Bishop. Furthermore, Regulars, (that is, those who are bound by the rules of some religious order, as Dominicans, Franciscans, &c.) except by license had from their prelates, cannot read or buy the bible."

It will be perceived that this law places the reading of the scriptures among Romanists, entirely under the *control of Bishops and Inquisitors.* Without their consent and approbation, the bible cannot be sold, bought, read or possessed. Is it wonderful, therefore, that Pope Pius VII, in the nineteenth century, (June 29, 1816,) should have used the following language concerning Bible Societies?—"We have been truly shocked at this most crafty device, (Bible Societies) by which the very foundations of religion" (Roman Catholicism) "are undermined. We have deliberated upon the measures proper to be adopted by our pontifical authority, in order to remedy and abolish this *pestilence,* as far as possible,—This defilement of the faith so imminently dangerous to souls. It becomes episcopal duty, (i. e. the duty of the Roman Catholic Bishops,) that you first of all, expose the wickedness *of this nefarious scheme.* It is evident from experience, that the holy scriptures, when circulated in the vulgar tongue, have, through the temerity of men, produced *more harm* than benefit. Warn the people entrusted to your care, that they fall not into the *snares prepared for their everlasting ruin*" (that is, as you value your souls, have nothing to do with Bible Societies, or the bibles they circulate.) "The deep sorrow we feel on account of this new species of *tares,* which an *Adversary* has so abundantly sown." *

It requires only the *power* in the hands of the Roman Catholic church to make the Word of God a *prohibited book* in every land.

Opus Operatum, or the Efficacy of the Sacraments.

Romanists hold that the Sacraments " confer grace," *ex opere operato,* i. e. by the work wrought, or " by virtue of the work and word done and said in the sacraments." Accordingly, to instance one ordinance, they hold that every person baptized is thereby justified; and that none are ever justified without baptism:—"instrumentalis (causa) justificationis Sacramentum Baptismi; quod est Sacramentum fidei, sine qua nulli umquam contigit Justificatio.—(Concillii Trid. Sess. VI. Cap. VII.) " Faith in the receiver giveth no efficacy to the sacrament, but only taketh away the lets and impediments which might hinder the efficacy of the sacraments; as the dryness of the wood maketh it to burn the better, yet it is no efficient cause of the burning, which is the fire only, but only a help." —(Willet. Synop. Papismi. Bellarm. Lib. 2, De Sac. Cap. 1.) Protestants deny that the ordinances have any power to confer grace " ex opere operato:" they regard these simply as the means under the influence of the Holy Spirit of strengthening faith and other graces, wrought in the heart by the same spirit. If there is no faith exercised, it is unscriptural and unreasonable to suppose there can be any blessing in the participation of an ordinance. On the contrary, such participation is to

---

* The above Denunciatory Epistle, e Bull, was addressed to the Primate of Poland

profane God's institution, and brings own condemnation on the head of the guilty.

From the superstitious notion that the sacraments "confer grace," ex opere operato, have arisen manifold and most enormous abuses. Such a principle carried out into practice, must necessarily destroy the spiritual character of Christ's church. All, according to this system, who come to the sacraments are Christians, and all ought to come, because grace is conferred ex opere operato. A church may in this way be built up entirely of worldly and unconverted men, who merely conform to the outward institutions of religion. How far such a state of things has been realized, facts but too plainly show.

That the reader may have more fully before him the views which the papal church maintains concerning the power of the sacraments, we subjoin a few passages from the proceedings of the Council of Trent. "Si quis dixerit, per ipsa novæ legis Sacramenta *ex opere operato* non conferri gratiam, sed solum fidem divinæ promissionis ad gratiam consequendam sufficere: ANATHEMA SIT." If any one shall say, that grace is not conferred by the sacraments of the new law (gospel) ex opere operato (by the work wrought;) but that only faith in the divine promise suffices to obtain grace: LET HIM BE ACCUR SED! (Sess. vii., Can. viii.) "Si quis dixerit, in tribus Sacramentis, Baptismo scilicet, Confirmatione, et Ordine, non imprimi characterem in anima, hoc est, signum quoddam spiritale et indelebile, unde ea iterari non possunt: ANATHEMA SIT." If any one shall say, that in the three sacraments, viz: Baptism, Confirmation, and Orders, there is not impressed on the soul a character, that is, a certain spiritual and indelible sign, on account of which these (sacraments) are not to be repeated: LET HIM BE ACCURSED! (Sess. vii., Can. ix.)

If any deny that by the grace of our Lord Jesus Christ, which is *conferred in Baptism,* the guilt of original sin is taken away,—or even assert that all *that* is not taken away (in baptism) which has the true and proper nature of sin, but that it is only erased (?) or not imputed: let him be accursed. For in those born again (that is *baptized*) God hates nothing.—(Sess. v. Decret. de pec. orig.)

But as it was perfectly manifest that baptized children, as well as others, when they grew up, exhibited evil inclinations and dispositions; so in order to get over this difficulty, the council boldly denies that such inclinations and dispositions, are truly and properly sin, and pronounces those accur-

Y

sed who think otherwise. If this procedure was not making void the law of God by man's tradition,. it is hard to say what constitutes such impiety. "Hanc concupiscentiam, quam aliquando Apostolus peccatum appellat, sancta synodus declarat Ecclesiam Catholicam numquam intellexisse peccatum appellari, quod vere et proprie in renatis peccatum sit, sed quia ex peccato est, et ad peccatum inclinat. Si quis autem contrarium senserit, ANATHEMA SIT." This concupiscence, (or lusting to evil,) which the apostle sometimes calls sin, the holy Synod (of Trent) declares that the Catholic church has never understood it to be called sin in such a sense, that there is truly and properly sin in those born again (baptized); but (it is called sin) because it proceeded from sin, and inclines to sin. If any man shall think otherwise, LET HIM BE ACCURSED! (Sess. v. ut antea.)

ORIGINAL SIN AND JUSTIFICATION.

The Council of Trent does not maintain the doctrine of total depravity in consequence of Adam's transgression; but simply that he was changed thereby for the worse in body and soul,—"secundum corpus et animam in deterius commutatum fuisse." (Sess. v. Decret. de Pec. Orig.) Accordingly Cardinal Bellarmine thus defines original sin: "Privatio seu carentia doni justitiæ originalis, vel habitualis aversio a Deo." A privation or want of the gift of original righteousness, or an habitual turning away from God. He denies that this sin is any evil disposition or quality inherent in us, but it arises only "ex carentia justitiæ originalis, *non ex insita aliqua qualitate.*" Of course he denies also, with the council of Trent, that the concupiscence, or lusting to evil which exists in baptized persons is truly and properly sin.

The Council of Trent declares also, as we have before seen, that original sin is altogether taken away in baptism—"totum tolli;" that without this ordinance none can be justified—and consequently that baptism is necessary to the salvation even of infants. "Si quis—negat ipsum Christi Jesu meritum per baptismi Sacramentum in forma Ecclesiæ rite collatum tam adultis quam *parvulis* applicari, anathema sit. Quod (originale peccatum) regenerationis lavacro *necesse* sit expiari ad vitam æternam consequendam. And though Bellarmine affirms also that infants dying without baptism are eternally punished, yet he maintains that it is only a punishment of loss (of heaven?), not of pain, or sensible fire"—damni, non sensus, sive ignis sensibilis."

On the subject of justification, Roman Catholics hold a doctrine entirely opposed to that of Protestants, and as this point is fundamental in Christianity, so the one or the other has here altogether departed from the faith of the Gospel. The latter assert that the obedience of the Saviour unto death, or in one word, the merits or righteousness of all done or suffered by the incarnate Redeemer, is the sole ground of a sinner's acceptance in the sight of heaven; that he stands on that ground simply by faith; and that Christian holiness or a good life is the *necessary* fruits and evidences of justification.— Good works, so far from being in any way the ground or cause of justification, are never performed until *we have been justified* through faith in the Lord Jesus Christ. This scheme, it will be perceived, takes away from the sinner all room for boasting, lays him in the dust, and gives the whole glory of his salvation from beginning to end to ' God our Saviour."

Protestants are very careful to distinguish between justification and sanctification,—the latter being in each penitent believer simply the consequence and proof of the former: So that no man, according to their views, can entertain a good hope that he has been justified, or pardoned, and regarded as righteous before God, who doth not bring forth the fruits of sanctification—who is not holy in heart and life.

What the views of Romanists are on this most important subject, may be seen in the subjoined extracts from the decisions of the Council of Trent:

The alone formal cause (of justification) is the righteousness of God—that righteousness with which he makes us righteous—with which forsooth we are endowed by him: we receiving this righteousness within ourselves, every one according to his measure, which the Holy Spirit divides to each as he wills, and according to each person's own disposition and co-operation. (Sess. vi., Cap. vii.)

Here we see that the " formal,"* that is, *essential* cause of justification, is the man's own holiness, or in other words, that righteousness with which the spirit of God endues him. Sanctification is the ground of justification. How large a space is here given for glorying in the merit of works!

And as according to the faith of Romanists a man is justified by his own holiness, so they assert, that *justification admits of*

* " Formal, having the power of making a thing what it is—constituent, essential." *Webster.*—When, e. g, the Saviour is said to be in the *form* of God—the meaning is, he is *essentially* God.

increase. " Sic ergo justificati, et amici Dei, ac Domestici fac-
ti euntes de virtute in virtutem, renovantur, ut apostolus in
quit, de die in diem: hoc est, mortificando membra carnis suæ,
et exhibendo ea arma justitiæ in sanctificationem, per observa-
tionem mandatorum Dei, et *Ecclesiæ*, in ipsa justitia per
Christi gratiam accepta, cooperante fide bonis operibus, cres-
cunt, atque magis justificantur." Thus, then, justified men,
made the friends and servants of God, going on from virtue to
virtue, are renewed, as the apostle says, from day to day; that
is, in mortifying the members of their flesh, and in using
these as instruments of righteousness unto holiness by observance of the laws of God and of the CHURCH, they increase in
that righteousness received by the grace of Christ, faith co-
operating with good works, and are MORE JUSTIFIED."—(Sess.
vi. Chap. x.)

" Si quis dixerit homines—per eam ipsam," (i. e. justitiam
Christi,) "formaliter justos esse; anathema sit." Sess. vi.
Canon x.) If any one shall say that men are formally (*essentially*) justified by the very righteousness of Christ, let
him be accursed.

" Si quis dixerit, homines, justificari—sola imputatione justitiæ Christi,—anathema sit." If any one shall say that men
are justified *solely by the imputation of Christ's righteousness;*
let him be accursed.—(Can. xi.)

"Si quis dixerit, fidem justificantem nihil aliud esse quam
fiduciam divinæ misericordiæ, *peccata remittentis propter
Christum;* vel eam fiduciam solam esse qua justificamur;
anathema sit." If any one shall say that justifying faith is
no other than a *reliance on divine mercy* REMITTING SIN FOR
CHRIST'S SAKE; or that it is this reliance (trust, or faith)
alone, by which we are justified; let him be accursed.—
(Can. xii.)

How could the great scripture doctrine of justification
through faith alone on the sole ground of the merits or righteousness of the Lord Jesus Christ, be more plainly expressed
than it is in the three preceding extracts from the Canons of
he Council of Trent? And yet this precious, fundamental
truth of the gospel, and the only foundation of hope to the really awakened, penitent, believing soul, is here condemned;
and all who hold it are *cursed* by the Church of Rome! And
now long such CURSED heretics would escape the flames of the
Inquisition, had "holy Mother Church" the power of erecting
one in this land, deserves the serious consideration of all who
value their religious and civil liberty.

Let the reader weigh well the following canon "Si quis dixerit, justitiam acceptam non conservari, atque etiam augeri coram Deo per bona opera: sed opera ipsa fructus solum modo et signa esse justificationis adeptæ, non autem ipsius augendæ causam; anathema sit." If any one shall say that justification received is not preserved, and also *increased before God through good works;* but that such works are only the ruits and signs of justification obtained, and not a cause of its increase; let him be accursed."—(Can. xxiv.)

How does the following canon agree with these scriptures? "There is not a just man upon earth that doeth good, and sinneth not.—If we say that we have no sin, we deceive ourselves, and the truth is not in us. If we confess our sins, he is faithful and just to forgive us our sins. Cursed is every one that continueth not in *all things* which are written in the book of the law to do them. The law of the Lord is perfect. The law is holy; and the commandment holy, just, and good."

If any shall say that a justified man sins venially, at least, in any good work, or, what is still more intolerable, that he sins mortally, and therefore deserves eternal punishments; and on account of that (the sin of his good work) he is not condemned only because God does not impute these works for condemnation; let him be accursed."—(Can. xxv.)

We subjoin but two more canons on the subject of justifica tion;—these, the serious reader of the Bible will allow, need no comment.

"If any one shall say that after the grace of justification is received, the sin of the penitent sinner so remitted, and his desert (guilt) of eternal punishment so blotted out, there remains no desert of temporal punishment to be paid in this world, or hereafter in Purgatory, before an access to the kingdom of heaven can be open to him;—let him be accursed."— (Can. xxx.)

"If any one shall say, that the good works of a justified man are so the gifts of God, that they are not the good merits of the justified man himself; or hat the justified man *by the good works* which are done by him through the grace of God and the merit of Christ, does not truly *deserve* the increase of grace, eternal life, and, provided he die in a state of grace, the attainment of eternal life itself, and the increase of glory; let him be accursed.—(Can. xxxii.)

TRANSUBSTANTIATION.

Roman Catholics believe that after the consecration of the bread and wine by the priest in the Lord's Supper, *these are changed into God*, and as such ought therefore to be *worshipped.*

Those, however, who have always had the scripture light and other religious advantages which are possessed in protestant communities, can scarcely suppose it possible that so monstrously superstitious and idolatrous a dogma as that of Transubstantiation, could be received by any body of professing christians. But such doubts will all be immediately removed by a reference to any of the doctrinal standards of the Church of Rome.

"In the first place, the Holy Synod teaches, and openly and simply professes, that in the holy sacrament of the Eucharist, after the consecration of the bread and wine, our Lord Jesus Christ, *true* God and man, is truly, really, and substantially contained under the form of these sensible things." That is, what *appears* still the bread and wine, is really no more so, but they are now "our Lord Jesus Christ, *true God and man!*" Such is the explanation given in the fourth chapter of the same session. This holy Synod declares that by the consecration of the bread and wine, a change is made of the whole substance of the bread into the substance of the body of our Lord Christ, and of the whole substance of the wine into the substance of his blood. Which change is suitably and properly called by the holy Catholic Church, Transubstantiation.

And as the bread and wine have thus become God, in the estimation of Romanists, so the next chapter directs that *the Sacrament be worshipped as the true God.* "Nullus itaque dubitandi locus relinquitur, quin omnes Christi fideles pro more in Catholica Ecclesia semper recepto latriæ *cultum, qui vero Deo debetur*, huic sanctissimo Sacramento in veneratione exhibeant." There is therefore no room for doubt but that all Christ's faithful people, according to the custom always received in the Catholic Church, should, in veneration, offer to this most holy sacrament, the worship (latriæ cultum) which is due to the true God. The council then goes on in the first and sixth canons to CURSE those who deny the doctrine of Transubstantiation, and hold the views of the protestants on the subject of the Lord's Supper, and those also who say that the worshippers of the Eucharist are idolaters.

As the church of Rome teaches that the elements of the Lord's Supper are really and substantially changed into the Divine Saviour, so she also teaches that this Sacrament is a sacrifice,—"sacrosanctum missæ sacrificium,"—the MOST HOLY SACRIFICE OF THE MASS,—and that it is "propitiatorum pro vivis et defunctis,"—a propitiation for the living and the dead; and that it is the same victim that was offered on the cross, so those who, with due preparation come to it, (mass,) will obtain grace and the pardon of their sins:—"non solum pro fidelium vivorum peccatis, pœnis, satisfactionibus, et aliis necessitatibus, sed et pro defunctis in Christo nondum ad plenum purgatis, rite, juxta apostolorum traditionem, offertur,"— that not only for the sins, punishments, satisfactions, and other necessities of the faithful who are living, but also for those who, having died in Christ, are not yet fully purified, (in purgatory,) it (sacrifice of mass) is rightly, and according to the Apostles' tradition, offered. (Sess. xxiii. cap. 1, 2.)

The doctrine of the mass is, therefore, that the elements, changed by consecration, are a real victim, the incarnate Saviour; that the officiating Priest offers the divine sacrifice; and that on the ground of this sacrifice or atonement, the pardon of sin and other benefits are obtained by the living and by the dead. That such a doctrine robs the Saviour of his glory and overturns the whole gospel system of salvation is most manifest. "Without shedding of blood" declares the Apostle, "is no remission" of sin. "By one offering he (the Lord Jesus Christ) hath perfected forever them that are sanctified." "The blood of Jesus Christ cleanseth us from all sin." Every reader of the word of God is aware that it abounds with similar testimonies.

PURGATORY.

Purgatory, according to the Romish creed, is a certain place to which are sent the souls of those who die in venial sin, or whose sins have been remitted, but the punishment of them not satisfied. These souls are purified by the fire of Purgatory, and thus made meet for heaven, to which at last they all safely arrive.

"Purgatorium esse;" declares the Council of Trent, (Sess. xxv.) "animasque ibi detentas, fidelium suffragiis, potissimum vero acceptabili altaris sacrificio juvari." There is a purgatory; and the souls there detained are helped by the suffrages (favors) of the faithful, but most of all by the acceptable sacrifice of the altar (mass.) What these suffrages are we are taught in the latter part of the decree—"Missarum sacrificia, orationes, eleemosynæ, aliaque pietatis opera, quæ a fidelibus pro aliis fidelibus defunctis fieri consueverunt." Sacrifices of masses, prayers, alms, and other works of piety which are wont to be performed by the faithful, for other faithful deceased.

The doctrine of Purgatory is most adroitly calculated to secure an irresistible influence over an ignorant and superstitious people. Only let it be believed that the soul is exquisitely tormented in a fire, from which the celebration of masses can deliver it, and the priest has at once a strong rein upon the necks of surviving relatives and friends, and a sure key to their pockets. Accordingly, masses for souls in Purgatory have always been a most gainful trade to the Church of Rome. It is not surprising, therefore, that the council commands that the existence of Purgatory be believed, held, taught, and every where preached, and curses those who deny the efficacy of mass in relieving souls there detained.

WORSHIP OF THE VIRGIN MARY, SAINTS, RELIQUES, IMAGES, &c.

Romanists are taught by their Church that the Virgin Mary and other saints in heaven pray for the faithful on earth, and that these ought to pray to Mary and other deceased saints to intercede with God for them. "Sanctos, una cum Christo regnantes, orationes suas pro hominibus Deo offerre, bonum atque utile esse suppliciter eos invocare, et ob beneficia impetranda a Deo per filium ejus, Jesum Christum—ad eorum orationes, opem auxiliumque confugere." The holy Synod commands the Bishops and other instructors in the Church,—to teach the people "that the saints reigning together with Christ offer their prayers for men to God; that it is good and useful suppliantly to pray to them; and for obtaining benefits from God through his son Jesus Christ, to fly to their prayers, help, and assistance."—(Sess. xxv.)

Having stated the doctrine of saint-worship, we will now subjoin two or three specimens of its fruits,—prayers addressed to saints.

"Holy Mother of God, who hast *worthily merited* to conceive him whom the world could not comprehend; by thy pious intervention wash away our sins, that so, *being redeemed by thee,* we may be able to ascend to the seat of everlasting glory, &c."

"O Martyr Christopher,—Confer comfort, and remove heaviness of mind: and cause, that the examination of the Judge may be mild toward all."

"O William, thou *good Shepherd*,—Cleanse us in our agony; grant us aid; *remove the filthiness of our life; and grant the joys of a celestial crown.*"

"O ye eleven thousand glorious Maids, lilies of virginity, roses of martyrdom, defend me in life by affording to me your assistance: and show yourselves to me in death by bringing the last consolation."—-(Collect. in Hor. ad usum sacrum, as quoted in Faber's Difficulties of Romanism, p. 191, 2.)

On the subject of relique-worship, the council decrees as follows: "Sanctorum quoque Martyrum, et aliorum cum Christo viventium sancta corpora, quæ viva membra fuerunt Christi, et templum Spiritus Sancti, ab ipso ad æternam vitam suscitanda et glorificanda a fidelibus veneranda esse: per quæ multa beneficia a Deo hominibus præstantur: &c.—(Sess.xxv.) The holy bodies of saints, also of martyrs, and of others living with Christ, which (bodies) have been living members of Christ, and the temple of the Holy Ghost, and which by him (Christ) are to be raised to eternal life and glorified;—(these bodies) are to be *venerated*.

What this religious veneration is, which the council here decrees to relics, we may learn from a late work on the doctrines of the Catholic church, by the Bishop of Aire. "From God, as its source," says the Bishop, "the *worship*, with which we honor relics, originates; and to God, as its end, it ultimately and terminatively reverts."—(Discuss. Amic. Lett. XV. Faber's Diff. of Rom. p. 194.) But the worship which originates from God, and reverts to him, must, if any species of religious service is entitled to the distinction, be the most exalted worship—it is true and proper worship, that which, according to the scriptures, is due to God alone.

The *Worship of Images* is enjoined in the following terms, "Imagines porro Christi, Deiparæ Virginis, et aliorum sanctorum, in templis præsertim habendas et retinendas, eisque debitum honorem et venerationem impertiendam," &c. (Sess. XXV.) Moreover, the Images of Christ, the God-bearing Virgin, and of other saints, are, in churches especially, to be had and retained, and due honor and *veneration* are to be given to them. That by this veneration, religious worship is really intended, is plain from what follows,—"honos, qui eis exhibetur refertur ad *prototypa*, quæ illæ repræsentant," &c. The honor which is shown to them (the images) is referred to the originals which these represent. In the case, then, of the image of

Christ, the identical honor which is given to him, is shewn to the image; but this is true and proper worship. The council apparently apprehensive, as well they might be, that they would be thought idolaters, thus endeavor, in anticipation, to escape the imputation, "non quod credatur inesse aliqua in iis divinitas vel virtus, propter quam sint colendæ," &c. Not that it is believed there is any divinity in the images, or virtue, on account of which they are to be worshipped, &c.; but the same reply was uniformly made by the ancient Pagan Romans, and when charged with idolatry, for worshipping before the images of Jupiter, &c. and yet the apostle does not hesitate to speak of them as heathens.

INDULGENCES.

Bellarmine, the celebrated defender of the Romish Church, tells us that indulgence is "remissionem pœnarum, quæ remanent luendæ post remissionem culparum:"—(Bellar. De Indulg. Lib. 1, ch. 1.)

The remission of the punishments which remain to be satisfied for, after the remission of faults. He who purchases an indulgence, procures thereby a remission of those purgatorial fires which otherwise he must suffer on account of his sins.— The sale of indulgences is a very extensive and gainful trade in Roman Catholic communities, and the effects of such a trade on the minds and manners of the people, cannot but be most deplorable. "That religion," says Dr. Johnson, a late traveller in Italy, "cannot offer very formidable checks to immorality, or even crime, which hangs up 'Plenary Indulgence' on every chapel-door. He who can easily clear the board of his conscience on Sunday, has surely a strong temptation to begin chalking up a fresh score on Monday or Tuesday." It was the shocking consequences of an extraordinary sale of indulgences, that opened the eyes of Luther to the abominations of Romanism, and thus led to the Reformation. The very bonds of society seemed to be loosening and dissolving, and crimes of the most frightful character obtained license by the flood of indulgences that was pouring in upon the country.

'Such indulgences were first invented in the eleventh century, by Urban II. as a recompense for those who went in person upon the glorious enterprise of conquering the Holy Land. They were afterwards granted to those who hired a soldier for that purpose; and in process of time were bestowed on such as gave money for accomplishing any pious work enjoined by the pope. The power of granting indulgences has been greatly abused in the Church of Rome. Pope Leo X., in order to carry on the magnificent structure of St. Peter's, at Rome, published indulgences, and a plenary remission to all such as should contribute money towards it. Finding the project take, he granted to Albert elector of Mentz, and archbishop of Magdeburg, the benefit of the indulgences of Saxony, and the neighboring parts, and farmed out those of other countries to the highest bidders: who, to make the best of the bargain, procured the ablest preachers to cry up the value of the ware. The form of these indulgences was as follows:— "May our Lord Jesus Christ have mercy upon thee, and absolve thee by the merits of his most holy passion. And I, by his authority, that of his blessed apostles, Peter and Paul, and of the most holy pope, granted and committed to me in these parts, do absolve thee, first from all ecclesiastical censures, in whatever manner they have been incurred; then from all thy sins, transgressions, and excesses, how enormous soever they may be: even from such as are reserved for the cognizance of the holy see, and as far as the keys of the holy church extend. I remit to you all punishment which you deserve in purgatory on their account: and I restore you to the holy sacraments of the church, to the unity of the faithful, and to that innocence and purity which you possessed at baptism: so that when you die, the gates of punishment shall be shut, and the gates of the paradise of delight shall be opened; and if you shall not die at present, this grace shall remain in full force when you are at the point of death. In the name of the Father, the Son, and the Holy Ghost." According to a book, called the Tax of the sacred Roman Chancery, in which are contained the exact sums to be levied for the pardon of each particular sin, we find some of the fees to be thus:

"Robbing a church, 2 dollars 25 cents. Simony, 2 dollars 25 cents. Perjury, forgery, and lying, 2 dollars. Robbery, 3 dollars. Burning a house, 2 dollars 75 cents. Eating meat in Lent, 2 dollars 75 cents. Killing a layman, 1 dollar 75 cents. Striking a Priest, 2 dollars 75 cents. Procuring abortion, 1 dollar 50 cents. Dead man excommunicated, 3 dollars. Priest to keep a concubine, 2 dollars 25 cents. * * * * Ravishing or deflowering a virgin, 2 dollars. Murder of father, mother, sister, brother or wife, 2 dollars 50 cents. Nun 'or frequent fornication, in or out of the nunnery, 5 dollars. Marrying on a day forbidden, 10 dollars. All incest, rapes, adultery and fornication committed by a Priest, with his relations, nuns, married women virgins and his concubines, with the joint pardon of all his whores, at the same time, 10 dollars. Absolution of all crimes together, 12 dollars."

"The terms in which the retailers of indulgences described their benefits, and the necessity of purchasing them, were so extravagant that they appear almost incredible. If any man, said they, purchase letters of indulgence, his soul may rest secure with respect to its salvation. The souls confined in purgatory, for whose redemption indulgences are purchased, as soon as the money tinkles in the chest, instantly escape from that place of torment, and ascend into heaven. That the efficacy of indulgences was so great, that the most heinous sins, even if one should violate (which was impossible) the Mother of God, would be remitted and expiated by them, and the person be freed both from punishment and guilt. That this was the unspeakable gift of God, in order to reconcile man to himself. That the cross erected by the preachers of indulgences was equally efficacious with the cross of Christ itself."

"Lo," said they, "the heavens are open: if you enter not now, when will you enter? For twelve pence you may redeem the soul of your father out of purgatory; and are you so ungrateful that you will not rescue the soul of your parent from torment? If you had but one coat, you ought to strip yourself instantly, and sell it, in order to purchase such benefit," &c.

Since that time the popes have been more sparing in the exercise of this power; although it is said, they still carry on a great trade with them to the Indies, where they are purchased at two rials a piece, and sometimes more. We are told also that a gentleman not long since being at Naples, in order that he might be fully ascertained respecting indulgences, went to the office, and for two sequins purchased a plenary remission of all sins for himself and any two other persons of his friends or relations, whose names he was empowered to insert.— [*Haweis's Church Hist.* vol. iii. p. 147; *Smith's Errors of the Church of Rome; Watson's Theol. Tracts,* vol. v. p. 274· *Mosheim's Eccl. Hist.* vol. i. p. 594, quarto.]

INFALLIBILITY.

The church of Rome claims to be infallible. In consequence of this attribute, she decides what is, and what is not scripture, and what the scriptures teach; she asserts the right also, to prescribe for faith and practice as necessary for salvation, other things than those contained in the scriptures; and all men are bound implicitly, to submit to her decision. Romanists, however, differ very much among themselves abou the seat of this tremendous power; some assert that it is in the Pope, others, that it is in a general Council, and others again, in the Pope and Council combined. This very doubt concerning the place of its existence, shews that the pretension itself is unfounded and ridiculous. For what is the use of infallibility, if none can with certainty, discover where it is, and by whom it is exercised?

But this is not all, the claim of infallibility is most blasphemous presumption. God alone is infallible,—his word alone cannot err,—in that are all things necessary to salvation, and to him alone ought we implicitly to submit. The man, or church, who claim to themselves infallibility, usurp the place of God, and exhibit the very character of Antichrist, "who opposeth and *exalteth* himself" says the apostle, "above all that is called God, or that is worshipped; so that he, as God, sitteth in the temple of God, *shewing himself that he is God.*" It were easy to swell out this article, so as to fill large volumes, with the account of the gross errors, oppressions, and enormities which have proceeded from infallible Popes, and an infallible church. It was by an almost universal acknowledgment of this impious claim to infallibility, that the spiritual despotism of the dark ages was maintained. Individuals and nations were stript of almost every civil and religious right, and trampled in the dust, beneath the feet of the Romish Hierarchy. The evils at last became intolerable, men almost every where endeavored to burst the yoke: the glorious reformation followed, and multitudes obtained the blessings of freedom. This liberty, purchased by the labors, and tears, and blood of thousands, it is ours to maintain against the claims of infallible "Mother Church."

As the church of Rome asserts her infallibility, she can never change; what she has once declared to be truth, must ever remain so—else what becomes of her infallibility? Such a claim then, it is manifest, makes all attempts to *reform* the Romish system of religion utterly hopeless. Being infallibly right in all its essential principles, it never can be altered.— There is no such thing, therefore, as getting rid of the evils of such a system, but by altogether abandoning it. They who would escape her plagues, must, in the language of God's word, come out of her.

We will present to our readers but one specimen of the fruits of infallibility—but *one*, because that will be sufficient to shew the character of the tree. By the third Council of Lateran, the *obligation to destroy heretics* was imposed upon

Z

the faithful; and by the same council, it was declared that all
oaths, which are against ecclesiastical utility, become, *ipso
facto*, null and void. "Non enim dicenda sunt juramer a, scd
potius perjuria, quæ contra utilitatem ecclesiasticam et sanctorum patrum veniunt instituta." Consequently, John Huss was
burnt, though he had received a safe-conduct from the Emperor Sigismund. The church authorities decided that the oath
of the Emperor was "contra ecclesiasticam utilitatem," and
therefore, he was bound to break it, and burn to death the man
whom he had sworn to protect.—(Faber's Diff. of Romanism,
page 42.)

Here then, the point is settled,—Roman Catholics, notwithstanding all oaths to the contrary, are bound to destroy all heretics, whenever their church requires it, and they have it in
their power. To deny the obligation to do this, would be a
denial of the infallibility of the Church.

Dr. James Johnson, a late traveller in Italy, gives a most
melancholy and disgusting view of its religion and morality.
After a short quotation upon these subjects, we will close the
present head with an extract from his book, giving an account
of one of the most imposing ceremonies, in honor of " *Infallibility personified*."

" The fundamental objects of every religion, I imagine tu be
these—first, to foster the good and check the evil propensities
of man's nature in this world; and, secondly, to procure him
immortality and happiness in the next. How far the Catholic system of faith and worship, as professed and practised on
the Classic soil of Italy, is calculated to secure the salvation of
the soul, I will not venture to judge, for the reason above mentioned. But I deem it not out of my province to form some
estimate of its influence over virtue and vice, and of its tend-
dency to good or evil actions in the common affairs of life.

" I humbly conceive, that there are two radical defects in the
Catholic religion, as practised in Italy: first, the facility of absolution, before alluded to; secondly, the perpetual intervention of saints and angels between the human heart, whether in
a state of contrition or adoration, and the throne of our Creator. I need not repeat that I have already said, as to the bale-
ful effects of cheap and easy remission of sins, through the medium of heartless ceremonies, if not virtual bribery. It is now
pretty well ascertained, that in proportion as the duty on contraband articles is diminished, the consumption will increase, so as that the revenue loses nothing by relaxation
of its demands. I believe the same maxim will hold good as

to moral articles of contraband, especially where no worldly *dishonor* attaches to breach of law. It is impossible to view the facilities with which sins are washed away in Italy, (not to speak of the *permission* to commit them,) without coming to the conclusion that one of the most effectual checks to vice, which religion affords, is thus rendered not only inefficient, but absolutely conducive to the evil which it is intended to remedy.

Forsyth, while speaking of certain scenes which took place at Naples, during a memorable epoch still fresh in the recollections of the present race, has the following passage:

" They reeled ferociously from party to party, from saint to saint, and were steady to nothing but *mischief and the church*

" Those Cannibals, feasting at their fires on human carnage, would kneel down and beat their breasts in the fervor of devotion, whenever the sacring bell went past to the sick; and some of Ruffo's cut-throats would never mount their horses without crossing themselves and muttering a prayer."

The perpetual intercession of saints and angels, not to speak of priests and relics of the dead, in pardoning sins and saving souls, must inevitably diminish, if not destroy that awful solemnity which ought to attend a direct appeal from man to his Maker.

In respect to the pompous formalities, the georgeous imagery, the superstitious rites, the solemn mockeries, and the sickening delusions of Italian worship, whatever influence they may have on people immersed in ignorance, and trammeled by priestcraft—they can have but one of two effects upon Englishmen—that of turning the Romish religion into ridicule, in strong minds; or that of overpowering and *converting* minds that are weak!

*   *   *   *   *   *   *   *

The Chapel of the Quirinal on Sunday mornings, is at last filled to suffocation. The tribunes on either side are occupied by *the elegantes of London and Paris, Petersburg and Vienna, Cracow or New York*. In the central nave the throng is composed of abbots, priors, and dignitaries in grand costume,—the Mamelukes of the church! Roman generals, all armed for the military service of the altar, the only service they have ever seen—monks, guards, friars, Swiss soldiers, and officers of state! Outside a *cordon* drawn round the choir, are placed the foreign gentlemen. The choir, the scene of action, all brilliant and beautiful, is still a void. When the signal is given, the crowd divides! and the procession begins!—Mutes and others form the *avantgarde* of the pageant, and lead the way. Then

comes, personified Infallibility! feeble as womanhood! help·
less as infancy! withered by infirmity; but borne aloft, like
some idol of pagan worship, on the necks of men, above all human contact.   The conclave follows, each of its princes robed
like an Eastern Sultan!   Habits of silk and brocade, glittering
with gold and silver, succeeded by robes of velvet, and vestments of point lace, the envy of reigning empresses.   The toi-
lette of these Church exquisites is perfect: not a hair displa-
ced, not a point neglected, from the powdered toupee to the
diamond shoe-buckle.   The Pope is at last deposited on his
golden throne: his ecclesiastical attendants fold round him his
ample caftain, white and brilliant as the nuptial dress of bridal
queens! they arrange his dazzling mitre; *they blow his nose,*
they wipe his mouth, and exhibit the representation of Divinity
in all the disgusting helplessness of drivelling caducity.   His
Holiness being thus cradled on a throne, to which Emperors
once knelt, the Conservators of Rome, the caryatides of the
Church, place themselves meekly at his steps, and the manikin,
who represents the Roman senate, precisely in his look and
dress resembling Brid'oison, in the *" Marriage de Figaro,"*
takes his humble station near the Imperial seat, more gorgeous
than any the Cæsars ever mounted.   Meantime, the demigods
of the conclave repose their eminences in their stalls, on velvet
cushions, and their *caudatorj* (or tail-bearers) place themselves
at their feet.   In the centre, stand or sit, on the steps of the
high altar, the bishops with their superb vestments.   Then the
choir raises the high hosannas; the Pope pontificates; and the
Temple of Jupiter never witnessed rites so imposing, or so
splendid.   Golden censors fling their odors on the air! har-
mony the most perfect, and movements the most gracious, delight the ear and eye!   At the elevation of the host, a silence
more oppressive than even this solemn 'concord of sweet
sounds' succeeds; all fall prostrate to the earth; and the military falling still lower than all, lay their arms of destruction
at the feet of that mystery operated in memory of the salvation of mankind.

'The ceremony is at last concluded.   The procession returns as it entered.   The congregation rush after: and the next
moment, the anti-room of this religious temple resembles the
saloon of the opera.   The abbots and priors mingle among the
lay crowd, and the cardinals chat with pretty women, sport
their red stockings, and ask their opinions of the Pope's Pon-
tification, as a *Mervillieux* of the Opera at Paris, takes snuff,
and demands of his *Chere Belle,* ' *Comment trowez vous ca*

Comtesse?' Bows, and courtesies, and recognitions—'nods, and becks, and wreathed smiles'—fill up the waiting time for carriages; and then all depart from the Quirinal, to re-congregate at St. Peter's to hear vespers, give rendezvous, and make parties for the opera."

Power of the Priest to Forgive Sins.

The doctrine of the Church of Rome on this point, is fully and clearly expressed by the council of Trent, in its fourteenth session, chap. 6.   The Holy Synod "teaches also, that even priests, who are held in *mortal sin,* do exercise, by virtue of the Holy Ghost, conferred in ordination, as Christ's ministers, the function of *remitting sins;* and that they think ill who contend there is not this power in *wicked Priests.*   And though the Priest's Absolution is the dispensation of another's benefit; nevertheless, it is not a naked ministry alone, either of announcing the gospel, or of declaring that sins are forgiven; but after the likeness of a judicial act, in which *by himself, as by a judge, sentence is pronounced.*"

In the ninth and tenth canons of this Session, those persons are, as usual, cursed, who deny the above doctrine of priestly absolution, and that even wicked priests have the power of remitting sins.

Impossibility of Salvation out of the Romish Church.

This point is a necessary consequence of infallibility, and of those anathemas with which its decrees are guarded.   If the Church of Rome is infallible, and has decided that her doctrine and sacraments are necessary to salvation—it follows that they who do not receive them must perish.   Accordingly, in the " Summary, &c." above given, the candidate swears that he will hold to the last breath of his life " this true Catholic faith," (i. e. the faith declared by the council of Trent)— " *out of which no one can have salvation.*"

Our readers cannot but have perceived, in examining the foregoing extracts from Roman Catholic authorities, that *the Church,* among professors of this faith, is the all in all;—it is the Church that is to be believed, and to be implicitly submitted to: whatever she has declared is infallibly and immutably true.   We must receive the scriptures on her authority, and hold them on all points as she is pleased to interpret them.— Now what is this but to put the church in the place of God? and to bow down in idolatrous homage to human authority?   A multitude of important reflections here crowd upon the mind, only

z 2

one, however, will our limits permit us to suggest. It is the utter hopelessness of all attempts to reform the church of Rome in any essential manner. As well, in the view of a conscientious Romanist, might we endeavor to change the eternal truth of God. That which is infallibly right it would be impious to alter, or even to indulge the wish that it were otherwise. " The principles of the Catholic Church," says the Bishop of Aire, " are *irrevocable*. She herself is *immutably chained* by bonds, which, at *no* future period, can she *ever* rend asunder."* To reform such a church, it is manifest, would be to destroy it. To those in this church, therefore, who have determined to make the *Word of God*, the holy scriptures, the supreme rule of their faith and life, a good conscience must compel to " come out of her."

* Faber's Diff. of Romanism, p. 283.

LETTERS FROM ROME.

The following Letters, dated at Rome, and written by a Physician, travelling in Italy for his health, to a brother in this country, contain many remarkable facts in reference to Romish doctrine and practice.

" Rome, ———, 16—.

"<i>Dear Charles,</i>—I am at length in Rome, and of all the pla·ces that I have yet seen, this is the most delightful. Where we have indulged in high anticipations, you know it is not often we find them more than realized, but mine were in this case

"Every thing which had particularly excited my admira·tion in my travels in the various cities through which I passed, awaited me at Rome in still greater perfection I had always ardently desired to view the <i>very place and scene</i> of those important events with which history had furnished me entertain·ment and instruction from my youngest years. I had promis·ed myself great pleasure in beholding the genuine remains of Pagan Rome—in visiting the sepulchres of her sages and heroes, and in searching out the place where each had lived, and walked, and held his disputations—in viewing the relics of her noble, ancient architecture—her temples—her sculp ture—her genius and taste; and though I expected to discover little comparatively, of old Rome, yet the bare view of the place where old Rome <i>stood</i> and her few noble remains I fan·cied would be sufficient to assist my imagination in portraying the rest. As for her religion, Popery, though I knew some of its superstitions, I knew comparatively little, and intended to lose no time in noticing its ridiculous ceremonies, but to devote myself to searching out her antiquities. But my first impres·sions were such, that I soon found myself regarding the Ro·mish worship with particular scrutiny.

"I find Popery, as it is exercised in Italy so nearly resem·bling the Paganism of old Rome, that, while witnessing her religious ceremonies, I am continually reminded of some pas·sage in a classic author where a similar ceremony was per·formed in the <i>same form and manner,</i> and in the <i>same place.</i> I can scarcely refrain from fancying myself a spectator of

271

some solemn act of ancient idolatry, rather than witnessing an
act of religious worship under the title of Christianity. The
first time I entered a church here, the smoke and smell of incense streaming from its numerous altars, transported me at
once to the description of Paphian Venus, in the first Æneid—

> " Her hundred altars there with garlands crown'd,
> And richest incense smoking, breathed around;
>   Sweet odors" &c.

And when I saw the little boy in surplice in the church of
Rome, waiting upon the Priest at the altar with the vessel of
incense and other sacred utensils, how could I but be reminded
of a *heathen sacrifice?*

" Nobody ever goes in or out of a church here without being
sprinkled with holy water, by the priest who attends for that
purpose, or else he serves himself with it, from a vessel placed inside the door resembling our baptismal fonts. Now this
custom is strictly derived from a heathen practice."

" I was present at one solemnity which was entirely novel
to me. I never saw any notice of any thing similar to it in
heathen worship, and conclude it to be an extravagance reserved for Popery alone. It is a yearly festival, celebrated
in January, to which I allude, called the 'benediction of
horses ——.' "

" It was commemorated with great solemnity. All the inhabitants of the city and neighborhood sent up their horses,
asses, and other cattle to the convent of St. Anthony, where a
priest in surplice sprinkles all the animals separately, with his
brush as they were presented to him; saying in Latin—
'Through the intercession of the Blessed Anthony Abate,
these animals are freed from all evils, in the name of the Father, of the Son, and of the Holy Ghost—Amen.' He received in return, a fee proportioned to the ability of the owner."

" I was amazed at such a display of lamps and wax-candles
as I find constantly burning before the shrines and images of
their saints. Many of these lamps are of massy silver; some,
even of gold, the gifts of princes and other distinguished per-
sonages. The number of offerings, too, presented in consequence of vows made in time of danger, and in gratitude for
deliverance, and cures, hanging up in the churches, is so great
as really to be quite offensive, and obstruct the sight of something more valuable and ornamental. These offerings consist
in a great measure of arms and legs, and little figures of wood
or wax, and sometimes fine pictures describing the manner
of the deliverance, obtained by the miraculous interposition

of the saint invoked, &c. As I was examining these various offerings, I could not but recollect an anecdote told by Cicero, of one, who, having found an atheistical friend in a temple, said, ' You, who think the gods take no notice of human affairs, do you not see here by this number of pictures, how many people for the sake of their vows have been saved in storms at sea, and got safe into harbor?' ' Yes,' says the atheist, ' I see how it is; for those are *never painted,* who happen *to be drowned.*'

"They pretend to show here at Rome, two original impressions of our Saviour's face on two different pocket handkerchiefs—one, it is said, was presented by himself to Agbarus, Prince of Edessa, and the other to a holy woman, named Veronica, at the time of his execution, (the handkerchief she lent him to wipe his face on that occasion.) One of these is preserved in St. Sylvester's church; the second in St. Peter's.

"I could tell you many more of the absurdities and superstitions of the Romish church, but time prevents now. I shall write you again soon; will then mention more facts, which I *know* to be true, and give you a faithful description of what I have seen with my own eyes in this Babylon, this city of abominations.

"You will be surprised at receiving so minute a statement of things relative to religious matters, and so few on other subjects, but I know Rome's state, in a moral view, will possess more interest for you, than aught else of her I could name.

"I must close—

"Yours, my brother in Christian love and affection,

"Henry Sturtevant."

———

" *Rome,* ——— ———.

"*My dear brother,*—I received your welcome letter last evening, and most cheerfully devote these, my first leisure moments since, to gratify the wish you expressed to be more particularly informed of some of the religious ceremonies of the Romish church. My curiosity has led me oftentimes to be a witness of various solemnities, and I will strive to detail the observations I made, and the information I have gained, with as much particularity as my time will allow.

"Soon after I despatched my last letter to you, I spent two or three days in visiting the several churches and noticing *particularly* every thing connected with Romish worship

which caught my eye.   Some of the numerous paintings which
adorn the altars I examined—they were very beautiful; indeed
I never saw any, that could compare with them for beauty of
execution.   I became less surprised, as I gazed at them with
admiration myself, at the reverence, solemnity and enthusias-
tic admiration with which they inspired those who had received from nature an eye to observe, and a heart to feel keenly
the beauties of this art—especially when I considered the ignorance and superstition of Papal worship which had shrouded
them from infancy, and led them to mistake these natural
sensibilities of a discriminating taste for true devotion and
holy love to the being whom they represented.

"The pomp and glory of the worship of this church is wonderfully calculated to awe and amuse the minds of a supersti
tious people.   The costly paintings—the images of saints, en-
riched with gold and pearl—the costly habits of the officiating
priests—the choice vocal and instrumental music—the public
processions and parades—in short, every thing combines, by
its magnificence, to win the attention and confidence of an un-
thinking people.

"But I am more and more astonished at the gross frauds,
practised in connection with supposed relics, and the credulity
of people in regard to them.   Among other relics which they
pretend to show here, are *the heads of St. Peter and St. Paul,*
encased in silver busts, set with jewels—*a lock of the Virgin
Mary's hair—a phial of her tears—a piece of her green petticoat—a robe of Jesus Christ, sprinkled with his blood—some
drops of his blood in a bottle—and some of the water which
flowed out of the wound in his side—the nails used in the crucifixion—and a piece of the very same porphyry pillar on
which the cock perched when he crowed after Peter's denial of
Christ—the rods of Moses and Aaron—and two pieces of the
wood of the real ark of the covenant.*   Many of the churches
are most abundantly supplied with relics of a similar charac
ter—there is one in Spain, I understand, which possesses *eleven
thousand,* among which are several of our Saviour; *a sacred
hair of his most holy head* is preserved in a vase—*several
pieces of his cross—thirteen thorns of his crown—*and *a piece
of the manger in which he was born.*   There are many relics
also of the Virgin Mary—*three or four pieces of one of her
garments—*and *a relic of the handkerchief with which she
wiped her eyes at the foot of the cross, &c.*   But enough of this.

"It would be a vain attempt, were I to undertake to tell you
the number of *saints* and *angels* who share in the devotions

of this superstitious people; indeed they are countless. And as every Pope takes the liberty of introducing one or several into the calendar of saints during his Pontificate, we need not wonder at the man who said on visiting one of these Papal cities, 'it was easier to find a god, than a man in it.'

"But I am perfectly amazed at the extravagant honors and blasphemous adoration paid the Virgin Mary. They have in fact Lighly exalted her, and given her a name above every name—I doubt whether their worship (even nominal) of the blessed Saviour exceeds that of the Virgin.

"Churches and chapels are consecrated to her service—five solemn festivals are annually paid to her honor, besides one day in every week set apart as especially for *her* worship as Saturday is for the *Son.* There are also seven hours in each day, called the seven canonical hours, which her most industrious worshippers devote to her service.

"From childhood, the Roman Catholic is taught to cherish for her the most profound reverence and the strongest affection. He addresses his prayers to her as being the 'queen of heaven' and 'the mother of God'—as 'being all-powerful to obtain from God by her intercessions all she shall ask of him.' A Catholic school-book inculcates this sentiment: 'Being mother of God, he cannot refuse her request; being our mother, she cannot deny our intercession when we have recourse to her—our necessities urge her —the prayers we offer her for our salvation bring us all that we desire—never any person invoked the mother of mercies in his necessities, who has not been sensible of the effects of her assistance. Among the reasons given why we should apply to the Virgin for salvation rather than to Christ, I have heard these two named—that 'she *being a woman* is more *tender-hearted*'—and 'being a *real mother* is therefore *indulgent.*' Such petitions as these following are addressed to her in the devotions of her worshippers: 'Succor the miserable,' 'help the faint-hearted,' 'comfort the afflicted,' 'loosen the sinner's bands,' 'bring light unto the blind,' 'our lusts and passions quell,' 'preserve our lives unstained,' 'guard us,' 'deliver us from all dangers,' 'lead us to life everlasting,' and innumerable others of similar import.

"Now, to whom, my dear brother, but a Power possessing all the attributes claimed by Divinity itself, should we think mortal man would address such service? and yet after all this, and in the midst of all this, they affirm that they worship 'the one only and true God,' and that 'Him alone they serve.'

"I find in the conclusion of the Biblia Mariæ, the Bible of

the Virgin Mary, (for you must know she has one composed
and provided for her especial service,) a prayer of this sort:—
'Oh Queen of mercy, grace and glory! Empress of all the
creatures, blot out all my transgressions, and lead me to life
everlasting!'

"I have been told, that, in a procession made here a few
years ago, the following inscription was placed over the gate
of one of the principal churches:

" 'The Gate of celestial benefit. The Gate of salvation.
Look up to the Virgin herself. Whosoever shall find me will
find life, and draw salvation from the Lord. For there is no
one who can be delivered from evils but through thee—there
is no one from whom we can obtain mercy but through thee.'

"I will just add a part of the litany of 'Lady of Loretto,' to
show you the extent of their extravagant and blasphemous
adoration:

"'Holy Mary.
Holy Mother of God.
Holy Virgin of Virgins.
Mother of Christ.
Mother of divine grace.
Mother most pure.
Mother most chaste.
Mother undefiled.
Mother untouched.
Mother most amiable.
Mother most admirable.
Mother of our Creator.
Mother of our Redeemer.
Virgin most prudent.
Virgin most venerable.
Virgin most renowned.
Virgin most powerful.
Virgin most merciful.
Virgin most faithful.
Mirror of justice.
Seat of Wisdom.
Cause of our joy.

Spiritual vessel.
Vessel of honor.
Vessel of singular devotion
Mystical rose.
Tower of David.
Tower of Ivory.
House of Gold.
Ark of the covenant.
Gate of Heaven.
Morning Star.
Health of the weak.
Refuge of sinners.
Comfort of the afflicted.
Help of Christians.
Queen of angels.
Queen of Patriarchs.
Queen of prophets.
Queen of apostles.
Queen of martyrs.
Queen of confessors.
Queen of virgins.
Queen of all saints.'

PRAY FOR US!'

"She wears a golden crown, set with precious stones of inestimable value—her fingers glisten with rings, and her neck
is tastefully adorned with several chains of gold, to which
medals and hearts of gold are appended, presents from devout
Catholic princes. She has changes of clothes for all work-days,

holidays and Sundays, of all colors, and even a *suit of mourning for passion-week!!*

"I have not time to say more of the idolatrous worship paid the Virgin Mary— yet I have given you scarce an idea of its extent; were I to tell you half the extravagancies I have seen and heard, you would believe I had made shipwreck of the credit for truth which I used to have, and would be incredulous of all I have yet to say on other points—but this much I m ist affirm: the *half* has not been told.

"I must describe to you, my dear brother, some of the famous *miracles* performed by the saints, images, relics, &c. They are really *wonderful.* No saint, it seems, can be admitted into the calendar, whatever may have been the sanctity of his life, unless it can be testified that he has *wrought miracles.*

"The tales of visions, apparitions, and miracles which are kept in circulation, and which are, in fact, necessary to uphold such a system of spiritual tyranny as the Popish religion is, among a superstitious and ignorant people are so absurd and monstrous, it would seem scarcely possible they should gain any credence at all.

"In several parts of Italy are shown the marks of hands and feet on rocks and stones, miraculously effected by the apparitions of some of their saints. Several images have been pointed out to me since I have been in Rome, which on certain occasions have *spoken—wept—sweat and bled.* One of the images of our Saviour, it was seriously averred, wept so profusely before the sacking of Rome, as to *employ all the good fathers in the monastery in wiping its face.*

"What is most wonderful of this picture is, that the Virgin Mary herself, attended by Mary Magdalen and St. Catherine, condescended to come down from heaven three or four centuries ago, to bring and introduce it to the special notice of papists. We must infer, as *the picture itself came down from heaven,* that it is imposed on the people as the workmanship either of the Virgin Mary, some of the angels or saints, or of God himself!! How shocking—outrageous!

"Of Thomas à Becket, perhaps as many miracles are recorded as of any saint. It is said, 'he outdid Christ himself in this particular.' Two volumes of them were preserved in Canterbury, where his shrine flourished, and a book has been published in France, containing an account of two hundred and seventy. It is remarkable that he works no miracles in England where his bones are deposited, but works abundantly in other countries.

A 2

"St. Francis Xavier turned a sufficient quantity of salt water into fresh to save the lives of five hundred travellers, who were dying of thirst, enough being left to allow a large exportation to different parts of the world, where it performed astonishing cures. St. Raymond de Pennafort laid his cloak on the sea, and sailed thereon from Majorca to Barcelona, a distance of a hundred and sixty miles, in six hours.

"At Mantua, I am told, there may be seen a bottle of the *real blood* of Christ. It was dug up a number of years since in a box containing a paper with an account of the circumstances of its deposit. It seems one Longinus, a Roman centurion, who was present at the crucifixion of Christ, became converted and afterwards left Judea for Mantua, carrying with him this phial of blood; he buried the sacred relic, and was so thoughtful as to enclose it in an envelope, stating all these facts. It is very remarkable that the writing, the box, the bottle, the blood and all should be perfectly fresh as it was when found, after lying in the ground sixteen centuries!!!

"A certain friar had preached a sermon during lent, upon the state of the man mentioned in Scripture possessed with seven devils, with so much eloquence and unction, that a simple countryman who heard him, went home, and became convinced that these seven devils had got possession of him. The idea haunted his mind, and subjected him to the most dreadful terrors, till, unable to bear his suffering, he unbosomed himself to his ghostly father and asked his counsel. The father, who had some smattering of science, bethought himself at last of a way to rid the honest man of his devils. He told him it would be necessary to combat with the devils singly; and on the day appointed, when the poor man came with a sum of money to serve as a bait for the devil—without which, the good father had forewarned him no devil could be dislodged—he bound a chain, connected with an electrical machine in an adjoining chamber, round his body, lest, as he said, the devil should fly away with him—and having warned him that the shock would be terrible when the devil went out of him, he left him praying devoutly before an image of the Madonna, and after some time gave him a pretty smart shock, at which the poor wretch fell insensible on the floor from terror. As soon, however, as he recovered, he protested that he had seen the devil fly away out of his mouth, breathing blue flames and sulphur, and that he felt himself greatly relieved. Seven electrical shocks, at due intervals, having extracted seven sums cf money from him, together with the seven devils, the man was cured, and a great miracle performed!"

Rome, Monday eve, —— ——.

"You will see from the above date, my dear brother, that this letter has lain untouched several days. I have been so completely engaged in the continued round of ceremonies, which engross the hearts and time of this people during the 'holy week' as to leave me no leisure to finish the accounts I had already begun. Rome is filled with pilgrims, and all the churches with worshippers—devout ones—save here and there a heretic, whose curiosity, like mine, has led him to mingle with the crowd, and follow the footsteps of the multitude through the endless absurdities, which tread hard on the heels of each other.

"Processions of penitents are seen silently wending their way along the streets, clothed in long dark robes, preceded by a black cross, and bearing in their hands skulls, and bones, and contribution-boxes for souls in purgatory.

"A most superb procession took place on the morning of the festa of the annunciation, which I, with thousands of others, ran to see.

"The Pope, riding on a white mule, (I suppose to imitate our Saviour's entry at Jerusalem,) came attended by his horse-guards who rode before to clear the way, mounted on prancing black horses and accompanied by such a flourish of trumpets and kettle-drums as to wear far more of the appearance of a martial parade than of a religious proceeding. All were dressed in splendid full uniform, and in every cap waved a myrtle sprig, the sign of rejoicing. The cardinals followed; and the rear was brought up by a bare-headed priest on a mule, with the host in a golden cup, the sight of which operated like a talisman on every soul around me, (for every knee bent,) save here and there one, who like myself stood heretically amid the kneeling mass, looking about panic-struck at this magic-like movement.

"The Pope himself was clothed in robes of white and silver, and as he passed along the crowds of gazing people that lined the streets and filled the windows, he forgot not incessantly to repeat his benediction—a twirl of three fingers, typical of the Father, Son, and Holy Ghost,—the little finger representing the latter.

"Many áresome ceremonies followed his entry into the church. He was seated on his throne; all the cardinals successively approached—kissed his hand—retired a step or two —gave three low nods—one to him in front, as personifying God, the Father, one to the right, intended for the Son; and one to the left for the Holy Ghost.

"I am sure, my dear brother, as this ceremony passed, the blood curdled in my veins—I was transfixed to the spot. I saw not what passed without me, but this text of holy writ stood like letters of fire, glaring upon me from within:—

" 'Who, *as God,* sitteth in the temple of God, *showing himself that he is God.'*

"When the first shock of this blasphemy had passed away, the inferior priests were bowing, each in their turn, and in adoring attitude *kissing the toe,* as it is called, which is in fact, the embroidered cross on the shoe of this lord of lords. High mass then began; during the elevation of the host, the Pope knelt before the high altar and in silence prayed—then followed an infinitude of gettings up and sittings down—of sayings and dead pauses, which I am sure those around me did not half comprehend; and of which I could—*nothing.*

"A lighted taper was then brought, (though it was broad daylight,) and held for the Pope, while he read something, I know not what, from a great volume before him, and after several other ceremonies, as comprehensible and edifying as those I have named, he rose and retired, twirling his benediction all the way out, as he twirled it all the way in. After this I had little running to do, till palm Sunday came. You know I am far-famed as a punctual man—and a full hour I had been seated in the gaze of expectation, waiting the Pope's appearance in the chapel, when he came. He was clothed this time in scarlet and gold, and a most sumptuous figure he made. The Cardinals were dressed in their mourning robes, of a violet color, richly trimmed with antique lace, with mantles of ermine and scarlet trains—but these were soon changed for garments of gold. The same round of ceremonies toward the Pope was performed as I related on the festa of the annunciation. Two palm branches received the Pope's benediction, after having passed through a cloud of incense. Smaller ones, artificial, composed of plaited straw or dried reed leaves, to which crosses were appended, were presented to each cardinal, archbishop, and to all the inferior orders of the clergy, to deacons, canons, choristers, cardinals' trainbearers, &c. as they individually descended the steps of the throne after per-

'orming the ceremonious routine I have mentioned before. The procession then began to move off, two and two, beginning with the lowest clerical rank, and at last the Pope himself in his chair of state, under a crimson canopy and borne on the shoulders of four men. Great pomp and splendor marked this parade. The crowns and mitres of the bishops and patriarchs, white and crimson, glittering with jewels, and set with precious stones—their long, rich dresses—the slow and uniform march of the procession, and the gay crowds surrounding, presented quite an imposing appearance. The procession issued forth into the hall in the rear of the chapel, and marching round it, entered again and seated themselves as before. A multitude of tedious services then followed—with frequent kneelings—the tinkling of bells, dressings, undressings, &c.; then the cardinals all embraced each other, gave the kiss of peace, and the scene closed.

"The next service I attended was three days after on Wednesday, in the same chapel at half past four, P. M. The house was filled to overflowing. I had a conspicuous place, and could distinctly see all that passed, and amused myself through a long and tedious chant with my own reflections on the varied scenes before me. My attention was then arrested by a row of *mourning candles*, fifteen in number, all lighted, though still broad day; the central one overtopped the others, they retreating in size each way. I learned the *tall* mourning candle was the Virgin Mary; the nearest each side, like maids of honor, were the two Marys, and all the rest apostles. As the services proceeded, the candles, one by one, were extinguished, a typical representation of the falling off of the apostles in the hour of trial. The Virgin was at last left alone in the midst, and she at length was set under the altar. As it grew dark, only light enough was allowed to make the darkness visible—to give a sombre, chilling melancholy to the whole aspect of things. Strains of music then commenced of such unearthly pathos as never before fell on my ear. I will not attempt to describe it; for a time I seemed to forget where or what I was, so deeply was every faculty of my soul absorbed in the plaintive, heart-stirring swellings that rose, and then melted away among the suppressed breathings of awe-stricken listeners. The lady who sat next me heard till nature fainted—and many on my right and left listened till too deeply agitated to suppress the keenness of their emotion.

"*Holy Thursday*, the succeeding day, was the interment of Christ; nearly the same ceremonies were performed as I have

2 A 2

already related, with the addition of the deposit of the host by the Pope in the sepulchre beneath the altar at the close of the procession.

"Then came the washing of feet, in imitation of our Saviour's washing the disciples' feet. This was performed by the Pope himself, officiating in a long white linen robe, and wearing a bishop's mitre.

"A silver bucket of water was presented to him by an attending Cardinal. The Pope knelt before the first of the pilgrim-priests, immersed one foot in water, then touched it with a fringed towel—kissed the leg, and gave the cloth and a sort of white flower or feather to the man—then went on to the next. The whole ceremony occupied but a few moments; the Pope then returned to the throne, changed his dress for the robes of white and silver, and proceeded to the next service. The twelve priests seated themselves at a table, loaded with various dishes and flowers; and the Pope, after pronouncing a blessing, handed to each from a side-table, bread, plates, and cups of wine, which each rose to receive from his highness' hand; a few forms having passed, he gave a parting benediction and withdrew."

"The next day was Good Friday; went early in the morning to the chapel to witness the 'adoration of the cross'—a long, tedious service of mass, chantings, kneelings, and prayings to the cross, from which the mourning-cloth had been removed. Then came the service of the 'three hours' agony' of Christ upon the cross, which I viewed with feelings so indescribably horror-struck, that I shall attempt no minute description of the ceremonies. I still shudder, as a confused remembrance of the representation of Mount Calvary, with its trees, rocks, and thickets, passes before me in review—the dying, agonized contortions of the muscles in the face of Him, who redeemed us, so strikingly and horribly depicted, that the cold chills came over me—the nails, with the spear and the crosses—the two dying thieves—the centurions, the horses, and the glittering swords—but my head swims at the recollection of the unhallowed sight of scenes, too sacred ever to attempt portraying. The whole scene, which is a complete drama, is divided into seven acts, composed each one of the seven sayings*

* The seven sayings are these—
. "Father, forgive them, for they know not what they do."
2. "To-day thou shalt be with me in Paradise."
3. "Woman, behold thy Son. Son, behold thy mother."
4. "My God, my God, why hast thou abandoned me."

of Christ on the cross; a tirade of the priest, consisting of apostrophes, ejaculations, and exhortations, calculated to excite the natural feelings of the auditors, by the help of surrounding scenes even to nature's highest pitch; and when the scene was perfect—when the whole multitude sank, exhausted with feeling and drowned with tears—when the whole church seemed to breathe in one loud burst of agony, as the melting sounds of infinite love faintly uttered, '*It is finished*,'—a band of friars, clothed in black, came noiselessly issuing from behind; they toiled up the steep, winding, and bushy ascent of the mountain, emerging now from the thicket, and then from the shade of a rock, to remove the body of Him, whose last life-drop was spilt for us. The nails were loosened, and the body removed and laid on a bier, amid the shrieks and agonizing groans of the people, who hastened, one by one, to pay it the last tribute of a kiss, before it was borne away. I staid till I could stay no longer, and retired amid the prayers, and sighs, and tears that found vent from almost every soul but mine, with a grieved and melted heart, and a conscience deeply reproaching me for witnessing a mock-scene like this.

"But I have spun this letter to quite an immoderate length I must close, but you shall hear from me again in a few days.

"Your affectionate brother,

"HENRY S————————."

————

"*Rome*, ————.

"*My Dear Brother*,—I am still busied in attendance on Roman Catholic ceremonies. Curiosity led me, a short time since, to witness the holy rite of Baptism, performed on a young lady in the family of Mr. R. with whom I am on terms of considerable intimacy. The ordinance of baptism, as administered in a Romish Church, is so encumbered with ceremonies, that it can be scarcely recognized as the simple seal of the gospel-covenant. There are the forms observed before coming to the font—those at the font—and those which follow the administration of the ordinance. A long series of catechetical instruction precedes the rite itself, succeeded by ex-

5. "I thirst."
6. "It is finished."
7. "Father, into thy hands I commend my spirit."

orcism—which is using 'words of sacred and religious import, and of prayers, to expel the devil, and to weaken and crush his power.' Salt is put into the mouth—the sign of the cross is made with the holy oil upon the forehead, eyes, ears, breast and shoulders—the nostrils and ears are touched with spittle—the crown of the head is anointed with chrism, after the performance of the baptismal ceremony—a white garment is given, and a wax taper, burning, is put into the hand. All these various rites are typical of the several effects which the sacred ordinance is said to confer; viz: 'To remit original sin and actual guilt, however enormous—to remit all the punishment due to sin—to bestow invaluable privileges, such as justification and adoption —to produce abundance of virtues—to unite the soul to Christ —and to open the portals of heaven.'

"Such are the unwarranted, efficacious virtues which the Romish church have ventured to ascribe to this simple ordinance, which the Bible recognizes only as the visible sign of an inward union, and which *of itself* and *in itself* confers no grace.

"Now, see the young lady, of whom I have been speaking, pass through the ceremony of taking the veil!! Miss Celia R. is a beautiful girl of 17—only daughter of the brother of Mr. R., who deceased about a year since, consigning this, his dearest earthly treasure, to his brother's care. Mr. R. is a native Italian, and stanch in his Roman belief—though his lady, I suspect, submits with great repugnance to an observance of the indispensable mummeries of her husband's faith. Miss R. came to Italy, overwhelmed with the sense of melancholy and loneliness, which her father's death and her present state of orphanage, (though independent in point of fortune,) has occasioned; her sadness was not at all lessened by the change of customs, of scenes and companions, which her removal from the land of her nativity and the associations of early youth has produced. She has yielded a listening ear to the counsels and persuasions of the friends she has acquired since her arrival, and with a firm faith in the represented advantages and pleasures of the life of a *nun*, she has this morning taken upon herself all the solemn, unwarranted, and irrevocable vows of monastic life!

"Poor girl! in the depth of her present sorrow, the world seems dark and cheerless: she knows not that youth, in its elasticity, *bends* only beneath the weight of sorrow, to rise again when the fury of the storm is past, and look out upon the charms of social life, with all its wonted freshness and delight. Her vi-

Pope washing the feet of Pilgrim Priests.

sions of futurity are now clothed in the sombre shadows which her spirit wears; she dreams not that the bright sun of youth and hope, though enveloped now, will soon emerge cloudless, and free, and brilliant as it was before. She thinks her sadness is religion; her voluntary renunciation of all earth offers, an offering acceptable in the eyes of Him, who disdains every sacrifice but that of a broken and contrite heart for *sin;* and she seeks the comfort which is found only in repentance and faith in the merits of her Saviour, in the cold, dull, monotonous round of duties she herself imposes, and the costly sacrifice of what her heavenly father never required her to forego.

"But enough of this—though I am in quite a moralizing mood, and heartily sick of cold externals, warmed by no life-throb—of a religion all *body* and no *soul.*

"It was a most delightful morning—one of Italy's brightest days—and one who has never roamed abroad amid all the beauties of Italic scenery, and the soothing mildness and fragrance of her atmosphere, can scarcely conceive how delightful her bright days are; and I thought, as I bent my steps at an early hour to the chapel in the convent of St. Sylvestro, that when the young lady came to look for the last time upon the beauties and pleasures she was about to renounce, for the cold, cheerless imprisonment of this living tomb, her heart must misgive her, and her soul recoil from the rash, fatal vow ————and I *hoped* it would be so; for I knew she had voluntarily, unadvised by her uncle or aunt, and strongly opposed by the latter, formed this inconsiderate resolution, and chosen this living death. But she came at last, and two footmen, in splendid liveries, made way for her entrance. She was in full dress, sparkling in brilliants, her dark hair blazing in diamonds, her cheeks unblanched—rather deepened by the excitement of the moment, and I think I never saw her more beautiful. She pressed forward amid the gazing crowd with a firm, though gentle step, while the fixed purpose of her soul beamed full in her eye; the path-way and altar were strewed with flowers—the public applauding—strangers admiring—cardinals blessing—priests flattering—friends weeping—nuns chanting—and *I*, inwardly execrating a practice unauthorized by the Bible, uncommanded by Jehovah, yet encouraged and insisted upon by those, who unworthily call themselves the messengers of the will of the Highest.

"The ceremonies commenced. You can scarcely imagine the indignation that by this time boiled within me, as I listened to the discourse pronounced from the pulpit by an old, fat

Dominican monk, who poured forth such a volume of rhapsody —with not a particle of sober reason or religion in it; or any thing, except what was calculated to inflame an inexperie nced imagination; calling her 'the affianced spouse of Ch ist,' a saint on earth,' 'one who had renounced the vanities of the world for a foretaste of the joys of heaven,' &c.—such as you, my brother, with all *your fire,* would not have staid to hear.

"The sermon closed, and at the altar the beautiful victim knelt—and on it laid her youth and beauty, wealth—the pleasures and refinements of life, the delights of friendship, the charms of nature and of freedom—every thing—all that nature *has* to give, she gave; she sacrificed them *all* on the shrine before her, and pronounced those vows which severed her from them forever.

"As the chant of her fatal vow died away in melting recitative, every eye was moistened, as far as my vision reached, save hers for whom they wept.

"Her diamonds were then removed; and her long dark tresses, in all their native polish and beauty, fell clustering about her shoulders—one lock of it was monopolized by the cardinal—then the grate opened, the choral voices of the black sisterhood chanted a strain of welcome, as she retired from the benediction of the cardinal and the embraces of her friends, within her future tomb. She renounced her name and adopted a new one—her beautiful garments were removed, and the plain, coarse dress of the Franciscan order was assumed; her ornaments were laid away forever, and nature's beautiful covering, that richly polished hair, was severed by the sisters' fatal shears.

"The white veil was thrown on, (which is a very different thing from what I had supposed, being simply 'a piece of white linen, fixed on the top or back part of the head, and falling down behind or on each side, as on a veiled statue.') Attired in the sober dress of a noviciate nun, the beautiful Celia R. appeared to view again behind the open grate—not otherwise, for she and the world, (save seen through the bars of her life-prison) were now parted forever. We all agreed the simple dress of the new nun had not at all abated from her beauty, for her bright eyes, and the lovely expression of her fair countenance had not departed with her brilliant attire. *I* thought her, indeed, even prettier than before.

"She appeared calm and firm until the last, when nature *would* have its gush, and while receiving the praises, congratulations and sympathy of friends and acquaintance, in spite of her, her tears fell fast and fi ee. We left her—the heroine of an hour.—But oh! how often in the long, dark flight of the tedious hours to which she has doomed herself, wil' she sigh over that fatal moment with bitter repentance, but it will come too late!"

"In my next letter, I intend to tell you about the immense stock of 'merits,' which have been, and are still accumulating —an inexhaustible fund from which they presume on their indulgences, but have not time now; indeed I must postpone what I had intended to say on other points, for urgent duties demand my attention.

"But believe me, my dear brother, as ever, your affectionate,
                                        " HENRY ———."

                                        " Rome ———.

" *My dear brother,*—This is my last letter from Rome; my health has wonderfully improved, and I intend soon to set my face homeward.

"Before this reaches you, I shall probably be on my way. I shall have bid adieu to all the beauty and splendor of this classic city, once mistress of the world, and be quite beyond the charms of her scenery, the balmy breath of her delightful hills, and all her romantic associations; and indeed the latter have long since floated from my memory, so absorbed have I become in the interests of her future spiritual welfare —but I shall carry with me many new thoughts and new feelings, which, by the blessing of God, will prompt to many new efforts and to many new plans.

"Henceforth, my brother, I will be the *Lord's* ! I will live for Him, act for Him, think for Him, and direct every effort of my soul to co-operate in bringing back this darkened, deluded world of immortals, to the standard of the holy and peaceful allegiance of Jesus; to hasten that latter-day glory, which my soul never longed with such intensity to see, as since I have contrasted its brightness and purity with the depressing gloom and abominations of the superstitious ages behind us, yet lingering in their retreat My heart has almost melted within me, as I have watched the thick, dark clouds, which have settled over this people, and the horrible blackness of darkness which has shrouded, and still envelopes so many millions of perishing immortals, as they make their final plunge into the fathomless gulf of eternity, blindly unprepared, deceived by

blind guides, and eternally lost. Oh! the wo reserved in the
dregs of the cup of antichrist, the indescribable torments that
await him at the decisions of the last great day!

"Every delusion I find in the 'cup of abominations,' prepared for the nations by the 'mother of harlots,' and greedily
drank by easily-deceived souls, thirsting for a blessed immortality, awakens new and deeper pangs of indignation and
grief, till my heart, at times, is ready to burst in the depths of
its distress for souls.

"I thought when I last wrote to you, that I had some fain.
glimpse of the deceits and delusions practised on the followers of Popery. I could see depths, frightful and immense, of
treasures of gold and silver, which Papal imposition had ex-
torted from the ignorant and superstitious, to pamper and uphold the dominion of the prince of darkness; but I had not
fathomed, with my imperfect vision, the greatest reservoir of
all, with its endless channels and its untold bounds—I mean
that of 'indulgences.' I was not, to be sure, ignorant of the
existence of such a fraud to obtain the mammom of unrighteousness, for I had found scarcely a church in Rome, where
'plenary indulgence' did not blaze in tempting letters—but of
the extent to which this fraud was carried, and the immense
source of revenue it has become, I was uninformed. I had
been rather startled, I confess, at the full pardon of sin which
a few prayers before certain shrines, and a few pence, slipped
into the hand of a priest, would procure; but my hair stood
almost upright, when I learned, that by the performance of a
few trifling, heartless ceremonies, and the payment of certain
sums of money, 30 or 40,000 and even 500,000 years of in
dulgence might be purchased. I find indulgences are of dif
ferent degrees—'full,' 'more than full,' 'fullest.' A *full* indulgence will 'clear you of all that can be laid to your charge.
and bring you to a baptismal innocency till the time and date
of the indulgence; but in case you live longer, though but a
fortnight, your total indulgence is spent, and therefore to help
you out here, you may have a fuller indulgence, which will
carry you to the end of your journey.'

"You may buy as many masses as will free your souls
from purgatory for 29,000 years, at the church of St. John's
Lateran, on the festa of that saint.

"Those that have interest with the Pope, may obtain an absolution in full, from his Holiness, for all the sins they ever
have committed, or may choose to commit.

"Certain prices, it seems, are affixed to certain sins, and

entire absolution may be obtained for any sin you can name, by paying the stipulated sum.

"For sins which in the Holy Scriptures we find called down the terrific judgments of heaven, a man may obtain absolution from the Pope for two shillings, two and sixpence, and perhaps less. It is almost incredible what a source of revenue the sale of nulls of indulgences has been to the Romish church —what uncounted treasures have been amassed in the Pope's coffers by this means."

"No measures are untried, that crafty policy suggests, to extort *masses for the dead*—to solicit contributions for the relief of suffering souls in purgatory. Strange tales of frightful visions and apparitions are circulated, 'of souls standing in burning brimestone, some up to their knees, and some to the chin— of others swimming in cauldrons of melted lead, and devils pouring metal down their throats,' with many such stories, greedily swallowed by superstition and ignorance. Solicitors, or agents, bearing lanterns with a painted glass, representing naked persons enveloped in flames, parade the streets and enter houses with tales that alarm, and appeals that excite the compassion for these 'holy souls.'

"So great is the dread of the horrors of purgatory, that besides the satisfactions they make in their life time, many deluded souls leave large legacies to the church to procure masses daily, weekly, monthly and yearly, as far as their money will go. Thus also are multitudes of the living induced, through compassion for the supposed sufferings of their deceased relatives, to spend large and frequent sums; sometimes even to forego many comforts and necessaries, to redeem by masses the souls of those they love from the horrors of the middle state. Many would rather starve their surviving families, than neglect the souls of the departed. This doctrine is a mine, as profitable to the church, as the Indies to Spain."

"You cannot conceive, my dear brother, of the depravation of morals here. If nothing enters heaven 'that defileth,' it must be a comfortable thought to the *priests* as well as the people, that a place is mercifully provided to cleanse them from the impurities of the debauchery they indulge on earth. The celibacy of the priests is but a cloak for the most shameless wickedness, so frequent and impudent as scarce to seek concealment—the day of judgment will reveal such enormities as will make every ear to tingle."

"I wonder not, my brother, at the indignation which boiled in the breast of the bold and fearless Luther, at the shameful

2 B

and infamous raffic of indulgences. 'Behold how great a matter a little fire kindleth!' Little did he imagine the flame that burned within his own breast was the torch to kindle Christendom—a light to turn the eyes of ages towards the rising of that better day, so dear to the hearts of all Christ's followers. How great should be our gratitude, that we were not nurtured in the long reign of darkness, which shrouded this and other countries before the deep, loud blast of Luther's trumpet sounded the alarm among sleeping Christians. He began a noble work; may all our energies be enlisted in its advancement, till He, whose right it is, shall rule and reign from sea to sea—from the river to the ends of the earth. Great is the work, even of a private Christian, I believe, it he stands in his lot, doing with his might what his hands find to do.

"May you and I, my dear brother, be watchful and diligent in our Master's work, that when he cometh, he may say, " Well done, good and faithful servants, enter thou into the joy of thy Lord."

"Yours, in the bonds of the strongest affection,

HENRY S————."

APPENDIX,

CONTAINING THE PRESERVATIVE AGAINST

POPERY;

BY THE REV. JOSEPH BLANCO WHITE.

Formerly Chaplain to the King of Spain, in the Royal Chapel of Scville,—-now a Clergyman of the Church of England.

DIALOGUE I.

Containing an account of the Author; how the Errors of the Roman Catholic Church made him an Infidel; and how, to avoid her Tyranny, he came to England, where the knowledge of the Protestant Religion. made him again embrace Christianity.

Reader. Well, Sir, since you are pleased to wish for a conversation with me, may I make bold to ask who you are?

Author. By all means, my good friend. The truth is, that unless you know who I am, and by what strange and unforeseen events I happen to be here, our conversation would be to little purpose. You must, then, know, in the first place, that I am a Spaniard, and have been regularly bred and ordained a Catholic priest.

R. Indeed, Sir! Perhaps you are one of those poor creatures who, I hear, have been driven out of Spain for having tried to give it a better government.

A. No, my friend: I have been now (1825) more than fifteen years in England, and came hither of my own accord, though I left behind every thing that was most dear to me, besides very good preferment in the church, and the prospect of rising to higher places of honor and emolument.

R. Why, Sir! that appears strange.

A. So it must to those who are not acquainted with the evil from which I resolved to escape, at the expense of every thing I possessed in the world. You, my dear friend, have had your lot cast in a country which is perfectly free from *religious tyranny.* Were it possible for you to have been born in Spain, and yet to possess the free spirit of a *Briton,* you would not wonder at the determination which made me quit parents, kindred, friends, wealth and country, and cast myself upon the world at large, at the age of five and thirty, trusting to my own exertions for a maintenance. All this I did merely to escape from *religious tyranny.*

R. You quite surprise me, Sir! But I wish you would tell me what it is you mean by that *religious tyranny,* which you seem to have feared and hated so strongly.

A. You will easily understand it as I proceed with the story of my own life. I was born of gentle parents, and brought up with great care and tenderness. My father's family were Irish, and the English language being spoken by him and many of his dependants, I learned it when a boy; and thanks to that circumstance, which I consider as a means employed by Providence for my future good, I can now thus freely converse with you. Both my father and mother were Roman Catholics, extremely pious from their youth, and devoted to works of charity and piety during the whole course of their lives. It was natural that such good parents should educate their children in the most religious manner; and they spared themselves no pains to make me a good Roman Catholic. My disposition was not wayward; and I grew up strongly attached to the sort of religion which was instilled into my mind. I had scarcely arrived at my fourteenth year, when, believing that the life in which I could most please God was that of a clergyman, I asked my parents to prepare me for the church; which they agreed to with great joy. I passed many years at the university, took my degrees, and at the age of five and twenty, was made a Priest. It is the custom in Spain, when certain places become vacant in cathedrals, and other great churches, to invite as many clergyman as will allow themselves to be examined, before the public, to stand candidates for the vacancy. After the trial of their learning, the judges appointed by law, give the place to him whom they believe to be the most competent.—I should be ashamed to boast, but so it happened, that soon after my becoming a Priest, I was made one of the Chaplains of the King of Spain, in the way I have just told you. All had been, hitherto, well enough with me; and I thank God that the ease and good fortune which had always attended me, did not make me forget my duties as a Clergyman.—Doubts, however, had occurred to me now and then, as to whether the Roman Catholic religion was true. My fear of doing wrong by listening to them, made me hush them for a long time: but all my peace of mind was gone. In vain did I kneel and pray: the doubts would multiply upon me, disturbing all my devotions. Thus I struggled month after month, till unable to answer the objections that continually occurred to me, I renounced the Roman Catholic religion in my heart.

R. In your *heart*, Sir! I hope you do not mean that when you had settled with yourself that the Popish religion was false, you pretended still to be a Roman Catholic.

A. What would you think of a power, or authority, that would force you to act like a hypocrite?

R. I should think that it was no better than the government of the Turks, which, as I hear, treats men like beasts.

A. Well; now you will be able to understand what I mean by *religious tyranny.* The Popes of Rome believe that they have a right to oblige all men who have been baptized, but more especially those who have been baptized by their Priests, to continue Roman Catholics to their lives' end. Whenever any one living under their authority, has ventured to deny any of the doctrines which the Church of Rome believes, they have shut them up in prisons, tormented them upon the rack, and, if they would not recant, and unsay what they had given out as their real persuasion, the poor wretches have been burnt as heretics. The kings of Spain, being Catholics, acted upon these matters according to the will of the Pope; and, in order to prevent every Spainard from being any thing, at least in appearance, but a Papist, had established a court called the *Inquisition,* where a certain number of Priests tried, in secret, such people as were accused of having denied any of the articles of the Roman Catholic faith. Whenever, moved by fear of the consequences, the prisoner chose to eat his own words, and declare that he was wrong; the Priests sent him to do penance for a certain time, or laid a heavy fine upon him: but if the accused had courage to persist in his own opinion, then the Priests declared that he was a heretic, and gave him up to the public executioner, to be burnt alive.

R. You astonish me. Have you ever seen such things, Sir?

A. I well remember the last that was burnt for being a heretic, in my own town, which is called *Seville.* It was a poor blind woman. I was then about eight years old, and saw the

2 B 2

pile of wood, upon barrels of pitch and tar, where she was
reduced to ashes.

R. But are there many who venture their lives for the sake
of what they believe to be the true Gospel?

A. Alas! there was a time when many hundreds of men
and women sacrificed themselves for the love of the Protestant
religion which is professed in England. But the horrible
cruelties which were practised upon them, disheartened all
those who were disposed to throw off the yoke of the Pope
and now people disguise their religious opinions, in order to
avoid the most horrible persecution.

R. And you, Sir, of course, were obliged to disguise your
own persuasion, in order not to lose your liberty and your life.

A. Just so. I lived ten years in the most wretched and
distressed state of mind. Nothing was wanting to my being
happy but the liberty of declaring my opinions; but that is
impossible for a Roman Catholic, who lives under the laws
which the Popes have induced most of the Roman Catholic
princes to establish in their kingdoms. I could not say, as a
Roman Catholic may, under the government of Great Britain and Ireland, " I will no longer be a spiritual subject of
the Pope: I will worship God as my conscience tells me I
should, and according to what I find in the Bible." No: had
I said so, or even much less; had any words escaped me, in
conversation, from which it might be suspected that I did not
believe exactly what the Pope commands, I should have been
taken out of my bed in the middle of the night, and carried
to one of the prisons of the Inquisition. Often, indeed, very
often have I passed a restless night under the apprehension
that, in consequence of some unguarded words, my house
would be assailed by the ministers of the Inquisition, and I
should be hurried away in the black carriage, which they
used for conveying dissenters to their dungeons. Happy indeed are the people of these kingdoms, where every man's
house is his castle; and where, provided he has not committed
some real crime, he may sleep under the protection of a mere
latch to his door, as if he dwelt in a walled and moated for-
tress! No such feeling of safety can be enjoyed where the
tyranny of Popery prevails. A Roman Catholic, *who is not
protected by Protestant laws,* is all over the world a slave, who
cannot utter a word against the opinions of his church, but at
his peril. " The very walls have ears," is a common saying
in my country. A man is indeed beset with spies; for the
Church of Rome has contrived to employ every one as such,

against his nearest and dearest relations. Every year there is publicly read at church, a proclamation, or (as they call it) a *bull* from the Pope, commanding parents to accuse their children, children their parents, husbands their wives, and wives their husbands, of any words or actions against the Roman Catholic Religion. They are told, that whoever disobeys this command, not only incurs damnation for his own soul, but is the cause of the same to those whom he wishes to spare. So that many have had for their accusers their fathers and mothers, without knowing to whom they owed their sufferings under the Inquisitors; for the name of the informer is kept a most profound secret, and the accused is tried without ever seeing the witnesses against him.

R. I am perfectly astonished at the things you say, Sir; and did I not perceive by your manners that you are a gentleman, I should certainly suspect that you were trying to trepan us poor unlearned people.

A. I neither wonder, nor am offended at your suspicion. All that I can say to remove it is, that I am well known in London; that for the truth of every thing you have already heard, and will hear from me, I am ready to be examined *upon oath;* and that there are many hundreds of Spaniards at this moment in England, who will attest every word of mine about the Inquisition of the Pope in Spain. I say the Inquisition of the Pope, because that horrible *court of justice* was established, kept up, and managed by and under the Pope's authority. And now I must add one word as to the effects of the Pope's contrivance to make spies of the nearest relations, against those who might not believe every tittle of the Roman Catholic Religion. I have told you that my parents were good and kind. My mother was a lady whom all the poor of the neighborhood loved for her goodness and charity; and indeed I often saw her denying herself even the common comforts of life, that she might have the more to give away. I was her favorite child, being the eldest; and it is impossible for a mother to love with more ardent affection than she showed towards me. Well, as I could not entirely conceal my own mind in regard to Popery, she began to suspect that I was not a true Roman Catholic in my heart. Now, she knew that the Pope had made it her duty to turn informer even against her own child, in such cases; and dreading that the day might come, when some words should drop from me against the Roman Catholic religion, which it would be her duty to carry to the judges, she used to avoid my company, and shut herself

up, to weep for me. I could not, at first, make out why my
dear mother shunned my company; and was cut to the heart
by her apparent unkindness. I might to this day have believed that I had lost her affection, but that an intimate friend of
hers put me in possession of the state of her mind.

R. Upon my word, Sir, you give me such horror of Roman
Catholics, that I shall in future look with suspicion on some
neighbors of mine of that persuasion.

A. God forbid that such should be the consequence of my
communication with you. The Roman Catholic religion in
itself, and such as the Pope would make it all over the world,
if there were no protestant laws to resist it, is the most horrible system of tyranny that ever opposed the welfare of man.
But most of the Roman Catholics in these kingdoms are not
aware of the evils which their religion is likely to produce.
They have grown up under the influence of a constitution,
which owes its full freedom to Protestantism; and many of
them are Protestants in feelings, whom their priests, I am
sure, must lead with a very light rein-hand, for fear of their
running away. There is, indeed, no reason for either fear or
suspicions, with regard to the Roman Catholics of these king
doms, so long as both the Government and Parliament remain
purely Protestant; but I would not answer for the consequences if the Pope, through his priests, could obtain an underhand influence in either.

R. But, Sir, I want to know the rest of your own story, and
how, through obliged to appear outwardly a Roman Catholic,
you settled within yourself what you were to believe.

A. I will not delay to satisfy your curiosity, though that
part of my story is the most painful to me. At all events,
you will be sure, when you hear it, that I am telling the truth,
the whole truth, and nothing but the truth, since I do not spare
myself.—You must know, then, that from the moment I believed that the Roman Catholic religion was false, I had no
religion at all, and lived without God in the world.

R. I am sorry to hear that, Sir. But surely you might
have tried some other church before you became an Infidel.

A. Ah, my honest and worthy friend, your expressions deserve my praise, though I feel humbled and rebuked by their
truth. Yet you forget that I was in a country where the
Roman Catholic religion played its accustomed game of
Christ with the Pope, or no Christ. The first thing that a
true Roman Catholic teaches those who grow under his care
is, that either all that the Church of Rome believes is true, or

all that is contained n the Scriptures is false. To believe that
the Church of Rome can be; or is wrong in one single article
of her creed, is, according to that Church, the same as to disbelieve the whole Gospel. That is the reason why in countries where the Roman Catholic religion is strictly observed,
every one who rejects Popery in his heart, looks immediately
upon Christianity as a fable.

R. Pardon me, Sir, I do not mean to offend you; but I
should wish to know if you still continue of the same opinion,
and believe with Hone and Carlile, and all that kind of people, whose books are sometimes secretly sold among country-
folks, that there is no truth in the Bible.

A. I am so far from being of that mind, that I do humbly
and earnestly pray to God he will rather deprive me of every
temporal comfort, and make my sufferings in this world equal
to those of the most unhappy wretch that ever breathed,
than withdraw from me his grace, whereby I believe in his
Son, Jesus Christ, and hope, through his merits, for eternal
salvation.

R. I have not the heart to say *Amen* to the first part of your
prayer, though I cordially join in the last. But will you have
the goodness to inform me how it was that you came to believe
again in the Bible, in spite of your former opinions? For I
have often heard a neighbor of mine, who frequently boasts
that he is an infidel, say, that the man whose eyes are once
(as he calls it) open about the Bible, can never be made again
to believe in it.

A. I wish I could relate my own history to that neighbor
of yours. Perhaps, by God's mercy, he might himself use
some of the means which Providence has employed in my
own conversion. Of one thing I feel quite assured on this
point, that if by God's grace, which always assists the honest
inquirer after religious truth, your infidel neighbor would
abstain from open sin, and pray daily to his Maker, (for I hope
he has not gone so far as to deny the being of a God,) to lead
him into the truth, he would soon become a sincere Christian.
But I will proceed with the account of myself. When I had
in my own mind thrown off all allegiance to the Christian religion, though I tried to enjoy myself, and indulge my desires,
I could find neither happiness nor comfort. My mind was
naturally averse to deceit, and I could not brook the necessity
of acting publicly as the minister of a religion which I believed
to be false. But what could I do? As for wealth and honors,
heaven knows they did not weigh a straw against my love of

manly openness and liberty. I once, indeed, went so far as to
write to a friend who lived at Cadiz, and whom, after many
years' absence, I have lately seen in London, to procure me a
passage to North America, whither I wished to escape; trusting to my own labor for subsistence. But when I looked
round and saw my dear father and mother on the decline of
life; when I considered that my flight would bring their grey
hairs with sorrow to the grave, tears would gush into my
eyes, and the courage which I owed to anger, melted at once
into love for the authors of my being. Ten years of my life
did I pass in this hot and cold fever, this ague of the heart,
without a hope, without a drop of that cordial which cheers
the very soul of those who sacrifice their desires to their duty,
under the blessed influence of religion. At last it pleased
God to afford me a means of escaping from the tyranny of
the Pope, and make me willingly and joyfully submit to the
easy yoke of his blessed Son, Jesus Christ. The ways of Providence for my change appear so wonderful to me, that I feel almost overcome when I earnestly think upon them. In the
first place, it was certain that I could not leave Spain for a
Protestant country, without giving a death-blow to my parents.
Could any human being have foreseen, in the year 1807, that
in 1810, my own father and mother would urge me to leave
my country for England? And yet, so it came to pass. You
have heard how Bonaparte entered Spain with the design of
placing his brother Joseph upon the throne of that country;
how for a time he seemed to have obtained his wishes when
his armies advanced till they came within view of Cadiz, and
threatened to extinguish the last hope of the Spaniards. I
was at that time at Seville, my native town. As the French
troops approached it, all those who would not submit to their
government, and had the means of removing to another place,
tried to be beforehand with them, by taking their flight to
Cadiz. My parents could not abandon their home; but as
they abhorred the French troops, and hated the injustice of
their invasion, they were anxious that I should quit the town.
Here I saw the most favorable opening for executing my
long delayed plan for escaping the religious tyranny under
which I groaned; and pretending that I did not feel secure at
Cadiz, prepared in four days to leave my country, for England
I knew it was forever, and my heart bleeds at the recollec
tion of the last view I took of my father and mother. A few
weeks after I found myself on these shores.

  R. Indeed, Sir, I think you did right. Poor as I am, had I known your case when you arrived, I would have shook you by the hand, and welcomed you to my cottage.

A. If I should tell you all the gratitude I feel for this country, and my sense of the kindness and friendship with which I have met from the moment I landed, you might suspect me of flattery.—But how different appeared England to me from what I had imagined it to be!

R. What, sir, did you fear that we should behave rudely to a foreigner, who came for shelter among us?

A. No, indeed; that was not my mistake. I found England as hospitable and generous as it had always been described to me. But one thing I found in it which I never expected; that was, true and sincere religion. I have told you that in Popish countries people are made to believe that whoever is not a Roman Catholic is only a Christian in name. I therefore supposed that in this Protestant country, though men appeared externally to have a religion, few or none would care any thing about it. Now observe the merciful dispensations of Providence with regard to me. Had I upon my first arrival fallen in with some of your infidels, I should have been confirmed in all my errors. But it pleased God so to direct events as to make me very soon acquainted with one of the most excellent and religious families in London. I had in my former blindness and ignorance, believed that since in Spain, which is the most thoroughly Roman Catholic country in the world, the morals in general are very loose; a nation of Christians only in name, (for such was my mistaken opinion of you) would be infinitely more addicted to vicious courses. But, when I began to look about me, and observed the modesty of the ladies, the quiet and orderly lives of the greatest part of the gentry, and compared their decent conversation with the profane talk which is tolerated in my country, I perceived, at once, that my head was full of absurd notions, and prepared myself to root out from it whatever I should find to be wrong. In this state of mind I went one Sunday to Church, out of mere curiosity; for my thoughts were at that time very far from God and his worship. The unmeaning ceremonies of the Roman Catholics had made me sick of churches and church-service. But when in the course of the prayers, I perceived the beautiful simplicity and the warm-heartedness, if I may say so, of your prayer-book, my heart, which, for ten years, had appeared quite dead to all religious feelings, could not but show a disposition to revive, like the leafless trees when breathed upon by the first soft breezes of spring. God had

prevented its becoming a dead trunk: it gave indeed no signs
of life; but the sap was stirring up from the root.   This was
easily perceived in the effect which the singing of a hymn had
upon me that morning.   It begins—

> When all thy mercies, O my God,
> My rising soul surveys,
> Transported with the view, I'm lost
> In wonder, love, and praise.

The sentiments expressed in this beautiful hymn penetrate
my soul like the first rain that falls upon a thirsty land.   My
long, impious disregard of God, the father and supporter of
my life and being, made me blush, and feel ashamed of myself;
and a strong sense of the irrational ungratefulness in which I
had so long lived, forced a profusion of tears from my eyes.
I left the church a very different man from what I was when
I entered it; but still very far from being a true believer in
Christ.   Yet, from that day I began to put up a very short
prayer every morning, asking for light and protection from my
Creator, and thanking him for his goodness.   It happened
about that time that some books concerning the truth of religion—a kind of works in which this country excels all
others—fell in my way.   I thought it fair to examine the matter again, though I imagined that no man could ever answer
the arguments against it, which had become quite familiar to
my mind.   As I grew less and less prejudiced against the
truth of Divine Revelation, I prayed more earnestly for assistance in the important examination in which I was engaged.
I then began a careful perusal of the Scriptures, and it pleased
God, at the end of two years, to remove my blindness, so far
as to enable me with humble sincerity to receive the sacrament according to the manner of the Church of England;
which appeared to me, in the course of my inquiries, to be of
all human establishments, the most suited, in her discipline, to
promote the ends of the Gospel, and in her doctrines as pure
and orthodox as those which were founded by the Apostles
themselves.   It is to me a matter of great comfort that I have
now lived a much longer period in the acknowledgment of the
truth of Christianity, than I spent in my former unbelief.

R. You have indeed great reason to thank God.   But have
you never had any doubts about our church, since you became
a member of it.

A. Never, my friend, as compared with the Roman Catholic.   I am so fully persuaded that the doctrines properly called
Popish, and which make the real difference between Protes

ι ·ɔts and Romanists, are false, that they would shake my faith
i.ₓ the Gospel, if one could prove to me that they are part of
iι. That I am sure can never be done; and since I learnt to
separate the chaff of Rome from the true grain of Christ, I
have never turned my back on my Master and Redeemer. I
will, however, confess to you, that several years after I embraced the Protestant religion, I was strongly tempted in my
faith; not, however, as I said before, from any leaning to popery, but from a doubt whether the doctrine of the people called
Unitarians—I mean those who say that Christ was nothing
but a man, the son of Joseph and Mary—might not be true.
This was a very severe trial to me; for as I had so long renounced the Christian faith, my mind required an uncommon
assistance of Divine grace, to prevent it from relapsing, like a
person recovered out of a long illness, into my old habits of
unbelief. In this state of doubt, but without any rash positive-
ness on either side (for, thank God, my past errors had made
me well acquainted with my weakness,) I carefully examined
the Scriptures, never omitting to pray to the Almighty that he
would make me acquainted with the truth. Clouds of doubt
hovered, a long time, over my soul, and darkness increased
now and then in such a degree that I feared my Christian faith
had been extinguished. Had I, in consequence of this disposition to unbelief, returned, as is often the case, to a course of
immorality, nothing could have saved me from a relapse into
infidelity. But the grace of God was secretly at work in me,
and whatever doubts I had about the doctrines of the Gospel,
I never deemed myself at liberty, openly and wilfully to offend
against its commandments. I sincerely wished to find the
truth; and though in my distress I felt often inclined to doubt
again the truth of Revelation, my knowledge of the vanity and
flimsiness of infidelity, made me turn to Christ, and say (I can
assure you I often uttered the words aloud in tears,) "To whom
shall I go? thou hast the words of eternal life."* Partly from
these doubts, and partly from a long and lingering illness
which the change of climate had brought upon me, I passed
the greatest part of a year without receiving the sacrament.
Had I, as far as it was my own fault, abstained much longer
from that appointed means of grace, I fear I should have fallen
a second time from the faith; but, by God's mercy, I examined
myself upon that point, and finding that my conscience did not
charge me with any true impediment to the reception of the

* John vi. 68.
2 C

Holy Sacrament and that, as to the doubts on my mi d hey
were involuntary, and accompanied with a sincere desire of
finding the truth, I presented myself at the sacramental table,
with feelings, similar to those which I conceived I should have,
if, as it was then probable, death had sent me with my doubts,
before the judgment seat of Christ. I threw myself, in fact,
wholly upon his mercy. My trust was not in vain: for calm
was soon restored to my soul; and I found myself stronger than
ever in the faith and profession which I made when I became
a member of the Church of England. You see, my friend, that
I disguise not my weakness from the world. You may suppose,
that for a man who has spent his whole life in the pursuit of
learning, it must be very mortifying to publish so many errors,
so many doubts, in a word, to shew the utter feebleness of his
mind and soul, when unsupported by Divine grace. But I
conceive this to be a duty which I owe to the truth of the Gospel, and to the spiritual welfare of my fellow-creatures. How
happy should I be if the humblest individual, when tempted.
should take courage from the knowledge of my case, and cling
to prayer whilst he examined, like the noble Bereans, "whether
these things were so."*

R. Sir, I pity what you have suffered; but I must say it com
forts me to find that doubts and errors upon religious subjects
are not confined to the unlearned.

A. They are not, indeed; on the contrary, the pride of human knowledge is often the rock on which the faith of the higher classes of society is wrecked. It is the true character of
the Gospel to be "hid from the wise and prudent, and to be
revealed unto babes;"† not that true learning or knowledge is
in opposition to spiritual truth, but because the best dispositions
for faith are humility and singleness of heart. The appointed
ministers of the Church of Christ are indeed commanded to
"be able by *sound doctrine* both to exhort and to convince the
gainsayers,"‡ but, though this direction of the Apostle Paul
does not exclude the laity from religious learning, and every
man, according to his ability, should make himself acquainted
with the unanswerable reasons on which the truth of the Gospel is founded, the saving faith of Christianity requires no
book-learning to have its full effect on the heart. Happy indeed are those millions of humble Christians, who, from the
publication of the Gospel to our own times, have received the
doctrines of the Bible by the simple means of their Catechism

*Acts xvii. 11.   † Luke x. 21.   ‡ Tit. i. 9.

and the instructions imparted by their Christian Pastors, and so ordered their lives as not to wish those doctrines to be false! How infinitely more happy is the lot of these humble Christians, than mine! After spending my whole life in reading; after trying, by ten years' incessant study, to obtain a complete assurance that Christianity was a fable, and finding out, at last, by great attention and labor, that such books as engaged to prove it, had deceived me; I have to thank God that by his grace, I find myself, as to Christian faith, upon a level with the humblest and most illiterate disciple of Christ, who trusts in his redeeming blood for salvation.—Yet the ways of God are wonderful; and it is not presumptuous to hope that the bitter struggles of my mind may be made the means of confirming the faith of many.

R. I feel assured they will. Without flattering you, sir, or supposing that your talents or knowledge are above the common run of gentlemen of your class, it stands to reason, hat the religion, which, after being so many years an unbeliever, you have embraced so earnestly, must have a very strong evidence in support of its truth.

A. So strong, my friend, that whoever takes proper pains to examine it, if he really acknowledge that there is a living God, a Being who concerns himself in the moral conduct of mankind, will never be at rest, till he has either believed in Christ, or succeeded in making himself completely blind and careless on spiritual subjects, allowing himself to be drifted by the rapid stream of life, without ever giving a thought to the unknown shores on which he is sure soon, very soon, to be cast. The greatest part of those who pretend to believe in a God, and yet reject the Gospel where it is publicly taught without the errors of Popery, do not mean by the name of the Deity, any thing like the Supreme Being, the living God, the intelligent Creator of mankind revealed in the Scriptures; but some unknown cause of what we call Nature, to which the good or bad conduct of men is equally indifferent. If it were not so, they could never suppose that a religion like the Christian, supported by proofs so superior to those of all the other religions of the world, so infinitely above them all in the purity of its laws, and so effectual in allaying the storms of evil passions, and bestowing peace and happiness on the breast that fairly gives it room to act; it is impossible, I say, that a man who really believes in an all-seeing, and all-wise God, could at the same time believe *that* religion equally a cheat with all the other superstitions of the world; and that it is indifferent to

Him, whether men, who can make the comparison, receive or reject it. This consideration was, my dear friend, my sheet-anchor, in the fierce tempest of my doubt, which, for a time, threatened to sink my faith after my conversion to Protestant Christianity. When nearly overcome by a multitude of little infidel arguments (for they are all like a swarm of puny in-sects, and can never form a well-connected band, as the proofs of Christianity do,) I turned, in the anguish of my soul, to seek for a resting place, out of the "Rock of ages," Christ the Sa-viour. The view around me was dismal indeed; a dark gulph, with small spots, every one of which I had tried, and found un-able to support me, and from which the fall, I well knew, would inevitably plunge me into the bottomless abyss of *Athe-ism*. It was in this distress of mind that I exclaimed with the Apostle Peter, *To whom shall I go?* and clung to the cross of Christ.

1?. Your reasons appear to me very strong, and such, that no man who feels a real concern for his soul, can shut his eyes to them. I clearly understand that a living God—a God to whom the man who murders, and he who feeds the hungry; the man who oppresses, and he that protects the orphan and the widow; the man who promotes virtue in his house and neighborhood, and he who spreads vice and misery for the gratification of his brutal passions, are not equally acceptable or indifferent; cannot be supposed to have allowed a religious cheat, to appear so beautiful and desirable as true Christianity shews itself to every honest and upright heart. But what have you, sir, to say to the existence of so many false religions as there are in the world? Would God permit them to exist, to the spiritual ruin of millions of men, if these matters were of real consequence in his eyes?

A. Suppose yourself obliged to penetrate through a dark forest, full of wild beasts and precipices, and crossed by innu-merable paths. On the side by which your entrance lies, there stands the son of the king of the country, who with the greatest kindness offers to a great multitude of the new comers a little map, with a clear view of the paths, which he tells them, must lead to certain ruin; while others are distinctly marked, which if they carefully follow, he promises to meet them at the other side of the perilous wood, and make 'hem rich and happy in his kingdom. You inform yourself, by every possible means, of the character of this man, and find no reason to doubt that he is able and willing to fulfil his engagements. Yet, upon observing great crowds of men and women, who are allowed to enter with little or no advice respecting their way, you rather pertly begin to question the prince about them. He will not, however, condescend to answer these questions, but urges you to avail yourself of his advice, and to consider how unjust and unfeeling it is, when he takes such pains for *your safety,* to question his justice and benevolence in his conduct towards his apparently less favored subjects. Suppose, lastly, that your pride and conceit get the better of your reason, and that you address the prince in such words as these · "Sir, though I have no reason to suspect your veracity, yet your conduct towards those people whom I see wandering without maps, about the forest, is not at all to my fancy. You must, therefore, either explain to me every plan and reason of your government, or I will throw this map in your face, and trust my own endeavors to find my way through the forest."— Would you deserve compassion, if this your proud rashness carried you to inevitable perdition?

R. Certainly not: God forbid I should ever act in such an ungrateful manner.

A. Yet this is exactly what men do, who object to their reception of the Gospel, that God has not made it equally known to all nations of the world. They, in fact, cast away the 'pearl of great price,' because they have been chosen amongst millions to possess it. They see the real and substantial value of the gift; they cannot but believe that he who puts it into their hands, must be infinitely kind and merciful; but still their pride will prevail, and they had rather be left to their own ignorance and weakness, than give glory to God for what they themselves receive, and trust that his goodness will, in some way, provide for his other creatures, and finally judge the world in righteousness.

R. I only put the question, because I have heard it from others. But, as to myself, I feel satisfied that every man's duty is to receive God's gifts with thankfulness, and without questioning the wisdom and justice of his government. I will, however, before we part, take the liberty to ask you why, when you became convinced of the truth of the Gospel, you did not return to your parents and friends in Spain? Surely there cannot be such difference between Romanism and Protestantism, as to force a man to become a stranger and an outcast to his own flesh and blood, and (as I believe you have done) turn his back upon all the hopes and prospects of life, and trust to chance for his subsistence. But perhaps, Sir, you have availed yourself of the liberty to marry, which

2c2

Priests have in this country, and cannot leave your wife and children.

A. You are mistaken, my friend, in your conjecture. I lost my health soon after my arrival in this country, and have not had the means of supporting a wife, in such comfort as might make her amends for devoting her life to the care of a sickly husband. But I do not like to speak upon these subjects, more than is absolutely necessary to remove all suspicion as to the motives of my change My voluntary exile has been attended to me with every thing that can make me thankful, yet without any circumstance that could bribe my will against my sincerity.—As to the principal part of your question, I can assure you that the difference which I find between the Roman Catholic and the Protestant religion, is so great and important, that had there been no Protestantism in the world, I cannot conceive how I should be a Christian at this moment.

R. Do you believe then, Sir, that the Roman Catholics are not Christians?

A I have known most sincere followers of Christ amongst them; but am perfectly convinced that Catholicism, by *laying another foundation than that which is laid, that is Jesus Christ;** by making the Pope, with his church, if not the *author*, certainly the *finisher* of their faith; exposes the members of that communion to the most imminent danger from the arguments of infidelity. What happened to me in my youth is the lot of a great part of the clergy, and the higher classes of Spain. The lower classes, and those who among the higher read little, and for that little confine themselves to the books approved by their church, are fierce bigots, who would, if they had it in their power, spread desolation and havoc among the nations who do not bend the knee before the saints and relics of Rome. But, amongst such as read and think for themselves, I seldom found a sincere christian. By the intolerance which Catholicism exercises, wherever it is the religion of the country, those men are forced to be hypocrites; but they are generally so uneasy and restless under the restraint imposed on them by the threats of the law; that a very slight acquaintance with another unbeliever will be sufficient to open their hearts to each other, and make them attack, in private, with great violence or levity, the most sacred mysteries of religion. There are few practical observations of my own, which I look upon with more confidence than the direct tendency of the Roman Catholic religion to produce infidelity. I suppose you either

*1 Cor. iii. 11.

recollect, or have heard, the almost universal contempt in which the christian religion was held in France during the Revolution. Now, had the French people been sincere christians, as they appeared just before their revolution broke out, they could not possibly have been changed in a few months into such horrible infidels, as that there should have been a doubt in their sort of parliament, whether they were or not to pass a law against the belief in a God. Here, therefore, you may observe the common effects of Catholicism, where it has the upper hand. It first disfigures and distorts the gospel, so as to make it appear absurd and ridiculous in the eyes of men that are bold enough to use their judgments. Then it stops their mouths, and makes their thoughts rankle in their hearts, till when, at last, some great commotion releases them from the fears of religious tyranny, they abhor the very name of religion, under which they have been forced to bow to the most barefaced impostures and vexations; and shake off, in desperate impiety, their allegiance to God; taking it to be one and the same thing with the yoke so long and heavily laid on their necks by the Pope and his emissaries.

R. You think, then, Sir, that a Protestant is safer from the attacks of infidelity than a Roman Catholic.

A. Incomparably safer. I do not, in matters of religion, much like illustrations or comparisons taken from subjects which may lead the mind to levity. But I cannot help comparing the question between a Romanist and an Infidel to one of the bets which you call *neck or nothing.* As a Roman Catholic is bound to believe that the Scriptures would be useless without the infallibility of the Pope and his church, he must be ready to cast off the whole Bible, as soon as he shall be obliged to confess that there is the least error in their creed. The Romanist grounds his belief of the Bible on his belief in the Church of Rome; the Protestant, on the contrary, grounds his respect for the church to which he belongs, on his belief of the Bible. The whole building of religion has been placed upside down by the Romanist, and the original foundations been made to stand upon the spires and pinnacles of the superstructure. Knock one of these down, and the whole tumbles to the ground. It is not so with the Protestant. He also has a church, but it is a church that leaves him free to try her authority by her conformity with the Scriptures. She does not, like Rome, teach her children that nothing can be true christianity but what is professed under her control; and that Christ will not acknowledge as his disciples such as learn his doctrines thro'

any other channel. A true Protestant Church, rather than
endanger the saving faith of her members, by riveting upon
their minds the notion of no alternative between the absolute
rejection of Christ, and perfect submission to her own declarations; will sacrifice every view of advantage to herself, and
even afford matter of exultation to her implacable enemies, the
Romanists, by leaving her members in perfect freedom to desert her, and choose their own christian guides. But God has
rewarded this generous forbearance, by appropriating it to
Protestant churches, and especially to our own, and making
them wear it, as the badge by which men can know the true
flock of Christ. " By this," says our Saviour, " shall all men
know that ye are my disciples, if ye have love one towards another."—" Thanks be to God! (exclaims a pious and amiable-
Bishop* of our church, in one of the most eloquent passages to
be read in any language,) thanks be to God, this mark of our
Saviour is in us, which you (the Roman Catholics,) with our
schismatics and other enemies want. As Solomon found the
true mother by her natural affection, that chose rather to yield
to her adversary's plea, claiming her child,† than endure that
it should be cut in pieces; so may it soon be found, at this day,
whether is the true mother, our's, that saith, give her the living child, and kill him not; or your's, that if she may not have
it, is content it may be killed, rather than want of her will.—
' Alas! (saith our's, even of those that leave her) these be my
children! I have borne them to Christ in Baptism; I have
nourished them as I could with my own breasts, his Testa-
ments. I would have brought them up to man's estate, as
their free birth and parentage deserves. Whether it be their

---

*Bishop Bedell. He was promoted in 1624, to the see of Kilmore, in
Ireland. The spirit of retaliation, which the previous persecutions of Rome
still kept alive, found the greatest opponent in Bishop Bedell. His meekness
and universal charity had so gained him the hearts of the Irish Roman Catholics, that in the rebellion of 1641, the Bishop's palace was the only dwelling
in the county of Cavan, which the fury of the rebels respected. As that palace
was, however, the shelter of several Protestants whom the Papists had doomed
to die, the Bishop, who firmly resisted the demands for their surrender, was
seized and carried away with his whole family. The horrors which surrounded him broke his heart, and he soon died. The very rebels, in a large body,
accompanied his remains to the grave, over which they fired, in honor to his
memory.—The passage above quoted is from a letter to a person who had
turned Papist. I have copied it from THE FRIEND, a work of Mr. S. T.
Coleridge, which is much less known than its eloquence, piety, and learning deserve.

†Read the third chapter of the first book of Kings.

lightness, or discontent, or her enticing words, and gay shows,* they leave me; they have found a better mother. Let them live yet, though in bondage. I shall have patience; I permit the care of them to their Father. I beseech him to keep them, that they do no evil. If they make their peace with him I am satisfied: they have not hurt me at all.' Nay, but saith your's (*the Church of Rome*) ' I sit alone as Queen and Mistress of Christ's family; he that hath not me for his mother, cannot have God for his father. Mine therefore are these, either born or adopted; and if they will not be mine, they shall be none.' So, without expecting Christ's sentence, she cuts with the temporal sword, hangs, burns, draws those that she perceives inclined to leave her, or have left her already. So she kills with the spiritual sword those that submit not to her; yea thousands of souls, that not only have no means so to do, but many which never so much as have heard whether there be a Pope of Rome, or not. Let our Solomon be judge between them,— yea, judge you—more seriously and maturely, not by guesses, but by the very mark of Christ, which, wanting yourselves, you have unawares discovered in us: judge, I say, without passion and partiality, according to Christ's word, which is his flock, which is his church.'—Oh, my friend, if the deluded Protestants, who allow themselves to be entrapped by the cunning arts of Popery, knew, as I do, by a long and sad experience, the proud, fierce, and tyrannous spirit of the Church to which they submit, by their recognition of the Pope and his laws; they would weep with more bitter tears than Esau, the loss of that Christian liberty, which is the birth-right of every one who is born a Protestant. A true Roman Catholic is the slave of the slaves of the Pope, the priesthood, all over the world. If you hear them talk loud and boldly in these kingdoms; if they appear to you as free and independent as other men, they owe it to the Protestant laws, which protect them against the church tyranny to which their religion binds them. They owe it also to the cunning system pursued by the Pope himself, who, by allowing to them, in silence, this apparent freedom, acts like the huntsmen in India, who let their tame elephants roam at large in the forests, that they may entice the yet untamed and free into the pitfalls. No; trust them not! Had I a voice that could be heard from north to south, and from east to west, in these islands, I would use it to warn

*The arts employed by the Church of Rome to gain proselytes, and her gaudy and showy Church service.

every Protestant against the wiles of Rome; wiles and arts in deed, of so subtle and disguised a nature, that I feel assured, many of the free-born Britons, who are made the instruments and promoters of them, do not so much as dream of the snare into which they are trying to decoy their countrymen. Such as believe that Popery, if allowed to interfere with the laws of England, would not most steadily aim at the ruin of Protestant-ism, even at the plain risk of spreading the most rank infidel ity, should be sent to learn the character of that religion where it prevails uncontrolled; where I have learnt it during five and twenty years, in sincere submission, and for ten in secret re-bellion. Would you form a correct idea of the character and spirit of that church which the Roman Catholics bind them selves to obey, as they hope for salvation; of that church, to be free from whose grasp, I deem my losses clear gain, and my exile a glorious new birth to the full privileges of a man and a christian—grant me another patient hearing, at your own convenience, and you shall see the Pope's church, such as she is, and without the disguises in which she begs for power.

R. I will hear you again, whenever you are disposed to speak on so important a subject

DIALOGUE II.

Reader. I cannot tell you, Sir, how anxious I have been for your return.

Author. It cannot be more, my good friend, than I myself have been to come to you. But as I know that I must be either a welcome or an unpleasant visitor, according as people dwell upon or reject the words of my first conversation; I feel some misgivings within me when I approach them the second time. Now, I can tell you with a certainty, which I do not derive from any confidence in myself, but from my experience of the nature of truth, that since you have given some thought to the subject of our first conversation, you will with God's blessing, bear with me to the end of our conferences.

R. That I will, Sir, for I love the truth in all matters; and much more so, of course, in those which concern my salvation. Now, I must tell you, my head has been at work upon things that I had never thought of before. When I formerly met my Roman Catholic neighbors, or saw their chapel, these things appeared to me as natural as the large yew-tree in our church-yard, or the holly-hedge before the Rector's house. There they are; and I never troubled myself to know how they came there. But I now say to myself, I am a Protestant; and farmer such a one is a Roman Catholic. The reason of this I know to be, that my father, and my father's father, and so on, were Protestants, and his were Catholics. But was this always so? How did this great division begin among christians? I have, of course, heard of the *Reformation,* and of Luther, who, according to a little penny book, which is frequently hawked among the country folks, seems not to have been a good man; for, it is said, he himself declares that the Devil taught him what he was to write against the Roman Catholics. I can hardly believe this to be true: I wish, Sir, you would

311

set me right, about the Protestant religion, and who it is that we Protestants follow: Is it Luther?

A. The Roman Catholics would fain persuade the world that Luther is the author of our religion; but it is to be hoped that their partiality deceives them, and that they do not use a deliberate untruth out of pure spite. Such as are really learned among them, cannot but know that Protestants acknowledge no master, on religious points, but Christ, whose instructions they seek in the inspired writings of his Apostles and Evangelists, contained in the New Testament. It is, however, a great shame that some learned men among the Roman Catholics, should employ themselves in writing and sending about such trash as *The confessed Intimacy of Luther with Satan,* when they must know, in the first place, that the story is a downright misrepresentation; and that, if Luther had really been the worst of men, (which is the very reverse of the truth) it would be the same, with regard to us Protestants, as if a thief had, by some strange chance, put an honest individual in the way of recovering a great fortune, which a cunning set of men had converted to their own profit. I wish you, my friend, to remember the comparison I have just given you, whenever the Roman Catholics, or those writers of no religion, whom they employ to seduce the unlearned, come to you with stories about the wickedness of the Reformers, and the vices of Henry the Eighth. Surely, it is nothing to us by what instruments and what means God was pleased to deliver us from the impostures and tyranny of the Church of Rome,—of that Church, which, having seized our rightful inheritance, the Bible, doled it out in bits and scraps to the people, mixed up and adulterated with human inventions. It is for them to be ashamed of the men they reckon among their Popes; poisoners, adulterers, and much worse still; a fact which they will not venture to deny. It is for them, I say, to be ashamed, that they believe and declare that such men held the place and authority of Christ upon earth; and that all Roman Catholics are bound still to believe their declarations, as if they had been given by Christ himself and his Apostles. We Protestants do not receive revealed truth through such channels.— We feel grateful, indeed, to the Protestant Reformers, all of whom, at the risk, and many at the expense of their lives, roused the attention of the Christian world, to the monstrous abuses which the Popes had introduced into the Church. Our Reformers encouraged the world to shake off the yoke of iron, which, in the name of Christ, the Popes had laid upon it; but did not claim any authority over the Protestant Churches, similar to that which Rome had usurped. The great and essential difference between the Romanists and ourselves is this:—the Romish Church says to all christians, "Follow not the Scriptures, but me;"—the Protestant Church, on the contrary, says, "Follow me as long as I follow the Scriptures." Now, if Satan himself had directed us to the pure fountain of Revelation, to the genuine word of God, would it not be our duty still to follow the Scriptures in preference to all human authority?

R. But is there any foundation for the story which the Roman Catholics are so busy to spread among the poor people, that Luther used to converse with the Devil?

A. No other foundation, my friend, than the spite which has rankled in the hearts of the Roman Catholic clergy, since Martin Luther opened the eyes of men to their spiritual tyranny. Luther was called by the Romanists, an instrument of the devil, and all his words were said to be put into his mouth by the Prince of Darkness. In this manner they tried to frighten the simple and ignorant, that they might stop their ears to the powerful arguments of the great Reformer. Well, then, said Luther, addressing himself to his calumniators, the Doctors of the Roman Catholic Church, see if you can answer the reasons by which the devil proved to me that the Mass is an idolatrous and unscriptural manner of worship; and he overwhelms the said Doctors with unanswerable reasons drawn from the holy scriptures. What better method could he employ to refute their abominable and silly calumny, than by showing that what the Romanists attributed to the devil, was the true and genuine declaration of the word of God? I have carefully examined the works of Luther, and can assure you that what the Roman Catholics circulate in their penny tracts, is a most ungrounded calumny. Were we mean enough to retaliate, we might give a history of their Popes—a history which they cannot gainsay, which would prove many of them to have been, not in communication with Satan, but possessed by him, body and soul. I will, however, mention to you one of them, a Spaniard by birth, whom the Roman Catholics acknowledge as the head of their Church, and whom they declare to have been tne representative of Christ upon earth. The Pope I speak of, whose name is Alexander the VIth, had four sons by a concubine, with whom he lived many years. The crimes he committed in order to enrich his children, exceed those of the most wicked heathen Emperors. After a life of the most diabolical profligacy, he died of poison, which he took by mistake, having prepared it for some person who stood in the way of his son. This happened only twelve years before Luther's appeal to the Scriptures, against a church which recognized the supreme authority of men like Pope Alexander, and blasphemously called them the Vicars of Christ upon earth. From this fact alone, you may judge on which side the devil was most likely to be.

R. Good heaven, sir! have the Roman Catholics had such monsters for their Popes?

A. They have, indeed, and not a few.

R. And do they bind themselves to obey any one who may happen to be Pope, whether he be good or wicked?

A. They certainly do, in all spiritual matters. I will explain to you the whole Church-system of the Romanists in a few words. The Pope is their spiritual king; and what they call their Church, that is, their Bishops all over the world, is, one may say, their Spiritual Parliament. Now, as this Parliament of Bishops from all parts of the world cannot meet without great difficulty, and as no one but the Pope can call it together, it is the Pope alone, who in reality, holds supreme authority over his spiritual subjects, the Roman Catholics. The way in which the Pope governs his churches all over the world is this: He publishes a kind of Proclamation, which they call a Bull, and sends it round to all places where there are Roman Catholics. As every Bishop by himself, is a subject of the Pope, who calls himself the *Bishop of Bishops,* the bull must be obeyed by them. Every Bishop commands all his Priests to see that the orders of the Pope be obeyed by all those who are under their charge. The priests preach the necessity of complying with the orders of the Pope; and when people come to get absolution of their sins, by privately confessing them, they are told that they cannot be forgiven, unless they obey the Bull from Rome. So, you see, that if all the world were true Roman Catholics, the Pope would do what he pleased every where. Such, in fact, was the case for many centuries before the Reformation. The Popes, in those times, boldly declared that they had authority from God to depose kings from their thrones, and many a fierce war has been made in consequence of the ambition of the Popes, who wished all christian kings to recognize their authority. King John of England was obliged by the Pope to lay his crown at the feet of a Priest who was sent to represent him. That king was, moreover, made to sign a public deed, by which he surrendered the kingdoms of England and Ireland to the Pope, reserving to himself the government of these realms under the control of the Bishops of Rome; and finally, as a mark of subjection, bound himself to pay an annual tribute. The Priest who represented the Pope, took away the crown, and kept it five days from the King, to show that it was in the Pope's power to give it back or not, as he pleased.

R. But did not you say, sir, that the Pope only claims authority in spiritual matters, that is, in things that concern the soul?

A. Yes; but as the soul is in the body, the Pope has always begun his spiritual government by things which are corporal and temporal. The Pope used to argue in this manner: "I am the Vicar and Representative of Christ upon earth, and the souls of all men are in my charge. There is a King in such a kingdom, (say England) who will not believe the doctrines which I teach. He naturally will spread his own religious views in that country; and consequently it is my *spiritual* duty to take the crown off his head. His subjects (supposing them true and stanch Roman Catholics) are obliged, as they wish to save their souls, to obey my spiritual commands. I will, therefore, send a Bull, or Proclamation, desiring them not to acknowledge for their King a man, who, how well soever he may govern his temporal interests, is sure to ruin their spiritual concerns, and lead them all to eternal perdition."

R. But is it a doctrine of the Pope, that all men who are not of his opinion, must be lost to eternity?

A. It is, indeed. It is an express article of their creed which it is not in their power to deny, without being accursed by their own church, and ceasing to be Roman Catholics.

R. I cannot comprehend how the Christians, all over the world, came to believe that men could not be saved unless they pinned their faith on the Pope and his Church. I believe, sir, no one doubted that point before the Reformation.

A. So the Roman Cotholics give it out; but the true fact is not so. You must know that there exists a very ancient and numerous Church, which is called the *Greek,* which has never acknowledged the Pope. There are also the Churches of the Armenians and Ethiopians, which were established by the Apostles, or their early successors, and have no idea of the necessity of submission to the Pope, in order to be true christians. Christianity, indeed, had been long established before the Popes bethought themselves of claiming spiritual dominion over all christendom. But I will tell you how they accomplished their usurpation, and you will see that the progress of their tyranny was perfectly natural. If you read the **Acts** of the Apostles, where we have the inspired history of the first Christian Churches, you will find no mention of any authority like that which Rome claims for herself and her head, the Pope. Rome, however, was at that time the mistress of the world, which was governed without control by the Roman Emperors. At first, those Roman Emperors made the fiercest opposition to Christianity; and the Christian Bishops of Rome, being persecuted, and in danger of their lives, had neither spirit nor leisure to imagine themselves superior to all other Bishops. But the persecutions ceased; and the Emperors themselves becoming Christians, the Bishops of Rome began to think themselves entitled to be that in the Church of Christ, all over the world, which the Emperors were in the whole Roman state. It was then that the idle and ungrounded report that St. Peter had been Bishop of Rome, grew up into a common belief: then it was said, that the Popes were St. Peter's successors: that as St. Peter was the Head of the Apostles, so the Pope was the head of all Bishops: and that as Christ had said to St. Peter, tna. he was a rock, on which he would build his Church, every Pope, good, bad, or indifferent, must also be a rock, on which the whole of Christianity depends. The temporal power of Rome gave a certain color to these absurd fancies; for Rome was at that time, to the greatest and best part of the world, what London is now to England and all her possessions. People, you know, attach ideas of superiority to every thing that comes from the capital town of a great empire. It happened, however, that not long after the Popes had begun to hold up their heads in this way, the whole Roman Empire was invaded by immense armies of barbarous people, who broke in from the North, where they had till then lived in the forests, unconquered and untamed by any human power. In the course of a few centuries these barbarians became masters of the Roman empire. They were all ignorant idolaters; but by mixing with christians, they were converted to Christianity. The Christian Religion, indeed, though ever so disfigured with the errors of those who profess it, is so holy, and has such power over the soul, that the barbarian conquerors of Europe could not but respect it. The Priests who worked in their conversion, were in the Pope's interest, and took care to instruct those ignorant men in all the false pretences on which the Bishops of Rome had built their assumed superiority. Every thing that the Roman Priests said was received as Gospel: for our forefathers (you should know that we are

all chiefly descended from those northern warriors) could neither write nor read, and were more illiterate than the merest
clown in our own times. Thus things proceeded for ages;
whilst error grew more and more rooted as it descended from
father to son. There were now and then a few men, who,
notwithstanding the general ignorance, applied themselves to
the study of the Scriptures, and some were bold enough to declare that the Popes were usurpers over Christian liberty. But
the pretended successors of St. Peter were not so mild as that
holy Apostle, who submitted to rebukes*; but had grown into
proud tyrants, who commanded all Christian princes to put to
death every one that dared to contradict Papal authority. Many
massacres were committed by order of the Popes, and even
good men were ready to dip their hands in the blood of those
whom Rome had declared heretics. The spiritual usurpers
had a great advantage in those times, when the art of printing
was unknown. Perhaps you are not aware, my friend, that
for ages of ages, the only way that people had to publish books
was to get them copied out by hand; so that one hundred Bibles could not be procured under the expense of seven thousand days, or nearly twenty years' labor, which it was
necessary to pay to the men who lived by writing out books.
Consider then, the ignorance of the Scriptures in which the
mass of the people must have lived, when none but very
wealthy men could afford to purchase a Bible.

The Romanists boast, to the ignorant and unlettered, that
the religion of Rome had been acknowledged as the only true
one over all the world; and that it was uncontradicted till the
time of Luther. In this they tell you what is not a fact; but
observe besides, that the silence of the Christian people, till
that period, is a poor sort of approbation, for it is the approbation of gross ignorance. In proportion as knowledge increased,
so complaints and protestations against Rome became more
frequent. But in every case they were answered by fire and
sword. The Popish Clergy used, besides, another shameful
trick. Whenever there arose a set of men who opposed their
usurpations, they published the most infamous calumnies
against their opponents, and charged them with the grossest
crimes of the most filthy and disgusting lust. This they did
in the same manner, and on the same ground, that the old
Pagans had done against the primitive Christians For as
both the early Christians, and the opposers of the tyranny of
Rome, were obliged to avoid death by holding their religious

*See St. Paul's Epistle to the Gallatians, c. ii.

2 D 2

assemblies in secret, their enemies made the world believe that they did shut themselves up for vicious and infamous purposes. This trick was the more hateful, as the clergy of the Church of Rome, at that very time, were the most dissolute and profligate set that ever lived; and this I can prove by the confession of their own writers. But Providence could not allow this state of things to continue much longer; and, as learning increased, so the opposition to Rome grew stronger. From the beginning of the twelfth century, the numbers which in various and distant parts of Christendom, stood up against the errors and tyranny of the Popes, were every day upon the increase, and that in spite of the most fierce persecution on the part of the Romanists. The very means which were employed against them, however, contributed, under God's providence, to prepare the great defeat of the Papal See, which took place four hundred years afterwards by the preaching of Luther. As those who opposed the corruptions of Popery, were put to death, or spoiled of their property, and turned adrift upon the world, many of them took refuge in distant countries, such as Bulgaria, Hungary, and Bohemia, from whence their descendants, who had learned to hate the oppression of the Popes, returned in after times, and swelled the number of their opponents. There were also some clans or families of simple shepherds, who, like the highlanders of Scotland, had lived all along confined to the valleys of the mountains which separate France from Italy. They were so poor, and unknown, that the Popes had either been ignorant of their existence, or thought it not worth the trouble to teach them their adulterated Christianity; so that these happy rustics preserved, by means of their poverty and simplicity, the doctrines of Christ, such as they had received them from the early Christian Missionaries, who spread the Gospel before the Popes had disfigured it with their inventions. Their descendants live to this very day in the same spot, and are Protestants, notwithstanding the murders and burnings by which their sovereigns, the kings of Sardinia, strove, till very lately, to make them Romanists. An English Clergyman, whom I have the pleasure of knowing, visited those good people not long ago, and found them most excellent Protestants. They have their bishops, priests, and deacons, and agree with us of the Church of England, in every essential point of religious belief and practice. These simple, and truly primitive Christians, are known by the name of *Vaudois.*—Well, to return to my narrative: the persecuted opponents of the

Pope who returned from the lands of their exile, having joined with those who remained concealed in Europe, re-appeared in growing numbers, and were called Albigenses. Pope Innocent III. in the year 1198, despatched several priests with orders to destroy them wherever they might be found. One of those who made most havoc among them, is known and worshipped by the Roman Catholics, by the name of St. Dominic. He was the founder of the Inquisition, a court of judges whose only employment is to discover and punish those who reject the authority of the Church of Rome. A large province of France had become, almost to a man, stanch opposers of Popery. But the Pope promised remission of all their sins to the King of France and his Lords, if they would join to destroy his enemies. The horrors which the friends of the Pope committed in that war, exceeds all imagination. You may judge by what happened on the taking of a town called *Bezieres.* The Albigenses had shut up themselves in it, though there were also many Roman Catholics within its walls. The Pope's troops were on the point of storming it, when the doubt occurred to the soldiers, how they were to distinguish the Papists from the Albigenses, in order to spare the first, without letting the Pope's enemies escape. A Priest, whom they consulted, answered them in these words: *Kill them all! God will know his own.* Upon hearing this the soldiers entered the city, and put to the sword fifteen thousand persons. The same persecution, though not so fierce, was extended to Spain, and even to England, where thirty Albigenses were starved to death at Oxford.

R. I beg your pardon, Sir, for interrupting you; but I am longing to know whether you believe that those unfortunate creatures were real Protestants like ourselves.

A. They were certainly Protestants as far as opposition to the Pope's tyranny and usurpation over the Church of Christ is concerned, though I cannot answer for every point of doctrine which they held. But consider, my friend, the circumstances of those unhappy Christians. Their fathers had grown up under the dominion of the Popes, in an age of universal ignorance. The Bible had been carefully kept from them, and it was with great difficulty and danger that they could meet to read some portions of it which had been translated into their language. How then, could these poor people find out at once the truth, and avoid all sorts of errors, without competent and well-educated teachers, and left, as they were, to grope for the true Gospel, not only in the dark, but under all the irritation and fear of a violent persecution? You see that it was impossible. This was only the breaking out, through the thick clouds of Popery, of a beam of light which gradually increased till the appointed time when Luther and the grea. Reformer of England, were enabled to make a perfect separation of the truths contained in the Bible, from the errors in which the Church of Rome had involved them. My object in mentioning these facts is to show you, that in proportion as learning and an acquaintance with the Bible increased, the opposition to the Pope's encroachments grew; and that the Papal Church was not without public opponents, but when ignorance had overrun the world, and the Bible was unknown.— The present Pope is so well aware of this, that he has published a Bull against the English and Foreign Bible Society; because wherever the Bible makes its appearance without his own notes and interpretations, it never fails to raise him enemies. Can that be the *only true* Church of God, whose greatest enemy is the pure word of God himself?

R. Surely not, Sir. But was there no true Church of God from the time that Popery began, till the *Reformation?* I recollect to have seen a Roman Catholic tract, where it was very strongly urged, that since Christ has promised that the gates of hell should not prevail against his Church, the Roman Catholic Church must all along have been in the right.

A. That is a very common argument of the Romanists; but it has no foundation except their own fancies about the infallibility of the church. Our Saviour did not promise that any particular church should never err; but that the light of his Gospel should never be completely put out by the contrivances and attacks of hell. Such is the meaning, you well know, of the words *to prevail*, or gain a victory. The light of revelation was very much dimmed and obscured, before Luther and the Reformers who established our Church. Others had, long before them, complained of the obscurity, and tried, as well as they could, to rekindle it; but the means of Providence were not yet ready. Learning was very scarce till the invention of printing multiplied all sorts of books, and put the Bible into the hands of many. The printing-press had been spreading knowledge far and wide for about seventy years, when Luther raised his voice, and the light of the Gospel shone again in its full splendor. The candle was the same that Christ had set on the candlestick; the Pope had hid it under a bushel; but Luther, despising the threats of the spiritual tyrant, took it out of his keeping, and made it shine again as free as when the

Apostles held it up to the eyes of the world. Whoever attentively considers the state of the Gospel before the Reformation, must be convinced that Luther was the instrument by which Christ prevented the victory of Satan over his Church.

R. I am always at a loss when I would clearly understand what is meant by the Church. Where is that Church against which Christ tells us that Satan shall not prevail?

A. Let me answer you by a question, though I fear it will appear to you rather out of the way. Where is the plough that we pray God to speed?

R. Oh, Sir! we do not mean any particular plough. We only pray God to prosper and bless the labors of man to produce the staff of life.

A. Very well. Now, suppose that God had in the Scriptures promised, that evil should never prevail against the *plough.* What would you understand by such words?

R. I believe that they would mean that there should never be a famine over all the world, or that all the crops should never fail at once, so that it would be impossible to grow any more grain.

A. And what would you think if a club of farmers, with a rich man at their head, had established themselves in London, and wished to have a monopoly of all the corn on earth, saying to the government, "you must go to war to defend our rights: for God has said, that evil shall not prevail against the *plough;*—and who can be the *plough,* but the head and company of farmers of the county of Middlesex, wherein stands the great city of London, which is the first city of the world?"

R. I should certainly say that they were a set either of madmen or rogues, who wished to levy a tax upon all farmers, wherever they were.

A. I will now leave you to apply what we have said, to the use which the Pope and his Cardinals have made of Christ's promise, that Satan should *not prevail against his Church.* Church, in this passage, must be understood in the sense in which we understand *Plough,* speaking of agriculture in general. It must mean *Christianity* in general, not Christianity confined to the walls of any town: the meaning, therefore, of Christ's promise must be, that the Devil shall never succeed in abolishing the faith in God through Christ, which has been published in the Gospel; not that the Pope must always be in the right,—and much less that he is to be the Spiritual Lord of all the Christians on earth.

R. I can understand very well, that the promise of Christ cannot be confined to the Church of Rome. But yet, Sir, is not the Church of Rome the *Catholic* Church; and do we not say in the Creed, that we believe in the holy Catholic Church• One might suppose that, by these words, we bind ourselves to believe in the Church of Rome.

A. The Romanists, my friend, have on that point, as on many others, taken an unfair advantage, which they employ to seduce the simple. *Catholic,* you must understand, is a word which means *universal.* Just at the times when the Apostles, and their immediate followers, had preached the Gospel to all the world, their doctrine was *Catholic,* that is *universal.* Wherever there were Christians, their belief was the same; and as that belief exactly agreed with the doctrines of the Apostles, *Catholic,* or universal belief, was the same as *true* belief Errors, however, began very soon to multiply in the Christian Churches, and these errors were called *heresies,* which means, *separations*; because those who set up their own conceits as the doctrine of the Gospel, *separated* themselves from the *universal* belief, which at that time was the *true* one. These heresies or *separations* became, in course of time, so numerous, that the true Christian belief could no longer be called *Catholic* or universal, with respect to the number of Christians who held it; so that to say I believe in the *Holy Catholic Church,* was not the same as if one said, I believe in the *true* Church. You will, therefore, observe a change on this point, in the creed which is used in the Communion Service—a creed which the Roman Catholics receive, and which is about fifteen hundred years old. In that creed it was found necessary to add the word *Apostolic* to the word Catholic; and consequently, we find there, "*I believe in one Catholic* and Apostolic Church:" which is as much as to say, I believe that there is spread over the world a *true* church of Christ, which was known in the beginning of Christianity, by its being *Catholic or Universal;* but which, since error became more general than the true faith, must be known by its being *Apostolic.* By this you will perceive the artful contrivance of the Romanists, who knowing that what in the times of the Apostles was *Catholic,* was therefore true Christianity, wish us to call them *Catholics* in the same meaning, even after Rome had made her errors so common in the world, that they appeared at one time to be *Catholic,* that is, *universal.* Protestants, therefore should be aware of this trick, and never call them *Catholics,* but *Roman Catholics, Romanists,* or *Papists,* though as this last name seems to hurt their feelings, I seldom make use of it myself, and never with an intention to offend them. Every one, my friend, all over the world, who holds the pure doctrine of the Apostles,—every *Apostolic* Christian is a true *Catholic*,—a member of that *one true* Church which the Apostles made *Catholic* or *universal;* but which continued being *universal* a very short time. The members of that *heretical,* that is, *particular* Church of the Pope,—that Church of the individual city of Rome, cannot be *Catholic* or universal, except as far as they are *Apostolic.*

R. And how, Sir, are men to judge what Christian churches are Apostolic?

A. By the words of the Apostles and their Divine Master, which we have in the New Testament.

R. But does not the Church of Rome receive the Scriptures?

A. She does; and so far as she regulates her doctrine and practice by that standard, we believe her to be a part of the true universal Church of Christ. But in regard of her inventions, whereby she has nearly made void the spirit and power of the Gospel, we are bound to declare her a corrupt and heretical Church; a church which has degenerated from the *Apostolic* rule of faith, and, in proportion to the additions which out of her own fancy she has made the Gospel, has separated herself from the *one Catholic,* or universal church of Christ; which is that multitude of persons, of all times and countries, who being called by the grace of God to believe in his Son Jesus Christ, have conformed and do now conform, their faith and lives to the rule of the Scriptures, and ground their hopes of eternal salvation on the promises made therein.

R. I believe you said, Sir, that the Church of Rome has made additions to the Gospel out of her own fancy: has she also made any omissions in the articles of her faith?

A. No. It pleased Providence to preserve the whole of the Christian faith in her keeping, without diminution or curtailment. The true Gospel was thus kept entire during the ages of general ignorance, under the heap of her superstitions, like live seeds, which want nothing to spring up, but the removal of some layer of stones and rubbish. Had she been permitted to cast off some of the essential articles of the Apostolic doctrine, as other sects do, the work of the Reformation would have been difficult. But when Luther and the other Reformers had removed the superstitious additions of the Romanists, the whole truth, as it is in Christ, appeared in its original purity; and as both Rome and the Protestant Churches agree in every thing which is really a part of the Apostolic doctrine, we cannot be charged with innovation.

R. Yet they say that ours is a new religion.

A. Any Protestant may rebut that charge with the Bible in his hand. The New Testament is the original charter of Christians; any thing under the name of Christianity which we do not find there, must be an abuse of more modern date than the Charter. The additions made by the Church of Rome are it is true very old; but the foundations over which she has built her fantastic structure must be older still. That foundation, the *Testament,* is our religion, and we do not wish to prove our religion older than Christ.

R. I wish you would have the goodness to mention the additions and innovations which the Church of Rome has made to the true and Scriptural religion of Christ.

A. I will, with great pleasure, in our next conversation

DIALOGUE III.

Conduct of the Church of England and of the Roman Catholic Church compared; a true Account of the Innovations made by Rome. Tradition: Transubstantiation: Confession: Relics and Images.

Author. I PROMISED, at our last meeting, to give you an account of the innovations which the Church of Rome has made, and the human additions by which she has adulterated the pure doctrines of the Gospel. But before I begin, I must ask your opinion upon a case which I heard some time ago.

Reader. I will give it you, Sir, to the best of my knowledge.

A. The people of two neighboring islands, which acknowledged the authority of the same Sovereign, received each a governor from the metropolis. One of the Governors presented himself with his commission in one hand, and with the book of the Colonial Laws in the other. " Gentlemen," he said, " here is the King's commission, which authorizes me to govern you according to these laws. I will direct my officers to get them printed, and every one of you shall have a copy in his possession. If ever any one of you should think that I am stepping beyond my powers, or governing against the laws, he may examine the point and consult his friends about it; and if, after all, he feels inclined not to be under me any longer, I will not at all molest him in his removal to the neighboring island, carrying away every thing that belongs to him." The other Governor pursued quite a different course. He appeared in the capital with all the pomp and show of a King. He gave out, that he had authority from the Sovereign, not only to govern according to the standing laws, but to make new statutes at his will and pleasure. At the same time, he employed his officers to deprive the people of all the copies of the Colonial Laws that were to be found, and published heavy penalties against any one who should possess or read them without leave, or in a copy which had not his own interpretation of the statutes. Some high-spirited individuals presented a petition to the new Governor, stating, " that they were perfectly willing and ready to obey any one commissioned by their King; but, still they conceived themselves entitled to possess a

copy of the laws of the country; that if the Monarch himself
had empowered him to make additional laws, they would make
no objection to that, provided he showed an authentic copy of
his commission." The Governor grew quite furious upon
reading this remonstrance, and answered that he would not
show any document relating to his power of making new laws
that the king had conferred upon him this privilege, not in
writing, but by a message; and, finally, that if the petitioners
did not obey him in silence, he would employ force against
them.—" Do, Sir, but prove to us your commission from the
King, and we are ready to obey without a murmur."—" Take
those fellows," said the Governor, " and let them die by fire."
The order being executed, a number of citizens tried to escape
from the island, but troops were stationed at every port and
creek, and such as were found in the act of getting away were,
without mercy, put to the sword or confined to dungeons, till
they swore that they would receive whatever the Governor
commanded, as if it had been a part of the book of the laws.
To complete the picture of this Governor, I will tell you that
there was not one among the laws which he added to the written statutes of the colonies, but evidently procured both to him
and to his officers, an increase of wealth and power.—The
question I wish you to answer is, under which of these two
Governors would you advise a man to place himself?

R.   I answer without a doubt,—under the first.

A.   What! without any further inquiry; without examining
the book of colonial laws; without hearing the reason of the
other governor?

R.   If I understood you rightly, the tyrant Governor (for he
deserves no better name) does not wish to settle the matter by
reasoning: he wishes to be believed on his word, and puts to
death even those who would avoid his power by flight.   He
must be an imposter,—an usurper, who grounds his authority
on his own word, and his word on his tyranny.

A.   Oh, my friend, how justly you have given your verdict!
The Pope is the man.   My parable applies literally to the
case between the Roman Church and the Protestants.   We,
the Protestant Clergy, declare to the world, that our Bishops,
Priests, and Deacons, have no authority but what the Scriptures confer upon us, for the instruction and edification of the
people.   We show them our commission in the book of God's
word, and leave them to judge whether they are bound or not
to listen to our instructions.   If any one wishes to leave us,
he is at liberty to do so: we use no arts, no compulsion to keep

any one within the pale of our church. To those who remain under our guidance we give no other rule or law but the Scripture; our articles declare that nothing contained in them is to be believed on any other consideration, but the clear warrant of the Holy Scriptures. But hear the conditions which the Pope presents to mankind: " Come to me," he says, " as you wish to be saved; for none can escape the punishment of hell who reject my authority." I ask him for the proof that God has limited Salvation, by making it pass exclusively through his hands. He answers me, that he has received the power of interpreting the Scriptures, and adding to them several articles of faith: and that, by virtue of that power, I must believe what he affirms. I rejoin, that if the Scriptures said that the Bishop of Rome and his Church were to be the infallible interpreters of the written word of God, and that they had power to add to the laws therein contained, I should be ready to obey; but since the Scriptures are silent upon a point of such importance, I will not believe the Pope, who is the party that would gain by the forced interpretation of those passages on which he wishes to build his power over the whole church. He now grows angry, and calls me a heretic, protesting that the Scripture is clear as to his being the head of the church and Vicar of Christ. Are the Scriptures so clear in favor of your authority, my Lord the Pope? Why, then, are you and yours so alarmed when you see the Scriptures in the hands of the people? If your commission from God is clear, why do you not allow every man, woman, and child to read it? Because (says the Pope) they are ignorant.—Ignorant, indeed! is the meanest child too ignorant to know the person whom his father appoints to teach him? Is a stranger to drag a child away and keep him under his control without the father saying, " this is to be your teacher; I wish you to obey him like myself?" The only thing, in fact, which the child can perfectly understand, is the appointment of the person who is to be his tutor: and are we to be told that because the mass of Christians are children in knowledge, they must blindly believe the man who presents himself, rod in hand, saying to them, " follow me, for I have a letter of your father's in which he desires you to be under my command?" " Shew me the letter," says the Christian. " You are a silly babe," says the Pope, " and must let me explain the letter to you." "Yes," says the Christian, " but all I want is to see that my father mentions your name, and desires me to obey you." " No:" is the Pope's answer; " my name is not in the letter, but St

Peter's name is there: St. Peter was at Rome, and I am at Rome, and therefore it is clear that you must obey me."— "But tell me, I pray you, my Lord the Pope, does the letter say even that St. Peter was ever at Rome?" "No; but I tell you he was," says the Holy Father. "Still another question: is it in the letter that Peter was to govern all Christians more than any other of the Apostles as long as he lived?" "The letter does not say it, but I do." "So it seems that all your authority must depend, not upon any command of my heavenly Father, but upon your own word. If so, I will not follow you; but put myself under instructors who will read my Father's words to me, without requiring from me more than I find therein enjoined." Happy, my friend, is that Christian who can speak thus out of the Pope's grasp; for he is a fierce school-master, and would tear the skin off any one's back who should not take his word on points relating to his authority. You know that I should be made to endure a lingering death, for what I say to you at this moment, if the Pope or his spiritual subjects, could lay hold on me in any part of the world, but where Protestants are in a sufficient number to protect me.

R. I see, Sir, that the Pope is just like the proud, usurping Governor you described. He grounds his claims on his own authority, and supports his authority by the sword. But what strikes me above all, is his fear of the Scriptures. If the Scriptures were favorable to him, he would not object to their free circulation. I believe you said that the Pope had introduced many things in the Church which are not to be found in the Scriptures.

A. Very many, indeed; and what is still more remarkable, not one of which but is decidedly to his own profit. Here again the comparison between the Pope and the Protestant clergy is enough to decide any rational man in doubt what Church to follow. Any one who is capable of making the comparison, will clearly perceive, that on whatever points the Church of Rome and the Protestant Churches (especially ours of England) agree, the Scriptures are their common foundation. But as soon as they begin to disagree, the Church of Rome is seen striving after wealth and power in the articles which she adds to the Scriptures, while the Protestant clergy evidently relinquish both emolument and influence, by their refusal to follow the Romanists beyond the authority of the word of God. I will give you instances of this, as I proceed in the enumeration of the principal points of difference.

Tradition is one of the most essential subjects of dispute be-

tween Protestants and Romanists. The Romanists declare
that the Scriptures alone, are not sufficient for Salvation; but
that there is the word of God, by *hearsay*, which is superior to
the word of God in *writing*. By this *hearsay*, for tradition is
nothing else, they assure the world that the Scripture must be
explained; so that if the Scripture says *white*, and tradition
says *black*, a Roman Catholic is bound to say, that *white* means
black in God's written word.

R. But, sir, how can they be sure of that hearsay or tradition? Every one knows how little we can depend upon
reports.

A. They pretend a kind of perpetual inspiration, a miraculous knowledge which can distinguish the true from the false
traditions. The existence, however, of that miracle, people
must take upon their assertion.

R. And who do they say has that miraculous knowledge?

A. Their divines are not well agreed about it. Some say
the miracle is constantly worked in the Pope; others believe
that it does not take place but when the Pope and his Bishops
meet in council.

R. Then, after all, the Romanists cannot be certain at any
time that the miracle has taken place. Would it not be better
to abide by the Scriptures, and judge of those *hearsays* or traditions by what we certainly know to be God's word?

A. That is exactly what we Protestants do.

R. Yet one difficulty occurs to me. Is it not by a kind of
hearsay or tradition that we know the New Testament to have
been really written by the Apostles and Evangelists?

A. What then?

R. You see, sir, that tradition seems to be a good ground of
Faith.

A. Now tell me: if you had the title-deeds of an estate,
which had descended from father to son, till they came into
your possession, what would you say to an attorney who should
come to you with a *hearsay*, that the original founder of the
estate had desired his descendants to submit their lands and
chattels to the family of the said attorney, that they might keep
it and manage it for ever, explaining every part of the title-
deeds according to the traditional knowledge of their family?

R. I should be sure to show him the way out of my house,
without hearing another word about his errand.

A. Yet he might say, your title-deeds are only known to be
genuine by *tradition*.

R. Yes, sir; but the title-deeds are something substantial,

2 E 2

which may be known to be the same which my father received from my grandfather, and again my grandfather from his
father, and so on; but there is no putting seals or marks on
flying words.

A. Well, you have answered most clearly one of the strongest arguments by which the Romanists endeavor to foist their
traditions on the world. As long as the Christians who had
received instructions from the mouth of the Apostles were
alive, St. Paul, for instance, might say to the Thessalonians
*"Hold the traditions which ye have been taught, whether by
word or our epistle;"** because they could be sure that the
words they had heard were St. Paul's; but what mark could
have been put on these unwritten words, to distinguish them
as the true words of the Apostle, after they had passed through
the hands of three or four generations?

R. What is, after all, the advantage which the Pope derives
from these traditions?

A. They are to him of the most essential service. Without *tradition*, his hands would be tied up by Scripture; but, by
placing the Scripture under the control of these hearsays, the
Pope and his Church have been able to build up the monstrous
system of their power and ascendancy. You know that one
of the principal articles of the Roman Catholics is *transubstantiation*. This article would be searched for in vain in the
Scriptures; for though our Saviour said of the bread, "this is
my body;" and of the wine, "this is my blood," the Apostles
could not understand these words in a corporal sense, as if
Christ had said to them that he was holding himself in his own
hands. Consequently, St. Paul did not believe that the bread
and wine were converted into the material Christ, by the
words of consecration; but though he calls these signs the communion of the body and blood of Christ, he also calls them
Bread and cup.† The Romanists, however, found out that by
making the people believe, that any Priest could make Christ
come to his hands, by repeating a few words, they should enjoy
a veneration bordering upon worship, from the laity. But
how could this be done without the help of tradition? The
people were therefore told that the Pope knew by *tradition*,
that after the words of consecration, every particle of bread
and wine was converted into the body and soul of our Saviour:
that if you divide a consecrated wafer‡ into atoms, every one

---

* 2 Thess. ii. 15.   † 1 Cor. x. 16.

‡ The Roman Catholics use not common bread for the Sacrament, but a
white wafer with the figure of a cross made upon it, by the mould in which

of those atoms contains a whole God and man; and that the presence is so material, that (I really shudder when I repeat their most irreverent language) if, as it has happened sometimes, a mouse eats up part of the consecrated bread, it certainly eats the body of Christ; and that, if a person should be seized with sickness, so as to throw up the contents of his stomach immediately after receiving the sacrament, the filth should be gathered up carefully and kept upon the altar:—this I have seen done. I could relate many more absurdities, which would shock any but a Roman Catholic, to whom habit has made them familiar. I must not, however, give up this subject without pointing to the advantages which the doctrine of Transubstantiation brings to the Roman Catholic Clergy, that you may see the use they make of tradition.

I have already told to you the superstitious veneration which the Roman Catholics pay to their Priests. A Priest, even when raised to that office from the lowest of the people, is entitled to have his hands kissed with the greatest reverence by every one, even a Prince of his communion. Children are taught devoutly to press their innocent lips upon those hands to which, as they are told, the very Saviour of mankind, who is in heaven, comes down daily. The laws of the Catholic Countries are, with regard to Priests, made according to the spirit of these religious notions:—a Priest cannot be tried by the judges of the land for even the most horrible crimes. Murders of the most shocking nature have often been perpetrated by priests in my country; but I do not recollect an instance of their being put to death, except when the murdered person was also a Priest. I knew the sister of a young lady who was stabbed to the heart at the door of the church, where the murderer, who was her confessor, had, a few minutes before, given her absolution! He stabbed her in the presence of her mother, to prevent the young lady's marriage, which was to take place that day. This monster was allowed to live, because he was a Priest.—What but the belief in transubstantiation could secure to the clergy impunity of this kind? Even in Ireland, where the law makes no difference between man and man, a Priest can take liberties with the multitude, and exert a despotic command over them, which the natural spirit of the Irish would not submit to from the first nobleman in the kingdom. For all this, the Catholic clergy have to thank *tradition,*

the wafer is baked. By this means they remove the appearance of bread, which would be too striking and visible an argument against their doctrine.

for without that pretended source of Revelation, it woud have been impossible to make whole nations believe that a Priest (as they declare) can turn a wafer into God.

R. Was it not in the power of the Reformers to have pre served the same veneration to themselves, by encouraging the belief in transubstantiation?

A. It was so much in their power, that even after England had shaken off the authority of the Pope, many were burnt alive for denying the corporal presence of Christ in the Sacrament. The mass of the people were so blind and obstinate upon that point, that not one of the Protestant Martyrs of the reign of Queen Mary, but could have saved his life by declaring in favor of transubstantiation. Nothing, indeed, but an almost supernatural courage, and an apostolic love of revealed truth, could have enabled the Protestant clergy to oppose and subdue the Romanist doctrine of the Sacrament.

R. I believe, sir, that the doctrine you speak of, was valuable to the clergy in other respects.

A. It was, and is still to the Romanist Priesthood, a never-failing source of profit. The notion that they have the power of offering up the whole living person of Christ, whenever they perform mass, paved the way to the doctrine which makes the mass itself a repetition of the great sacrifice of Christ upon the cross. Under the idea that the Priest who performs the bloodless sacrifice, as they call it, can appropriate the whole benefit of it to the individual whom he mentions in his secret prayer before or after consecration, the Roman Catholics are eager all over the world, to purchase the benefit of masses for themselves; to obtain the favor of Saints, by having the masses done in their praise; and finally, to save the souls of their friends out of Purgatory, by the same means.

R. I have heard a great deal about Purgatory; but I do not exactly understand what the doctrine is which the Romanists hold about it.

A. They believe that there is a place very like hell, where such souls as die, having received absolution of their sins, are made to undergo a certain degree of punishment; like criminals who, being saved from the gallows, are kept to hard work as a means of correction. There is a strong mixture of a very ancient heresy in the religious system of the Catholics, which leads them to attribute to pain and suffering, the power of pleasing God. It was that notion that first produced the idea of purgatory; and it is the same notion that induces the devout and sincere among them almost to kill them selves with stripes, and flogging, with fasts, and many other self-inflicted penances,

R. I have heard that the heathen in India do the same.

A. The religious practices of those heathen, and many among the Roman Catholics, are remarkably similar. But we must not lose sigh. of the offspring of Roman Catholic *tradition*, and the profitable account to which the Church of Rome has turned it. *Tradition* alone must have been brought to the aid of Purgatory. But the doctrine once being received by the people, became a true gold mine to the Pope and his priesthood. This was obtained by teaching the Roman Catholics, that the Pope, as Vicar of Christ, had the power to relieve or release the souls in Purgatory, by means of what they call indulgences. These indulgences were made such an open market of, throughout Europe, before the Reformation, that kings and governments, even such as were stanch Catholics, bitterly complained that the Popes drained their kingdoms of money. Incalculable treasures have flowed into the lap of the Roman Catholic clergy, for which they have to thank the doctrine of Purgatory. The reason is clear, the Pope knew too well his interest, not to tack the doctrine of Transubstantiation and the Mass on that of the souls in Purgatory fire. If a mass, they said, is a repetition of the great sacrifice on the cross, and it is in the power of the Priest to apply the benefit of it to any one, then, by sending such a relief to a soul in Purgatory, that soul has the greatest chance of being set free from those burning flames, and of entering at once into heaven. Who that believes this doctrine will spare his pocket when he thinks that his dearest relations are asking the aid of a mass to escape out of the burning furnace! You will find, accordingly, that no Roman Catholic who can afford it, omits to pay as many priests as possible to say masses for his deceased relations and friends; and that the poor of that persuasion, both in England and Ireland, establish clubs for the purpose of collecting a fund, out of which a certain number of masses are to be purchased for each member that dies. Their accounts are regularly kept, and if any member dies without having paid his subscription, he is allowed to be tormented to the full amount of his debt in the other world, where the difference between rich and poor, according to these doctrines, is greater than in this life. A rich man may sin away, and settle his debt with masses; the poor must be a beggar even at the very gates of heaven, and trust to his savings properly kept and improved by a club, or to the charity of the rich, to escape out of that Purgatory which you may properly call the *Debtor's side* of hell.

R. Perhaps the Romanists will say that God will not allow the rich people to get off by the great number of masses, but will give the benefit of them to the poor.

A. So they say, when the abusurdity of their doctrine stares them in the face. But even this contrivance to evade the difficulty objected to their doctrine, has been turned into an increase of profit to the clergy. "Since," it is said, "no man can be certain that one or more masses, indulgences, or any of the various Purgatory bank-bills, will be allowed to avail the person for whom they are purchased, it behoves those who have worldly means to repeat the remittance as often as possible, that your friend or yourself may at last have his turn." You see, therefore, that even the doubts which might have endangered the sale of the Popish wares, are made by an effort of ingenuity to increase demand in the market. Without the fresh discovery, that God appropriates to the more deserving poor the masses and indulgences sent to the wealthy dead, a mass or plenary indulgence a head, would be more than sufficient to keep purgatory empty. The case is very different when you are acquainted with the doubt in which you must be left as to the effect of your purchases; so that, if possible, you must continue them forever.

R. What do you mean by indulgences?

A. That wonderful storehouse of knowledge, *Tradition*, has informed the Popes that there is somewhere an infinite treasure of spiritual merits, of which they have the key; so that they may give to any one a property in them, to supply the want of their own. A man, for instance, has been guilty of murder, adultery, and all the most horrid crimes, during a long life; but he repents on his death-bed; the Priest gives him absolution, and his soul goes to Purgatory. There he might be for millions of years; but if you can procure him a full or plenary indulgence from the Pope, or if he obtained it before death, all the merits which he wanted are given him, and he flies direct to heaven.

R. Sir, are you really in earnest.

A. You have only to look into the *London Roman Catholic Directory*, and will find the appointed days, when every individual of that persuasion is empowered by the Pope to liberate one sóul out of Purgatory, by means of a plenary indulgence. These indulgences are sold in Spain by the King, who buys them from the Pope, and retails them with great profit. I have told you, my friend, and will continue to prove it, that there is not a doctrine for which the Church of Rome contends against the protestants, but is a source of profit or power (which comes to the same) in the hands of the clergy. Indeed, I could fill volumes upon this subject; but time presses, and I must not omit saying a few words about confession. Do you not perceive, in an instant, that whoever has a man's conscience in his keeping, must have the whole man in his power?

R. It appears to me impossible to doubt it; and, in fact, the better the man, the more he must be in the power of his priest, for the Priest is his conscience, and the good man is most anxious to follow that which conscience suggests.

A. Never, my good friend, was a plan of usurpation and tyranny set up that can equal that of the Church of Rome in boldness. Her object is to deprive men both of their understanding and their will, and make them blind tools of her own. She proclaims that the perfection of faith consists in reducing one's mind to an implicit belief in whatever doctrines she holds, without any examination, or with a previous resolution to abide by her decision whether, after examination, they appear to you true or false. She then declares a renunciation of one's conscience into the hands of her Priests, the very height of human perfection. Let those who in England are trying every method of disguising the Roman Catholic doctrine, shew a single pious book of common reputation in the Roman Catholic Church, which does not make unlimited obedience to a confessor the safest and most perfect way to salvation. No, I should not hesitate to assert it in the hearing of all the world: in the same proportion as a Roman Catholic has an understanding and a will of his own upon religious matters, or matters connected in any way with religion, in that same degree he acts against the duties to which he is bound by his religious profession.

R. I do not well understand the Romanist belief on the necessity of confession.

A. The Romanist Church makes the confession of every sin by *thought*, *word*, and *deed*, necessary to receive absolution from a Priest, and teaches that, without absolution, when there is a possibility of obtaining it, God will not grant remission of sins. The most sincere repentance, according to the Catholics, is not sufficient to save a sinner, without confession and absolution, where there is a possibility of applying to a Priest. On the other hand, they assert that even imperfect repentance, a sorrow arising from the fear of hell, which they call *attrition*, will save a sinner who confesses and receives absolution. The evident object of doctrines so inconsistent with the letter and spirit of the Scriptures, is no doubt, that of making the priesthood absolute masters of the people's consciences. They must some time or other (every Roman Catholic is, indeed, bound to confess at least once a year, under pain of excommunication) entrust a Priest with the inmost secrets of their hearts; and this, under the impression that if any one sin is suppressed from a sense of shame, absolution makes them guilty of sacrilege. The effects of this bondage, the reluctance which young people, especially, have to overcome, and the frequency of their making up their minds to garble confession, in spite of their belief that they increase the number and guilt of their sins by silence, are evils which none but a Roman Catholic Priest can be perfectly acquainted with.

R. I thought, Sir, that confession acted as a check upon men's consciences, and that it often caused restitution of ill gotten money.

A. I never hear that paltry plea, so frequently used by Roman Catholic writers in this country, without indignation. It seems as if they wished to bribe men's love of money to the support of their doctrines. In a case where the main interests of religion and morality are so deeply concerned, it is a sort of insult to hold up the chance of recovering money through the hands of a Priest, as if to draw the attention from the monstrous evils which are inseparable from the Romanist confession. The truth is, that restitution is not a whit more probable among Roman Catholics, than among any other denomination of Christians. There is not a Protestant who does not firmly believe the necessity of restitution in order to obtain pardon from God. Though I have lived only fifteen years in a Protestant country, the voluntary restitution of a sum of money by a poor person, whom the grace of God had called to a truly christian course of life, has happened within my notice. I acted as a Confessor in Spain for many years, and from my own experience can assure you, that confession does not add one single chance of restitution. I believe on the contrary, that the generality of Roman Catholics depend so much on the mysterious power which they attribute to the absolution of the Priest, that they greatly neglect the conditions on which that absolution is often given. The Protestant who earnestly and sincerely wishes for pardon from God, knows that he cannot obtain it unless he is equally earnest in his endeavors to make restitution ; but when the Romanist has assured to the Confessor, that he will try his best to indemnify those he has injured, the words of absolution are to him a sort of charm, that removes the guilt at once, and consequently relieves his uneasiness about restitution.   One of the greatest evils of confession is, that it has changed the genuine repentance preached in the Gospel—that conversion and change of life, which is the only true external sign of the remission of sins through Christ —into a ceremony which silences remorse at the slight expense of a doubtful, temporary sorrow for past offences.   As the day of confession approaches (which, for the greatest part, is hardly once a year) the Romanist grows restless and gloomy.   He mistakes the shame of a disgusting disclosure for sincere repentance of his sinful actions.   He, at length, goes through the disagreeable task, and feels relieved.   The old score is now cancelled, and he may run into spiritual debt with a lighter heart.   This I know from my own experience, both as Confessor and as Penitent.   In the same characters, and from the same experience, I can assure you that the practice of confession is exceedingly injurious to the purity of mind enjoined in the Scriptures.   "Filthy communication" is inseparable from the confessional : the Priest, in discharge of the duty imposed on him by his Church, is bound to listen to the most abominable description of all manner of sins.   He must inquire into every circumstance of the most profligate course of life.   Men and women, the young and the old, the married and the single, are bound to describe to the Confessor the most secret actions and thoughts, which are either sinful in themselves, or may be so from accidental circumstances.   Consider the danger to which the Priests themselves are exposed—a danger so imminent, that the Popes have, on two occasions, been obliged to issue the most severe laws against Confessors who openly attempt the seduction of their female penitents.   1 will not, however, press this subject, because it cannot be done with sufficient delicacy.   Let me conclude by observing, that no invention of the Roman Church equals this, as regards the power it gives to the Priesthood.   One of the greatest difficulties to establish a free and rational government in Popish countries, arises from the opposition which free and equal laws meet with from the Priests in the confessional.   A Confessor can promote even treason with safety in the secrecy which protects his office.   But without alluding to political reforms, the influence of the King's Confessors, when the

2F

monarch is a pious man, is known to be so great in Catholic
countries, that when there was a kind of Parliament in Arragon, a law was made to prevent the King from choosing his
own Priest, and the election was reserved to the Parliament
called *Cortes.*

R. I cannot help wondering how the Church of Rome
could persuade men to submit to such a revolting and dangerous
practice as that of confession.

A. This enormous abuse grew up gradually and impercep-
tibly, together with the whole of the Romanist system. It
was the practice, in the beginning of the Christian Church, to
exclude the scandalous sinners from public worship, till they
had shown their repentance by confessing their misconduct
before the congregation. This discipline was found, in the
course of some time, to be impracticable; and the act of humil-
iation, which at first was required to be public, was changed
into a private acknowledgment to the Bishop, of such sins only
as had occasioned the exclusion of the sinner from Church at
the time of worship. The Bishops, a little after, began to refer
such acts of public reconciliation with the Church to some of
their Priests. The growing ignorance of after times made
people believe that this act of external reconciliation was a real
absolution of the moral guilt of sin; and the Church of Rome,
with that perpetual watchfulness by which she has never omitted an opportunity of increasing her power, foisted upon the
Christian world what she calls the Sacrament of Penance,
obliging her members, as they wish for pardon of their sins, to
reveal them to a Priest.

R. Is there nothing in Scripture to support that practice?

A. Nothing but the word *confessing*, which, as you will
observe, means only, whenever it occurs, the acknowledgment
of our sins before God; or that of our mutual faults to our fellow Christians. "*Confess your faults to one another*," says
St. James.* The Romanist will make us believe, that by *one
to another* the holy Apostle means confessing to the Priest.—
By thus distorting the sense of the Scripture, and calling in
the convenient help of their own invented tradition, they have
set no limits to their encroachments upon the spiritual liberty
of the Christian world. Their love of power had, indeed, carried them so far, that in enlarging the foundations of their influence, they established some of their doctrines without even
a word in the Scriptures on which to build their fanciful sys-

* Chap. iii. ver. 16

tems. Did you ever find any mention of relics in the Bible : or do you recollect that it ever mentions images, but to forbid the worshipping of them ?

R Certainly not. But do you believe, Sir, that relics and images are also instruments of power to the Church of Rome ?

A. The city of Rome has carried on, for ages, a trade in bones, which, besides the donations in money, made by those who, from all parts of the world, came or sent thither to procure them, has been the cause of building churches, with large endowments for the clergy, in almost every province in Christendom.

R. But were those bones really from the bodies of the Saints, whose names they gave to them ?

A. Nothing can equal the impudence with which the bones really taken out of the public burial grounds, where the ancient Romans buried their slaves, have been sent about under the names of all the Martyrs, Confessors, and Virgins, mentioned in the Roman Catholic legends. The Pope claims the power of what is called *christening* relics, and the devout Romanists believe, that when their Holy Father has thus given a name to a skull or a thigh-bone, it is equally valuable, as if it had been taken from the body of their favorite Saint. They are not generally aware that what is thus *christened* is probably part of the skeleton of some ancient heathen. But to give you an idea of the credulity which the Popes have encouraged on this point, I have seen the treasury of relics which belongs to the kings of Spain ; where the Monk who keeps it, shows to all who visit the Church of the *Escurial*, near Madrid, the whole body, as it is pretended, of one of the children who were put to death by Herod. But there is still a more monstrous piece of impudence in the same exhibition. A glass vial, set in gold, is shown, with some milk of the Virgin Mary. These and a hundred other such relics are presented to be worshipped by the people ; all duly certified by the Pope or his ministers. At the Cathedral at Seville, the town where I was born, there is, among other relics, one of the teeth of Christopher, a Saint who is said to have been a giant. The tooth was procured from Rome, and is to be seen in a silver and glass casket, through which the holy relic may be admired by the worshippers. It is clear, however, that the tooth before which the Pope allows his spiritual children to kneel, belonged to a huge animal of the elephant kind. These impositions have been at all times carried on so carelessly by the Romish Priesthood.

that it was necessary, in some cases, to declare that the bodies of some Saints had been miraculously multiplied ; else peo ple would have discovered the fraud by finding the same Saint at different places. The Priests themselves are often aware of these absurdities; but they must bow their heads in silence. I will, however, tell you a good joke of a French Priest of high rank, who, having no religion himself, as it often happens to those of his profession in Roman Catholic countries, submitted quietly to the established superstition, though he would now and then give vent to a humorous sneer. He had been travelling in Italy, and in the Catholic parts of Germany, where the collection of relics, kept in every great Church, had been boastingly displayed to him. The Priests of a famous abbey in France were doing the same, when, among other wonders, " here," they said to the traveller, " is the head of John the Baptist."—" Praised be Heaven !" an- swered the waggish Priest, " this is the third head of the holy Baptist which I have been happy enough to hold in my hands."

R. I hope the jolly Priest did not pay dear for his wit.

A. It would have been a serious matter in Spain ; but there has always existed a very strong party of distinguished infidels in France, where the Pope never succeeded in his attempts to establish the Inquisition. The consequence was, that the Priests were greatly checked by the general laugh which was often raised against them. He that would know genu- ine Popery must go to Spain—the country where it has been allowed to grow and unfold itself into full size. There you would see all the engines of Rome at work, and perfectly un- derstand the true and original object of her inventions. To show you at one glance the benefit derived by the Priests from image worship, I will tell you what happened at Madrid, dur- ing a residence of three years, which I made in that most Catholic capital. In one of the meanest parts of the town the ragged children, who are always running about the streets, found an old picture, which had been thrown, with other rubbish, upon a dunghill. Not knowing what the picture was, they tied it to a piece of rope, and were dragging it about, when an old woman in the neighborhood, looked at the canvass, and found upon it the head of a Virgin Mary. Her screams of horror at the profanation which she beheld scared away the children, and the old woman was left in pos- session of the treasure. The gossips of the neighborhood were anxious to make some amends to the picture for the past neglect and ill-treatment, and they all contributed towards the expense of burning a lamp, day and night, before it, in the old woman's house. A priest, getting scent of what was going on, took the scratched Virgin under his patronage, framed the canvass, and added another light. All the rich folks who heard of this new-found image, came to pray before it, and gave something to the Priest and the old woman, who were now in close partnership. In a very short time the amount of the daily donations enabled the joint proprietors of the picture to build a fire chapel, with a comfortable house adjoining it for themselves. The chapel was crowded from morning till night; not a female, high or low, but firmly believed that her life and safety depended upon the favor of that particular picture : the rich endeavored to obtain it by large sums of money for masses to be performed, and candles to be burnt before it, and the poor stinted their necessary food to throw a mite into the box which hung at the door of the chapel. I do not relate to you old stories ; I state what I myself have seen. Yet, what happened at Madrid, under my own eyes, had constantly taken place in the Popish kingdoms of Europe, till the Reformation gave a check to the Romanist Priesthood. There is scarcely a town or a village of some note in Europe but had a rich sanctuary, where Monks lived, mostly in vice and idleness, at the expense of the neighborhood. The origin of these places was perfectly similar everywhere ; a shepherd found an image of the Virgin in the hollow of a tree, (most assuredly placed there on purpose to be thus found;) an old woman drew another from the bottom of a well ; a stranger had asked for lodgings for a night at a cottage—he was not to be found in the morning ; but, on searching the room where he slept, a small Virgin Mary was discovered. The nearest Bishop was sure to come with his Priests, holding lighted tapers, and carry such images in procession to his church ; and declare that they had been miraculously sent to the faithful! Those found in the tree and well had fallen from heaven : the vanished stranger was an angel, who had carved the image during the night.

R. Such images put me in mind of what is said, in the *Acts of the Apostles*, about the great Diana of the Ephesians, which had fallen from heaven, and for the sake of which the people made a riot, in which they would have murdered Saint Paul.*

A. The Church of Rome has so closely copied the idolatrous superstitions of the Pagans, that all persons not blinded

* Acts xix. 37
2 f 2

by the fanatic zeal of that Church, are struck with the great similarity. Their lighted candles, their frankincense, images from heaven, many ceremonies of their mass, many forms of their private worship, are just the same as formed a part of the service done formerly to the idols of the heathens. Even the manner of acknowledging the pretended miracles by hanging up in the temples little figures of wax, or pictures representing the part of the body which is supposed to have been supernat urally healed, or the accident from which the person escaped, is constantly practised, wherever the Pope alone directs his flock, without fearing a laugh from Protestant neighbors. If the figures acknowledging miracles performed by images throughout the realms of Popery, were to be reckoned, the miracles would amount to some hundreds a day.   •

R. But how can people believe in such a number of mir acles ?

A. The Church of Rome, my friend, is like a large and showy quack-medicine shop. There is not a disease, not an evil, for which the Pope has not a *labelled* Saint. People, when in fear or actual suffering, are apt to receive a certain relief from hope. You have only to say, try this or that med- icine, and you will see the patient's eyes lighted up, like the poor man who has a kind of foretaste of riches from the mo- ment he purchases a lottery ticket. The Pope's spiritual quack-medicines are to be applied without doubt or hesita- tion, and not to be given up in despair; all you are allowed is to add some new Saint to your former patron. Well, a poor creature is writhing with the tooth-ache ; he goes to the Pope's shop, and finds that Saint Apollonia had all her teeth pulled out, and therefore takes pity on those who suffer in a similar way. He prays, buys a print of the Saint, and lights up a candle before it. If the pain goes off, Saint Apollonia cured him ; if at last the tooth is drawn, Saint Apollonia blunted the pain of the operation. So it is with every disease, with every undertaking,—a journey, a speculation ; even the most sinful and wicked actions are often commended by the lower classes of Roman Catholics to the care of their patron Saint. Of this I have the most positive certainty. Miracles being thus expected at all times, and means supposed to possess a super- natural virtue, being constantly used, under the idea that the most effectual way of receiving the looked-for benefit is a strong persuasion of their efficacy, and a rejection of all doubt, which, they believe, offends the implored Saint ; every acci- dent is construed into a wonder ; the failures are attributed to ı want of faith, and the success, either complete or partial, which would have infallibly taken place in the natural course of things, is confidently proclaimed as a display of supernatural power. Add to this, that there is a very common feeling among the Roman Catholics, of the same kind as that which anticipates thanks for the sake of securing favor.— They, in fact, give credit to their Saints beyond what they really believe, and flatter them by public acknowledgments, which they mean as a beforehand payment, which, in common honesty, must bind the receiver to complete the work. All this is done, not with an intent to deceive, but from that utter weakness of mind which a man cannot fail to contract, when brought up under a complete system of quackery, either spiritual or temporal ; a system which encourages all sorts of fears, to ensure the sale of imaginary remedies against them.

R. Do you think, Sir, that all Roman Catholics are in such a state of mind ?

A. By no means. There are various circumstances which make individual minds resist, more or less, the influence of their Church. But this I can assure you before the whole world, that whoever submits entirely to the guidance of Rome, must become a weak, superstitious being, unless his natural temper should dispose him to join with superstition the violence and persecuting spirit of the bitterest bigotry.

R. If you can prove what you so broadly assert, I shall infer, that while the Roman Catholics uphold their Church for the sake of possessing an unerring guide, and thus having a decided advantage over the Protestant Churches, who allow their members to exercise their judgment upon religious matters ; it is only individual judgment and natural good sense that make Romanism assume a decent appearance among us.

A. Keep to your inference till we can renew this conversation, when I trust I shall satisfy you that it is supported by the most undeniable facts. Remember that I undertake to prove, that the Church of Rome leads her members into the most abject and lamentable superstition, cruelty, and bigotry ; that she keeps her subjects in bondage by the most tyrannical means ; and that she is always ready to force men into subjection to her authority, in the same measure as they are off their guard to resist her encroachments.

DIALOGUE IV.

Author. I COME prepared to describe to you the character of the Church of Rome: and in the first place I am to prove that she exerts her whole power in making her members superstitious. I must, however, ask you, before I proceed, whether you have a clear idea of what is meant by the word *superstitious.*

Reader. I believe I have a tolerably good notion of it; but to say the truth, I should be at a loss to state clearly what I understand by that word.

A. My notion of it may be expressed thus: superstition consists in credulity, hopes, and fears, about invisible and supernatural things, upon fanciful and slight grounds. We call that man superstitious who is ready to believe any idle story of ghosts and witches; who nails a horse-shoe upon the ship or barn, which he hopes, by that means, to preserve in safety; and dreads evil consequences from going out of doors the first time in the morning, with his left foot foremost.

R. Does the Church of Rome encourage superstitions of this kind?

A. She certainly encourages the same state of mind, though not exactly upon the same things. Every church may be compared to a great school or establishment for religious education. I will represent to you a pupil of that school, that you may infer what is taught in it, and I will draw the picture from various Roman Catholics whom I have intimately known. Imagine my Romanist friend retiring to his bed in the night.— The walls of the room are covered with pictures of all sizes. Upon a table there is a wooden or brass figure of our Saviour nailed to the cross, with two wax candles, ready to be lighted at each side. Our Romanist carefully locks the door; lights up the candles, kneels before the cross, and beats his breast with his clenched right hand, till it rings again in a hollow sound. It is probably a Friday, a day of penance; the good

344

man looks pale and weak. I know the reason — he has made but one meal on that day, and that on fish ; had he tasted meat, he feels assured he should have subjected his soul to the pains of hell. But the mortifications of the day are not over. He unlocks a small cupboard, and takes out a skull, which he kisses and places upon the table at the foot of the crucifix. He then strips off part of his clothes, and with a scourge, composed of small twisted ropes hardened with wax, lays stoutly to the right and left, till his bare skin is ready to burst with accumulated blood. The discipline, as it is called, being over, he mutters several prayers, turning to every picture in the room. He then rises to go to bed ; but before he ventures into it, he puts his finger into a little cup which hangs at a short distance over his pillow, and sprinkles, with the fluid it contains, the bed and the room in various directions, and finally moistens his forehead in the form of a cross. The cup, you must know, contains holy water—water in which a priest has put some salt, making over it the sign of the cross several times, and saying some prayers, which the Church of Rome has inserted for this purpose in the mass-book. The use of that water, as our Roman Catholic has been taught to believe, is to prevent the devil from approaching the places and things which have been recently sprinkled with it ; and he does not feel himself safe in his bed without the precaution which I have described. The holy water has, besides, an internal and spiritual power of washing away venial sins—those slight sins, I mean, which, according to the Romanist, if unrepented, or unwashed away by holy water, or the sign of the cross made by the hand of a bishop, or some other five or six methods, which I will not trouble you with, will keep the venial sinner in Purgatory for a certain time. The operations of the devout Roman Catholic are probably not yet done. On the other side of the holy-water cup, there hangs a frame holding a large cake of wax, with figures raised by a mould, not unlike a large butter-pat. It is an *Agnus Dei*, blest by the Pope, which is not to be had except it can be imported from Rome. I believe the wax is kneaded with some earth from the place where the bones of the supposed Martyrs are dug up. Whoever possesses one of these spiritual treasures, enjoys the benefit of a great number of indulgences ; for each kiss impressed on the wax gives him the whole value of fifty or one hundred days employed in doing penance and good works ; the amount of which is to be struck off the debt which he has to pay in Purgatory. I should not wonder if our good man, before laying himself to

sleep, were to feel about his neck for his rosary of beads.
Perhaps he has one of a particular value, and like that which
I was made to wear next my skin, when a boy. A priest had
brought it from Rome, where it had been made, if we believe
the certificates, of bits of the very stones with which the first
martyr, Stephen, was put to death. Being satisfied that the
rosary hangs still on his neck, he arranges its companion, the
scapulary, formed of two square pieces of the staff which is
exclusively worn by some religious order. By means of the
scapulary, he is assured either that the Virgin Mary will not
allow him to remain in Purgatory beyond the Saturday next
to the day of his death; or he is made partaker of all the penances and good works performed by the religious of the order
to which the scapulary belongs. At last, having said a prayer
to the angel who, he believes, keeps a constant guard over
him, the devout Romanist composes himself to sleep, touching
his forehead, his breast, and the two shoulders, to form the
figure of a cross. The prayer and ceremonies of the morning
are not unlike those of the night. Armed with the sprinkling
of holy water, he proceeds to mass : if it happens to be one of
the privileged days in which souls may be delivered out of Purgatory, you will see him saying a certain number of prayers
at different altars. He will repeat his rosary in honor of the
Virgin Mary, dropping through his fingers either fifty-five or
seventy-seven beads, which are strung in the form of a neck-
lace. There may be a blessing with the *Sacrament*, which the
good Catholic will not lose, for the sake of the plenary indulgence which the Pope grants to such as are present. On that
occasion you would see him kneeling and beating his breast,
while the priest, in a splendid cloak of silk and gold, in the
midst of lighted candles and the smoke of frankincense, makes
the sign of the cross with a consecrated wafer, inclosed between two pieces of glass set in gold. It would, indeed, be an
endless task were I to enumerate all the methods and contrivances of this kind recommended by the Church of Rome to
all her members, and practised by all who are not careless of
their spiritual concerns.—These are facts which no honest
Roman Catholic will venture to deny. I therefore ask whether, since revelation is the only means we have of distinguishing between religion and superstition,— between things and
acts which really can influence our manner of being when we
shall be removed to the invisible world, and fanciful contriv
ances which there is no reason to suppose connected with
our spiritual welfare,— ask whether the whole system of the

Church of Rome, for the attainment of Christian virtue, is not a chain of superstitious practices, calculated to accustom the mind to imaginary fear, and fly to the Church for fanciful remedies? Saint Paul had a prophetic eye on this adulterated Christianity when he cautioned the Colossians,* saying : *Let no man therefore judge you in meat or in drink, or in respect of a holyday : Let no man beguile you of your reward in a voluntary humility and worshipping of angels, intruding into those things which he hath not seen, vainly puffed up by his fleshly mind, and not holding the head, from which all the body, by joints and bands, having nourishment, ministered and knit together, increaseth with the increase of God. Wherefore, if ye be dead with Christ from the rudiments of the world, why, as though living in the world, are ye subject to ordinances (touch not, taste not, handle not, which all are to perish with the using) after the commandments and doctrines of men? Which things have, indeed, a shew of wisdom in will-worship, and humility, and neglecting of the body.* I cannot conceive a more perfect resemblance than that which exists between the picture of a devout Romanist, and the *will-worship* described in this passage. Observe the distinction of days, the prohibition of certain meats, the worshipping of angels, the numerous ordinances, the mortification and neglect of the body ; and, most of all, the losing hold of the head, Christ, and substituting a constant endeavor to *increase* spiritually by *fleshly,* that is, external means, instead of fortifying, by a simple and spiritual worship, the *bands and joints,* through which alone the Christian can have nourishment, and *increase with the increase of God.*

R. I confess that the likeness is very striking. But I wish to know if all the *will-worship* of the Romanists is fully recommended by their Church.

A. It is in the most solemn and powerful manner. You have only to look into the devotional books which are used among the Romanists, and you will find their bishops encouraging this kind of religious discipline in the most unqualified terms. I could read to you innumerable passages confirming and recommending more *fleshly ordinances* than ever the Jews observed ; and this, too, in English Roman Catholic books, which, for fear of censure on the part of the Protestants, are generally more shy of disclosing the whole system of their Church, than those published abroad. But what settles the point at once, and shows that it is the Church of Rome,

* Chap ii

and not any private individual, that adulterates 'ne character
and temper of Christian virtue, I have only to refer you to
their Common Prayer-book, which they call the *Breviary.*—
Now, that is a book not only published and confirmed by three
Popes, but which they oblige their whole clergy to read daily,
for at least an hour and a half.   Such, indeed, is the importance which the Church of Rome attaches to that book, that
she declares any Clergyman or Monk who omits, even less
than an eighth part of the appointed daily reading, guilty of
sin, worthy of hell,— a mortal sin, which deprives man of the
grace of God.   The *Breviary* contains Psalms and Collects,
and lives of Saints, for every day of the year.   These lives
are given as examples of what the Church of Rome declares
to be Christian perfection, and her members are, of course,
urged to imitate them as far as it may possibly be in every
one's power.   Now, I can assure you, having been for many
years forced to read the Breviary daily, that there is not one
instance of a Saint, whose worship is not grounded, by the
Church of Rome, mainly upon the most extravagant practice
of external ceremonies, and the most shocking use of their
imaginary virtue of penance.

R. What do they mean by penance ?

A. The voluntary infliction of pain on themselves to expiate
their sins.

R. Do they not believe in the atonement of Christ ?

A. They believe that the atonement is enough to save
them from hell, but not from a temporal punishment of sin.

R. But have they not *plenary indulgences* to satisfy for that
temporal punishment ?

A. So they believe ; but the truth is, that they cannot understand themselves upon the subject of penance and indulgences.   Penance, however, the Romanist Church recommends, even at the expense of depraving the sense of the Gospel in their translations.   As there is nothing in the New Testament which can make self-inflicted pain a Christian virtue,
the Romanists, wanting a text to support their practices, have
rendered the third verse of the 13th chapter of Luke, " Unless
ye be *penitent,* ye shall all alike perish."   Yet, this was not
enough for their purpose, and as the same sentence is repeated in the fifth verse, there they slipt in the word *penance.*—
Their translation of that verse is, " Unless ye shall do *penance,*
you shall all alike perish."   By the use of this word they
make their laity believe, that both confession, which) ey call

penance, and all the bodily mortifications which go among them by the same name, are commanded by Christ.

R. That, Sir, I look upon as very unfair.

A. And the more so, my friend, as, in the original Gospel, the word used by the inspired writer is the same in both verses, and cannot by any possib.lity mean any thing but a *change of the mind*, which we properly express by the word *repent*.

R. What, Sir, is the origin of their attachment to bodily mortification ?

A. A mean estimate of the atonement of Christ ; and the example of some fanatics, whom, at an early period of the corruptions of Christianity, Rome declared to be saints and patterns of Evangelical virtue. The Monks, who took them for their models, gained an unbounded influence in the Church ; and both by the practice of some enthusiasts among them, and by the stories of mirac.es, which they reported as being the reward of their bodily mortification, confirmed the opinion of the great merit of penance among the laity. Here, also, the mutual aid of the doctrines invented by Rome contributed to increase the error ; for, as the Popes teach that the *indulgences* which they grant are taken from the treasure of merits collected by the Saints, it is the interest of those who expect to escape from Purgatory by the aid of indulgences, that the treasure of penances be well-stocked ; and they greatly enjoy the accounts of wonderful mortifications which their Church gives them in her Prayer-book.

R. Do you think those accounts extravagant ?

A. I will give two or three, and you shall judge. You know that Saint Patrick is one of the most favorite Saints among the Irish Roman Catholics, as having been the first who introduced Christianity into their island. The Church of Rome gives the following account of his daily religious practices, holding him up, of course, as a pattern, which, if few can fully copy, every one will be the more perfect as he endeavors to imitate. The *Breviary* tells the Roman Catholics, that when their patron Saint was a slave, having his master's cattle under his care, he used to rise before daylight, under the snows and rains of winter, to begin his usual task of praying *one hundred times* in the day, and again *one hundred times* in the night. When he was made a Bishop, we are told that he repeated every day the one hundred and fifty Psalms of the Psaltery, with a collection of canticles and hymns, and two hundred collects besides. He made it also a

2 G

daily duty to kneel three hundred times, and to make the sign, of the cross with his hand eight hundred times a day. In the night he recited one hundred Psalms, and knelt two hundred times—passed one third of it up to the chin in cold water, repeating fifty Psalms more, and then rested for two or three hours on a stone pavement.

R. I cannot believe it possible for a man to perform what you have said, unless he had the strength and velocity of a steam engine.

A. I will not enter into the question of its probability. External ceremonies, and a course of self-murdering practices, are proposed by the Church of Rome, in nine out of ten lives of their Saints, as objects of imitation. In the same spirit, St. Catherine of Siena is represented as so addicted to the practice of fasting, that Heaven, to indulge her in the performance of that pretended virtue, kept her, by miracle, without food from Ash-Wednesday till Whit-Sunday. So the *Breviary* proclaims before the face of the world.

R. But does not our Church recommend fasting as a religious practice ?

A. The practice of checking our appetites, even those which we may indulge without sin, is a most useful exercise of the powers of the will over the inclinations of our passions. The man who cannot abstain from some savory food, and is a slave to the cravings of his stomach, is little apt to control his inclinations when tempted to open sin. Upon this principle, and justly fearing that if the memory of fast was abolished, men might be inclined to believe that Protestantism encouraged gluttony and excess ; the Church of England recommends a rational abstinence on certain days, which, especially when it is made to produce some savings to bestow upon the poor, must be acceptable in the sight of God. But neither are these fasts enjoined under the threat of damnation, as we find them in the Church of Rome, nor do they consist in a superstitious distinction, or quantity of food. The Roman Catholic fast is intended to produce pain and suffering, which is the object of their penances ; ours is a mere check laid upon indulgence, and even that is left to the discretion and free will of every individual.

R. How far does the Church of Rome recommend the infliction of pain, as penance ?

A. To an excess that destroys every year many well-meaning and ardent persons, especially young women of that communion. These deluded creatures lead the lives of Saints set

forth by their Church, and there they find many females who
are said to have arrived at great perfection by living, like St.
Elizabeth of Portugal, one half of the year on bread and water; besides the constant use of scourging their bodies, sleeping on the naked ground, wearing bandages with points that
run into the flesh, plunging into freezing water, and ten thousand other methods of gradually destroying life.

R. I cannot help thinking, that though the Church of Rome
is not the best school for Christian instruction, it must afford a
kind of spiritual amusement (spiritual, I say, because I cannot
find another word) to her followers. Her ceremonies, her miracles, her relics, must afford an agreeable variety to those who
have never doubted her creed.

A. Ah, my friend, nothing can be more deceitful than the
appearance of that Church. There is more misery produced
by her laws and institutions than I can possibly describe,
though I have drunk her cup of bitterness to the dregs. In the
first place, a sincere mind which is made to depend for the
hope of salvation on any thing but faith and unbounded trust in
the Saviour, can never enjoy that Christian peace " which
passeth all understanding." I have known some of the best
and most conscientious Roman Catholics which that Church
can ever boast of; my own mother and sisters were among
them; I have been Confessor not a few years, and heard the
true state of mind of the most religious nuns, and such as were
looked upon as living saints by all the inhabitants of my town.
From this intimate knowledge of their state, I do assure you,
that they are, for the greatest part, so full of doubts about their
salvation, as not unfrequently to be driven to madness. In their
anxiety to accumulate *merits* (for their Church teaches them
that their penances and religious practices are deserving of
reward in heaven) they involve themselves in a maze of external practices. Then come the fears of sin in the very things
which they undertake under the notion of pleasing God; and
as they believe that their works are to be weighed and valued
in strict justice, the sincerity of their hearts cannot help discovering not only that they are nothing worth, but that sin is
often mixed with their performance. In this state they are
never impressed with the true scriptural doctrine, that the
blood of Christ cleanseth from all sin, whenever the sinner,
with a lively faith, receives him as his only Saviour. They are
not taught that good works are the fruit of true faith; but that
they bear a true share with Christ in the work of our salvation. They re thus forced, by their doctrines, to look to them-

selves for the hope of heaven; and what can be the consequence but the most agonizing fear? With the view of heaven
and hell perpetually before their eyes, and a strong belief that
the 'obtaining the one and avoiding the other depend on the
performance of a multitude of self-imposed duties, as complicated and more difficult than those of the ceremonial law of the
Jews; what can be the result but distracting anxiety? When
a Protestant is conscious that he does not make the doctrine
of salvation by faith in Christ a means to deceive himself and
indulge his passions; his trust in the "full, perfect, and sufficient sacrifice, oblation, and satisfaction for the sins of the
whole world," which was made on the cross, removes all fear
from his soul. In his progress through the stormy sea of life,
he does not, as the Romanist, cling with one hand to Christ,
and depend on the strength of the other to break the waves.—
The poor, deluded pupil of the Popish school, looks (as man always does in cases of great danger) not to the stronger, but
the weaker ground, for his dependence for safety. Fear, consequently, predominates in his heart. "Mind your swimming hand," say his Priests; "ply it stoutly, or Christ will
allow you to sink." "Hold fast on Him who is powerful to
save," says the Protestant Church, in the language of the Bible; "all that you have to do, is to throw the weight of your
sins and infirmities upon Christ." This is the only faith that
can produce the fulness of "joy and hope in believing."

R. But are not good works necessary to salvation?

A. The truly Apostolic doctrine on that point will be best
understood by looking to the direct consequence of sin. Besides that, the whole scripture is full of loud warnings against
wickedness; the Apostle expressly says: *Know ye not that the
unrighteous shall not inherit the kingdom of God? Be not deceived; neither fornicators, nor idolaters, nor adulterers, nor
effeminate, nor abusers of themselves with mankind, nor thieves,
nor covetous, nor drunkards, nor revilers, nor extortioners, shall
inherit the kingdom of God.** So that there can be no doubt,
that if we wish to be saved, we must renounce sin, or, as we
are told by our Saviour, we must repent; that is, as the original word expresses it, we must *change our mind,* from the
pursuit of unrighteousness. By turning away from sin, and
placing our full trust or faith in Christ, we are pardoned and
become justified in the sight of God. We then are made living
branches of the true vine, and the spiritual life, which we re-

* 1 Cor. vi. 9, 10

ceive from the trunk, cannot fail to produce fruit unto life eternal. Here, then, is the essential difference between the Protestant and the Roman Catholic doctrine of justification. The
Roman Catholic believes that his good works are, in part at
least, the means of his justification, and is anxious to secure
and increase it by numerous external practices, especially by
self-inflicted misery; the true Protestant feels assured, on the
strength of revelation, that, as he turns with his whole heart,
and accepts pardon through Christ's blood, his sins are pardoned without reserve. The work of justification, or acquittal,
is thereby perfect; and the spirit of Christ proceeds without
delay subsequent to the work of sanctification. The Protestant has but one ground of salutary fear, lest he should wilfully and deliberately turn again from Christ to sin; but this fear
is allayed by the certainty given him by the same Scripture,
that God is faithful, and that it is God "who worketh in us
both to will and to do, of his good pleasure."*—The system of
Popish justification is, I repeat to you, in the words of that
truly great and calumniated man, Luther, "a plain tyranny, a racking and crucifying of consciences." He knew
this from his own experience, for, like myself, he had in his
youth, tried it in the full sincerity of his heart. In order to secure his salvation, and following the advice of the Church of
Rome, he made himself a Monk, and most conscientiously kept
the rule of his order; but he found, what I have frequently
seen in those who bind themselves with Popish vows, that he
was on the way to distraction and downright madness. "When
I was a Monk," he says, "I endeavored, as much as possible,
to live after the strait rule of my own order; I was wont to
shrive (confess) myself with great devotion, and to reckon up
all my sins, being always very contrite before, and I returned
to confession very often, and thoroughly performed the penance
that was enjoined unto me; yet for all this my conscience
could never be fully certified, but was always in doubt, and
said this or that thou hast not done rightly; thou wast not contrite and sorrowful enough; this sin thou didst omit in thy confession, and so forth. Therefore, the more I went about to
help my weak, wavering and afflicted conscience by men's traditions, the more weak, and doubtful, and the more afflicted, I
was. And thus, the more I observed men's traditions, the
more I transgressed them; and in seeking after righteousness
by mine order, I never could attain unto it."—To the truth of

* Phil. ii. 13

2 G 2

this statement I myself can bear most ample testimony. In fact, with the exception of the persecuting spirit of the Church of Rome, I know nothing more odious and mischievous than her contrivances after the righteousness or sanctity which she recommends ; they are indeed *a plain tyranny, a racking and crucifying of the conscience.*

R. What contrivances do you mean?

A. I mean the Popish laws, by which, in order, as they say, to make their clergy more perfect, men are led into the most fatal snares, even to the loss of their souls, or at least to the ruin of their happiness. It is, indeed, a consequence of the Romanist doctrine of good works, or works through which men acquire a title to salvation, that they should lay intolerable burthens on the necks of well-disposed Christians. Hence the Pope has made it necessary for his Clergy never to marry ; and for both men and women who, striving after the imaginary perfection of works, make themselves Monks, or Friars, or Nuns, to make vows of never marrying, of obeying the superior of their Convents, and possessing no money. They also oblige themselves to keep the rule of their order, which gives forty or fifty commandments, besides those of God ; and which, by their vows, they consider as binding, as if they were all in the Bible. As far as this goes such a system would be a dangerous absurdity ; for what can be more unreasonable than to endanger salvation by self-imposed duties, when we know how difficult it is for man to keep the plain laws of God ? But, as the object of all these human ordinances is, that the Church of Rome may be able to make an external show of the sanctity of her unmarried Priests, and the self-denial of her professed Monks and Nuns ; the Popes, fearing lest those who undertake these duties, should soon find them impracticable, and shame the Church by resuming their Christian liberty—the Popes, I say, most unfeelingly, and with the greatest disregard of men's salvation, have induced all Roman Catholic governments to force Clergymen, Friars and Nuns, to abide by their profession ; so that whoever finds himself unable to live in celibacy, or within the walls of a convent, must fly his country, under the dreadful certainty, that, if taken in the attempt, he shall be punished with a cruel imprisonment during the rest of his life.

R. That is certainly a piece of tyranny which I have not sufficient words to describe.

A. You would, indeed, want words to express your feelings, if you had seen the effects of that proud and insolent despot-

rsni of the Romish Church, as I have. Indeed, I am touching
upon a subject of which I cannot speak without the most lively pain and indignation. When Saint Paul enumerates the
advantages which the unmarried Christians had in the early
days of the Gospel, he uses the greatest caution. "This (says
the Apostle) I speak for your own profit, not that I may cast a
snare upon you." The Church of Rome, on the contrary, carried away by her pride, uses every art to induce young persons of either sex to bind themselves with religious vows of
chastity for life. All her books of devotion, and especially her
established Prayer-book, are full of the praises of virginity.
She carries her absurd, not to say wicked, extravagance to
the point of asserting of one of her female Saints, (Saint Rose
of Lima, whom I have already mentioned,) that she made a
vow of perpetual chastity at the age of five years. There was
indeed a time when children were bound by their parents to
become Monks and Nuns for life; an engagement which they
were forced to keep when they grew up. But now the Church
of Rome allows boys and girls of sixteen to take the religious
vows, and, having done so, she puts them under the guard of
the Roman Catholic Governments, who, frightened with the
spiritual threats of the Popes, employ their force to make them
prisoners of the Church for life. It would make your very
heart sick to see the nunneries abroad. They are large
houses, with high walls like prisons; having small windows at
a great distance from the ground, and guarded by strong and
close iron bars, bristled over with long spikes. As it is the custom among Roman Catholics to send most of their little girls to
be educated by the Nuns, the poor innocents become attached
to their teachers, who are besides exceedingly anxious to gain
recruits to their order. The girls are petted till they come of
age to take the vows. The priests, who, being not allowed to
marry, feel a strong jealousy of those who take a young and
amiable wife, are always ready to advise their young penitents
to take the veil. In this manner a great number of unsuspecting girls are yearly entrapped in the Roman Catholic Church.
Even in England, nunneries have been on the increase of late
years. Some of these poor prisoners continue in their slavery
without reluctance; many feel unhappy, but submit from the
shame of changing their minds, and because, even in this country, where the Protestant law would protect their leaving the
convent, their relations would look upon them as reprobates,
and their Priests would harass them to death. In Roman
Catholic countries, the hopelessness of their case obliges many

to bear their unhappy lot patiently. But some are driven to desperation, and I have known instances which prove that the Pope is a more unfeeling tyrant than any slave-master in Algiers.

● *R.* Have you really seen a poor female dying for liberty, and yet kept like a criminal in bondage ?

A. I have known many; but there was one among those unhappy victims whose sufferings harrow my mind and hear' whenever they come to my recollection. You must, however, be made acquainted with her melancholy story; but, to save myself the pain of telling it anew, let me read it out of my *Evidence against Catholicism :*

"The eldest daughter of a family intimately acquainted with mine, was brought up in the convent of Saint Agnes at Seville, under the care of her mother's sister, the abbess of that female community. The circumstances of the whole transaction were so public at Seville, and the subsequent judicial proceedings have given them such notoriety, that I do not feel bound to conceal names. *Maria Francisca Barreiro*, the unfortunate subject of this account, grew up, a lively and interesting girl, in the convent, while a younger sister enjoyed the advantages of an education at home. The mother formed an early design of devoting her eldest daughter to religion, in order to give her less attractive favorite a better chance of getting a husband. The distant and harsh manner with which she constantly treated Maria Francisca, attached the unhappy girl to her aunt by the ties of the most ardent affection. The time, however, arrived when it was necessary that she should either leave her, and endure the consequences of her mother's aversion at home, or take the vows, and thus close the gates of the convent upon herself forever. She preferred the latter course; and came out to pay the last visit to her friends. I met her, almost daily, at the house of one of her relations; where her words and manner soon convinced me that she was a victim of her mother's designing and unfeeling disposition. The father was an excellent man, though timid and undecided. He feared his wife, and was in awe of the Monks, who, as usual, were extremely anxious to increase the number of their female prisoners.— Though I was aware of the danger which a man incurs in Spain, who tries to dissuade a young woman from being a Nun, humanity impelled me to speak seriously to the father, entreating him not to expose a beloved child to spend her life 'n hopeless regret for lost liberty. He was greatly moved by my reasons; but the impression I made was soon obliterated. The day for Maria Francisca's taking the veil was at length fixed, and, though I had a most pressing invitation to be present at the ceremony, I determined not to see the wretched victim at the altar. On the preceding day, I was called from my stall at the Royal Chapel to the confessional. A lady quite covered by her black veil, was kneeling at the grate through which females speak to the confessor. As soon as I took my seat, the well-known voice of Maria Francisca made me start with surprise. Bathed in tears, and scarcely able to speak without betraying her state to the people who knelt near the confessional box, by the sobs which interrupted her words, she told me she wished only to unburden her heart to me, before she shut herself up for life. Assistance, she assured me, she would not receive; for, rather than live with her mother, and endure the obloquy to which her swerving from her announced determination would expose her, 'she would risk the salvation of her soul.' All my remonstrances were in vain. I offered to obtain the protection of the Archbishop, and thereby to extricate her from the difficulties in which she was involved. She declined my offer, and appeared as resolute as she was wretched. The next morning she took the veil; and professed at the end of the following year. Her good aunt died soon after; and the Nuns, who had allured her into the convent by their caresses, when they perceived that she was not able to disguise her misery, and feared that the existence of a reluctant Nun might by her means transpire, became her daily tormentors.

"After an absence of three years from Seville, I found that Maria Francisca had openly declared her aversion to a state from which nothing but death could save her. She often changed her confessors, expecting comfort from their advice. At last she found a friend in one of the companions of my youth; a man whose benevolence surpasses even the bright genius with which nature has gifted him; though neither has been able to exempt him from the evils to which Spaniards seem to be fated in proportion to their worth. He became her confessor, and in that capacity spoke to her daily. But what could he do against the inflexible tyranny in whose grasp she languished!

"About this time the approach of Napoleon's army threw the town into a general consternation, and the convents were opened to such of the Nuns as wished to fly. Maria Francisca whose parents were absent, put herself under the protec-

tion of a young prebendary of the Cathedral, and by his
means reached Cadiz, where I saw her on my way to England.
I shall never forget the anguish with which, after a long conversation, wherein she disclosed to me the whole extent of her
wretchedness, she exclaimed, *There is no hope for me!* and
fell into convulsions.

"The liberty of Spain from the French invaders was the
signal for the fresh confinement of this helpless young woman
to her former prison. Here she attempted to put an end to her
sufferings by throwing herself into a deep well; but was taken
out alive. Her mother was now dead, and her friends instituted a suit of *nullity of profession,* before the ecclesiastical
court. But the laws of the Council of Trent were positive;
and she was cast in the trial. Her despair, however, exhausted the little strength which her protracted sufferings had left
her, and the unhappy Maria Francisca died soon after, having
scarcely reached her twenty-fifth year."

R. Sir, the history of your unfortunate friend is so horrible,
that I wonder how whole nations can conspire to support a
tyranny wicked enough to sacrifice not only the body but the
soul of the helpless creatures who fall into its snares. I know
that God is infinitely merciful; but does it not strike you that
the Pope and his Church, provided they keep their slaves, do
not care if they are driven to suicide, and all the sins which
follow and attend despair?

A. I know that the Pope and his Counsellors are perfectly
indifferent about moral evils which arise from the laws which
keep up the appearance of infallibility in their Church.—
Rather than alter her law of celibacy, Rome has allowed her
Clergy to be for many ages exposed to the most fatal tempta
tions; and for the most part to be involved in the guilt of many
a secret, and many an open sin, which might be avoided by
the repeal of that law.

R. Does not the Pope ever dispense with the law of celibacy?

A. Rome, my friend, never draws back but when fear compels her. The only dispensation I ever heard of, was obtained
by Bonaparte for Talleyrand, a French Bishop. The whole
history of Papal Rome proves that nothing but absolute compulsion will ever make her change her conduct. Even when
the Popes have been forced to yield to necessity, they have always done it in sullen silence, and never by publicly disclaim-
ing even their most unjustifiable and tyrannical laws. At this
moment, when the Pope knows that by a short declaration he

should instantly remove all the difficulties which oppose the termination of what is called the Catholic Question, and dispel the well-grounded fears which most Protestants have of the admission of Roman Catholics to seats in Parliament,— the Pope lets them struggle on towards the object of their am bition; with the view, no doubt, of reminding them, in case they should gain the point, that it is the duty of every spiritual son of Rome to exert himself in the destruction of Protestantism, and consequently so to behave themselves in Parliament, as to undermine the foundations of every Christian denomination which does not acknowledge the Pope as the Vicar of Christ on earth.

R. I know, Sir, many Roman Catholics who are most excellent people, and who appear to bear no malice against the religion of their neighbors.

A. I have no doubt that there are many such persons among them; but am equally certain that every spiritual subject of the Pope is bound to oppose Protestantism, by the same conscientious principle which makes him a Roman Catholic.— Why is he a Romanist? Because he thinks the Pope's religion the safest way to save his soul. Would he then endanger that soul by acting against the principles of that religion, merely for the sake of the Protestants?

R. I wish you would tell me the real belief of the Church of Rome with regard to Protestants?

A. The Church of Rome declares, as positively as she does the doctrine of the Trinity, and the Death and Resurrection of our Saviour, that there is no salvation out of her pale; that is to say, that the promises of the Gospel are exclusively made to those who acknowledge the Pope as the representative of Christ. This doctrine has been repeatedly established by the highest authority of the Church of Rome, which is the Pope and his Bishops met in council. The same authority has declared and bound all Roman Catholics to believe, that every person who has received baptism, either in their church, or out of it, is obliged *to obey all the precepts of the holy Church, either written or delivered by tradition ; and that whoever denies that such baptized persons should not be forced to obey those precepts by any other punishment than that of excommunication, is to be accursed.* Such is the declaration of the Council of Trent,* whose infallibility no Roman Catholic can disbelieve. He is therefore *accursed* by the Church of Rome who supports religious toleration. Nothing, conse-

* Session VII. Canon IV. and XIV.

quently, can be more evident, than that sincere Roman Catholics are bound to be intolerant; for the Roman Catholic religion does not consist only in believing certain doctrines, but
in believing them in obedience to that Church of which the
Pope is the head. The sincere Roman Catholic cannot, therefore, explain away the practical consequences of his creed.—
He believes what his Church believes: his Church believes
that whoever denies that baptized persons should be forced to
obey the traditions of Rome, is accursed; he must therefore
deem himself *accursed* if he omits any opportunity of forcing
people into the Romish communion. Besides, if you see the
Roman Catholics incessantly at work to make converts by
persuasion, because their Church declares it to be their duty
to snatch the souls of Protestants from eternal damnation; how
can you suppose that, if they had power, they would not use
it for the same purpose and under the same authority? But
we are not left to inferences and conjectures upon this subject. The Church of Rome is so fully determined to impress
upon her children their duty of forcing Romanism upon all
who may be under their influence, that she enjoins that intolerant principle under an oath. The most solemn declaration
of the Romanist faith ends in words which, translated into
English, are as follow: " *This true Catholic Faith, out of which
none can be saved, which I now freely profess and truly hold,
I promise, vow, and swear, to retain (with God's assistance)
whole and entire to my life's end, and to procure to the extent of
my power, that all my subjects, or those who, by virtue of my office, may be under my care, shall hold, teach, and preach the
same.*" This oath was framed by the Council of Trent, with
a determination to tender it to all persons in power; and is
taken, even in this Protestant kingdom, by all Romans, Bishops and dignitaries. If this be not a proof, that checking and
opposing every religion but that of the Pope, is considered a
strict duty by the Church of Rome, all sound reasoning is at
an end.

R. Do you suppose that any free-born Briton could approve
of anything like the Inquisition?

A. I have a very high opinion of the British character; but,
on the other hand, I am too well acquainted with the baneful
effects of the Roman Catholic religion upon the mind. I hope
that few among the subjects of Great Britain are, in their
hearts, abetters of that darling of the Romish Church—the
Inquisition. But I know that a dignified Spanish Clergyman, who was in London a few years ago, met with English

Roman Catholics who declared their approbation of the Inquisition. In the preface to a history of that infamous tribunal, which he published in the year 1818, he has the words which I am going to give you translated from the French: "*During my residence in London, I heard some Roman Catholics say, that the Inquisition was useful in Spain for the preservation of the Catholic Faith; and that it would have been well for France if it had had a similar establishment.*"* This he asserts, not to attack the Roman Catholics, for he died in the communion of their Church, but as a simple fact.

R. I am quite surprised!

A. I am not surprised at all. It is when I hear of Roman Catholics who engage not to persecute Protestants, even if they had the power, that I am seized with astonishment.— How can the spiritual children of Rome be so unlike their mother? Was it not the church of Rome that in Spain, urged the burning of *thirty-one thousand nine hundred and twelve* dissenters from her doctrines, and that punished with imprisonment, fine, confiscation, and public infamy *hundred and ninety-one thousand four hundred and fifty,* who saved their lives by recantation? Was it not by the same authority that in this kingdom of England, and during the four years of the reign of Queen Mary, *two hundred and eighty persons* were burnt alive; the number of those who perished in prison, for not turning Papists, being unknown? If this sanguinary church acknowledged her error, if she confessed that she was misled by the ignorance and bigotry of old times, (though she herself had undoubtedly caused that ignorance and bigotry,) we might believe that her children had also put off their persecuting character. But when has mortal man heard that the Church of Rome ever whispered a regret for the torrents of blood with which she has drenched the earth? Her Spanish Inquisition existed till within the last five years. The Pope restored it in 1814, and his Bishops are at this moment doing every thing to revive it. But what is the existence or abolition of the Inquisition, but a mere external symptom of power or want of it, to put the invariable principle of Romanist intolerance into practice? The cruel deeds of the Romish Church are nothing but a republication, in blood, of the articles of her Faith stamped in every copy of the decrees of Trent. How then can I believe that sincere Roman Catholics have renounced persecution? When a man's hopes of

*Llorente's History of the Spanish Inquisition. Paris edition, 1818, vol. l. p. xxii.

2 H

eternal happiness are bound up in a persecuting creed, he may indulge in toleration as he does in sin, under a sense of spirit ual danger, and a hope of future amendment: in the hey-day of life he will be for letting every man have his way; but I would not trust my liberty and my life into his hands, differ ing, as I do, from his creed, when he turns his thoughts to religion, and begins his course of Romish repentance

R. I had never till now believed that intolerance and per-secution could be taught by Christians as necessary for sal-vation.

A. One benefit, I trust in God's grace, you will at least derive from the clear proofs I have given you, that such is the doctrine of the church of Rome. Convinced as you must be, that she makes persecution an essential part of her creed, you will bear that fact in mind, if ever her emissaries should try their arts to seduce you from your Protestant profession.— Whenever you shall hear the often told story of St. Peter and his Primacy, you have only to remember the tyrannous doc-trine and conduct of the Popes which have grown out of that threadbare fiction. Compare the government of the pretend-ed successors of Peter, with the model of a Christian Pastor which Peter himself has left in his first Epistle. " Feed," he says, "the flock of God which is among you, taking the oversight thereof, NOT BY CONSTRAINT, but willingly; not for FILTHY LUCRE, but of a ready mind; NEITHER AS BEING LORDS over GOD'S HERITAGE, but by being ensamples to the flock."* There needs not much learning to rebut all the pretensions of the Romish Church, when you compare her Popish government with this passage. You have only to remember the constraint and bloodshed by which the Popes obtained at one time the *oversight* of the flock of God: the *filthy lucre* which at this very day is the effect of their indulgences and dispensations; and lastly, to observe the *lordly* manner in which they still claim the spiritual dominion of this and all other countries which have shaken off their tyrannical and usurped authority. Remember all this, and beware, my friend, of the guiles and arts of a Church, which, even at this moment, looks upon you and your brother Protestants as runaway slaves, whom she does not punish, from mere want of power, and rest as-sured, that where there is so much spirit of pride and ambi-tion, the Christian spirit must have been nearly quenched.

* 1 Peter v. 2. 3.

DEFECTS OCCURRING IN THE MASS.

NO. I.

A curious extract from the Roman Missal, p. 53, &c. " respecting Defects occurring in the Mass." Thayer's Contro. p. 71. 79.

'Mass may be defective in the Matter to be consecrated, in the form to be used, and in the officiating Minister. For if in any of these there be any defect, viz. due Matter, Form, with Intention, and Priestly Orders in the celebrator, there is no sacrament consecrated.'

The defects in the bread.

1st. " If the bread be not of wheat, or if of wheat, if it be mixed with such quantity of other grain, that it doth not remain wheaten bread; or if it be in any way corrupted, it doth not make a sacrament."

2d. 'If it be made with rose or other distilled water, 'tis doubtful if it make a sacrament.

3d. 'If it begin to corrupt, but is not corrupted: also, if it be not unleavened according to the custom of the Latin Church, it makes a sacrament; but the Priest sins grievously.

Of the defects of the Wine.

'If the wine be quite sour, or putrid, or be made of bitter or unripe grapes: or if so much water be mixed with it, as spoils the wine, no sacrament is made.

'If after the consecration of the body, or even of the wine, the defect of either kind be discovered, one being consecrated, then, if the matter which should be placed cannot be had, to avoid scandal, he must proceed.

The defects in the form.

" If any one shall leave out, or change any part of the form of the consecration of the body and blood, and in the change of the words, such words do not signify the same thing there is no consecration.

The defects of the Minister.

" The defects on the part of the Minister, may occur in these things required in him. These are first and especially

363

Intention, after that *disposition* of soul, of body, of vestments, and disposition in the service itself, as to those matters which can occur in it.

"If any one intend not to consecrate, but to counterfei also, if any wafers remain forgotten on the altar, or if any part of the wine, or any wafer lie hidden, when he did not intend to consecrate but what he saw; also, if he shall have before him eleven wafers and intended to consecrate but ten only, not determining what ten he meant, in all these cases the consecration fails, because *Intention* is required."

Reader, Art thou not astonished? It is admitted 1st, That to offer up a false Mass to God, or take a false sacrament, or worship a false host, is sacrilegious, and is damnable idolatry 2d, that one case is doubtful, but twelve are certain, in any one of which, the consecration fails, and there is no true sacrament, and then the Mass service is sacrilege and idolatry!! And should the priest, as he serves, discover any of these *defects,* but can't mend it; he must proceed, rather than let the people understand it, and therefore plunge them and himself into these miseries! Has Christ, I ask, ever taught such principles? And, if to guard against these dangers, is plainly impossible; then, for any man to be safe in that church must be clearly impossible. But let us see the rest of it.

'Should the consecrated host disappear, either by accident, or by wind, or miracle, or be swallowed by some animal, and cannot be found; then let another be consecrated.'

'If after consecration, a gnat, a spider, or any such thing, fall into the chalice, let the Priest swallow it with the blood, if he can; but if he fear danger and have a loathing, let him take it out, and wash it with wine, and when Mass is ended, burn it, and cast it and the washing into holy ground.'

'If poison fall into the chalice, or what might cause vomiting, let the consecrated wine be put into another cup, and other wine with water be again placed to be consecrated, and when Mass is finished, let the blood be poured on linen cloth, or tow, remain till it be dry, and then be burned, and the ashes be thrown into holy ground.'

'If the host be poisoned, let another be consecrated and used, and that be kept in a tabernacle, or a separate place until it be corrupted, and after that be thrown into holy ground.

'If in winter the blood be frozen in the cup, put warm cloths about the cup; if that will not do, let it be put into boiling water near the altar, till it be melted, taking care it does not get into the cup.'

'If any of the blood of Christ fall on the ground by negligence, it must be licked up with the tongue, the place be sufficiently scraped, and the scrapings burned; but the ashes must be buried in holy ground.'

'If the Priest *vomit the Eucharist,* and the species appear entire he must *piously swallow it again,* but if a nausea prevent him, then let the consecrated species be cautiously separated, and put by in some holy place till they be corrupted, and after, let them be cast into holy ground; but if the species do not appear, the vomit must be burned and the ashes thrown into holy ground.'—Marvellous!

The oath of the Papal Clergy is, "that the Host is Christ—body and blood, soul and divinity," (see their creed;) yet they confess, as above, this cannot be known, how desperate then is such oath! By this document they inform us, that their Host (i. e.) Christ, can be lost by accident or by wind, or be eaten by animals, as mites, or mice, or dogs, &c. or by the spider or fly which may fall into the cup, and which the priest must swallow if he can; or that he may be bound up in frost, and be released by hot water, &c. or be poisoned, and poured on tow, and dried, and then must be burned; or may fall, or be spilled and licked off the ground by the priest's tongue, and be swallowed, and may be eaten by him and vomited up again, and then must be taken out of the vomit, and be worshipped, and devoutly swallowed again! Shocking infatuation. Now will not common sense itself, ask, Do any of these things ever happen to the true Christ, the son of Mary? Has he been ever swallowed by spiders, or flies, mites, mice, or by priests, or lain in their vomit? Has he been ever frozen up in a cup, or poured out on tow, and burned? if not, then, Christ was not thus eaten by flies, rats, mice, priests, &c. &c. and, nevertheless, he was eaten by them, which involves many contradictions or falsehoods. But if the true Christ be not thus eaten by these things—the host, which, it is confessed, may meet all these accidents, is not the true, but a fictitious papal Christ. Had not these hideous doctrines and monstrous and degrading absurdities, been thus written, and openly avowed and defended in their own books, so that with our own eyes we can behold them, who could be persuaded to believe, that any church or society of rational beings, could for a moment entertain them? Strong indeed must be that delusion by which the Papal Doctors are thus so deeply infatuated and corrupted, as to adhere to such a religion!

NO. II.

The Trent Creed under Pope Pius IV. to which the Papal Clergy are bound by oath.

The Bull of Pius IV. by divine providence, Pope, relative to the FORM OF OATH or the profession of the faith.

Pius, Bishop, the servant of the servants of God, for the perpetual remembrance of this deed.

"*Injunctum nobis Apostolicæ servitutis officium, &c.*" "The office of our apostolical ministry enjoins us to hasten and execute these decisions of the holy fathers, with which the Almighty God has, for the good of his church, inspired them, &c. Whereas, therefore, by the decree of the Council of Trent, all pastors who shall henceforth be placed over cathedrals and superior churches and their dependencies, or who, entrusted with the care of souls, are provided for, must be obliged to make public profession of the orthodox faith, and to *promise and swear*, that they will continue obedient to the church of Rome: We, desirous, that all this should be diligently attended to by all so entrusted, and in whatsoever department, whether in monasteries, convents, houses, and such like places, whether called regular, military, or by what name soever, and that the profession of the same faith might be uniformly exhibited to all, and that one only and certain form of it, might be made known to all men, and published in every nation, by those whom, under the prescribed penalties, it concerns, strictly command, by our apostolical authority, that the following aforesaid profession of faith be solemnly made, according to this form only, &c.

"Ego, N. *firma fide credo, &c.*—I, N. firmly believe and profess all and every thing contained in this Creed, which the holy Roman Church useth, viz.

"I believe in one God, Father Almighty, maker of heaven and earth, and of all things visible and invisible, and in one Lord Jesus Christ, the only begotten son of God—by whom all things were made; who for us men, and for our salvation, came down from heaven, and was incarnated by the Holy Ghost of the Virgin Mary, and was made man; was crucified also for us under Pontius Pilate, he suffered and was buried; and rose again the third day, according to the Scriptures; and ascended into Heaven, and sitteth at the right hand of God the Father; and shall come again with glory to judge the living and the dead, of whose kingdom there shall be no end; and in the Holy Ghost, the Lord and giver of life, &c.—and one holy Catholic, and apostolic church," &c.

The oath on Schoolmasters and Doctors—

·*Ad hoc omnes ii ad quos universitatum,*" &c. "Moreover, all those to whom the care, visitation or reform of universities and general studies belong, must take diligent care, that the canons and decrees of this holy synod, be received entire by th·se universities, and that according to these rules, the master, doctors, and other teachers in such universities, may teach and interpret those things which belong to the Catholic faith, and that they bind themselves *by a solemn oath,* in the beginning of each year, to this observance." C. Trent, Sess. xxv. cap. 2.

Thus, by these authentic documents, it is evident, that the Papal Clergy are obliged to be *sworn on the Gospels, three times;* 1st. to the Church of Rome, 2d. to the Pope, and 3d. to believe and propagate her doctrines, and, by the *same oaths,* to oppose every thing contrary thereto,—(and so were schoolmasters sworn.) This accounts for that constant watch they keep lest the people should hear or read any doctrine but their own, lest they should get enlightened. How ignorant of all this craft are the people kept, and how astonishing, if not miraculous, that the Gospel of truth has broken forth from all those dire and ingenious trammels.

Observations on the above Papal Creed and its notorious contradictions.

Obser. 1—The Council of Nice, which in 325 framed the Nicene Creed, pronounces in one of its canons, any man, that shall thenceforth add any more articles of faith than those then specified, accursed. And Pope Celestine, an. 423, in his Epistle to Nestorious in defence of that creed, has these words, "Who is not adjudged worthy of an anathema, that either adds or takes away from it? For, that faith which was declared by the apostles requires neither addition or diminution." But the Council of Trent and Pope Pius, in 1564, fear not, in the face of all this, to add 12 new articles at a stroke, nor once blush to pronounce those who shall presume to refuse them, accursed. And although these Councils thus contradict and curse each other, yet the Papal Doctors *are sworn* to believe and teach both are infallible!! And that although both creeds plainly contradict one another, as shall presently appear, yet they are nevertheless one and the same true faith! *risum tencatis?*

Obser. 2.—The old part of this creed declares, "Christ was incarnated by the Holy Ghost of the Virgin Mary, and was made man." But in the 5th article of the new part of the same, it is defined and declared, " that Christ's body and blood are really, substantially, and truly made, by consecration, of the whole substance of the bread, and of the whole substance of the wine." Here then are two sorts of Christs, from entirely different sources, exhibited in one compound creed. By one part thereof, Christ was born, crucified and suffered, was buried, rose again, ascended into heaven, sitteth at the right hand of God, and shall come to judge all men, &c. But, by the other, he was not born, but made of bread, &c. nor did any of these things! and yet the Papal Clergy *are sworn*, to believe and teach they are the same! As all these contradictions are, to be sure, divine truths! so, their people, rational beings, must believe it, because their clergy direct them to do so!!!

Observ. 3.—By the 1st article, traditions, and Papal Decrees &c. (mere inventions of men) must be admitted *and embraced too;* but by the 2d, the holy scripture is, *coldly,* to be admitted *only, not embraced,* and that under most severe and cautious restrictions.—Who can forbear noticing this? And when we turn to, Sess. iv. *Decretum de Edit.* &c. An. 1546, and to the rules, *de libris prohibitis,* framed by the Council in March, 1564, their dread of the scriptures, it is manifest, cannot be concealed. From *her index,* take the following extracts—

Rule 4. *Cum experimento manifestum sit, &c.*—" Whereas, it is plain by experience, were the holy scriptures read every where in the vulgar tongue, more injury than good would follow, yet if permission to read translations of the Bible made by Catholics only, may be safely granted to some, who by such reading may reap godly benefit, must rest with the judgment of the bishop or inquisitor, together with the counsel of their parish priest. In such cases it may be given, but they must have a license from the bishop in writing. *Qui autem absque tali facultate ea legere seu habère presumserit, nisi prius bibliis ordinario redditis, peccatorum absolutionem precipere non posset, &c.* "But he that without such license, shall presume to read or have such books, unless he instantly deliver them up to the ordinary, cannot be capable of the forgiveness of his sins. And the bookseller, who without such license, shall sell or otherwise grant the bible in the vulgar tongue, &c. shall forfeit the price of the books, and be otherwise punished at the bishop's discretion, according to the nature of his offence—nor may the monks, without such license from their Prelates, read or buy them.

Rule X.—"Liberum tamen Episcopis, &c."—"But, yet, the Bishops or Inquisitors general, are by their license; which they have authorized to prohibit in their kingdoms, provinces, or dioceses, those very books that appear to be permitted by those rules, if they shall judge fit." So, after all the pains of procuring this said license, it can be rendered null in an instant, and then the Bible must not be read.

Ad extremum vero omnibus fidelibus, &c.—"Lastly, the faithful are commanded, that none must dare read or have any books contrary to the prescribed rules of this Index; but if any one shall read or have books of heretics, or of any author on heresy, or condemned and prohibited on suspicion of false dogmas, he instantly incurs the sentence of excommunication. And he that shall read or have books of any name that are so forbidden him, besides the guilt of mortal sin into which he falls, he must be severely punished, according to the judgment of the Bishops."

Behold how difficult it has been to obtain leave to read the word of God, even when translated by Roman Catholics themselves! See what dread this church ever had of the Bible.— Thank God! the darkness is greatly passed, and the true light is increasing.

Obser. 4.—This 3d new article of faith is unqualified jargon; for, seven christian sacraments, (as per. Sess. VII. Can. I.) are insisted on, as instituted by our Lord Jesus Christ, which is proved false.

Holy Orders and Ext. Unction clearly destroy each other; and if no sacrament can be without Christ's own institution, such as Baptism and the Eucharist alone have, then, none of the other five are christian sacraments, because, for them no institution from Christ can be found—"The matter or visible sign of Holy Orders," says Challenor, (p. 131, C. Chris. Inst.) "is imposition of hands by a Bishop and prayer, and the institution is from Luke xxii. 19. *Do this in remembrance of me,*" but Christ never laid his hands on the Apostles to make them Priests, nor commanded it; (nor ever made them Priests, as is proved, p. 156.) Hence Holy Orders, being without sign, matter, or institution from Christ, is no christian sacrament, but a papal fiction.

"As to Penance," says Challenor, p. 94. "it consists of contrition, confession and satisfaction, and the Priest's absolution. Confession, is a full and sincere accusation made to a Priest, of all mortal sins, a person can remember: and satisfaction is a faithful performance of the penance enjoined by the Priests, p. 163—which penance is enjoined, as an exchange which God makes of the eternal punishments which we have deserved by sin, into these small penitential works, p. 104.—Yet it is to be feared that the penance enjoined is seldom sufficient to take off all the punishment due to God's justice on account of our sins." p 105   The penitent after confession, must say, 'I beg pardon of God, and penance and absolution from you, my ghostly father,' and the Priest then gives the absolution, and adds, "May the passion of our Lord Jesus Christ, the merits of the blessed Virgin Mary, and of the Saints, and whatsoever good thou shalt do, or whatsoever evil thou shalt suffer, be to thee unto the remission of thy sins, the increase of grace, &c " Most shocking and anti-scriptural doctrine!

If Christ's death on the cross be a full, and the only satisfaction for all sin, and that his precious merits and intercession alone, be the sinner's only hope, as is testified by all the sacred writers; and if a wretched sinner, the moment he believes this, and submitting himself to Christ, calls upon his name, "hath everlasting life, passes from death unto life, and shall not come into condemnation," John v. 24. Rom. viii. 1.; If "the blood of Jesus Christ cleanseth from all sin," 1 John, i. 7. If "God was in Christ reconciling the world unto himself, not imputing their trespasses unto them," 2 Cor. v. 19.; And if "all that believe in Christ with a heart unto righteousness, are justified from all things." Acts xiii. 39; the above doctrine must be false.   Besides, if Christ never appointed any such private confession of mortal sin, nor any such penance or absolution, nor any visible sign of any such sacrament, nor was any such thing ever practised by the apostles, and hence, that it is therefore only a papal fiction, what can be imagined more blasphemous against Christ, and subversive of his gospel, more delusive to a sinner, and destructive of his true hope and salvation, and at the same time, more pharisaic and better calculated to enhance the Priest's power over the people, than the above mischievous and anti-christian doctrine of papal penance.   Yet, after all the parade about it, the hopes excited of its many and great benefits, p. 102, they grant, "If the Priest, to whom this confession is made, has not the necessary faculties and approbation, and also true intention, the penance is null."   But these things are impossible to be known or guarded against by Priests or people; hence, such penance is extreme folly.   But repentance towards God, and faith in Christ, is the only safe and gospel way; this can deceive no man.

With regard to *Invocation of Saints,* in addition to what has been already said, its novelty and impiety are set forth by the following striking testimonies.

"*Saith St. Augustine, de civ. Dei l. 8. Si rex constituerit intercessorem, &c.*—"When a king has constituted *one certain intercessor*, he is not pleased that any causes should be brought him by others. So, as Christ is appointed our High Priest and Intercessor, why do we seek others?

"*Solent tamen pudorem*," &c. saith St. Ambrose, "The Heathen Idolaters, to cover the shame of neglecting God, used this miserable excuse, that by *these mediators* they might go to God, as by his officers we may approach a king."

"Go to, is any man so mad, or unmindful of his own safety as to give the king's honor to his officers? whereas, if any be found even to treat of such a matter, they are justly condemned as guilty of insulting the king's majesty. It is for this reason that men go to a king by tribunes or officers, because the king is but a man, and knoweth not to whom he should entrust the commonwealth. But to procure the favor of God, from whom nothing is hid, and who knows the qualities of all men, we need no spokesman but a devout mind."—*Ambros ad Cap 1. ad Rom.*

Says St. Chrysostom, "when thou hast need to sue unto man, thou art forced first to deal with door-keepers, and entreat parasites and such like persons to go with thee a long way about; *epi de tou theou ouden toiouton estin*, but with God there is no such thing; without money, without cost, he yieldeth to thy prayer." Serm. 7. de pœnit. And again, *Ora gunaikos philosophia*, &c. "Mark," says he, "the wisdom of the woman of Canaan, she entreateth not James, nor beseecheth John, nor cometh to Peter, but brake through the whole company of them, saying, 'I have no need of such mediators, but taking repentance with me for a spokesman, I come to the fountain itself; for this cause did he take flesh that I might have boldness to speak to him. I have no need of a mediator, have thou mercy on me.' "—*Dimissum Chanaan. Tom. 5.*

Thus, these Fathers, who lived so near the Apostle's days, judged it idolatry, madness, and the height of impiety against God, when he has appointed Christ, his son, our high priest and only mediator, (who is ever ready and present to receive all sinners who humbly call upon him, and to hear their prayers,) to have recourse, nevertheless, to the intercession of angels or departed saints, "which manner," saith Chrysostom, "came in through the envy of the devil."

I must notice the Papal doctrine of Baptism by Bossuet and

the Trent Counc l, "As infants cannot supply the want of *Baptism*, by acts of faith, hope and charity, nor by the earnest desire of receiving this sacrament, *we believe if they do not really receive it, they have no share in the grace of the redemption, and thus dying in Adam, they have no inheritance with Jesus Christ.*" Con. Trid. Sess. vi. cap. 4. Bossuet. Expos. p. 42. Dublin. Edit. 1821.

Thus has the Papacy and its Doctors, to subserve their own purposes, poisoned almost every part of the christian religion. As this astonishing "Exposition" is as contrary to scripture, as it is insulting to common sense, and fraught with such inconceivable impiety, I shall now proceed briefly, by reason and scripture, to destroy it.

Arg. 1.—The j ist and merciful God does not require impossibilities. To say he does, is to say he is unjust and cruel, which is blasphemy. But to most infants, Baptism is totally, and to all, personally impossible. Hence, can no blame attach to them, and they can suffer nothing for dying unbaptized; and hence to affirm, "that such unbaptised infants have no share :n the grace of redemption, nor with Christ," as the Papacy and its doctors do, is to teach, God is unjust and cruel, which, as it insults reason, so is it monstrous blasphemy against God's mercy and justice!

Arg. 2.—That God instituted Baptism in the Christian Church, as he did circumcision in the Jewish, cannot be fairly denied; yet neither of them was absolutely essential to salvation; for, if it appear, the latter was not so, particularly that of infants, so neither can the former be. Circumcision was rather a sign of that of the heart, and a seal of the covenant, as St. Paul argues, Rom. ii. 26, and also as a distinction from the heathen world; for these uses, and because God commanded it, it was necessary, yet not essential to salvation; otherwise, all the infants that died before they were eight days old, were, by God's own will and fault, and contrary to his will and word, excluded from Christ's redemption, and heaven! which to affirm, involves unequivocal blasphemy. For, by his command, no child was circumcised before eight days old; and He declares *"he willeth not that any should perish,"* 2 Peter iii. 9. And Christ says, *"that all infants are of the kingdom of heaven."* Luke xviii. 16.—Now, if all the Jewish infants who died before eight days old, were fully saved without the sacrament of circumcision, so, (if *"God be no respecter of persons,"* as St. Peter says,) must all the infants of christians who may happen to die without Baptism, be saved likewise. If to con·

tradict this, is blasphemy against God, so therefore is Bossuet's, and the Trent doctrine, "that *unbaptised infants can have no part in Christ's redemption, nor in heaven*," a flat contradiction to truth, and palpable *blasphemy*.

Arg. 3.—St. Paul tells us, "that although condemnation came by one man, even Adam's offence, Christ brought justification to life to all men; and that no sin is imputed where there is no law," Rom. v. 18.—2 Cor. v. 19. But infants know not any law, and, therefore, according to St. Paul, no sin can be imputed to them; again, "*the son shall not bear the sin of the father*," except the son himself do evil.—Ezek. xviii. 20. Hence can no infant suffer for any sin. Once more, the holy Virgin and the Apostles tell us, "*that God's mercy is on them that fear him—that glory, honor, and peace shall be on even the Gentile that worketh good, for God is no respecter of persons*." Luke i. 50.—Rom. ii. 10—15, 26.—Acts x. 34, 35 If then such God-fearing Gentiles are saved without circumcision or baptism, as these affirm, so must their infants also.— Hence, to teach, "that the infants of Christians dying without Baptism, have no part in redemption, nor in heaven, is to contradict the Apostles and the holy Virgin, and all reason and scripture, and to be guilty of hideous impiety. And hence, what Christ says in John iii. 5, as he cannot require impossibilities, so it cannot apply to infants, but to those who hear of, and refuse baptism and regeneration.

With regard to confirmation and matrimony, however these may be proper, the latter especially as rites, either religious or civil, yet, as Christ appointed no visible signs of them, as he did of Baptism and Eucharist, how can they be christian Sacraments? Impossible; hence, there are no true christian sacramen's but Baptism and Eucharist; and the others, being proved Papal fictions, the oath of the clergy "that there are seven sacraments appointed by Christ," is most contradictory and desperate.

As pure christianity,—that rational and holy religion which Christ the Lord came to establish on earth, not by force or fraud, but by gentleness, prayers, and persuasion, requires for its propagation and support, no other weapons but those employed and enjoined by him; and, inviting investigation, calls for no other aid, but a fair exhibition of its own incomparable loveliness, and inestimable excellencies, .o recommend it to man, to lead him into the paths of peace and everlasting felicity, and thus at once displays its divine.origin: So, that system of eligion that, taking a directly contrary course, and because of its deformity manifestly dreading examination, hates the light, dreads the bible, insults reason, and the rights of conscience, and has recourse to various wiles, machinations and violences for its support and propagation, unequivocally proclaims to all men, it has emanated from a totally different source. Viewing, then, by the following additional documents, the line of conduct the Papacy has for ages pursued, to support itself and propagate its doctrines, the conclusion is most obvious, that its fountain is not pure,—is not the God of peace, of light, and love.

NO. III.

The Oaths to be taken to defend the Papacy.

THE POPE'S OATH.—By the general Councils of Constance and Basil, it is stated, *"That all Popes must be obliged to* SWEAR *that they will uphold and enforce (generalium concilio-rum fidem, &c.) the faith maintained in the general councils, to the least tittle, even to the shedding of their blood."* Concil. Const. Sess. 39, Basil, Sess. 37.

By the following Councils also, Constance, Sess. 12. 17. 37; Lyons, Tom. 11. Binii, p. 645. Pisa, Sess. 14. Basil, Sess. 24. 34. 40. 46, it is expressly decreed, "that the Pope shall depose and deprive Sovereign Princes of their dominions, their dignity, and honor, for certain misdemeanors," &c.

Hear the lofty language of Pope Gregory VIII. "On the part of the Omnipotent God, I forbid Henry IV. to govern the kingdoms of Italy and Germany; I absolve his subjects from all oaths which they have taken, or may take to him; and I excommunicate every person who shall serve him as King."— *Greg. lib.* 5, *Epist.* 24.

NO. IV.

The Pope's Bull, in Cœna Domini, &c. which per art. 28, *thereof must be diligently studied by the Clergy, and (per 27th Art.) solemnly published in the Churches once a year or oftener; and carefully taught the people,* 1638—*Tom.* 8, *p.* 183, *Constit.* 63, *Pauli V.—The Excommunication, &c.*

First Article—"We excommunicate and anathematize, in the name of God, Father, Son, and Holy Ghost, and by the authority of the blessed Apostles, Peter and Paul, and by our own, all Wicklifites, Hussites, Lutherans, Calvinists, Hugonots, Anabaptists, and all other heretics, by whatsoever name they are called, and of whatsoever sect they be; and also, all Schismatics, and those who withdraw themselves, or recede obstinately from the obedience of the Bishop of Rcme; as also their Adherents, Receivers, Favorers, and generally any defenders of them:—together with all who, without the authority of the Apostolic See, shall knowingly, read, keep, or print, any of their Books which treat on Religion, or by or for any cause whatever, publicly or privately, on any pretence or color defend them."

The Pope's joy at the murder of Protestants.

Pope Gregory XIII. in 1572, upon the massacre in Paris on St. Bartholomew's day, caused medals to be struck with this inscription about his image, "Gregorius XIII. Pont. Max. An. 1." and on the reverse side, a destroying angel holding a cross in one hand, and in the other, a sword thrusting, with these words, "Hugonotorum strages, 1572." "The slaughter of the Hugonots." Voyage to Italy, p. 15. An. 1688. See Rev. xvii. 6.

NO. V.

BISHOP'S OATH.—In addition to the *oaths,* stated in the Creed, on the priests; when they become Bishops, they must be again sworn. Richerius, an eminent papal divine of the 15th century, and Doctor of the Sorbonne, observed, "That Pope Gregory VII. contrary to the custom used in the church for more than a thousand years, introduced that order, "that all bishops must swear unlimited fidelity and obedience to the pope," whence, says he, *"the liberty of all succeeding councils was taken away."* Hist. Concil. lib. c. 38. Rich. Apol. Ax. 22.

"I, N. N. Bishop elect, of the See of N. do swear, that, from this time henceforth, I will be faithful and obedient to the blessed Apostle Peter, to the holy Church of Rome, and to our Lord the Pope, and his successors canonically appointed. I will to my utmost defend, increase, and advance, the rights, honors, privileges, and authority of the holy Roman Church of our Lord the Pope, and his successors aforesaid.—I will not join in any consultation, act or treaty, in which any thing shall be plotted to the injury of the rights, honor, state and power of our Lord the Pope, or of the said Church. I will keep with all my might the rules of the holy Fathers, (i. e. of the Council) the Apostolical (Papal) decrees, ordinances, disposals, reservations, provisions and mandates; and cause them to be observed by others. Heretics, Schismatics, and rebels to our said Lord the Pope and his successors aforesaid, I will to the utmost of my power persecute and destroy." Sub. Jul. iii. **An. 1551.**

Bishop's obligation, (*Conc. Benii. Tom.* 11. *p.* 152.) "If
any Bishop be negligent in purging his diocese of heretical
pravity, he, by the 3d canon of the 4th Lateran Council, must
be deprived of his episcopal dignity; and by the Council of
Constance (*Sess.* 45. *Tom.* 7. *p.* 1122.) and by the Canon
Law, (*Decretal lib.* 5. *tit.* 7. *cap.* 13.) Bishops, by their above
oath of consecration, are bound to do so. And the punishment to be inflicted on the heretics, must be excommunication,
confiscation of goods, imprisonment, exile, or death," as the
case may be. *Concil. Benii. Tom.* 8.

Concil. Tom. 11. p. 619, "All Inquisitors of heretical pravity appointed by the Pope, all Archbishops and Bishops, in
their respective provinces and dioceses, with their officials,
must search for and apprehend heretics.—The Civil Magis-
trate must assist them under severe penalties in enquiring
after, taking, and spoiling them, by sending soldiers with
them, p. 608.—They can compel the whole neighborhood to
swear they will inform the Bishops and Inquisitors of any heretics they shall know of, or of any who may favor them.—
Constit. Innoc. iv. c. 30.

By Later. IV. Con. Tom. 11. part. 1. p. 152. and Con. Constance, Sess. 45, Tom. 7. p. 1120. Benii. "Whoever appre-
hends heretics, which all are at liberty to do, has power to
take from them all their goods and freely enjoy them." And
Pope Innocent III. declares, "*This punishment we command to
.be executed on them by all Princes and secular powers, who shall
be compelled to do so by ecclesiastical censures.* Decret. 7.
lib. 5. tit. cap. 10.

NO. VI.

On Extirpation of Heretics.

OATHS ON KINGS—to extirpate heretics. The 4th Council
of Lateran, can. 3, has these words—"Pro defensione fidei
præstat juramentum, quod de terris suæ jurisdictionis subjec
tos universos hæreticos ab Ecclesia denotatos, bona fide pro
viribus exterminare studebunt." For the defence of the faith,
all Princes must SWEAR, that they will, *bona fide*, most diligently study to root out of their territories, all their subjects,
by the Church pronounced heretics, which, should they neg-
ect to do, they must themselves be excommunicated, and de-
posed. The Council of Constance confirms this Sess 45.

In the 5th Council of Toledo, the Holy Fathers say: "We
promulge this decree pleasing to God. That whosoever here-

after shall ascend to the kingdom, shall not ascend the throne all he has sworn, among other oaths, to permit no man to li·e in his kingdom, *who is not a Catholic;* and if, after he has taken the reins of government, he shall violate this promise, let him be anathema maranatha in the sight of God, and fuel of the eternal fire." Caranza, Sum. Concil. p. 404.

An Edict of Louis XVth of France, published in 1724, *consisting of* 18 *Articles; the* 1*st and* 2*d are as follows* "That the Catholic Religion be alone professed in our kingdom; forbidding all our subjects, of what estate, quality, or condition soever, to profess any other Religion, or assemble for that purpose in any place, under any pretence whatever, on pain, of Men for the gallies for ever, and Women to be shorn, or shut up for ever in such places as our Judges shall think proper, with confiscation of goods.

"We order, that all such Preachers as have convened assemblies, not according to the said C. Religion, or shall have preached, or discharged any other function therein, shall be punished with death!—We forbid all our subjects to receive such Ministers or Preachers, or to give them any retreat, succor, or assistance, or to have any manner of communication with them. And we order all who shall have any notice thereof, to discover it to the officers of these places, the whole on the aforesaid penalties."

That the Clergy did press this dire. law, is notorious, from the address of the assembly of Bishops to the King, in 1765.

"Give, Sire," say they, "Give to the laws all their force, and to Religion all its splendor, that the full revival of the Edict of 1724, may be the result of our humble remonstrances.—The plague we complain of, will continue to ravage your kingdom, till the press also shall be restrained by laws faithfully executed."

What man, of any name or nation, and in whose breast is any of the milk of human kindess, but must shudder at these fearful plans and exclaim, How could a church, so desperate against Bible Christians, be the mild, holy spouse of Christ?

A recent Conversation with a Nun

"Do you believe the sacred writers of the Scripture were infallibly inspired? N. 'I do.' 'If not, you could have no true foundation for a divine religion; would you, after they had finished their work, consent to their making any changes in it? 'No, for that would be denying they were rendered

2 I 2

infallible. 'In this, you agree with St. Paul, Gal. i. 8.—'that
nc apostle, angel, or man, must make any alterations in the
gospel. Now, were not the Apostles the true teaching church?'
'Yes, certainly.' 'But if you would not allow that church,
even the very apostles, to deviate from the scriptures, on what
ground can you permit any other church or teachers to deviate
from them? Hence, the infallible scripture, not any church
whatever, must be your only safe guide. I shall now prove
your clergy are on oath to teach you, what yourself know is
an untruth! Has there ever been a true, proper, and real sacrifice for sin on earth, but the death of Christ on the cross?"
'No.' 'What were all the sacrifices from Abel's, till then?'
'They were typical only.' 'But Christ's last supper or sacrament, which ye call his mass, being before his death or even
apprehension, could not, therefore, you own, be more than typical or figurative; yet, your priests are on oath to believe and
teach "that in the mass, there is a true, proper and propitiatory sacrifice for the living and the dead," which, you see, is a
plain falsehood!' Said her grand-father, who was present,
'There, indeed, you have them by the neck.' 'Yes, Sir, and
they can never get loose.'

NOTES.

Notices of the Papal Church in the United States

From the Quarterly Register of the American Education Society,
Vol. 2d, 1830.

The subject announced at the head of this article is one of great and increasing importance. Contemplated either in a civil or religious view, this is unquestionably the case; but it is more especially under the latter that it commends itself to the readers of this publication. We shall endeavor, in pursuing it, to bear in mind not only the imperious duty of the historian, to exhibit truth, but also that of the patriot and christian, to ascertain and feel its connexion and relations.

But in this paper it is not intended to enter at large into the long, protracted, and voluminous controversy with the Church of Rome. Such we style her, and are backward to admit her title to the usurped but ordinary appellation of 'Catholic.'— This controversy has occasionally occupied, for more than three hundred years, some of the most serious minds and able pens of Christendom; and indeed from an earlier age there have not been wanting individuals who have successively borne testimony against the assumptions, spiritual and temporal, of the Roman Court, or Church—terms, in this case, commutable—her growing superstitions, preposterous claims, and absurd pretensions.

Yet, while we waive, for the present, a professed entrance on this controversy, it is not because we are under no apprehension of evil, nor because we do not feel that it is matter of surprise that the evil should be extending its influence so widely in our country. For we cannot forget the apprehensions of our puritan ancestors, and their conscientious opposition; nor the sufferings of many who preceded them. And it is equally impossible to forget the invaluable privilege of possessing God's word, translated and accessible in our own language with the liberty of reading, expounding and practising its requirements, without fear of molestation.— That, in such circumstances, Rome should increase her votaries from among our freeborn citizens, in numbers almost equal to those who came as papists to this country from the shores of Europe, is indeed matter of surprise.

Our main design is to give a statistical view of Romanists in the United States, as has been done in reference to other denominations. But, with our opinions and feelings, it will be impracticable, and would also, we think, be improper, to exhibit such a view without remarks.

At the outset, however, it is to be distinctly and gratefully acknowledged, that, as in our own state government 'every denomination of Christians, demeaning themselves peaceably, and as good subjects of the Commonwealth, shall be equally under the protection of the law; and no subordination of any one sect or denomination to another shall ever be established by law:'* so likewise in the Constitution of the United States it is provided, that 'Congress shall make no law respecting an establishment of religion, or prohibiting the free exercise thereof.'† Whatever remarks, therefore, be made in reference to that branch of the Church of Rome which exists in these States, it is to be considered that they have an equal right with ourselves to their own views, and opinions, and forms of worship, while they infringe not on the rights of others. And, as a consequence, they have an equal right with ourselves to publish their own opinions, and send out their missionaries to promulgate them through the Union, and multiply their converts—it being only the force of truth and sound argument, and the influence of a holy and useful life, which can justly be allowed to sway the public sentiment, and establish the prosperity of any denomination: every tendency to the union of the Church and State, in establishments professedly religious, militating as much with our feelings, as with the spirit of our free constitutions of government.

Nor are the Romanists to be regarded as interlopers in the United States. One of the members of this Confederacy was indeed originally constituted, in great degree, by individuals of that faith. Maryland, settled by Lord Baltimore, was intended by him as a place of refuge for such, and for their enjoyment of religious liberty. However strange, therefore, it may seem to us, that our ears are saluted with reports of the extension of the Romish Church in this Protestant country—we must be prepared to contemplate the fact.

And why, some are ready to say, is this increase to be deprecated? Are we to charge on the modern professors of that faith the derelictions of their ancestors? Shall we hold the

*Constitution of Mass. Art. III.   †Amend. to Const't. of U. S. Art. III.

present Church of Rome responsible for the cruelties exercised against the Albigenses, six hundred years ago—and for
the fires of Smithfield, the *dragonnades* of the Cevennois, the
massacres of St. Bartholomew, and of 1641? Do we not find
in that communion men of humanity, of elegant literature, engaging manners. sound science, and fervent piety? These
questions would have weight, did we recognize in the acts of
the Court of Rome any compunction for her past violences; did
she express her abhorrence of the principle, ' that no faith is
to be kept with heretics,' and abjure the dogmas of Jesuitic
morality. But until this is done, she must be held responsible
to the world—as indeed she will be to God, *when he maketh
inquisition for blood.*

The refinement of modern manners, the withholding of ob-
jectionable articles of faith, in soothing conversations maintained with inquiries, the specious glosses put on expressions
startling to the lover of Scriptural simplicity—all these might
seem to say, Rome has changed, and is far different from that
power which Luther and Zuingle, Melancthon, Calvin and
Bucer, and the host of Reformers combatted. But the high
tone of her present publications claims* an unchanged and
unchangable character for her faith and her practice

It is not therefore to be wondered at, that this whole subject
is awakening investigation. Indeed, the wonder is, rather,
that curiosity has slept so long—and that watchmen themselves
have slumbered. Specially is it to be regretted, that that
important part of our territory, concerning which we are accustomed to hear that it will speedily, by its abundant population, give law to our Union, has been left open so long to the
enterprises of Rome; and has obtained from the elder portions
of our population so scanty means of resistance to a persevering and specious hierarchy. How important it is in the sight
of Romanists, this paper will soon evince. Had it been in
our eyes as important at the commencement of this century,
and had those means been in operation, which our tardy zeal
is now employing, how different the result from that we have
reason to apprehend?

We have before us the numbers of a French periodical publication for the year just closed, containing several deeply interesting statements. It is entitled ' Annals of the Association for the propagation of the Faith.' At what precise period
the Association was formed, or what station it holds in the Ro-

*See The Jesuit, a periodical published in Boston, passim.

mish Church, whether it has succeeded the 'College *de propaganda Fide*,' or is a new body altogether, we are not inform
ed.   These numbers are from xv to xviii inclusively, and we
propose to gather from them a few of the facts and represen-
tations which bear on the subject of this paper.

But, as the subject, in all probability, is comparatively new
to very many of our readers, it will be necessary to take previously a cursory view of what had been done antecedently to
this period, in reference to the Romish Church in the United
States.   For this we are indebted to a publication in 1822 in
New York, exhibiting its condition at that time.*   From this
we learn that a Jesuit priest accompanied the emigrants to
Maryland, in 1632, and from that date till the period of the
revolution, the American Catholics in Maryland and Virginia
were constantly served by Jesuit missionaries, successively
sent from England.†

The Rev. Dr. John Carroll having been elected the first
Bishop, by the clergy, through a special indulgence granted
them by the Pope, Pius VI. a See was constituted, and the
Bishop elect consecrated in England, Aug. 15, 1790.   He had
been chosen by twenty-four out of twenty-six priests, assem
bled for the purpose.

At length, in 1810, the increase of the Romish Communion
had become so great in the United States, it was judged best at
Rome to erect the Episcopate of Baltimore 'into a Metropolitan
or Archiepiscopal See, and to establish four new suffragan
dioceses; namely, Boston, New-York, Philadelphia, and Bardstown in Kentucky.'   This was accordingly carried into effect
' with great pomp and solemnity.'

Previous to this period, New Orleans had been erected into
a bishopric, and in 1820, those of Richmond and Charleston
were added.   All these are entitled from the places where they
are constituted, as in countries connected with the Romish
government, or as is done in Episcopal England—there being
no occasion, such is American liberality or indifference, for
the ecclesiastical figment, *in partibus infidelium*.   Singular,
therefore, as is the sound, Boston, the capital of the puritans,
is designated as an episcopate subject to Rome.   At her court,
doubtless, this has been regarded as no small triumph, and on
this side the water, appears no trifling anomaly.

---

*'The Laity's Directory to the Church Service,' revised and corrected by
Rev. Mr. Power, a distinguished Romanist.

† Id. p. 73.

To the above episcopal sees, that of Ohio has been subsequently added, and is denominated from Cincinnati, the principal town, where the Bishop's cathedral was consecrated, Dec. 17, 1826. Mobile has likewise been created an episcopate by Pius VIII, the present Pope.

It remains that something be remarked in reference to the resuscitation of the order of Jesuits, especially as this relates to their labors in the United States.

To no body of men whatever has the See of Rome been more deeply indebted than to this, for active, persevering, and devoted service. Of their former history, their flexible principles, the abilities and accomplishments of their most distinguished members—the extent of their missions, their estimation in courts, and influence in the cabinets of princes—little need be said. It is subject of general notoriety, and familiar to all who read. Equally known is the hatred this celebrated society excited even in kingdoms like France, Spain and Portugal, devoted, and the latter too almost blindly, to the interests of the See of Rome. This odium demanded at length the suppression of the order, which it was the glory of Ganganelli (in the eyes of the Protestants at least, as well as of the petitioners) ultimately to effect in 1776. Rumor said it cost his life.

From the time of Clement XIV. the society, which had been so powerful and so richly endowed, lay dormant for near forty years—at least so far as regarded its public appearance with its own name. It may, however, be useful to notice its previous extent. This we are able to do from a document, 'found among the papers of the society at the time of their expulsion from Spain,' in 1767, and entitled, 'A general enumeration of the houses, colleges, residences, seminaries and missions of the Jesuits in all parts of the world.' It states* that there were in the society

  39 Provinces,
  24 Houses (professed),
  669 Colleges,
  61 Houses of probation, or Noviciates,
  176 Seminaries, or Boarding houses,
  335 Residences,
  273 Missions,
22,819 Jesuits; among whom were
11,413 Priests.

* See 'Recueil des pieces concernant le bannissement des Jesuites,' etc. 1, suite, p. 46.

A subsequent note adds, 'We thus see that the world is as
it were, environed by an extended net, composed, it is true,
of wide meshes, if it were formed but of 22,000 Jesuits; but
these meshes are compressed when we inspect a copy found
in the Imperial College, enumerating such as were connected
with the Congregations throughout the Spanish Monarchy. In
the Imperial College of Madrid alone the number amounted to
near 2000 men or youths, and a thousand females; so that
their "Congregations" among the subjects of his Catholic Majesty surpass 60,000.*

It is not in our power to trace the members of this Society
during its suppression. The name of Jesuit was, suffice it to
say, but synonymous with all of ambition, craft, and treachery,
duplicity, and talent, to be conceived by the human mind. A
history of the order was printed in France, and its delinquen-
cies detailed in an elaborate manner. Of this work we have
seen five, closely printed, thick quarto volumes, and it was
then incomplete. The caustic pen of Pascal had long before
withered its laurels, and it seemed doomed to irremediable
death. But Pius VII. ventured to resuscitate it; and by his
bull of Aug. 7, 1814, brought it again into existence in all the
States acknowledging spiritual subjection to Rome. Let then
the Court of Rome bear the responsibility of its daring! Necessary indeed to its service may be the devotion of such a
band—but how perilous the determination to employ it!†

A word or two must also be said in regard to the College
de propaganda Fide. We confess we are not informed of its
present state. But it is not long since its funds appeared to
be wholly exhausted. However, Spain contributed, as the
public papers announced, an amount of 60,000 crowns, in the
depth of her national poverty, not long ago; and Austria, at
least, is able to furnish abundantly the cost of new and extended missions: and not only able, but, it is stated on good au-

* See 'Recueil des pieces concernant le bannissement des Jesuites,' etc.
page 48.

† See a Dissertation published in Paris, 1825, entitled, Les Jesuites et leur
doctrine, p. 287. In the introduction the author observes, 'There have appeared lately many histories of the Jesuits: but they have treated only of
their political intrigues, and very little respecting their doctrine—of which
many have heard a great deal, out do not comprehend it. This has caused
the production of the present work.'—'We presume to hope, that the public
will be gratified to know thoroughly a Society, which formerly rendered itself
so celebrated by its disorders, and which still, at the present day, threatens us
with the evils it has never ceased to bring upon our kings and upon our country:' pp. xiv. xv.

thority, actually engaged in doing it for the 'Mission to the United States.' Private intelligence also from Italy assures us, that, in the upper circles, the enterprise of reducing our Western States to spiritual subserviency and subjection under the See of Rome, or, in other words, *to convert them to the Faith*, is the subject of most frequent and interesting conversation.

In circumstances like these, we advert to the articles of information contained in those numbers of the 'Annals' before alluded to, occupying about 240 pages. They are introduced by the following editorial remarks.

'In the first and second number of these Annals we inserted two articles respecting Kentucky. We then stated the condition of the catholic religion in this vast mission. Since that time, the good which had been commenced, has been confirmed, and truth has obtained new triumphs over error. Daily conversions, although not of a splendid character, are crowning the labors and animating the zeal of the venerable bishop of Bardstown, and his indefatigable helpers. The Jubilee was preached in succession and with effect throughout all the parishes of the diocese. Infidels and the protestants of all denominations, who inhabit this country, were neither alarmed nor stirred up to opposition, as has often been the case elsewhere, at the sight of a few poor priests announcing to sinners the mercies of the Most High, or dazzling the eyes of heretics with the torch of the true faith.

'Beside the bishop and his coadjutor, Monseigneur* David, there are in all the diocese of Bardstown but twenty-one missionaries. This diocese is formed of the states of Kentucky, Tennessee, Indiana, and Illinois, the population of which amounts to 1,397,450 souls, comprising 207,930 slaves. This population, in which are found not more than 30,000 Catholics, is spread over a surface a hundred leagues wide, and two hundred and forty in length. The diocese possesses a Dominican convent, two nunneries, and thirty churches, of which eleven are built of brick and nineteen of wood. The convent of the Dominicans is at St. Rose, near Springfield in Kentucky. It was founded in 1806, by M. Edw. Fenwick, the present bishop

---

* The title of 'My Lord' is the qualification of bishops abroad; but, very properly, we think, the editor of the 'U. S. Catholic Miscellany,' published at Charleston, commenting on a notice copied from a Canada paper, objects to the use of it in this country. However, let it appear. It is only one exemplification of Romanist aberrations from the simplicity of Scripture, which allows not bishops to be '*lords over God's heritage--but ensamples to the flock.*' 1 Peter v. 3.

of Cincinnati, and has thus far furnished twelve priests. Some
years since Mgr. Flaget instituted a community of *Missionary
Friars.* They are intended for the office of catechists, schoolmasters, sacristars, etc. Their vow is for three years, and
they engage in manual labor, gardening, and agriculture.

'The nuns devote themselves to the education of young persons of their own sex. The *Sisters of Charity*, seventy in
number, were established by Mgr. David. Their chief town
is at Nazareth, one league from Bardstown. By the increase
of pupils, they have been necessitated to build a boarding-
house, that will contain a hundred and fifty. Nuns, of the
Dominican order, were established six or seven years ago, to
the number of fifteen, in the neighborhood of Springfield.—
They have but about thirty pupils, not being able to accommo-
date more. The *Sisters of the Cross, or of Loretto*, founded
by the venerable M. Nerinckx, amounting already to one hundred and thirty-five. Their principal establishment is at Loretto, near Bardstown, and they have six other secondary
houses, for country schools.

'Most of the churches of the diocese of Bardstown are very
destitute of linen and ornaments; many, in fact, are in want
of the objects most necessary for the celebration of sacred
rites. The Abbe Martial, whom Mgr. Flaget had sent to Europe in 1826, having shown the king of France the poverty of
the mission of Kentucky, His Majesty and Monseigneur, the
Dauphin, condescended to present him the altar furniture for
the cathedral of Bardstown: the tabernacle, cross, and six
chandeliers are of bronze, gilt, and of excellent workmanship.
M. Martial had previously received of the king of Naples six
paintings, of the Sovereign Pontiff four paintings and the sacred vessels, of the queen of Sardinia an *ostensoir*, inlaid with
vermillion, and of His Highness the Duke of Modena, an epis
copal ring for Mgr. Flaget. And when,' adds the editor, 'the
letters are read which are now published, it will appear that
these testimonials of esteem, given by the abovementioned
sovereigns to the venerable prelate and his missionaries, are
well merited.'

Of the three letters from the bishop of Bardstown, which
are then given, the first, directed to a friend who had been in
America, is dated in February, 1825, and states:

'The second wing of Bardstown college is nearly finished.
It has cost more than 7,000 dollars, and the whole is, unhap-
pily, not yet paid. Our Legislature has just incorporated the
college. The Bishops of Bardstown are constituted perpetu

ally its moderators or rectors. I might have dictated conditions, which I could not have made more advantageous or honorable; and what is still more flattering is, that these privileges were granted almost without any discussion, and with unanimity in both houses.'

After some further detail of plans, and prospects, and labors, and urging his friend to 'knock at every door, and try to obtain the aid necessary to meet his accumulated expenses,' the bishop says:

'There are fourteen or fifteen scholars in the little seminary, and new ones present themselves almost every week.— The spiritual call spreads, and offers a consoling prospect for time to come. Strangers who hear of our success wonder at it; but we who behold it, and who know the immense disproportion between our local resources and what is actually wanting, speak of it like men in a delirium, who follow the inspiration that conducts them, much more than the dim light of their own reason. This serves to guard us against the temptations of vanity, and inspires us with courage to struggle against the innumerable difficulties which surround our steps Pray much, my dear friend,' he continues, 'and urge others to pray, that we may be humble and grateful; then all will go well.'

Happy, we may add, happy would it have been for the Church of Rome and the world, had the excellent spirit of this last expression breathed ever in her councils and in the members of her communion!

In justice to the bishop, it must also be mentioned that, in the same letter, he says:

'You will recollect that I wrote you about fourteen years ago, that my great ambition was to make but one family with my venerable priests, and that we should have a *common purse;* that each of our members, whether in health or sickness, should have a right to a decent support, and that the remainder, if any, should be consecrated to good works. The incorporation of our college occurred most happily to bring into operation this family-contract, and to recall the lovely times of the primitive church. I am still engaged in executing this plan, and my young priests appear to enter into my views with much pleasure.'

In a subsequent letter of acknowledgment and solicitation, the bishop thus dilates on his situation, labors, and prospects:

'The providence of God has unquestionably been remarkable in regard to me, and even lavish of kindnesses; and had i the hearts of all the angels, I could not recount them. On my part I have endeavored to answer its designs, and my exertions have not been useless. In fact, what a consolation is it to me, that I have formed three female religious orders— the *Lovers of Mary*, the *Sisters of Charity*, and the Dominican Nuns! More than two hundred young women, who have taken their vows in these institutions, are principally devoted to the education of persons of their own sex. What a consolation, to have formed two seminaries, containing thirty-five or forty young people designed for the church; to have erected two schools for country children, and a little college for such as desire a classical education; to see that eight brick churches, without mentioning my cathedral, which is the wonder of the country, have been erected since my abode in Kentucky; that the two seminaries, the two schools, and the college, are also beautiful buildings of brick, erected and paid for by ourselves. It is true that we owe from 30 to 35,000 francs; but from the profits of the college and the contributions we expect, we may be freed in about four years. Still, had I treasures at my disposal, I would multiply colleges, and schools for girls and boys; I would consolidate all these establishments, by annexing to them lands or annual rents; I would build hospitals and public houses: in a word, I would compel all my Kentuckians to admire and love a religion so beneficent and generous, *and perhaps I should finish by converting them.*— The directors of the Association for the Faith ought not, in general, to scruple sending abundant alms to bishops whose wants plead more eloquently than their letters. By the fruits we judge of the tree.

'The following,' he adds, 'is the account of the ordination I administered the last December: one who received the tonsure, nine minorites, two sub-deacons, and one deacon; five or six children of the little seminary, after a trial of eighteen months or two years, may receive the tonsure; but garments must be bought for them, for I have not the means. In our two seminaries, we have one tonsured, eleven minorites, four sub-deacons, and three deacons, with seventeen or eighteen young persons more, who have been studying two or three years for the priesthood. This prospect in a diocese, existing only thirteen years, is consoling to the friends of religion, and merits encouragement.

The editor subjoins to this statement:

'Mgr. Flaget has established in his diocese many convents

of nuns devoted to the education of young females. These establishments do wonderful good. Catholics and Protestants are admitted indiscriminately. The latter, after having finished their education, return to the bosom of their families, full of esteem and veneration for their instructresses They are ever ready to refute the calumnies, which the jealousy of heretics loves to spread against the religious communities: *and often, when they have no longer the opposition of their relations to fear, they embrace the Catholic religion.*'

That such has been the frequent result cannot be denied; and that such a result has been anticipated, the above documents fully evince. Nor can the 'heretics' of these United States be too 'jealous' of the insidious influence of the religion of Rome on their unguarded population.

The following is an extract of another letter:*

'From time to time Protestants are converted. The disinterestedness of our clergy, their regularity and devotion to the good of the people, *from whom they gain nothing,* have more effect upon the minds of the Protestants than all the reasonings in the world. The Protestants are divided into an infinity of sects; but many of them are *nothing;* they are not even baptised. They come to our church, attracted by the music and the preaching. They behave there as well as the Catholics. In fact, the church is not here, as in Europe, a place for walking and meeting acquaintances. There reigns in it a silence and tranquility, which are astonishing when observed for the first time.'

We extract also a paragraph from the details of services in proclaiming the 'Jubilee:'†

'The same day on which the exercises ended at St. Thomas they were begun at Louisville. Two ecclesiastics from Bardstown came to assist the ordinary pastor of the congregation here. Its church, though ill situated for the greater portion of the inhabitants of this trading and populous city, was nevertheless filled with people. Beside the morning sermon, there was a conference at 4 o'clock, respecting indulgences and the jubilee. One of the ecclesiastics proposed the objections of the Protestants, and another replied, referring always to the testimony of the scriptures and tradition. Some days before, a Presbyterian minister of Louisville, by the ame of Blackburn, had declaimed publicly against the Cath

*Annales, etc. No. xv. p. 175. †Id. p. 178.
2 K 2

olic cleigy. The missionaries contented themselves with proving their doctrine and dispelling prejudices; but the church being found too small for the crowd of auditors, after Monday the conferences were held in the courthouse at seven in the evening. The multitude was very great, and sometimes the conferences lasted two hours and a half.— On Saturday, instead of the conference, there was a sermon on the necessity of baptism. On Sunday there were but sixty persons at the communion; but the Catholics are only a small part of the population, and beside it is known that this city, by its situation on the banks of the Ohio, and commercial connexion with all the West, is a species of market, where the tumult and dissipation are extreme. Others of the faithful are preparing to receive the communion, *and several Protestants have announced their design of joining the church.* The conferences have produced *a species of revolution* in ideas and feelings; the most important points have been discussed, as the authority of the Pope, the real presence, the worship of the saints, the reproaches against the priests, ecclesiastical celibacy, &c. On the day when the last point was handled, a Presbyterian minister thought proper to interrupt the preacher in a loud voice. Some zealous Irishmen went to him; but the preacher requested permission to answer the proposed questions; and, in fact, he replied with great animation, shewing, by St. Paul himself, the advantages of continence.' At another place: 'A conference on the infallibility of the church,* before a numerous body of Catholics and Protestants, closed this visit.' In other places: 'The missionaries proposed to answer, in a conference, some of the calumnies published by an Anabaptist journal. They aimed to show, that charity is the distinctive character of our religion, and they refuted the objections drawn from the Inquisition, and some other topics:'—'two priests, one deacon, four sub-deacons, all born in the United States, and most of them in Kentucky, were ordained:'—'the planters crowded earnestly to attend the exercises, and there were at the holy table two hundred and fifty believers, and about sixty received confirmation,

---

*From the apparent caution with which the subject of this conference is expressed, it might be supposed that the letter-writer and his friends were not of the High Church party, ascribing infallibility to the Pope. See the Rev. Mr. Faber's able and seasonable work on the Difficulties of Romanism, for the difference of opinion on this point, (if in an *invariable* church such a thing can be imagined,) between the Transalpine and Cisalpine parties. P. 40, Amer. dit.

one adult was baptized, and two others already baptized, entered the bosom of the church.' At Lexington, 'almost the whole
audience was Protestant, and the subject of conference was,
the power of the church to forgive sins. The other exercises
were held 'n St. Peter's Church, but the conferences at the
courthouse. There, the questions respecting purgatory, the
inquisition, and the reading of the Bible, were discussed, and
the church was defended on these points. Such peaceable conferences excited, as at Louisville, the chagrin of some ministers, who declaimed from their desks with warmth.'

Of these conferences, Bishop Flaget, in a letter to his friend,
remarks: 'It is impossible for me to tell you the good which
will result from this exercise. The Protestants are, perhaps,
more attached to it than the Catholics. We have had the consolation of seeing a great number of old sinners making considerable efforts to obtain the indulgence of the jubilee. Many Protestants are much shaken. Mad. B——, a widow of
this city, [Louisville] sister of your friend, ——, invited me
to see her, the day before yesterday, along with Messrs. Rey-
nolds and Kenrick. She is convinced that she cannot find
peace but in embracing the Catholic religion.' But, (adding
the fashionable French exclamation, which we cannot divest
of profaneness,) what difficulties to overcome, on the score of
the ministers, and of her relations!'

The remaining part of the letter is, mostly, a description of
the urgent wants of the mission, and a pressing request to
make every exertion for obtaining a supply.

The next year the same Bishop acknowledges the reception
of 13,200 francs, assigned to his use by the Association for the
propagation of the Faith.

'This sum,' he writes, 'has been a great help to me; but I
shall still need the good offices of the Association, during a
long time. For the love of God, plead the cause of the Mission of Kentucky with His Eminence, the Grand Almoner.—
No mission, I venture to say, *offers to religion greater hopes
than this:* but it has been compelled by circumstances, which
the Abbe Martial can recount to you, to incur necessary expenses, and those above its present means. The honor of
religion requires that they should be paid as soon as possible,
and I anticipate this distinguished favor, in a great degree,
from the generosity of the Association for the Propagation of
the Faith. Convince His Eminence that the money sent me
is not employed to maintain the luxury of my table, or pride of
dress or furniture. Perhaps there is not in Paris, or in all

France, one ecclesiastic in a hundred, who could satisfy himself with my daily fare; and last winter I constantly wore,
while at the seminary, a garment presented me at S. Fleur
sixteen years ago.   In truth, I have but one simple desire, and
I have the happiness of inculcating it on all my young priests,
—that of extending our holy religion, and laboring for the
glory of God.   Do not, however, I beg you, alarm yourself
with my debts and actual necessities.   I am, indeed, I confess,
in a painful condition now; but every thing promises me a
more tranquil issue.   Our buildings are nearly finished; we
have almost ninety boarders in the college, and more than a
hundred and fifty abroad.   Besides, our personal expenses
are moderate; so that I have the greatest confidence we shall
be able in a short time to liquidate our debts,—and shall then
have the opportunity of educating gratis a much larger number of pupils in our seminary for the good of the church in
Kentucky—and even of the Bishops, my neighbors, who have
no seminaries established.˙

Abundant proof seems to be offered in these extracts, of the
zeal, patience, labor, and indefatigable perseverance of the
Bishop and his helpers.   We wish it may stimulate to equal
exertions, many in whose faith, as Protestants, we have a
greater confidence.   It speaks loudly to all among us, who
value *the liberty wherewith Christ hath made them free,* and
cannot consent to be *brought again into bondage,* to use effort
for the propagation and establishment, among our brethren in
the West, of those wholesome institutions and religious advantages, of which the descendants and successors of the Ley-
den pilgrims are so justly tenacious.

We must proceed, however, in our extracts.   The bishop
feared his account was too flattering, and that the Association
thinking his establishments highly prosperous, would direct
their bounty to other less promising stations.   His next letter,
therefore, presents some interesting details: 'They write me,'
says he, ' from different quarters, that the principal directors
of the Association for the Propagation of the Faith, are scru-
pulous of aiding my diocess, because they believe it is sufficiently established, and because I have no stations among the
savages.   As you have been long my friend, and know perfectly the sincerity and frankness of all my words and actions,
I will enter into some details on the Western Missions of the
United States, where I have resided as Bishop sixteen years,
and was sent thirty-five years ago as a missionary.

'Generally, we ought to consider all the new bishoprics of

America as Sees destitute of all resources, which can never
be solidly established, unless for half a century they are aided
by rich and pious souls in Europe, with zealous and learned
missionaries, with money, and with all kinds of church vessels,
ornaments and decorations.

'To give you a clear idea of these bishoprics in the United
States, I will briefly narrate my own situation, when the court
of Rome, on the presentation of Mgr. Carroll, had nominated
me to the See of Bardstown. Willing or unwilling, I was obliged to accept it; I had not a farthing at my command; the
Pope and the Cardinals, who had all been dispersed by the
revolution, could make me not the smallest present; and M.
Carroll, although he had been for sixteen years a Bishop, was
poorer than I—for he was in debt, and I owed nothing. They
proceeded at once to consecrate me, on the 4th of Nov. 1810;
but for want of money to defray the journey, I could not set
out. It was not until six months after, that, in consequence of
a contribution made in Baltimore, I was able to reach Bardstown, my episcopal seat. On the 9th of June, 1811, I entered this little village, accompanied by two priests, and three
young men, students for the ecclesiastical condition. Not
only had I no money in my purse, but had been obliged to
borrow nearly two thousand francs for the journey. So, without cash, without a house, without possessions, and almost
without information, I found myself in the middle of a diocess
two or three times larger than all France, containing five large
States, and two immense Territories, and able to converse
but imperfectly in the language of the country itself. Add to
this, that almost all my Catholics were emigrants, and very
poorly accommodated.

'After this faithful description, which will suit all the Western bishoprics except New Orleans, where should I have been,
my dear D——, if my kind friends of America and Europe
had not generously succored me, and if I had not made the
best use possible of their abundant alms? Alas! I should have
done nothing—I should have vegetated—all would have yet
remained to be commenced. It is very true, that with the aid
of friends, and the grace of God, I have formed establishments
which excite the admiration even of those who have most ef-
fectually labored with me in erecting them. But, because I
have known how to put to profit the precious gifts I have received—because I have begun in an admirable manner, must
I be left there to behold the decay and ruin of what had offered such flattering hopes for the future? Would it not be better

to aid me still in consolidating what I had established with sweat and toil,—so that, in a few years, my seminaries should be, as it were, a branch of the Propaganda of Rome, in which might be trained a sufficiency of missionaries for Kentucky and the dioceses adjacent? Already am I furnished with buildings which can contain a hundred young persons, and this number I could procure, had I the means of feeding and decently clothing them, and could I furnish the books necessary for their education. I beg you, inform the directors, that our Americans are not like the people of the East Indies.* Sprung from Europeans, they have the intelligence, the resources, the customs and manners necessary for the most brilliant education, and are capacitated to receive it. Some of my Kentuckian preists would do themselves honor at Paris and at Rome, by their knowledge, quickness of perception, learning and extemporaneous eloquence. They easily bend to the rules of the seminary; acquire a piety more solid than showy; are fond of learning, and capable of great application. Give me only sufficient funds, and a few serious and well-instructed professors, and I can assure the gentlemen, Directors of the Association for the Propagation of the Faith, that I will soon form a sufficiency of priests for even the savages. I may indeed assert, that the savages can never be assured of having missionaries constantly, until it shall be found practicable to form them in the country itself. Finally, it is a falsehood to say that there are no savages in my diocess. Many nations of these poor barbarians inhabit the borders of Indiana and Illinois, *two States depending still on my jurisdiction*.† But I have yet so great need of priests for the Catholics around me, that it has not been possible I should employ myself in managing a mission altogether different from that I am now conducting. The almost invincible repugnance these savages show to civilization, the degeneracy and brutishness of their powers of mind, their implacable hatred and revenge, their almost constant and disgusting drunkenness, their insurmountable indolence, their roving, vagabond life, more necessary now since the vicinity of the whites has deprived them of game; all this united—with their continual traffic among the whites, which cannot be hin-

---

*See their case exhibited by the Abbe Dubois, and the reply of a Protestant missionary at Serampore.

† Less is probably meant than meets the ear in these unwelcome and even apparently arrogant sounds.

dered, *as long as the republican government shall subsist**—
must render the labors of missionaries among them, almost
fruitless.

'God forbid,' he adds, 'that I should decry such missions;
but I have been convinced for several years, that the missions
among whites are much more valuable, in regard to both the
progress and the honor of religion. For, since the holy Catholic religion has exhibited herself in Kentucky with a certain
splendor,—since schools for girls and boys, into which all
sects are admitted, have been multiplied, our many churches
built, and our doctrine clearly and solidly explained in them on
Sundays and festivals, the most happy revolution is effected in
her favor. To the most inveterate prejudices have succeeded
astonishment, admiration, and the desire of knowing our principles. Now the conversions are numerous. In twelve jubilees, wherein I have presided, more than forty Protestants
have entered the church; a great number are still preparing
to share the same happiness—and I have hardly gone over
the half of Kentucky.'

The next communication of the bishop covers a statistical
account of his diocese, drawn up by M. Kenrick, a young Irish
priest, of whom he speaks in the highest terms.

Did our limits permit, it would be gratifying to give this document entire. But, in fact, the preceding extracts will enable
our readers to form a judgment for themselves of the extent to
which this ecclesiastical enterprise, on the part of Rome, has
reached. Yet we must give another extract, and in addition
remark, that four letters are published from M. Champonnier,
'apostolic missionary' at Vincennes, with interesting details
respecting labors in that direction—for even parts of which,
however, we have, at this time, no room.

The extract we propose to give consists of editorial remarks
on intelligence, respecting the 'Mission of Ohio.' The editor,
at the commencement of No. xvi. published in Jan. 1829,
observes:

'In our 9th number, we gave the Association some interesting details respecting the establishment of the bishopric of
Cincinnati; we exhibited the wants of this immense diocese,
and recounted the first labors of the Prelate, to whom the Holy See has committed the charge of this rising church. Mgr.
Fenwick has already employed all his resources in laying the
foundation of a cathedral; aided by the Association for the

---

*And can Rome begin already to calculate on its termination? 'Timeo
Danaos et dona ferentes'—we may well exclaim.

Propagation of the Faith, he has seen this edifice gradually rise, and at length, on the 17th of December, 1826, he was enabled to celebrate its consecration. Eleven other churches or chapels have been built in different parishes. The Protestants themselves rejoice at the sight of these temples erected to the true God, and feel a peculiar attachment for the Catholic worship, *whose pomp and splendor form so striking a contrast with the barrenness and nudity of the Protestant worship.*

'The number of missionaries in Ohio has not increased; on the contrary, some of the assistants of the venerable Bishop of Cincinnati have quitted him for various reasons. One of the most zealous among them, M. Bellamy, who resided at Raisin River in Michigan, has embarked for the missions of the East. He has not been deterred by the poverty and wretchedness which were his lot. His apostolic courage has conducted him to a country where there are greater privations to support, greater conflicts to sustain, greater evils to endure.

'We ought here to notice the difference between the Oriental missions and the missions to America. In China, and at Tong-King is found a polytheism, less brilliant, indeed, than that of the Greeks and Romans, but equally as abject. Temples and idols are beheld in every place; courts, in which Christians are arraigned, and unjust judges who consign to punishment the worshippers of the true God. The Emperors, Ming-Meng and Tao-Kwang,* like the persecuting tyrants of ancient Rome, hate the religion of Jesus Christ, and proscribe his disciples; but they meet, among their own subjects, courageous imitators of the primitive martyrs, who repeat before the mandarin the heroic confession, I AM A CHRISTIAN! and mount the scaffold, singing the hymn of thanksgiving. The missionaries who are evangelising these countries, worthy successors of the Apostles, have more than once with their blood fertilized the soil, which before they had moistened with their sweat and their tears. Every year they have the consolation of causing many hundreds of infidels to abandon the worship of their false gods, and of regenerating, in the holy waters of baptism, many thousands of pagan children, in danger of death. Heresy has not followed us upon this field of battle; in her favor the voice of the blood of martyrs has never been heard; she cannot inspire her converts with courage to die for her.†

---

*Such is the English spelling authorized by Dr. Morrison. The French is Minh-Menh, Tao-Kouan.

†Are the martyrs under Mary of England, and the other persecutors of protestants, forgotten? But, possibly, they were not heretics.

'Let us now consider the missions of America. In this coun‑
try we find not, as in India, a government which proscribes
christianity. The government of the United States has thought
fit to adopt a complete indifference toward all the religions.
Missionaries, therefore, have neither persecution to fear, noi
protection to hope. Their ministry, however, is not the less
laborious.

'It is easy to conceive what fatigue must be endured, and
what perils must be incurred by those apostolic men who are
travelling without cessation the rugged mountains of Kentucky
and Tennessee, or the forests of Ohio, Missouri, Indiana, Illi‑
nois, etc. The traveller, whom necessity conducts into these
desert portions of the United States, cannot penetrate them
without trembling. He must scale precipices, traverse the
streams, the muddy marshes, the tangled woods; his progress
is disputed by ferocious beasts and loathsome reptiles; during
the day he is terrified at the vast solitude which surrounds him
—and fears he shall fall into the midst of some tribe of inhos‑
pitable savages; and when night arrives, he enjoys no repose
—for if he sleeps, it is but a disturbed slumber. His excited
imagination presents continually before him the rattlesnake,
the tiger of the forest, or bear of the mountain, or alligator of
the stream. Charity, evangelical zeal alone can engage the
missionaries to suffer exile in these distant regions. Each of
them is charged with a parish of sixty, eighty, or near a hun‑
dred leagues in extent. They traverse it unceasingly, to
furnish the Catholics confided to their care with the aids of
their ministry; and the year closes before they have been able
to visit them all. Genuine pilgrims on earth, they make no.
where a long abode; nothing stops them in their apostolic ca‑
reer, neither the penetrating cold nor the overpowering heat
—both excessive in this climate. They advance with no oth‑
er arms than a cross, for in the cross they find the necessary
strength to sustain such fatigue, and to despise the many dan‑
gers they meet at every step. Often does night overtake them
in the midst of the woods. The hissing of snakes, and cries of
ferocious beasts sound in their ears. The ruins of an Indian
hut afford them a retreat, and they fall asleep reflecting that
Providence is watching over them. Oh power of charity' O
prodigy of apostolic zeal!

'The missions of America are of high importance to the
church. The superabundant population of ancient Europe is
flowing towards the United States. Each one arrives, not with
his religion, but with his indifference. The greater part are

2 L

disposed to embrace the doctrine, whatever it be, which is first preached to them. We must make haste; the moments are precious. America may one day become the centre of civilization, and, shall truth or error establish there its empire?—*If the Protestant sects are beforehand with us, it will be difficult to destroy their influence.*

'Mgr. Fenwick,' adds the editor, 'is laboring with an admirable zeal to combat this influence of the Protestant sects in the mission entrusted to him. Numerous conversions have already crowned his efforts; and he has even been able to establish a convent, all the nuns of which are Protestants, who have abjured their former faith.'

But we have no space for further extracts from this deeply interesting, and to us, humiliating correspondence. It remains only to state briefly what was done in France for the last year, toward sustaining the Romish missions in our heretofore fondly-termed Protestant Republic;—concerning which we should not speak in such terms, were it not that we know the religion of Rome, to be precisely what the corrupt heart and the proud imagination of man craves—splendid, specious and superficial in its forms—indulgent in its permissions, especially to the rich—easy in its penances, which pacify the guilty, and encourage to new crimes, as easily pardoned—seductive and magnificent in its promises, but exalting itself against the Truth of God, and substituting for it the vanity of useless traditions—cruel and vindictive in its enmities, though it retain amiable and estimable men within its bounds—rotten as a system, and in regard to its factitious pomp of ceremonies, dignities and orders, though possessing many elements of truth—and in Scripture designated as the *mother of harlots, and of the abominations of the earth.*

In 1828 the Association for the Propagation of the Faith collected a sum, which, with an amount on hand, made 271,999 francs, 75 centimes; of which they were able to distribute among the several missions 254,939 fr. 70 c. Of this last amount there was assigned to the Missions of America the sum of 120,000 francs—being about $24,000. The items were as follows:

To Mgr. Fenwick, bishop of Cincinnati, in Ohio   20,000 fr.
To Mgr. Richard, bishop of Detroit, in Michigan   7,500
To Mgr. Flaget, bishop of Bardstown, in Kentucky 20,000
To Mgr. Rosati, bishop of St. Louis, and Adminis-
    trator of New Orleans: for Missouri   20,000
                     for Louisiana   10,000

To Mgr. Portier, bishop of Mobile, in Alabama   15,000   fr
To Mgr. Whitefield, archbishop of Baltimore,   5,000
To Mgr. Dubois, bishop of New York   7,500
To Mgr. England, bishop of Charleston   5,000
To M. Bachelot, Apostolic Prefect of the Sandwich
     Islands   10,000

We have not the means of giving an accurate, statistical view of the number belonging to the Papal Church in the United States. We shall endeavor to do this at a future day—perhaps in our next number. The population belonging to this church has been variously stated. We are inclined to believe it to be *half a million.* The archbishop of this church is James Whitefield, of Baltimore. Bishops, Benedict Josepr. Flaget, of Bardstown, Ky., John England of Charleston, S. C Edward Fenwick of Cincinnati, Ohio, Joseph Rosati, of St Louis Mo. Benedict Joseph Fenwick, of Boston, John Dubois, of New York, Michael Portier, of Mobile, John B. M. David, of Mauricastro, and coadjutor to the Bishop of Bardstown, Henry Conwall, of Philadelphia. They have periodical publications at Charleston, S. C., Hartford, and Boston. A Convention of the prelates met at Baltimore in October last, and addressed a pastoral letter to the laity in the United States.— The principal matters of exhortation are—necessity of greatly increasing the number of the priests—the importance of the education of children—influence through means of the press—interpreting the scriptures " according to the unanimous consent of the church"—adherence to the principles and govern ment of the church—urgency of efforts to disseminate the true faith, &c.—We trust in God that the " Mother Church" is not to become in the United States what she is now in southern or even in central Europe. But this is to be prevented, let it be remembered, and pondered well, by far greater efforts on the part of Protestants, to spread the Word of Life, and the blessings of a *Christian Ministry.* *The efforts of Jesuits are not to be despised.*

In the United States the Popish Hierarchy is composed of one Archbishop and eleven Bishops; the number of Priests is not far from 230. They have seven ecclesiastical Seminaries, ten Colleges and collegiate institutions, several Academies for boys, twenty nunneries, to which are attached female academies, besides numerous other primary and charity schools, under the instruction of priests and nuns, and according to the estimate of the late Council at Baltimore, a population of 500,000.

INQUISITION.

This tribunal, the most infamous by which the history of the world has been disgraced, was instituted in the beginning of the thirteenth century, for the purpose of completing the exter mination of heretical pravity from among mankind. Its intro duction and establishment constitute the most awful demon stration that could possibly have been given of the apostacy of the Papal church, and a most unequivocal and dreadful proof of her anti-Christian character. Any thing more abhor rent to justice than the procedure of this tribunal—any thing more revolting to humanity than the punishments which it im posed—any thing more at war with religion than the spirit which it displayed—any thing, in short, more entirely destruc tive to the peace and the happiness of mankind, than its exis tence and operation, it is impossible to conceive. It did not seem enough to the profligate ecclesiastics who sought to be come masters of the world, that they had imposed restraints upon liberty of thought, and induced an almost universal mid night darkness, and gained the implicit reverence of almost all the princes and the nations of Europe; there seemed to be some formidable institution still wanting in their system of degradation, by which their unhallowed triumph, wheresoever it was not fully achieved, might be completed, and which might seem like some mighty giant standing at the gate of the gloomy edifice which they had reared, and frowning destruc tion on all by whom it should be assailed. This institution they found in the court of the Inquisition. Organized for the avowed purpose of punishing and exterminating heresy, it came, in the course of a few years, in consequence of the ex tensive interpretation which that term received, to take cogni zance of every thing which the Inquisitors thought proper to regard as a crime. It was *heresy*, to reject even one tenet which had been sanctioned by the councils or the court of Rome; to read an interdicted book; to be kind to an excom municated person; to utter an unguarded expression respect ing the Papal authority; or even to manifest natural affection to the dearest earthly friend, who had incurred the censure of the church. In consequence of such an extensive interpre tation of the crime of heresy, the life of almost every man was put under the power of this most extraordinary tribunal. Soon after the establishment of the Inquisition, positive crime was not necessary in order to bring persons under the cogni zance of that ruthless court: it was sufficient to be suspected

of heresy, and the slightest degree of suspicion, however destitute of foundation, was enough to involve those to whom it attached, in proceedings which might terminate in their temporal ruin, and their death.   Even when no ground for suspicion
existed, accusations were basely fabricated, and the innocent
and unsuspecting were imprisoned, that their property might
be forfeited, and their all sacrificed to the avarice and villany
of the church.

The mode of proceeding which this court adopted in the
prosecution of its victims, was not less extraordinary and unjust, than that by which they were brought under its power.—
Secrecy, dishonest and tyrannical secrecy, under cover of
which the most flagrant crimes might be perpetrated, was its
peculiar characteristic.   The apprehension of the unhappy
victims of inquisitorial villany was not permitted to transpire.
Generally, in the dead hour of night this deed of darkness was
done; and with so much dexterity was it conducted by the familiars of the holy office, that not only those who lived in the
same neighborhood, but even those who were members of the
same family, in many instances, knew nothing of it.   One
striking example of this is mentioned by the historian of the
Spanish Inquisition, in case of a father, three sons, and three
daughters, who, although they lived together in the same
house, were all carried prisoners to the Inquisition, without
knowing any thing of one another's being there, till seven
years afterwards, when those who were alive were brought
forth to an Auto-da-fe!

Lest any of its infernal secrets might be disclosed, no
sounds were permitted to be heard throughout the dismal
apartments of the Inquisition.   The poor prisoner was not
allowed to bewail his fate, or, in an audible voice, to offer up
his prayers to Him who is the refuge of the oppressed; nay,
even to cough was to be guilty of a crime, which was immediately punished.   A poor prisoner, we are told by Limborch,
was on one occasion heard to cough; the jailors of the Inquisition instantly repaired to him, and warned him to forbear, as
the slightest noise was not tolerated in that house.   The man
replied that it was not in his power to forbear; a second time
they admonished him to desist; and when again, the poor man,
unable to do otherwise, had repeated the offence, they stripped
him naked, and cruelly beat him.   This increased his cough,
for which they beat him so often, that at last he died through
the pain and anguish of the stripes which he had received!

From the moment that the hapless victims of this dreadfu.

tribunal were arraigned before it, an utter violation of justice characterised every step of the proceedings that were institu ted against them. No information was given to the wretched prisoner respecting the crime of which he had been accused. The grand object of the Inquisitors was to make him inform against himself; with his accusers, or the witnesses against him, he was never confronted; nay, he knew not even their names. He was told that the holy fathers never proceeded save on the most unquestionable information; was exhorted to reflect on his past life, and to tell ingenuously the sins which he had committed; and was assured that ingenuous confession would procure for him a mitigation of the punishment which his crime might deserve. Rarely were their efforts unsuccessful. By operating successively on their victim's hopes and fears—now fawning and then frowning—one while affecting to pity, another while uttering dreadful menaces; at one time deluding him with promises of speedy deliverance, at another threatening racks, and dungeons, and burning flames; or if these methods availed not, by a train of excruciating torments, in the invention of which more than human ingenuity seemed to have been employed, and in the application of which more than human cruelty seemed to have been displayed; and, by tedious confinement in some solitary, noisome dungeon, where his eye never beheld the light of heaven, and no sounds ever fell upon his ear, save the clanking of his fetters, and the stern voice of the man who daily brought him his miserable pittance of bread and water;—in this way did the Inquisition generally bring their unhappy prisoner to accuse himself, to confess crimes of which he was innocent, and thus to become the instrument of his own destruction.

It was against the poor, but memorable people, known by the name of Waldenses, that the operations of this infernal tribunal were first directed. Dwelling in the deep sequestered valleys of the Alps, and greatly unknown and unheeded by the rest of the world, this interesting people preserved, for many ages, the purity of Christian worship and Christian manners: and their little region was the scene of light and verdure, while all around it was darkness and desolation. But persecution entered their peaceful retreats It was not to be brooked by the haughty priest at Rome, that this simple people should remain strangers to the Papal yoke, and be permitted, without interruption, to worship God according to his word, apart from the Roman abominations. In the ears of surround- ng princes their atrocious heresy was proclaimed; and it was declared to be more meritorious and pleasing to heaven, to undertake a crusade against them, than even against the infidel possessors of the Holy Land. Armies were accordingly assembled at the nod of the pontiff; against a people of whom the world was not worthy, was the tempest of their ungodly fury let loose; and the lone valleys of the Waldenses, where the sound of War had never been heard, became the scene of outrage and ruthless devastation. In this truly anti-christian work of extirpating heretics and heresy together, was the Inquisition devised and established to yield its aid—as if the ordinary operations of pontifical vengeance would have too tardily accomplished the annihilation of this weak, unresisting, harmless people. The detail of its atrocious proceedings in their ill-fated land—of the havoc which it made among the humble disciples of Jesus Christ—of the tortures which it inflicted—and of the martyring flames which it lighted up, will remain in the historian's page an indelible memorial of its character, and of the monstrous wickedness of the system that gave it birth. Over this devoted and truly christian people, among whom the truth of God was preserved, when all the surrounding world had forsaken it, did persecuting Rome, after ages of bloodshed and martyrdom, gain a melancholy triumph;—the crossed banners of Popery floated over deserted villages, and the wrecks of conflagrated towns, and the poor remains of the Waldensian church, driven to strange lands, or retired in the mountains and lurking-places of their own beloved land, wept in secret over its sad desolations, and cried to him who is the refuge of the oppressed, that he would arise and plead his own cause.

In other parts of Europe was this bloody court soon erected, and, that the poor heathen who had never heard of the name of Jesus, might have a specimen of the tender mercies of christian men, and might be gained over as converts to the christian faith, its establishment was extended to Pagan lands. Nowhere, however, has its operation been more powerful and terrific than in the kingdom of Spain. Eight hundred persons have been condemned at once by one of its tribunals; and, in the year 1481, the Inquisition of Seville condemned to the flames no fewer than two thousand persons, and nearly twenty thousand more to various inferior degrees of punishment.—During hundreds of years, the Inquisition has been the terror of the Spanish people, and has contributed more than any other institution to reduce to the lowest pitch of degradation their national character. "Its form of proceeding, is an infallible

way to destroy whomsoever the inquisitors wish. The prisoners are not confronted with the accuser or informer. Nor is
there any informer or witness who is not listened to. A public convict, a notorious malefactor, an infamous person, a common prostitute, a child, are, in the holy office, though no where
else, credible accusers and witnesses. Even the son may de-
pone against his father, and the wife against her husband.

This procedure, unheard of till the institution of this court,
makes the whole kingdom tremble. Suspicion reigns in every
breast. Friendship and quietness are at an end. The brother dreads his brother, the father his son."

This is the tribunal of the Inquisition!—a tribunal more
blasphemous, and dishonoring to the God of Mercy, and our
Saviour Jesus Christ, and more awfully degrading to mankind,
than any other institution that ever has existed upon earth.—
Everlasting infamy will rest upon its name; and the execra-
tions of the wise and the good in all ages, will light upon the
unhallowed system that gave it birth.

---

*Damnation and Excommunication of Elizabeth, Queen of
England, and her adherents.*

PIUS, FOR A PERPETUAL MEMORIAL OF THE MATTER.

I. He that reigneth on high, to whom is given all power in
Heaven and on Earth, committed one Holy, Catholic, and
Apostolic Church out of which there is no salvation, to one
alone upon earth, to Peter the Prince of the Apostles, and to
Peter's successor the Bishop of Rome, to be governed in fulness of power. Him alone he made prince over all people,
and all kingdoms, to pluck up, destroy, scatter, consume, plant,
and build, that he may retain the faithful, that are knit together
with the band of charity, in the unity of the Spirit, and present
them spotless and unblamable to their Saviour. In discharge
of which function, we who are, by God's goodness, called to
the government of the aforesaid church, spare no pains, laboring with all earnestness, that unity and the religion, which the
author thereof hath for the trial of his children's faith, and for
our amendment, suffered to be exercised with so great afflictions, might be preserved uncorrupted.

II. But the number of the ungodly hath gotten such power,
that there is now no place left in the whole world, which they
have not essayed to corrupt with their most wicked doctrines.
Amongst others, Elizabeth, the pretended Queen of England

a slave of wickedness, lending thereunto her helping-hand, with whom, as in a sanctuary, the most pernicious of all men have found a refuge, this very woman having seized on the kingdom, ano monstrously usurping the place of the Supreme Head of the church in all England, and the chief authority and jurisdiction thereof, hath again brought back the same kingdom into miserable destruction, which was then newly reduced to the faith, and to good order. For having by strong hand, inhibited the exercise of the true religion, which Mary the lawful Queen, of famous memory, had, by the help of this See, restored, after it had been formerly overthrown by King Henry VIII. a revolter therefrom, and following and embracing the errors of heretics, she hath removed the royal council, consisting of the English nobility, and filled it with obscure men, being heretics; hath oppressed the embracers of the Roman faith, hath placed impious preachers, ministers of iniquity, and abolished the sacrifice of the mass, prayers, fastings, distinction of meats, a single life, and the rites and ceremonies; hath commanded books to be read in the whole realm, containing manifest heresy, and impious mysteries and institutions, by herself entertained and observed, according to the precept of Calvin, to be likewise observed by her subjects; hath presumed to throw bishops, parsons of churches, and other priests, out of their churches and benefices, and to bestow them and other church-livings upon heretics, and to determine of church causes; hath prohibited the prelates, clergy, and people, to acknowledge the church of Rome, or obey the precepts and canonical sanctions thereof; hath compelled most of them to condescend to her wicked laws; and to abjure the authority and obedience of the bishop of Rome, and to acknowledge her to be sole lady, in temporal and spiritual matters, and this by oath; hath imposed penalties and punishments on those who obeyed not, and exacted them of those who persevered in the unity of the faith, and their obedience aforesaid; and hath cast the Roman prelates and rectors of churches into prison, where many of them, being spent with long languishing and sorrow, have miserably ended their lives.

III. All which things, seeing they are manifest and notorious to all nations, and by the greatest testimony of very many so substantially proved, that there is no place at all left for excuse, defence, or evasion; we, seeing that impurities and wicked actions are multiplied one upon another; and, moreover, that the persecution of the faithful, and affliction for religion groweth every day heavier and heavier, through the indigna

tion and means of the said Elizabeth: because we understand
her mind to be so hardened and indurate, that she hath not
only contemned the godly requests and admonitions of princes,
concerning her healing, and conversion, but also hath not so
much as permitted the Nuncios of this See to cross the seas in
to England, are forced of necessity to betake to the weapons
of justice against her, and not being able to mitigate our sorrow, that we are constrained to take punishment upon one, to
whose ancestors the whole state of Christendom hath been so
much bounden.

IV. Being therefore supported with his authority, whose
pleasure it was to place us, though unequal to so great a bur-
den in this supreme throne of justice, we do, out of the fulness
of our Apostolic power, declare the aforesaid Elizabeth, being
a heretic, and a favorer of heretics, and her adherence in the
matter aforesaid, to have incurred the sentence of anathema,
and to be cut off from the unity of the body of Christ. And,
moreover, we do declare her to be deprived of her pretended
title to the kingdom aforesaid, and of all dominion, dignity,
and privilege whatsoever: and also the nobility, subjects, and
people of the said kingdom, and all others which have in any
sort sworn unto her, to be forever absolved from any such
oath, and all manner of duty, of dominion, allegiance, and
obedience; as we also do, by the authority of these presents,
absolve them, and do deprive the same Elizabeth of her pretended title to the kingdom, and all other things aforesaid.—
And we do command and interdict all and every one of the
noblemen, subjects, people, and others aforesaid, that they presume not to obey her, or her admonitions, mandates, and laws;
and those who shall do the contrary, we do innodate with the
like sentence of anathema.

Given at Rome, in the year 1570.

---

*Excommunication pronounced by Philip Dunn, against Fran-
cis Freeman, who embraced the Protestant faith in 1765,
found among that Prelate's papers in his house, Wicklow.*

By the authority of God the Father Almighty, and the bles
sed Virgin Mary, and of Peter, and Paul, and all the Holy
Saints, we excommunicate Francis Freeman, late of the county of Dublin, but now of Juckmill, in the county of Wicklow,
that, in spite of God, and Peter, and in spite of all the Holy
Saints, and in spite of our most Holy Father the Pope, God's

vicar on earth, and in spite of Philip Dunn, our diocesan and worshipful Canons, who serve God daily, hath apostatized to a most damnable religion, full of heresy, and blasphemy; excommunicated let him be, and delivered over to the devil, as a perpetual malefactor and schismatic; accursed let him be in all cities, and all towns, in fields, in ways, in yards, in houses, and in all other places, whether lying or rising, walking or running, leaning or standing, waking or sleeping, eating or drinking, or whatsoever thing he does besides: we separate him from the threshold and all good prayers of the Church; from the participation of the Holy Jesus; from all sacraments, chapels and altars; from the holy bread and holy water; from all the merit of God's holy priests and religious men; and from their cloisters, and all pardons, privileges, grants, and immunities which all the Holy Popes have granted them; and we give him over, utterly to the fiend; and let him quench his soul when dead in the pains of Hell fire, as this candle is quenched and put out; and let us pray to God, our Lady, Peter and Paul, that all the senses of his body may fail, as now the light of this candle is gone, except he come, on sight hereof, and openly confess his damnable heresy and blasphemy, and by repentance make amends, as much as in him lies, to God, our Lady, Peter, and the worshipful company of this Church; and as the staff of this holy cross now falls down, so may he, except he recants and repents. PHILIP DUNN.

Dreadful form of excommunication denounced against the Pope's alum-maker, who, having abandoned his holiness, introduced the secrets of his trade into England.

"By the authority of God Almighty, Father, Son, and Holy Ghost, and of the holy Canons, and of the Immaculate Virgin Mary, the Mother and Patroness of our Saviour; and all the celestial virtues, angels, archangels, thrones, dominions, powers, cherubims, and seraphims; and of all the holy patriarchs and prophets; and of all the apostles, and evangelists; and of all the holy innocents, who, in the sight of the Lamb, are found worthy to sing the new song; of the holy martyrs and holy confessors; and of the holy virgins, and of all the saints, and together with all the holy and elect of God, we excommunicate and anathematize this thief or this malefactor N: And from the thresholds of the holy Church of God Almighty, we sequester him, that he may be tormented, disposed and deliv-

ered over with Dathan and Abiram, and with those who say
unto the Lord God, Depart from us, for we desire not the
knowledge of thy ways. And as fire is quenched with water,
so let the light of him be put for evermore, unless it shall repent him, and he make satisfaction. Amen.

May God the Father, who created man, curse him. May
the Son, who suffered for us, curse him. May the Holy Ghost,
who was given for us in baptism, curse him. May the Holy
Cross, which Christ, for our salvation, triumphing ascended,
curse him. May the holy and Eternal Virgin Mary curse him.
May Michael, the advocate of holy souls, curse him. May
John, the chief forerunner and baptist of Christ, curse him.
May the holy and wonderful company of Martyrs, curse him.
May Peter, Paul, Andrew, and all other Christ's Apostles, together with the rest of his disciples, and four evangelists,
curse him. May the holy choir of the holy Virgins, who, for
the honor of Christ, have despised the things of the world,
curse him. May all the Saints, who from the beginning of the
world, to everlasting ages, are found to be the beloved of God,
curse him. May the heaven and earth, and all the holy things
therein remaining, curse him. May he be cursed wherever
he be, whether in the house or in the field, or in the high way,
or in the path, or in the wood, or in the water, or in the church.
May he be cursed in living, in dying, in eating, in drinking,
in being hungry, in being thirsty, in fasting, in sleeping, in
slumbering, in lying, in working, in resting, ———— and in
blood-letting. May he be cursed in all the powers of his body. May he be cursed within and without. May he be cursed
in the hair of his head. May he be cursed in his brain. May
he be cursed in the crown of his head; in his temples; in his
forehead; in his ears; in his eye-brows; in his cheeks; in his
jaw-bones; in his nostrils; in his fore-teeth and grinders; in
his lips; in his throat; in his shoulders; in his wrists; in his
arms; in his hands; in his fingers; in his breast; in his heart;
and in all the interior parts to the very stomach; in his veins;
in his reins; in his groins; in his thighs; ————; in his lips; in
his knees; in his legs, in his feet; in his joints; and in his nails.
May he be cursed in the whole structure of his members.
From the crown of his head to the sole of the foot. May
there be no soundness in him. May the Son of the living
God, with all the glory of his majesty, curse him; and may
heaven and all the powers that move therein rise against him,
to damn him; unless he shall repent and make full satisfaction
Amen, amen,—so be it."

Printed in the United States
121130LV00004B/7/A

9 781428 620032